History
of
Grenada County, Mississippi

By: H.C.J. Hathorn

1968

New Material Copyright 2015
By: Southern Historical Press, Inc.

All rights reserved. No part of this publication may be reproduced, stored in a retrieval system or transmitted in any form or by any means without the prior permission of the publisher.

Please direct all correspondence and orders to:

SOUTHERN HISTORICAL PRESS, Inc.
PO BOX 1267
375 West Broad Street
Greenville, SC 29601

ISBN # 0-89308-425-5
ISBN # 978-0-89308-425-7

DEDICATION

To those thousands of boys and girls of Grenada and Grenada County with whom it has been my good fortune to have been closely associated for a period of forty years, I dedicate this history with the sincere hope that it will give them a better understanding and greater appreciation of the aspirations, hopes, struggles and triumphs of those pioneer spirits whose labors were largely responsible for the heritage now enjoyed by our people.

FOREWARD

This modest volume of local history is designed to make available to the people of this area historical information which is now found only in the dusty pages of old newspapers, land deeds, records, wills, personal letters and similar written sources. Another purpose is to either confirm, or correct, some of the traditions which have been handed down from generation to generation until they have come to be accepted as authenic historical facts. Since this book is intended for the casual reader rather than scholars interested in the various sources of the information contained herein, footnotes indicating sources have been omitted, but the information has been obtained from authenic documentary sources such as those mentioned above. The period covered is generally confined to those years elapsing between 1833 and 1900 although, in a few instances, some particular topic will be continued into the first few years of the 20th century.

CHAPTERS

I.	The Land From Which Grenada And Grenada County Were Created	1-4
II.	Town and Community Development In The Area Which Became Grenada County	5-35
III.	Transportation	36-51
IV.	Early Educational Development In Grenada And Vicinity	52-65
V.	Henrette Sims Lifts A Cloud From Title Lots In East Half Of Section Seven	66-70
VI.	Organization of Grenada County	71-77
VII.	Grenada During Civil War Years	78-87
VIII.	Reconstruction In Grenada And Yalobousah Counties	88-98
IX.	The Yellow Fever Epidemic of 1878	99-111
X.	Grenada Experiences Banking Difficulties and Triumphs	112-120
XI.	Founders and Builders of Grenada and Grenada County	121-135
XII.	Early Churches Of Grenada And Vicinity	136-144
XIII.	Grenada Newspapers And Newspaper Men	145-155
XIV.	Business And Industry	156-167
XV.	The Advent Of Utilities, Public and Private	168-174
XVI.	Hotels, Taverns and Inns	175-179
XVII.	The People - Origins and Characteristics	180-194
XVIII.	Six Tragic Years	195-203
XIX.	The Mel Cheatham Affair	204-210
XX.	Miscellaneous Items Of Interest	211-228

Chapter One

THE LAND FROM WHICH GRENADA AND GRENADA COUNTY WERE CREATED

Grenada City and Grenada County were located in that section of Mississippi which was opened for white settlement by the Third Choctaw Land Cession, which cession was provided by the Treaty of Dancing Rabbit Creek. The existence of Grenada as a town, or city, preceeded the creation of the County of Grenada by some thirty-six years. Actual settlement in the area which was to become the town of Grenada came at an earlier date than the creation of Grenada, two earlier towns having been organized at least three years before they combined to form the town of Grenada.

The first and second Choctaw land cessions had opened up most of the southern and central portion of the state to white settlement, and by the year 1830, the 19,000 Choctaw Indians of Mississippi were pretty much concentrated in the north-central portion of the state. Not much more than sixty per-cent of the lands opened for white settlement by the previous Choctaw cessions had been settled, but already the land hungry speculators were looking with envious eyes on the very nearly eight million acres of land still under Choctaw control.

Men, high and mighty, both in State and Federal circles, were interested in obtaining more and more speculative lands, and such lands were always cheaper and more easily obtained when Indians were either forced, or induced, to give up new areas of former Indian land. In early 1830, the Mississippi Legislature made the first move in the process of dispossessing the Choctaws of the remainder of tribal land in Mississippi. A law was passed which brought the tribal Indians under the laws of Mississippi. This would result in the end of the privilege which the Choctaw Nation had always retained of being able to regulate by their tribal law, the conduct of Indian individuals within the limits of the territory of the Choctaw Nations. The law also provided that it should be a crime for any person to act as Chief or Mingo of an Indian tribe. This law, if enforced, would mean that a nation of proud Indians would come under the provisions of white men's laws which they did not understand, and would no longer be able to look to their traditional chieftain to guide them in the future as in the past.

The United States Government advised the State to proceed slowly in enforcing this law, and no serious attempt was made to enforce it in the early months of the year. The threat of strict enforcement, the free use of whisky by men seeking to negotiate a treaty with the Indians, and the conviction of certain half breed Choctaw chiefs that the tribe would be better off in a western Indian reservation, led to the ratification of the Treaty of Dancing Rabbit Creek later in the year of 1830. There was much discontent in the tribe because of the acceptance of the treaty by those who ratified it. It was claimed that many of the tribe had gone home before the vote on ratification, and that those who did vote were less than a majority of the tribe. The claim was also made by some of the discontented that their leaders had sold them out and had obtained much land and money as a price of their support of the treaty. History has not authenticated that charge aganist the Indian leaders, but it does agree that there was much opposition, on the part of some of the Choctaws, to any deal whereby they would surrender the remainder of their tribal lands in the state of Mississippi.

Anticipating such opposition, the commissioners who negotiated the treaty tried to appease those members of the Choctaw Nation who wanted to remain in Mississippi by providing that for each family head who elected to remain, one section of Choctaw land, to be located at a later date, would be reserved. It also provided that for each child of such a family a half section of land would be reserved, if the child had attained the age of ten at the time of the treaty, and a quarter section for those who were younger than ten years. It was also provided that if any Choctaws who elected to remain in Mississippi changed their minds within a period of five years after the removal of the Choctaw Nation to the western reservation, such persons could rejoin the nation with full tribal rights.

Because of the necessity of a land survey of the area before claims could be located; the time required to remove the Choctaws from the state; and in an attempt to prevent white settlement and exploitation of Indians before they were removed to the west; the treaty provided that no legal titles could be secured, nor lands sold, before October 1833. This would give a period of about three years in which it was expected that there would be little or no land grabing. This provision did, in the main, serve the purpose, but did not prevent some of the shrewder land speculators from locating Indians who had proposed to remain in Mississippi and claim land reservations. Although land sales could not be made before October 1833, there was nothing to prevent these shrewd operators from buying from these Indians their reservation rights, and then, after the opening of the land office in October 1833, list the Indians reservation, locate them, show a transfer of title, and become owner of these choice lands at very low cost. The United States learned something from this practice, and thus when the Chickasaw lands were sold as a result of the Treaty of Pontotoc Creek in 1832, the sale had to be approved by two of more tribal chiefs, thereby lessening the chance of fraud on the part of the land speculators.

Land speculators bought up the reservations of Peggy Tryhan who was entitled to land under the general provisions of the Treaty of Dancing Rabbit Creek, and John Donley, mail rider and a general favorite with Indians of the Choctaw nations, who, at the requests of the Choctaws was granted a section of land by the treaty, both sold their land reservation rights. The purchasers of Peggy's reservation located it in the east on half of section 7, township 22 north, Range 5 east. This soon was laid off in lots in a town called Pittsburg. The purchasers of the reservation of Donley located it in section eight of the same range and township as that in which Peggy Tryhan's reservation had been located. Thus the East half of Section Seven was joined on the East by the West part of Section Eight. The land in the first named Section became the site of the town of Pittsburg and the West part of Section Eight became the site of the town of Tullahoma. These sites were surveyed and land sales of lots in them became legal in October of 1833, and after about three years, the two towns which were divided by only the sectional line between Sections Seven and Eight united to become the town of Grenada.

We give hereafter a brief account of the handling of three of these land reservations for individual Choctaw Indians. In the first we find that Tookloon Tuby conveyed to Hardy Perry (who seems to have been a half breed Indian) "one-half Section of land which said land was allowed the aforesaid Tookloon Tuby by the cultivation article of the treaty." (Reference of course to the treaty of Dancing Rabbit Creek.) Of course, most of the Indian land was held in common by the Choctaw nation, but some individual Indians had selected sites and improved them while still living under the laws of the Choctaw nation. The "Cultivation Article" of that treaty gave such an Indian the right to locate his land reservation on any land which he had improved or cultivated. The first transfer of claim (not title) to the land reservation was made on September 2, 1832, a little more than a year before legal title, or even legal land purchase could be made. Hardy then sold the claim to John H. McKennie, who gave a power of attorney to James Crowder to sell and give title to the land after the land office opened. All three of these transactions took place before the sale of lands in the area began at the Land Office in October 1833. In a second example of this early sale of Indian land reservations we find that in July 29, 1833, a little more than a month before the opening of land sales, Peggy Tryhan sold to Franklin E. Plummer a part of her land reservation right, who on October 9, 1833, just a few days after that purchase authorized George W. Martin to make a selection for the location of this reservation. The location was that fractional part of Section 7, Township 22 north, Range 5 east which was designated by the land survey as lots number one, six, seven, eight, nine, fourteen and fifteen. (Land in Sections along the Yalobusha was described in this way rather than in half sections, quarter section, etc., probably because of the possibility of a shifting of the river making it more difficult to keep the land measured in fractional parts of a section than would be the case in describing it in lots.) Evidently Peggy Tryhan sold to Plummer only a part of her total reservation right, as we find later transactions whereby she and her sons made other sales of land located on other areas of the cession.

The consideration paid to Peggy by Plummer is not given, but if it followed the usual pattern in such reservation sales, it was inconsiderable. In 1834, about a year after purchasing the reservation claim from Peggy, Plummer sold a fourth interest in the land to the firm of Joseph McRaven & Hiram Coffee of Hinds County, and another fourth interest to the firm of John Lane & John A. Lane of Warren County. He received four thousand dollars for the sale of these two quarter interests in the land, and, a little later, sold a third one-fourth interest in the land to John Smith for two thousand dollars. There is some indication that he may have sold another interest to the firm of Shields and Puckett, but if he did that firm must have defaulted in terms of the sale because we find that on August 15, 1838, he appointed James Sims to act as agent for Franklin Plummer who is identified as "One of the proprietors of the town of Pittsburg." In the W. P. A. Source Book of Grenada an erroneous statement is made to the effect that Franklin L. Plummer was "the founder of the town of Pittsburg," whereas the town was actually laid out, lots sold and all other matters of town business transacted by Mcraven & Coffee; John Land and John A. Lane, and John Smith, while Plummer shared, to some extent, in the proceeds of the lot sales while continuing as a silent partner, represented by his agent Sims. Plummer's failure to actively participate in the development of the town is understandable when we realize the extent of his involvement in state politics. During the years 1831-1833, inclusive, he served as a representative in the United States Congress. In 1835 he was an unsuccessful candidate for the United States Senate. Very popular while a congressman, he lost that popularity during the senatorial campaign of 1835 when he was accused of being the candidate of a banking company which had gained ill repute in the state. By the time of his death in Jackson, Mississippi, in 1847, he was in destitute circumstances as well as in political obscurity.

Another example of white land ownership resulting from purchase of lands reserved for individual Choctaw Indians was the sale by John Donley--the mail rider who was granted a Section of land by the Treaty of Dancing Rabbit Creek--of his reservation right to Henry W. Hill of Tennessee. In turn, Hill gave a power of attorney to W. M. Gwin, a government land agent, to locate and sell this land. Gwin located the reservation on Section Eight, Township 22 North, Range 5 East, which section of land joined on the east the land sold by Peggy Tryhan to Plummer. Under his power of attorney, Gwin sold this section of land to Hiram Runnels and John Watt. They, in turn, sold undivided shares in the section of land until ten men were listed as owners of the section. The price paid Hill by Runnels and Watt was four thousand dollars. These men formed the town company of Tullahoma and began to lay off a town. The W. P. A. History of Grenada county lists Runnels as "founder of the town of Tullahoma," whereas he, like Plummer in the town of Pittsburg, was more or less a silent partner in the development of the town. Runnels, like Plummer, was too busy to take much active part in the founding and development of the town. From 1820 to 1830 he was State Auditor. In 1830 he was a member of the State Legislature which passed the law which would subject the Choctaw Nation to the laws of the state of Mississippi. In 1831 he ran for State Governor but was defeated by Abraham Scott. In 1833 the date of the organization of the Town Company of Tullahoma, he was elected State Governor. In 1835 he entered the race for United States Senator, then in 1838, upon the organization of the Mississippi Union Bank, he was made president of that institution at a salary of ten thousand dollars per year. Being thus engaged during the years of the development of the town of Tullahoma, Runnels had little time to devote to its business affairs, although he continued to share in the proceeds of sales of lots, and in other land speculations. Incidentally, this was not his first venture in part ownership of a newly organized town. Records in the Chancery Clerk's office in Marion county list him as one of the commissioners who bought up shares of the place first called Lott's Bluff, and developed the town of Columbia, now the county seat of Marion County.

These two men were representative of their time and age. They lived in an age of optimism. New lands, available at small cost, opened up visions of great wealth. So, Plummer, Runnels, and many other of their contemporaries bought up large acreages of land, much of it on credit, and expected to reap a golden harvest from their investment. A number of connected events, which will be related later, conspired to ruin these optimistic dreams and resulted in financial ruin for many of the land speculators.

Chapter II

TOWN AND COMMUNITY DEVELOPMENT IN THE AREA WHICH BECAME GRENADA COUNTY

The people who came into the area opened for settlement by the Treaty of Dancing Rabbit Creek were optimists. They saw, or thought they saw, a golden opportunity to better their economic status in life. Unlike the early English settlers on the Atlantic seaboard, they were not fleeing from religious persecution, not from the arbitrary rule of kings. Some of them were land speculators who expected to build fortunes by rushing to the land offices and buying up large acreages of Indian land at low prices, and on the very favorable terms offered by the Federal Government. They expected to sell the lands at much higher prices to the johnnie-come-lately actual settlers who would follow after the speculators. Of course, there were the bolder spirits among the actual settlers who contended with the speculators in the land bidding. These were able to secure choice land at the prevailing low price being paid for these lands. Then, there were the promotors, frequently land speculators themselves, who dreamed of founding towns in strategic locations and amassing fortunes by the sale of towns lots. They established the towns, but none of them realized their dreams of attaining great wealth from these ventures.

Since the early settlers of the region were dependent on the Yalobusha River for the transportation of most of their supplies and produce, the most promising situations for proposed towns would be along the course of this river. Six early towns were located on this river within the boundaries of the area which later became Grenada County. There were some white settlers in the area before the Treaty of Dancing Rabbit Creek opened the area for the sale of land. The presence of a considerable number of half-breed Indians, as evidenced by the names of some of the Indians securing land under the treaty provisions, indicates that white traders and squaw men had been in the area for a considerable time before the negotiation of the treaty. The first documented information relative to the presence of white people in the area is found in the records of the Elliott Indian Mission School which was established in 1818. We shall discuss this mission and the several towns in chronological order of their establishment.

Elliott Indian Mission School

The presence of a considerable number of half-breed Indians in the area which now comprises Grenada county would seem to indicate that there had been some white men in the area long before the Treaty of Dancing Rabbit Creek. It is probable that most of these men were itinerate traders who established no permanent places of residence. The first attempt by white men to establish a permanent settlement was the establishment of the Indian Mission School. In the year of eighteen hundred and eighteen, twelve years before the Third Choctaw Cession, and fifteen years before the organization of the ceeded land into counties, this school was started at a point about a mile south of the present town of Holcomb. Of course at that time the land had not been surveyed and divided into townships, ranges and sections, but it was located on land now found in sections twenty six and twenty seven in township twenty two north, range three east. In the earliest land transactions taking place after the Indian lands were placed on sale, an area of eleven hundred and twenty acres in these sections is refered to as "the Elliott Plantation." The school was abandoned soon after the cession of the land by the Choctaw nation, and, in the public land sales which began in the fall of 1833, this land was purchased by Robert J. Walker, Pierce Nolan, James and Lewis Miller, Laurence Millander, John Smith and James A. Girault. Eventually Girault obtained a one half interest in the entire eleven hundred and twenty acre tract.

John Smith, listed as one of the purchasers, had been a member of the mission school staff.

The establishment of the school was the indirect result of an impromptu prayer meeting held by five young men in eighteen hundred and six. These men were students in Williams College which was located in the state of Massachusetts. During a storm they took refuge in a hay-stack, and began to pray for the evangelization of the people of the world. They determined to begin the work themselves. In the year eighteen hundred and ten, as a result of the zeal of these five men, there was a meeting in Farmington, Connecticut in which one lawyer and four ministers organized, in the name of the Massachusetts General Association of Congregational Churches, a commission to be known as the American Board of Commissions for Foreign Missions. A little later this board, in conjunction with a similar organization in the Presbyterian Church, established an Indian mission school at Brainerd near the site of the present city of Chattanooga. This school was, of course, for Indians of the Creek nation. In some way, some of the Choctaw leaders either observed, or learned in some other way, about the work of this school. Several Choctaw chiefs sent a request to the men in charge of this school that similar schools be established in the Choctaw Nation. The head of the Brainerd school was a man named Kingsbury, and among the men and women associated with him in the school there Mr. and Mrs. L. S. Williams. Since the Brainerd school was well established and well staffed, Mr. Kingsbury decided to resign his post and, under the direction of the American Board of Commissioners, to go into the Choctaw Nation and set up a similar school for the Choctaw Indians. He was able to induce Mr. and Mrs. Williams to go with him. They set out in wagons and made the long trip to the Choctaw Nation. They selected a site, according to their report to the Board of Commissioners, "about three and one half miles south of the Yalobusha river at a point about thirty miles before it joined the Yazoo river." Of course, their spelling of the name of the Yalobousha is not as we spell it today and rather than joining the Yazoo river, it joins the Tallahatchie to form the Yazoo, but there can be no doubt that this was a fairly accurate description of the location of their school.

Kingsbury and Williams, no doubt with the help of the friendly Indians began, soon after their arrival, the construction of log cabins. They reported to the Board of Commissioners: "Within fourteen months several commodious cabins, a school house, lumber house and grainery were erected. School opened with ten pupils, eight of whom had been brought one hundred and sixty miles." In eighteen hundred and nineteen the Choctaw Indians from the "Six Towns" agreed to make an appropriation of two thousand dollars a year, payable quarterly, for a period of seventeen years, to aid in the support of the school. The six towns mentioned were the chief towns of the Choctaw Nation. The school was established just about the time that the three half-breed Indian chiefs Greenwood Leflore, David Folsom and John Pitchlynn, decided that if the Choctaws were to remain in Mississippi it would be necessary for them to be educated to the extent that they could set up some kind of stable government. It was probably the encouragement of these three men to the establishment of the Indian Mission School at Elliott that brought about the financial support of the Choctaw Nation for the school. It is a matter of record that Pitchlynn, son of a Tory merchant, and himself a planter and trader of considerable means, contributed thirteen hundred dollars to the support of missionary schools.

We have little information relative to the people other than Kingsbury and Mr. and Mrs. Williams who made up the staff of the school. We do know that Mr. John Smith and his wife Hannah, came down from Massachusetts soon after the establishment of the school and remained with it in some capacity until it ceased operation. Smith became one of the earliest residents of the little town of Pittsburg which was laid off in the late months of eighteen hundred and thirty three. He operated a tavern called the Union Hotel, in the little town, and became the owner of considerable property in the town and vicinity. His daughter Harriett married James Sims, a merchant of Pittsburg. In time, Mr. and Mrs. Sims came to own many lots in what is now the West Ward of the city of Grenada, many of which were bought up at tax sales during eighteen hundred forty one and eighteen hundred and forty two, a period of depressed values following the Panic of eighteen hundred and thirty seven. Smith built his home on an elevation a few hundred feet south and west of the present Grenada Motel, located at the intersection of South and Commerce streets.

It is possible that John Smith may have been in charge of the farming operations at the mission school. A farm was maintained under the direction of a northern farmer. The boys were taught to hoe and plow, and the girls to spin, weave, sew, knit, and to make butter and cheese. An excerpt from the report of the Mission Superintendent to the Board of Commissioners in eighteen hundred twenty will give some insights into the condition of the school after it had been in operation less than two years: "Sixty male and twenty female scholars will show the prosperity and usefulness of the establishment. The chiefs have shown great liberality in providing for the education of their children by appropriating two thousand dollars annually out of their annuity for the purpose of schools and the American Board has taken measures for the establishment of other schools in the nation. The school at Elliott is on the Lancaster Plan. Since the last report thirty eight scholars have been admitted; ten have left and one dismissed for misconduct. Six more considered belonging but now home on a visit. Sixty males and twenty females all board in our family except ten who live in the neighborhood go home on Saturday and re-enter generally on the Sabbath morning. Fifty now belonging could not speak English upon admission. All have made progress in English, and several speak the language fluently. Twenty eight can read in the Testament. Lessons in writing begin on slates and then advance to paper. On paper thirty nine can write a plain hand. The boys, when out of school, are employed, as circumstances may require, in the various business of the farm and family. Each one, who is of sufficient size, is furnished with an ax and a hoe. We cultivated the last season about fifty acres of corn and potatoes, most of which was planted and hoed by the boys. The girls are in two divisions, and are employed alternately in the kitchen and in sewing, spinning, knitting, and other domestic tasks. Many full-blooded Indians have made application of late to have children admitted to the school. Strong desires are expressed to have other schools opened."

From the statement relative to full-blooded Indians beginning to become interested in entering their children in the school it may be well to explain that there was considerable difference of opinion between the full-blooded Indians and the half-breeds relative to the desirability of having the children educated in the white man's ways. As has been indicated the Indian Mission Station at Elliott, and other stations which were established later, were like plantations including schools, farming activity, instruction in homemaking and the teaching of both dicipline and Christianity. The half and quarter breed Indians frequently co-operated with the missionaries and became converts both to Christianity and the desire to have their children receive some formal education. The missionaries at the "stations" discouraged many of the Indian practices of ball-playing, dancing, smoking, and idleness. The full-blooded Indians did not take to these restrictions as well as the breed Indians did, and many of them at first refused to allow their children to attend the schools. As time went on they began to see that the Indian children attending the schools were becoming more prosperous and more influential in the Choctaw Nation. This probably explains the statement relative many of the full blood Indians beginning to request that their children be admitted to the school at Elliot. Early in 1826 the Federal Government began to try to negotiate a treaty with the Choctaws to buy their Mississippi lands and remove the tribe to Indian reservations in the west. The general opinion was that the full-blood Indians, because of their resentment of white man law and white man religion, would be willing to accept such a treaty. But the breed Indians such as LeFlore and Folsom, and, at first, Pitchlynn, were hostile to the proposal. They were frequently men of considerable property and felt that they were better off by remaining as leaders in the Choctaw Nation. Later, when the Federal negotiators began to offer inducements in the nature of large land grants to the chiefs, most of them changed their minds and favored the treaty. This caused suspicion on the part of many of the full blood Indians who, under the leadership of Moshulatubbee opposed a treaty proposed by Greenwood LeFlore. One ground of the chief's opposition to the **treaty** proposed by LeFlore was that it was drawn up by a Methodist preacher. The old chief didn't want any part of the white man's religion and was afraid that the ways of his people would be destroyed by the efforts of the missionary preachers. This opposition resulted in the failure of the treaty proposed by LeFlore. Later the treaty of Dancing Rabbit Creek was accepted over the opposition of many of the full blood Indians. There has been considerable controversy over the change in attitude of the half-breed chiefs which resulted in the adoption of the treaty. Friends of the chiefs contend that they changed their attitude because they realized that the many full blood Indians could never adjust to white civilization and law. Many of the full blood Indians felt that they had been sold out by the breed chiefs who received generous land and money grants. In addition to the grants to these breed chiefs their "family connections" also received generous land grants, seventeen sections going to LeFlore's relatives; ten to Pitchlynn's, and eight or nine to Folsom's.

Since the signing of the treaty in 1830 would ultimately mean the end of the school at Elliot, it probably closed soon thereafter. We have no information relative to the date of the closing of the school. The last record we have relative to any Indian connection with Elliott Station is an instrument, dated at Elliott, in which Judy Turnbull sold a quarter section of land, granted her as her land reservation to Angus Campbell. We wonder if she could have been one of the Indian girls who had attended the Mission School and had remained there until the school closed. She probably did not go west with the people of the Choctaw nation since we know that her father, Chief Turnbull, remained in the area until his death, and that she had a sister who married a man by the name of Foster who made a crop in 1832 in that area of Tallahatchie county, which later became a part of Grenada county.

The Sale of Indian Land Begins

In anticipation of the removal of the Choctaw Nation from Mississippi and the opening of a land office to begin the sale of Indian land on October 23, 1833, The Mississippi Legislature had organized the land, obtained through the provisions of the Treaty of Dancing Rabbit Creek, into a number of counties, among those newly created counties were Carroll, Choctaw, Tallahatchie, and Yalobousha, all of which were, at a later date, to contribute land to the formation of Grenada County. The land office set up to carry on the sale of Indian land in that part of the Choctaw purchases in which the above named counties were located was located at Chocchuma on the Yalobousha River, and in the county of Tallahatchie. To this point came Samuel Gwin, Registrar of the land office, James A. Girault, Receiver of Public Monies, at the same office, and William Huntly, employee in the same office, and husband of one of the daughters of John Smith the missionary, who was a member of the staff of the Elliott Indian Mission until it closed down after the Treaty of Dancing Rabbit Creek.

Land sales were to begin early in the morning of the date mentioned above. At this date there were few buildings in the new land office town of Chocchuma, and little lodging facilities for the people who came flocking in to buy up land. But the people who came to the opening land sales were land-hungry, some for large areas of speculative land, and others for smaller areas on which they could build homes and clear farms. During the three years elapsing since the land cession by the Choctaw nation, the area had been surveyed and marked off in townships and sections. It is quite probable that many of the prospective land purchasers had spent some time in the area viewing out and locating the lands which they wished to purchase. Some of the big land speculators probably had sent agents into the area to get this information and have it available when the sales began. Since the sales were to be conducted as public sales, a person would hardly make a bid of a piece of land about which he had no information. The supposition is that most of the early land purchasers had information about the land they bought. The location of the early land purchases, mostly the better land of the area, bears out this supposition.

From the date of the beginning of the land sales through the last day of December in 1833 was just seventy days. These must have been days of feverish activity at the land office. During that period two hundred and four individuals and partnerships bought eighty thousand five hundred and ninety two acres of land in the area which is now Grenada County. Thus, in a period of seventy days, thirty per cent of the land area which is now in Grenada county was bought up by the above-mentioned number of individuals and partnerships. Since many of the two hundred and four purchasers made a number of different purchases, the number of land transactions during this period was much greater than the number of purchasers. Many of these early purchasers continued to buy other lands for several years after the opening of the land office, so, in reality, they came to control much more than the thirty per cent of the land of the future county of Grenada.

The land was sold on very liberal terms, one third down, with ten years to pay off the balance, at which time they would become entitled to a land patent on their purchases. The prices paid ranged from seventy five cents per acre to a high price of six dollars. The average price paid was about one dollar per acre. At this price, and under the liberal terms of payment, many of the men buying land were tempted to pay only the down payment required so that they might get larger acreage by obligating themselves to pay the balance in ten years. A man with one hundred dollars could have bought outright one hundred acres of land, or could have made the required down payment on three hundred acres of land incumbered by the two thirds balance to be paid within the next ten years. Most of the purchasers were optimistic relative to the prospect for enchanced land values, and their ability to sell off part of the land at higher prices, or to pay for it by the returns from the farms which they intended to establish. There were three general classes of men buying land. There were the land speculators, who were not looking for places in which to establish homes and farms, but were buying up the land in expectation of making a killing when land prices went up and new settlers came into the area in which much of the best land was owned by the speculators, and available for sale to the late comers. A larger number of the men buying land were legitimate settlers--men who were buying more modest acreages. They were buying quarter and half sections, with some of them increasing these holdings as the years passed by. Some of them were buying larger acreage, but, at the beginning, most of them were modest in their buying. The last, and the smallest class of those seeking land were those Choctaw Indians who had announced their intention to remain in the area and to exercise their treaty right to reserve land for themselves and their children. The head of a family was allowed to claim a whole section of land for himself; a half section for any children over ten years of age, and a quarter section for younger children. In order to perfect title to any land obtained in this way the Indian had to reside in Mississippi for a period of five years after the removal of their kindred to the Western Reservation. It would have been much better for the early land buyers to have paid their cash for lessor areas of land, rather than for equities in larger acreage, since the Panic of 1837 was to cause much of the land to be forfeited because of inability of purchasers to meet the installments. Although some of the smaller operators lost their lands during the period of financial depression, it was the large land speculators who suffered the most severe results of the depression. Owing two thirds of the purchase price; required by the Andrew Jackson Specie Circular of 1836 to pay off their installments in either gold or silver, and unable to sell their lands for this type currency, most of the large speculators lost out and their lands became available for later settlers.

A few of the men regarded as land speculators, most of whom were severely hurt by the depression of land values and lack of hard money with which to pay off the installments on their land purchases will be named hereafter. Robert J. Walker purchased nine thousand nine hundred and two acres of land in the area presently to be included in the boundaries of Grenada County, and bought many other acres in other areas of the Choctaw lands. According to the records available, he received patents on less than two hundred acres. The rest was either sold or lost. Most was lost. James A. Girault, being a member of the Land Office Staff, was in a position to know the best land. During the seventy days he purchased twenty eight hundred acres of the best land in the area. Later, he bought other large acreages of land, including 1920 acres located near Holcomb, Mississippi, which had been located for Jefferson Military College of Washington, Mississippi. This land had been made available to the Mississippi school by an act of the Federal Congress entitled "An Act In Aid Of Jefferson College." Girault, like the other speculators, had his financial troubles, and soon the College bought up the land under the provisions of a deed of trust given the College by Girault to secure payment of the purchase price. Unlike most of the big land purchasers, Girault continued to live in the area and was able to save part of his property. He lost much of his land under a mortgage given the Mississippi Union Bank to secure his subscription to a large number of shares of stock in that ill-fated institution. Malcolm Gilchrist, about whom we know little other than that he bid in five thousand eight hundred and seventy one acres of land, was another speculator who never realized much on his speculation. The firm of John & John A. Lane bought three thousand four hundred and ninety acres during this seventy day period; later they purchased a fourth interest in the town of Pittsburg. These men were residents of Warren County. George W. Martin, who had been a Federal Land Office official appointed to locate reservation claims by Indians, must have done some good locating for himself, since he bought five hundred and forty three acres of choice land for himself. He should not be classified as a real speculator since he resided in the area and was actively engaged in its development. William B. Beale was a resident of New Orleans who acquired nine hundred and thirty four acres of land during the early sale period. A. S. Campbell, like Martin, lived in the area, and although he traded extensively in lands, he bought up only six hundred and thirty four acres during the last part of the year 1833. James Hayden of Yazoo County bought eighteen hundred and thirty five acres, but soon sold at a profit to other buyers. Later he bought smaller acreage and became a resident of Tallahatchie County. Thomas G. Ellis was another of the real speculators. During the seventy day period of sales in 1833 he purchased eight thousand two hundred and forty acres. The largest acreage bought up by any one man in the early land sales was the ten thousand two hundred and seventy seven acres secured by Robert Jameson. He may have been mostly speculator, but he was also the operator of extensive farming operations. The extent of his involvment in agricultural pursuits is evidenced by a Deed of Trust given him to secure payment of a large obligation. He gave this deed of trust on considerable land in Tallahatchie County, many slaves, much livestock, and considerable personal property. Thacker Winter bought up eight hundred and seventy one acres at the early sales, and although he did trade in lands, he seems to have settled in the county and cultivated part of his land. During this period Green and R. B. Crowder acquired thirteen hundred and ninety five acres. In the years to follow, they bought a great deal more land, some at public sale of Indian land, and a considerable acreage from other settlers who needed to sell off a portion of their lands in order to meet obligations, or because they had enough of the pioneer conditions under which they were living and desired selling out and seeking homes in other localities.

The promoters and land speculators have their place in the development of any new area. This was as true in the area which was to become Grenada County as it was in other pioneer areas of the nation, but the people who made up the backbone of any new pioneer locality were the men and women who erected houses and carved farms, some large, but mostly small, during the early years of their venture. It is our purpose to list the names of most of the purchasers of small or medium size areas who obtained their land during the first seventy days of the Indian land sales. Perhaps the list will be monotonous reading for any reader who has no particular interest in the identity of these men, but it is possible that in the list, some reader may find listed the name of some early ancestor about whom they have no definite information. By listing these names we do not intend to convey the impression that they were the only pioneering spirits who built up the area which is called Grenada County. Following fast upon their footsteps, in early 1834, 1835, and 1836, came those other people, who along with those listed herewith changed the pioneer country of 1833 to the prosperous area of the period just before the Civil War. Few areas have made such rapid progress in approximately a quarter of a century. Crude cabins, had in many places, been replaced by substantial homes; two small villages on the Yalobousha River had developed into a prosperous trade center and railroad shipping point; the slave population had increased greatly and the area had definitely become a part of the "Cotton Kingdom." In a discussion of this sort it will be impossible, within the space available for the subject, to list all those settlers of the years indicated above, but the list given of those who came and purchased lands by December 31, 1833, is representative of the pioneer settlers who made up the driving force responsible for the rapid settlement and development of the area. History has a way of recording the contributions of a few outstanding leaders who make their contributions to the development of a new community, but of necessity must remain silent on the contributions of many unsung men and women who have made their contributions to the same end. Such individuals are represented in the list to follow of men who came, many with their families, into this area of Mississippi during the last months of 1833. We have been able to obtain some small information about a few of these individuals, and such information shall be given along with the names, but the major portion of the list will be names of people who lived and worked in the obscurity which is the fate of many of our pioneer forefathers.

These are the names of the individuals who made small, or medium sized, purchases of land during the first seventy days of public land sales: William Anderson, R. W. Anderson, Elizabeth Anderson, Loflin Barnes, William B. Bodley, William Beal, Hiram Coffee, James Beasley, James Blackburn, Peter Bridges, Bowling, C. Burnett, Alfred Battle, Benjamin Bradford, Timothy Bloodworth, Richard Coleman, Samuel C. Caldwell, William Cargile, Peter Chambliss, James Crofford, Thomas Coopwood, Stancil Cobb, Samuel Colson, Moses Collins, William Clark, David W. Connely, William R. Campbell, Matthew C. Clanton, Samuel Carson, Joseph Collins who became an extensive land holder in and about Grenada, John M. Curry, Wiley Davis who later became one of the Proprietors of the Town Company of Tullahoma, R. W. Driver, E. M. Driver, John Donly who was probably the same John Donly who was given a reservation of a section of land by the Treaty of Dancing Rabbit Creek, which land eventually came into the possession of Hiram Runnels and John Watts and the location of the town of

Tullahoma, William Edgar, John M. Evant, Alvon Fisk, John G. Freeman, Joseph Forgay, Nicholas Fisher, Berry Green, Andrew Govan who was a native of the Orange District of South Carolina and served for a time as a Federal Congressman from that district. He moved to Holly Springs and became a large land owner in Marshall and Tippah counties. During the few years following the beginning of the sale of the Choctaw lands he obtained considerable land in and about the town of Grenada. The name Govan applied to one of our streets derives from this man. Like many of the other large purchasers of land, he eventually lost most of his holdings. A deed of Trust in on record in the Grenada County Chancery Clerk's office by which he gave, as security for a loan of well over one hundred thousand dollars, several thousand acres of land, some two hundred slaves, several saw mills and a considerable amount of personal property such as watches, silverware, etc.) Samuel H. Ford, David Isiah, Joseph B. Gleen, Daniel Greer, David Gleen, Allen Gattis, Daniel Green, Nicholas Gray, Littleberry Gilliam, Luther A. Gonodough, Daniel Halkens, John Hammond, James Howley, Jeremiah House, Augustus Hester, Augustus Hastin, Jeromiah Hendrick, Thomas Harris, Daniel Harris, Asa Holland, Thomas Howard, Sterling Harrison, Titus Howard, Bostic & Hardeman, Thomas B. Ives, H. L. Irish, John Jones, Bently Jarrett, Allen K. Jones, James B. Jones, Samuel Jackson, Lemuel Jackson, Thomas Kirkman, Franklin L. Lane, Joseph Logan, Henry Logan, Samuel McCracken, William Minter, Alexander McCullogh, S. McCrelah, Andrew McDaniel, George W. Martin, James B. March, Samuel B. Marsh an attorney who practiced in the early courts of Yalobousha county and who was given a deed of trust on land to secure a fee of one thousand dollars to defend the sons of the grantor who, according to the deed of trust, "are in the jail at Coffeeville charged with murder;" John C. McLemore, Laurent Millanden, William McCoy, John Myers, Thomas Martin, George Myer, Charles Miles, Duncan McIvan, John McSwine, James Mathews, Joel McGuire, C. Mithcell, Thomas Nixon, Pierce Noland, Calvin Nicholson, William Norman, Caswell Newsome, Ransom Newsome, John Newbell, John Noland, William J. Oldham, Jacob H. Oaks, John F. Ormond, Joseph Penon, Henry Penon, Joseph Persons, Abraham Penquite, Isaac Perry, Franklin L. Plummer who played his part in the establishment of Pittsburg; Thomas Powers, Lewis B. Powers, N. E. Powers, James W. Perkings, Jones W. Perkins, John B. Peyton, David C. Pane, John W. Pegram, John Rowles who later became owner of several thousand acres of land in the area; John S. Rhea, John Robinson, Harden D. Runnels who also later came to be the owner of considerable land which was located within the boundaries of the present county of Grenada; William Sims, Louis Stigher, John S. Skinner, Henry Staeen, John Seagers, Anderson C. Smith, George H. Sykes, Virgie H. Stewart, John Tabb, Edward Tucker, William Truit, Parham Thompson, Stephen Threlkell, Enos Ward, Elijah S. Watson, Isham Wooten, William Winter, John D. Wyatt, Jordan Williams, Perry Widdon, Philip A. Weaver, John Williams, Allen Walker, Robert Williams and William S. Young. It is very probable that the spelling of some of these names is in error. The educational level of some of the land purchasers was such that their spelling was rather uncertain, and the faded handwriting in the Original Tract Book, from which these names were taken, sometimes make it impossible to distinguish certain letters in the name given. The spelling given here is substantially the same as in the Tract Book.

The names given above were of white men coming into the lands of the Choctaw nation, but there is in the Tract Book a shorter list of names of people native to the land. This is the list of reservations made for Choctaw Indians who claimed lands, provided by the Treaty of Dancing Rabbit Creek, for those Indians who determined to remain in the area. All of these reservations were entered in the first seventy days of land sales. Through the negligence of certain Indian Agents, other reservations claimed by Indians were not made until later, hence are not on the list which we shall give. Because of the delay in entering these names, some of the lands claimed by individual Indians had been sold to others, so it was necessary for them to be allowed "float reservations" which allowed them to pick out any unsold land and recompense them for land selected by them and sold to others. The names of Indians reserving land will indicate that some were half-breeds. The names are as follows: Children of James Oxberry under age of ten years 478 acres; Sarah, one of Deliah's daughters, 160 acres; Conncontontah, 80 acres, David Oxberry 476 acres, Jessie & William Turnbull, both over ten years of age, 640 acres, Tuckloon Tubby 318 acres, Peggy Tryhan 320 acres, Fish o pi a 80 acres, Hardy Perry, 160 acres, John Perry 657 acres, Captain Turnbull 798 acres, Isaac Perry 640 acres. From the small acreage reserved by some of the above, whose names indicate fullblood Indian ancestry, we presume that they were entitled to reserve the rest of the acreage to which they were entitled in some other area at some other time. Only a few of the names in the list were well enough known to deserve comment. James Oxberry was the interpreter employed at the land office to aid in the land sales; Peggy Tryhan was the Indian woman who had earlier sold a half section of her claim to Franklin L. Plummer, at a date before the land sales began, so in the Tract Book that land, the half section on which the town of Pittsburg was established, was listed under the name of Plummer in a transaction taking place early in the year 1834. The land reserved for her in the early land sales was the other half section to which she was entitled. Later she registered reservations for her two sons in another area part in what was to become Grenada County and part in Holmes County. Captain Turnbull was an Indian chief who had a daughter married to a whiteman named Foster who had come into the Tallahatchie County and made a crop in the year 1832. He had another daughter Judy, who evidently had attended school in the Indian Mission School at Elliott, since she dated a deed of conveyance for sale of land later reserved for her as having been made at Elliott Station.

Chocchuma

The first town established in the area which is now Grenada County was Chocchuma which was to be the United States Land Office for the Northern District. Since the Land Office was set up before actual sale of land could begin the Federal government must still have been in possession of the land, lots eleven and twelve in Section 19, Township 22, Range three east, on which the town of Chocchuma was established. On the Original Entry Book that land is listed as a "float reservation" for "Sarah, older daughter of Deliah" Since, under the Treaty of Dancing Rabbit Creek, the heads of Indian families desiring to remain in Mississippi were entitled to lands, both for themselves and their children, the land upon which the land office was located evidently was first reserved for an Indian girl, daughter of the head of a family desiring to remain in Mississippi after the Choctaw Nation moved west. In explanation of the term "float reservation," it should be remembered that because of some carelessness of the Indian Agent for the Choctaw Nation reservations made by some of the Indians desiring to remain in the state were not filed before the land sales began, and, as a result of this negligence, some of the land which the Indians had selected as their reservations was sold to other people. In order to compensate for this negligence on the part of the Indian agent, the Indians having lost their earlier reservation selections were allowed to claim any other similar area of land not yet sold to some other person. When such an area of unsold land was located for the Indians, these were called "float reservations." Franklin Plummer, land speculator and Congressman from Mississippi, probably realizing the importance of the location of the office, evaded the provision that no land sales could begin before October 1833, by securing from Sarah, a release of her reservation. This was done on July 29, 1833, about three months before the land sales opened at Chocchuma. Incidentally Plummer used the same means of securing the half section of lands on which the town of Pittsburg was later established. In this transaction he bought part of the reservation from Sarah, and almost two months before the legal sale of the land opened at the Land Office, Plummer sold this land after the Land Office opened for business in October 1833 Sterling became the first person to obtain legal title to land on which Chocchuma was located.

Evidently Franklin Plummer had other associated with him in the purchase of the original Indian reservation, and had conveyed only his interest in the land, since on January 2, 1835, we find Wiley Davis, Mary J. Davis, and Joseph R. Plummer conveying to Sterling, for a consideration of eleven hundred dollars, "all that piece or parcel of land on which the town of Chocchuma is situated in Tallahatchie County and state of Mississippi it being one undivided half of lots number eleven and twelve on the southeast quarter of Section 19, Township twenty two, Range Seven." These lots mentioned were not town lots but much larger areas of land. When the original land survey was made the sections of land along the Yalobousha river were not marked in quarter and half sections only, but those fractional sections were divided into lots. Lots eleven and twelve comprised the entire southeast quarter of the section on which the town was located.

We do not know when the town was surveyed and laid off, but it must have been after 1832 when the Land Office was first located, and before 1835, because as of the last named date, town lots were being sold by number in the town which now seems to have been owned, in its entirety, by Robert Sterling. It is very probable that the town plat may have been delayed until after legal title to the land could have been established some time after October 1833 when the land sales began. It is possible, but not probable, that the town was laid out after Robert Sterling secured sole possession of the land in 1835. On August 18, 1836, the same year when the two small towns of Pittsburg and Tullahoma joined to establish the town of Grenada, we find that Sterling sold to Robert and Joseph Miller, for a consideration of $450 "Town lots 13, 14, and 15, and 16 in square number one; agreeable to the plan of the said town situated in Lots 11 and 12, of section 19, Township 22, Range 3 East." Presumably square number one must have been the center of the town, so the establishment of Grenada, about fourteen miles to the east, must already have cast a shadow of pessimism as to the future of Chocchuma, since the consideration involved seems very small for four choice lots in a town which had any real future. In the same month Sterling sold number 2 to Daniel Stanford for a consideration of $126. Some time in 1837 Henry and Hiram Hagen purchased lots number 17 and 24 in square number four for a consideration of $400. All improvements on the lots were a part of the sale and they are identified in the following manner: "with all improvements including the houses now in the occupance of James Kendall and James Crump." Kendall and Crump had lived in Montgomery County, North Carolina, and evidently came to Mississippi about the same time. In 1838 we find the following transaction recorded: "Daniel Ferguson for the love and esteme which he bears his son A. P. Ferguson grants all his interest in the following described land in the town of Chocchuma, Lots number 23 and 25 as will more fully appear on the plan of the map of the town." In 1838 Sterling conveyed to E. P. Grayson lots 19 and 20 for a consideration of $2100. In May 1839, Samuel C. Caldwell sold lots 3, 4, 5, and 6 and other land outside the town for the sum of $3000. On September 17 of the same year, Caldwell bought back the town lots sold by the sheriff for taxes. Five dollars was the sum brought by the tax sale. In March 1841 Caldwell sold these lots and forty acres of land located elsewhere to William Tergartern for a consideration of $1700. In July of 1840 James A. Girult bought for a bid of fifty dollars at a tax sale, lots 23 and 25. Lots 2 and 7 belonging to Joseph B. Lyons sold on a tax sale to Ralph Montgomery for $13.64. These tax sales indicate the beginning of the end of the town of Chocchuma. The Land Office was to be moved to Grenada in 1842. James Girault who was an official at the land office, and a big land speculator, was involved in the final episode in the demise of the town of Chocchuma. On October 18, 1841, in order to satisfy claims against Girault, lots 19 and 20 "with frame house and kitchen formerly known as land office at Chocchuma" and lots 7 and 8 square five "including two story tavern house known as the Planters Hotel in the town of Chocchuma, also lot number 5 in square number eleven containing one two story house and a frame ware house" was sold by the sheriff. Evidently J. Duvaney was the successful bidder at the tax sale, for we find that in May, 1856, he sold the whole of lots 11 and 12 consisting of 113 acres for a consideration of $372. Since the land office was to be moved to Grenada in 1842, the tax sale of the area on which Chocchuma was located only three months before the removal of the office may be considered as an indication of the end of the town of Chocchuma as a place of any importance. In 1857 James Hayden and his wife sold the property, bought from Duvaney, to James M. Duncan for a consideration of $1130. An old newspaper has as a new item that James Duncan stated that at the time of the publication of that issue of the paper he had made fifty two crops on lots 11 and 12. Part of the property still is in the possession of his descendants.

Today there is nothing to indicate the early presence of a town at the old town site except some rutted trails which the imagination may conceive of as the location of the old Charleston-Carrollton road which wound its way thru the town to cross the Yalobousha at the "Chocchuma" ferry. Its location about three miles southwest of Holcomb was on the last high ridge of land, before the river fell away into the low lands of the Yazoo-Mississippi delta.

There can be no doubt that Chocchuma was a busy place during the early years of its existence. It was here that the several million acres of land, formerly known as the Choctaw Nation and occupied by about 19,000 Choctaw Indians, was to be sold to the hungry white land speculators. Here they held the public land sales, and here they registered their purchases. Important men in state and national potitics either came here or sent agents to represent them. Franklin L. Plummer, Mississippi representative in the lower house of the National Congress was certainly here at the time the sales began October 24, 1833. Mississippi governor elect, Hiram J. Runnels, attended the sales. Robert J. Walker, later a United States Senator from Mississippi and purchaser of huge tracts of land in what is now Grenada County, was either there or had his representative present. Samuel Gwin, head of the land office, made his headquarters here. Later he was killed in a duel with Issac Caldwell, law partner of United States Senator Poindexter, Caldwell being mortally wounded in the duel. Poindexter had appointed Gwin to the land office position, and Gwin later supported Robert J. Walker in an election in which Walker financially involved; lost practically all his land, and left Mississippi when appointed as Territorial Governor of Kansas. As a law partner, Walker had the famous Mississippi orator Sargent S. Prentiss. W. M. Gwin, brother of Samuel Gwin, was appointed Marshall for the United States Court of the Northern District of Mississippi, and was much in evidence as the man who acted as agent for locating reservations for Indians who desired to remain in Mississippi. Accused, but never convicted of defrauding some of the Indians, he left Mississippi and became an United States Senator from the new state of California. During the Civil War he was arrested and charged with treason against the United States because of his efforts to aid the Confederate States in the war. He again escaped conviction. He was supposed to have tried to get Emperor Maximillion of Mexico to recognize Southern Independence. James A. Girault was appointed "Receiver of Public Monies" at the land office. He was the son-in-law of William Dunbar, a large land owner of Adams County. Incidentally, the Gwins, Walker, and Girault were all residents of Natchez. Girault was a heavy speculator in Indian lands, and during the early years was considered wealthy, but like most of the other speculators, lost most of his possession. When a Congressional "Act for the Relief of Jefferson College in Mississippi" alloted some 1900 acres of Indian land for the school Girault located the land for the College, and then purchased it for himself for a consideration of $17,244. He made the purchase in 1833, and being well versed in land locations, had located for the college the fertile lands in the vicinity of the present village of Holcomb. In August 1844, a Commissioner of the

Chancery Court sold the land at public auction, and it was bought up by representatives of Jefferson College for $24,611.61. Evidently the College had to pay this higher price to protect against other bidders who realized the value of the land. The school never became a real college, but continued for many years as a military school for boys, and closed only a year or so ago.

Chocchuma is now but a ghostly memory in the minds of some of the oldest citizens of our county who have heard of it from their ancestors, and an interesting study for those who like to turn the dusty pages of history; but its rise and fall, and the era of land speculation at the expense of the ill treated Choctaw Indians have been sadly neglected by historians.

Pittsburg

The first official record of anything having to do with the founding of the town of Pittsburg is the bare record in the Original Entry Book--sometimes called Tract Book--indicating that the East one half of Section 7, Township 22, Range 5 East was entered as a "float" reservation for Peggy Tryhan. Behind that simple entry there is much of land manipulation, political influence and erroneous tradition relative to the founding of the town. Peggy Tryhan was an Indian woman, who, as a small girl, was a survivor of the virtual extermination of the tribe of Chocchuma Indians by a war party of Choctaw Indians. She was adopted into the Choctaw tribe, but because of not being a Choctaw Indian, it seems that for her to be able to receive a land reservation under the original Treaty of Dancing Rabbit Creek, it was necessary for a supplementary article to be added to the treaty to enable her to receive a reservation, whereas members of the Choctaw tribe were to receive their reservations under the general provisions of the treaty.

We have been unable to find any record of the transaction by which she sold part of her reservation right to Franklin E. Plummer, but in deeds to the lots later sold in the town we find statements indicating that Peggy sold on July 29, 1833, the land on which Pittsburg was to be located. This date was approximately three months before the public sales of land began.

At the instigation of unscrupulous land speculators, many Indians who did not intend to remain in Mississippi after the tribe was removed to the western reservation, were induced to claim reservations and give these speculators power of attorney to locate and purchase these reservations at a very low price. Samuel Gwin, Registrar of the land office at Chocchuma, was aware that this condition prevailed and was very much disturbed because of what he considered wholesale frauds being perpertrated against both individual Indians and the Federal Government. His concern was probably compounded because his brother William M. Gwin, Federal District Marshall, had obtained some land by this method. On August 26, 1835, he expressed his concern in a letter to the Commissioner of the General Land Office: "Under the eighth paragraph of the Supplemental Treaty of Dancing Rabbit Creek there is a reservation in favor of Peggy Tryhan and her fatherless children, and Deliah and her five fatherless children to be located under the direction of the President of the United States. Under this clause the following lands have been reserved from sale, and that the orphans may have full benefit of the donations, I recommend that the lands be sold at public sale and that the money be paid over to them, or otherwise be disposed of for their uses as may be determined by the President of the United States." Gwin then gave a description of the land which had been reserved for the children of Deliah and then proceeded to get back to the question of the land reserved for Peggy Tryhan and her children. He described their reservation as follows: "Peggy Tryhan Lots 1, 6 and 7, Township 22, Range Five East, and lots 8, 9, 14 and 15, these are believed to be for the children of Peggy Tryhan, for Governor Runnels purchased the mother's claim, if I mistake not. It has been represented to me that fraud has been practiced on these orphans by a person having himself appointed their guardian; ordering the lands to be sold; and he, himself, becoming the purchaser for little or nothing. From the whole tenor of the treaty I think that it may be rationally concluded that the President is by it the guardian of these orphans, and for their use the lands ought to bring as much as they are worth."

Gwin seems to believe that Peggy had sold her own reservation to Governor Runnels, and that her children were in the process of being defrauded by the unnamed person who had acted in the manner described in his letter quoted above. In all probability the unnamed person was Franklin E. Plummer, since he is reported to have brought the land from Peggy Tryhan--who probably acted for her children. On December 18, 1845, there is recorded a transaction by which Jerry Tryhan, for a consideration of two hundred dollars, conveyed to L. W. Edington "a certain tract of land lying and being situated in the county of Yalobousha known and designated as the east half of lots number one, six, seven, eight, nine, fourteen, and fifteen." This, of course, is the same land alleged to have been sold by Peggy Tryhan to Plummer, and on which the town of Pittsburg had been established ten years earlier. Since the records never show a transfer of this property by Edington to anyone else, it leads to the presumption that Edington may have felt that because of the fraud mentioned by Gwin, Plummer's title was defective, and that he had bought the land from Jerry hoping to use the threat of alleged defective title to gain some financial return from the proprietors of the town who had warranted title to the various lots sold, and who would be responsible to the purchasers of the lots should their own title to the town prove defective. An example of the results of such a defective title was the removal of the original county seat of Tallahatchie County from Tillatoba to Charleston when the title to the land on which Tillatoba was located proved to be defective. Another evidence that Plummer was probably the person to whom Gwin had reference in his letter to the Commissioner of the General Land Office is the fact that Plummer also became owner of part of the land reserved for Deliah's children.

In deeds to land sold by Plummer, he is referred to as Franklin E. Plummer of Simpson County. He was a native of Massachussetts who came by ship to New Orleans and from there to Simpson County. He settled in the now extinct town of Westville. He taught school there for a time, and later practiced law at that place. He became a Congressional representative from Mississippi; later ran for the United States Senate in which race he was defeated. This ended his political life and with this defeat, he began a moral and physical decline which ended with his death under destitute circumstances in a miserable hotel in the city of Jackson. So far as we have been able to ascertain, he never had a permanent residence in the town which was founded on his original purchase, although his widow who ran a private school met her death, along with some of her pupils in a tornado which struck Grenada in 1846.

In early 1834 the fortunes of Plummer seem to have been at flood-tide. He was a successful politician and had secured an advantageous town site situated on the Yalobousha river, an important channel of commerce, as well as other well located land all at a very low price. There exists traditions, established by the dim memories of men and women in their old age, and compounded by errors in the W. P. A. Source Book in Grenada County, that Plummer and Runnels were the founders of the two rival towns of Pittsburg and Tullahoma, separated only by the sectional line which came to be known as Line street. This tradition is not true. Plummer was the owner of the land on which Pittsburg was established, but had sold out his interest in the land before its development as a town began, although apparently, at a later date, one of the purchasers, the firm of Shields & Puckett, defaulted and assigned their share of the Town Company to Plummer and James Sims. The earlier deeds to lots in the town list Shields & Puckett as among the proprietors of the town, while later deeds list "Plummer & Sims, Assignees" as being among the proprietors of the town. The land on which Tullahoma was established was bought by Hiram Runnels and John Watt. They sold eight tenths of their interest in this land to eight other men before the town was established. After this sale Runnels never owned more than one tenth share in the land, and was never active in its development. In early 1834 Plummer made three different conveyances by which he sold out his entire interest in the future town site. (A summary of these three transactions are found in deed by the Proprietors of the Town of Pittsburg to Michael Melton recorded in 1837. An excerpt from that deed reads as follows: "Whereas the portion of the second article of the suppliment to the treaty of Dancing Rabbit Creek there is given and granted unto Peggy Tryhan a reservation of land to be located at the descretion of the President of the United States, and whereas the said Peggy Tryhan by her certain instrument of writing, signed, sealed, and delivered on the 29th day of July in the year of our Lord eighteen hundred and thirty three conveyed all her right and title in and to the said reservation to Franklin E. Plummer, and whereas George W. Martin, the agent for that purpose appointed under the direction of the President of the United States on the 9th day of October in the year of our Lord eighteen hundred and thirty three located said reservation of land in the east half of Lots No. one, six, seven, eight, nine, fourteen and fifteen of fractional section No. seven, Township Twenty Two, Range No. Five East, and whereas the said Franklin E. Plummer has conveyed the said described tract unto the following persons and in the following proportion towit: Unto Hiram Coffee & J. A. McRaven and John & John A. Lane, one undivided half interest, and unto John Shields & G. M. Puckett one undivided fourth, and unto John Smith one other undivided fourth of the said before described tract or parcle of land, and whereas the said Coffee & McRaven, J. & J. A. Lane, Shields and Puckett and John Smith have formed themselves into a company under the style of Pittsburg Town Company and have laid off a town on the said described land according to the form of a plot of survey signed by the members of the said company. . ." Then the instrument gives a deed to lots 195-203, inclusive.) This deed seems conclusive evidence that the tradition of the town of Pittsburg being founded by Plummer had no basis in fact. From other instruments we know that the firm of Coffee & McRaven was domiciled in Hinds county and that John and J. A. Lane were residents of Warren county, and that the two firms paid four thousand dollars for their undivided half interest in the land involved. Shields & Puckett, whose one fourth interest cost them two thousand dollars, do not have their place of residence indicated. John Smith, who paid two thousand dollars for his undivided fourth interest, is the only one of the proprietors who has been definitely established as a resident of the town. He is the same John Smith who was a member of the staff at the Elliott Indian Mission, and whose daughter Harriett married James Sims, a merchant of Pittsburg, and along with Plummer an assignee of the interest of Shields & Puckett.

    The original survey of the town consisted of thirty five blocks which were subdivided into two hundred and forty nine lots. Commerce street on the west; Margin street on the south; Line street on the east, and the Yalobousha river on the north were the boundaries of the town. Streets running east and west were, beginning at the northern boundary, Promanade, Pearl, Cherry, Vine (now called Union), South and Margin. Streets running north and south were, beginning at the western boundary, Commerce, Water, West, Pittsburg, (now called College), East, and Line. Sale of lots in Pittsburg began in 1835, and houses were built and businesses established that year, but the majority of lots sold by the Pittsburg Town Company were sold after the town of Pittsburg had become the West Ward of the town of Grenada. As a going town, Pittsburg had an existence of less than two years, before its union with the town of Tullohoma to form Grenada. During the early years of its existence as either Pittsburg, or a ward of Grenada, we know that the following business firms were doing business in Pittsburg: John Smith Proprietor of Union Hotel; James Sims, Merchant; R. T. Bryarly, Merchant; Pryor & Howard; R. Coffman &

Company; Morris, Howard & Company; and Smith & Simms. In connection with the name "Howard" being connected with two of the firms we might note that from Goodspeed's Memoirs of Mississippi we find that one E. N. Howard had established a trading post in a cane-break on the Yalobousha river in the year 1832 at a place about where the town of Grenada is located. It is probable that the Howard mentioned as doing business in Pittsburg may have been this early trader. Other business and professional men located in the town of Pittsburg were: E. P. Davidson & Thomas Davidson, merchants; Dr. Gillespie and Dr. Douthet, physicians; C. D. Mitchell, teacher; M. H. Melton, blacksmith; Jonathan Carl Miller, and W. A. Thompson, building contractor. It is probable that some of the men or firms may have been established after Pittsburg had been consolidated with Tullahoma to form Grenada. It is also quite probable that, as the former town of Tullahoma gradually became the business center of the new town of Grenada, some of the business firms may have moved their operation to the area which is now the business district of Grenada.

Among those buying lots from the Pittsburg Town Company during the early years of its operation were Absolan Bew, W. H. Danthit, Peter Doman, J. F. Edmunson, William J. Marshall, Ralph & Joseph Coffman, John Smith, James Stanley, Jerry Taylor, J. W. King, Robert Williams, T. G. Logwood, J. M. Tate & Company, James and Harriett Sims, M. H. Melton, Thomas Williams, J. P. Crittendon, M. M. Drake, M. Mays, Samuel Pool, D. M. Dukley, N. Fitzmore, John Balfore, R. D. Flack, J. N. Shaw, D. M. Beck; Trustees of Baptist Church; W. C. Paine, John Moore, W. C. Chambers, J. R. Plummer, and Bacon & Crenshaw. There were many other transactions during the same period by which some of the original purchasers sold their newly acquired lots to late comers, usually at an increased price for the lots involved. Either because of the removal of business houses to the East Ward of Grenada, or because of the tight money situation in 1847, possibly because of both, many of lots in the original Pittsburg town site were sold for taxes at public sale, or by private sale at very low prices. An example of a private sale of considerable property for a low price was the transaction by which Septimus Caldwell and wife Mary conveyed to Harriett Sims for a consideration of two hundred dollars: "Lots number one hundred ninety six and one hundred ninety seven on which lots are situated the Tavern House occupied at this time by William Allen, also lots one hundred seventy two, one hundred seventy three, one hundred seventy four and one hundred seventy five, on which stands an office occupied by Septimus Caldwell." On August 13, 1839, Caldwell had bought part of this property from Samuel C. Caldwell and Theopulos Knox for a consideration of three notes of three thousand dollars each. On March 1, 1841, Caldwell had purchased the lots numbers one hundred ninety six and one hundred ninety seven, on which the tavern house was located, at a sheriff's sale under a court judgement against Thomas Davidson, John A. King, Granville A. Morris and James Howars. This property which brought twenty one dollars at the sale, is described in this manner: "Lots number one hundred ninety six and one hundred ninety seven lying in the west ward of Grenada on which there is a large, comodious Tavern House and other buildings known as the Union Hotel." This was the tavern first operated by John Smith, one of the proprietors of the Pittsburg Town Company. Just about two years earlier, on September 7, 1839, this same John Smith and his wife Hannah had sold to James Standley thirteen lots in the town for a consideration of six thousand and ten dollars. The fact that the property sold to satisfy the judgement should have sold for such a small sum indicates a serious depreciation in lot values, since the Smiths sold their lots for a good price two years previous to the court judgement sale. Another indication of financial distress and falling property values of the time are three transactions, one in 1841 and two in 1847, by which Harriett Sims bought, at public tax sales, thirty lots in the town for the small total consideration of three dollars and eight cents. Most of these lots were never redeemed by their former owners. The probable cause of such drastic reduction in land values, and frequent tax sales during this period, was the Panic of 1837 which lasted for six years, and caused the nation-wide financial depression which resulted in the shut-down of ninety per cent of the factories in the East, and business failures throughout the nation. Mrs. Sims continued to buy up lots at subsequent tax sales and soon became the chief property towner in the town. In 1846 there was a strange transaction by which Harriet Sims, now owner of much of the property in the town, purchased from Peggy and Jerry Tryhan lots 1, 6, 7, 8, 9, 14, and 15. These lots make up the east one half of Section 7, Township 22, Range 5 East, the same property which Plummer had purchased from Peggy in 1833 and on which Pittsburg was located. We can only speculate as to the reason for this transaction. It brings about the possibility of fraud being perpertrated in the original purchase, and the desire of Mrs. Sims to clear any possible defect in title to the considerable property which she owned in the town. It is possible that this factor may have contributed to the fact that so many property owners in Pittsburg allowed their lots to sell for taxes. It would seem that, at the time of the union of Pittsburg and Tullahoma to form Grenada, Pittsburg was rapidly being overshadowed by the sister town to the east.

Tullahoma

Although tradition, accepted by the compilers of the W. P. A. Source Book on Grenada county, names Hiram G. Runnels as the founder of the town of Tullahoma, this is not true so far as the founding of the town being the individual project of Runnels. The first official record relative to the Tullahoma Town Company, which record is quoted hereafter, does not even mention Runnels who was never more than an absentee one tenth owner of the town project, although before the founding of the town he had obtained a one half interest in the section of land on which the town was to be established. The original reference to the town is as follows: "The Board of Commissioners of Tullahoma Company met at Chocchuma on the 4th of November 1833. Present John L. Orwin, President; George W. Martin and W. M. Gwin, Treasurer. It was resolved that L. Cleveland is hereby authorized to sell at private sale any lot of ground in the town of Tullahoma, reserving every other square entire, and at least half of the lots in each square thus subject to private sale, to be sold at public sale of the lots thereafter to take place. Resolved that the said Cleveland is hereby authorized to divide the said lots into halves and quarters to suite purchasors. Resolved that the said Cleveland is hereby authorized to sell the cite (sic) at the best possible price at twelve months credit, giving bond for title when money is paid, providing no corner business lot shall be sold for a sum less than fifty dollars."

For some unexplained reason Clevelnad was, one day later on November 5, released from the agreement with the company and Uriah Tyson empowered to do all things which Cleveland was authorized to do, and in addition, he was empowered "to make any contracts concerning the ferry, also to employ a surveyor to finish laying off the remainder of the land intended for town lots and family residences." Tyson was also authorized to "call on the Treasurer of the said Company to pay L. Cleveland forty eight dollars, that being the price of the entry book furnished by the said Cleveland to the said Company. If there is no monies in the treasury, the said Treasurer is authorized to call on the Proprietors for that amount. Resolved that Public Sale of lots take place at Chocchuma on the third Monday in February, 1834."

In its description of the transactions by which the town site came into possession of the Proprietors of the Tullahoma Town Company the W. P. A. Source Book has this statement: "John Donly was a white man who had for many years carried mail for the Indians. When the treaty of Dancing Rabbit Creek was drawn up, the Indians, out of consideration for him, stipulated that the government should give him a tract of land which he might choose from any part of the Choctaw Nation. He decided on a section adjoining that belonging to Peggy Tryhan. Later he sold it to Henry R. W. Hill of Nashville, Tennessee who conveyed it to S. M. Gwin, then United States Marshall for Mississippi, from whom H. G. Runnels acquired it." This statement is in error in at least three particulars. In the first place, Donley, who was the father of the first wife of Greenwood Leflore, did not choose the land. He merely sold his unlocated section of land to Hill. All land reservations granted under the treaty were located by a government locating agent. Hill did not convey the land to Gwin, but gave him a power of attorney to sell the land for the original purchasers. Hiram G. Runnels did not become sole owner of the section of land. He and John Watt paid Hill four thousand dollars for a joint and equal interest in the land. The land sold them by Hill was located for them in Section 8, Township 22, Range 5 East. Since the price paid for this section of land was far greater than was paid for most of the other land in the area, it is very probable that Gwin, who being a Federal employee, had inside information relative to land locations, was able to assure Runnels and Watts that the locating agent would locate their purchase in the advantageous position which they secured when the locating agent certified the section mentioned above as the location of the reservation which they had purchased. The Source Book also states, in reference to the towns of Pittsburg and Tullahoma, "About 1820 a town was platted on each of the land claims." This, of course, is a very obvious error, perhaps a typographical one, since neither of the land transactions by which the two town companies came into possession of the land could take place before the signing of the treaty which took place in 1830.

    A power of attorney by John C. McLemore to John A. King, authorizing King to sell McLemore's one tenth interest in Section 8, Township 22, Range 5 East gives us the identity of the men who were the original Proprietors of Tullahoma. By that power of attorney McLemore authorizes King "to sell my one tenth interest in Section 8, Township 22, Range 5 East, the same section of land reserved for John Donley and fully described in Articles of Agreement between H. G. Runnels, and John Watt, Parties of one part and J. R. Plummer, William G. Covington, John B. McLemore, George Martin, Wiley Davis, L. Cleveland, John L. Irwin, William Terry, and Allen Sharkey." Most of these men mentioned had bought one tenth shares from Runnels and Watt, although the number of partners indicates that some of them owned less than a one tenth share. The original partners soon sold part, or all of their shares. In one transaction we find a sale of a one fortieth share. W. M. Gwin never owned any part of the Town Company, although he served briefly as the treasurer of the organization. Runnels and Watt were absentee part owners and had little to do with the actual development of the town. Irwin, Martin, Cleveland and Davis were either temporary or permanent residents of the area. John H. McKinnie purchased a one tenth interest from Covington, but died soon thereafter, and after his death most of the deeds to lots in the town designated the grantors of the lots as "Proprietors of Tullahoma, Survivors of John H. McKinnie," such deeds then being signed by the individual proprietors of their agents. As time went on the make-up of the proprietors changed as original members sold their interests to others. Among those buying interests in the Town Company were: A. S. Brown, William B. Beall, Andrew R. Govan, William P. Byron, Uriah Tyson, Thomas B. Ives, John J. Claw and John Balfour. A number of the proprietors bought individual lots from the Town Company. Runnels, Balfour, Cleveland, and Brown were most active in securing these individual holdings.

    The original survey contained in excess of two hundred and fifty lots. Streets in the town were very much as they are today in the East Ward of Grenada. Lots were marked off all the way to the Yalobousha river with the most northern east and west street being Front street which ran along the line of the old "Peavine" railroad tract which has been discontinued. From east to west lots were marked off all the way from Bogue Creek to Line street. Some town maps show Depot street, but, in all probability the name of this street was changed, since at the time of the original survey of the town the arrival in Grenada of the Mississippi Central Railroad and the construction of a railroad depot, which probably gave rise to the name "Depot Street," was some twenty three years in the future.

We have little or no information relative to most of the Town Proprietors. We know, of course, that Hiram G. Runnels was a native of Lawrence county and had been long a politital power in the state. He served as State Auditor from 1822 to 1830. About 1820 he was one of the founders of the present town of Columbia in Marion county. He was elected as a member of the State Legislature in 1830. In 1831 he made an unsuccessful race for State Governor, being defeated by about two hundred votes. In 1833 he was elected Governor over his previous opponent, Scott, who was running for re-election. During his administration as Governor he directed the building of the first capitol building in the newly located town of Jackson which had been selected as the State Capitol. Defeated for re-election as Governor he became president of the ill-fated Mississippi Union Bank. He evidently then, or sometime thereafter, left the state, since we find on record a transaction by which in 1857 he sold a lot in Grenada to A. S. Brown, and is identified by the deed of transfer as a resident of Harris county, Texas. Andrew R. Govan was a resident of Holly Springs, Mississippi, who owned much land, several mills, and many slaves. His land holdings were in Marshall, Tippah and Grenada counties. His slaves were on his Marshall and Grenada county lands. There is on record a deed of trust, dated in 1841, by which, in order to secure varied indebitiness amounting to ninety eight thousand five hundred and thirty dollars, he mortgaged 9600 acres of land, two hundred and one slaves; all his livestock; his gold and silver watches; his carriage; farm utensils; saw mills; lumber and his town lots in Holly Springs and Grenada. Govan was a native of South Carolina and, before removing to Mississippi had represented the Orange District of that state in the Federal Congress. Like many of his contemporaries he over-extended his credit and lost most of his possessions. John Balfour was an early settler in the town. He served as a ferryman on one of the two Yalobousha river ferries in the area. His wife was one of the first persons to be buried in the old cemetery across from Highway 51. A. S. Brown was one of the proprietors who invested heavily in town lots bought from the Town Company. During the years 1837-1840, inclusively, he bought twenty six lots at a total cost of six thousand five hundred and thirty dollars. He was also a considerable land owner throughout the area. His prize property was a two thousand acre plantation called Emerald Garden on which he built, in the 1840's, the house recently owned by Mrs. C. C. Provine. The plantation name derived from the extensive flower garden which surrounded the house. Mr. Brown was a native of Nashville, Tennessee who came to the area in the early years of its development and prospered. After the Civil War he moved to Memphis in an endeavor to restore his fortune, but died there before he accomplished his purpose. George W. Martin served the Federal Government as a locating agent of the many Indian land reservations claimed by members of the Choctaw Nation. L. Cleveland was a merchant in the town of Tullahoma and owner of considerable land outside the town. William M. Beall was a New Orleans business man who invested heavily in lands in the Choctaw Land Cession.

In the original survey, Tullahoma was divided into two hundred sixty five lots. The first recorded conveyance of a lot in the town is dated November 5, 1833, and the last such transaction by the Town Company occured in 1855. Thus, the Tullahoma Town Company had a life span of twenty two years. During the course of its existence the company sold two hundred and one lots for a total sum of sixty one thousand three hundred two dollars and ninety two cents. Since many of the sales were made on liberal credit terms, it is probable that, because of default of payment on some of the lots, the Company actually received considerably less money from the sale of lots than is indicated above. Most of the remaining sixty four lots not recorded as having been sold by the

Company, were sold for taxes during the period of financial depression which reached its crisis during the early 1840's. Although the Company continued to sell lots until 1855, most of the sales made by the Company occurred during the years 1835-1839, inclusive. It was during these years that choice lots brought good prices. It seems that some people had selected lots before the formal sale of lots began. On November 5, 1833 the Proprietors of the company authorized Larkin Cleveland to donate to Matilda Price and David Daughlin lots 66 and 68 on which they had made improvements. We have no indication as to why these lots should have been donated just because improvements had been made upon them. For some reason there was a dispute between David Daughlin and Shubal Foot over the ownership of lot 66. To settle the dispute they agreed to arbitration by a group of three men whose decision was to be final. They must have found for Foot since the transaction ended with Daughlin conveying his interest in the lot to Foot. This lot was located on the north side of the square where Gordon's store is presently located. Lot 66 is the lot on which Grenada Theater is located. At an early date a hotel was located on this lot. In 1855 lot 68 was bought by W. M. and H. S. Lake, and about the same time they acquired lot 67; the two purchases giving the brothers ownership of the south half of the block which was just north of the public square. The two hundred one lots sold by the Company during its existence were sold to seventy seven individuals who bought one or more lots. Some of the purchasers built homes and set up businesses in the town. Other purchasers were absentee speculators who bought early, hoping to sell later at increased prices. One of these speculators was John R. Marshall of New York City. He obtained several choice lots; did some trading, and ended by having the Yalobousha county sheriff sell several of his lots for taxes. The heaviest investors in town lots included A. S. Brown, who bought twenty six lots for six thousand five hundred and ninety dollars; A. C. Baine, purchaser of eighteen lots at a total price of four thousand one hundred forty dollars and one cent; John Moore, who invested thirty six hundred and fifty two dollars in the purchase of eleven lots; and John Balfour who paid eight thousand three hundred and sixty three dollars for ten well located lots, and the Lake brothers, either individually or in partnership, spent three thousand six hundred sixty eight dollars and eighty cents for six lots.

Brown and Balfour have heretofore been identified as being among the Proprietors of the Tullahoma Town Company. A. C. Baine was an extensive land owner both of lots in the town and farming land in the vicinity of the town. William, H. S., George and Levin Lake were four brothers who came to Grenada from Maryland in 1835. From time to time they engaged in mercantile business, banking, insurance, warehousing, and other ventures. For almost one hundred years they and their descendants continued active in the business and civic affairs of the early town of Tullahoma, and the later town of Grenada. The brothers bought some of their lots along the Yalobousha river front, and it was one of these on which they built a cotton warehouse which stored much cotton during the days when the river was about the only way by which cotton could be shipped to the cotton factories in New Orleans. John Moore was an architect and builder who constructed some of the more pretentious houses built in the two towns, the houses presently occupied by J. L. Townes and Mrs. R. S. Jackson being two examples of his architectural and building skill. The lots along the north side of the town square were purchased by L. Cleveland, David Daughlin and Subal Foot. Those on the east side of the square were originally purchased by A. C. Baine, N. S. Neal and G. K. Morton. Those on the south side of the square were first purchased by J. Abbott, S. Tyson and A. S. Brown. On the west side of the square W. H. Whitaker and G. K. Morton were the original purchasers. The lot on which Grenada Bank is now located was purchased by G. W. Parker and John B. Pass. Other early purchasers of lots were G. Phillips, Sam Smith, Robert and John Williams, A. B. Jones, J. D. Melton, Green Crowder, J. D. Thomason, J. A. Mitchell, and J. A. Wilson. It is indicative of the importance which the Town Proprietors placed on the ferry which they controlled that, in each lot sold which had a river front, there was a stipulation that no ferry rights were conveyed. Some of the early business firms established in the town, on or soon after its consolidation with Pittsburg, were those of L. Cleveland; Clark Daugan; Armour, Lake & Morton; as well as other businesses run by the Lake Brothers. Marshall was a silversmith, Major Jack Williams and Mrs. Annie Parker operated hotels.

Tullahoma, having made an earlier start in organization and sale of lot than in its neighboring town to the west, seems always to have been a place of more importance than Pittsburg. Beginning even before the union of the two towns, and continuing for several years thereafter, the business firms of Pittsburg gradually moved their locations to Tullahoma which became the chief business section of the united towns. Although the hard times of the period hit Tullahoma, it seems that it hit with less force than it did in Pittsburg. Fewer tax sales of lots in Tullahoma probably indicate that, because of its increasing importance as a business center, lots were more valuable in Tullahoma than in Pittsburg, and owners less likely to allow them to be sold for taxes. The increasing importance of Tullahoma as a trade center as early as 1835 is evidenced by a paper written or dictated by L. Lake. He states that he and his brothers moved from Maryland in 1830 to Jackson, Tennessee. In 1834 they moved to Hendersonville, an early town located about four miles south of the present town of Coffeeville. This town was started earlier than Coffeeville, and aspired to become the seat of county government. The first meeting of the Board of Supervisors of Yalobousha county was held at Hendersonville, but since the newly organized town of Coffeeville became the county seat, Hendersonville, after a very brief existence, was abandoned and its site became part of a plantation owned by Franklin E. Plummer, and called Oakchickamau. Soon thereafter the Lakes moved in 1835, to the town of Tullahoma. Mr. Lake lists the following business firms as being located in Hendersonville: Martin, Edwards & Company; John H. McKinnie; Armour, Lake and Bridges; H. S. & W. Lake; and McCain and Company. We have evidence that three of these firms later located in either Tullahoma or in Grenada after the consolidation took place.

As will have been seen elsewhere, the growth which made the consolidated rival towns Pittsburg and Tullahoma into the chief trade center of the area came from the removal of people and business firms from the other small towns of the area which towns were founded, flourished, and then declined, to the extent that most of their people and business firms removed to more favorable situations, of which the new town of Grenada was the most favored. During the first few years of their existence, neither of the two towns of Pittsburg and Tullahoma had any pretentious buildings. Practically all buildings, both residences and businesses, were frame buldings of no considerable value. It was only after the union of the two towns, and the growth of a well-to-do class of farmers and plantation owners in the new, rich lands of the area, that a better class of buildings were erected. As time passed it took at least two disasterous fires to remove all of the shoddy buildings ranged around the public square, the fires resulting in an ordinance forbiding the erection of any more frame buildings in the business section of the town. The story of this transformation will be related in the account of the union of Pittsburg and Tullahoma.

Tuscahoma

Located about three miles up the Yalobousha river from Chocchuma, the town of Tuscahoma began its existence slightly later than Chocchuma and lasted a few years longer. During its heyday it was probably the second largest town in what is now Grenada county. Of course, for the years of its existence as a town, it was located in Tallahatchie county. The second road established in Tallahatchie county was "viewed out," that is, it was located from Parsalia to Tuscahoma. Parsalia was established in 1833 or 1834 and was located on the south bank of the Yocona river in the northeastern part of Tallahatchie county, near the present village of Enid. It is probable that the first road located in the county was the road from Charleston to Carrollton by way of Chocchuma. Since there were ferrys at both Chocchuma and Tuscahoma, and since early roads led to each place, it was as a result of both these favorable circumstances that both became shipping points and places of some importance during the early years of the settlement of the area.

Tuscahoma seems to have been a project started by James A. Girault who was "Receiver of Public Monies" at the land office in Chocchuma. It was located in section sixteen, township 22, range 3 east. Since each sixteenth section of land in the Choctaw purchase was ear-marked for school purposes, it became necessary for the promoters of the town to obtain a lease from the school trustees of the township in which the section was located. Girault received a ninety nine year lease on the northwest quarter of the section, the lease beginning in September, 1834. Evidently other men were associated with Girault in the project since there is on record the following account of the organization of the Association of the Tuscahoma Company:

> "The undersigned agree to form themselves into an association or company to be styled the Tuscahoma Company and agree by one of their members to buy the east half of the northwest quarter of Section 16, Township 22, range 3, east, provided the sum does not exceed in amount more than twenty per cent of the amount of shares recorded by the undersigned. Each of the subscribers is to secure, according to the laws of the state in relation to leasing of sixteenth sections, his proportion of purchase money to the satisfaction of the trustees within ten days or forfeit his share; each share to be one hundred dollars; half shares may be subscribed. Those who reside on improved lots are at liberty to take said lots at a fair valuation to be assessed by three dis-interested individuals of fair intelligence unless the parties themselves shall agree upon the valuation. If the holder of any lot, or lots, shall not accept the same at its fair valuation within ten days after the same shall be assessed, he shall forfeit his pre-emption right to the said lot, or lots. The value of such improved lots shall be applied first to the payment of the debts contracted by the company, to be paid to the school trustees of the township, and if the same shall not be sufficient for that purpose other lots shall be sold as early as practicably to raise a sufficient sum to pay said debts, the payment for improved and unimproved lots until said principal debt is paid shall be in one, two, three and four years from the 12th instance, after which the remaining lots shall be sold on such terms as the subscribers, or a majority of them shall agree, and the net profits are to be divided among the subscribers in proportion to the shares or half shares subscribed by each co-partner. If the said site of land should not sell for more than the amount of shares subscribed and not to exceed the sum more than twenty per cent then each subscriber is bound to supply his pro-rata share of the excess."

Shareholders in the Association and the numbers of shares subscribed for by each subscriber were as follows: A. S. Campbell 10, Samuel B. Marsh 15, James A. Marsh number of shares not listed, A. F. Stacey 4, G. M. Savage 8, Charles P. Flackly 2, Cyrus Parkhurst 5, James A. Girault 10, Thomas R. Girault 5, William Hunley number of shares not listed, E. L. McCracken 3, J. D. Carroll 5, L. McLaughlin 5, John Miller 6, Eli McMullen 5, and C. P. Alexander 5. The ninety nine year lease was purchased for the sum of eight thousand six hundred and sixty four dollars. From the reference in the agreement to surrender of pre-emption rights to lots it would seem that some of the persons involved had settled in the area of the town before land sales began and expected to be granted leases on the pre-empted area as soon as such leases could be made. Evidently L. McLaughlin was one of the early settlers and, under the agreement, wanted to purchase his property from the Association, since we find a deed, or rather a lease, by which Girault, as President of the Tuscahoma Company, gave a ninety nine year lease to McLaughlin for a consideration of six hundred and twenty five dollars on lots thirty, forty one and forty two "payable in four annual installments evidenced by four notes of one hundred fifty six dollars and twenty five cents each." On May 3, 1835, he leased lot number six in square number 12 to M. G. Shumate for a consideration of fifty eight dollars payable in three annual payments. In 1836 Tuscahoma was incorporated by an act of the state legislature. The first license to operate a saloon in Tallahatchie county was granted to a firm at Tuscahoma for a fee of fifteen dollars.

A. L. Campbell operated the ferry at Tuscahoma. Some of the business firms in the town were Girault & McRea; Campbell & Adams; Tulson and Company, J. Y. Blocker; Adams & Wilcox and J. D. Carroll & Company. Mr. and Mrs. Williams operated the Wayside Inn, the remains of which still existed as late as 1930. Tuscahoma Academy was not located in the town, but about a mile and a quarter southeast of the town at Guy's Corner, near the site of the present Holcomb Elementary school. E. Percy Howe began publication of a newspaper THE TUSCAHOMIAN in 1835. Like the town of Troy, a few miles up the Yalobousha river, Tuscahoma prospered for a few years, but, from a letter published in 1842, seems to have about reached the end of its existence as a place of importance. The letter, addressed to "Mr. Tyler" by an unidentified writer reads in part:

"A few days ago in company with Major James A. Girault, a planter residing near Tuscahoma, I visited that place, once the principal commercial emporium of North Mississippi, but now a deserted village...The scence was more forcibly impressed on the mind as the Major pointed here and there to improvements made by him at a time when the investment was considered one that would prove of permanent value. Major Girault was a liberal patron toward the improvements of this town; he was the prime mover in various branches of business such as merchandising, tavern-keeping, painting, brickmaking, carpentering, & all of which, I was inferred, caused an outlay which was never realized. There are yet remaining in this town two large two-story frame tavern houses one of which belongs to the Major, as also a large commodious mercantile house about 100 feet in length-many of the buildings have been moved, some for dwelling houses in the country..one store house has been removed..a distance of twelve miles...One of the buildings in Tuscahoma to which my attention was more particularly called, was the one formerly occupied by E. Percy Howe...I recollect well the "TUSCAHOMIAN"; that proved champion of Democracy...The building, to which I have alluded as the consecrated temple of Democracy, Major Girault was having removed to his residence for a schoolroom as he is educationg his children under the care and supervision of a private instructress; a highly capable lady from one of the New England states."

Although his dream of a prosperous outcome to the Tuscahoma town project had not been realized, it would seem that Girault was still a man of considerable means, as evidenced by the fact that he was employing a private teacher for his children when the Tuscahoma Academy was still operating and that he was still the owner of considerable property in and about Tuscahoma. At the time of the publication of the letter, Girault was living on the plantation known as Bellview Place. This place, which was later bought by D. L. Holcomb, was about a mile southeast of the area where the town of Holcomb is now located. Before Girault moved to this place, he had lived on a part of the land formerly used as the Elliott Indican Mission School. This place was about one mile south of the present town of Holcomb.

Although Tuscahoma was abandoned a town project when most of its inhabitants moved away, it still continued to be the center of some activity. The ferry which continued to operate until well after the Civil War was rather busy as there was a road connecting Grenada with Tuscahoma, and also a road running from Tuscahoma to Charleston. Before the creation of Grenada county people living in the vicinity of Tuscahoma had to go to Charleston for any business necessitating a trip to their county seat, so, many people from that part of Tallahatchie County, continued to cross the river at the defunct town, and perhaps to stop in the Wayside Inn which continued in operation for several years after the town had been very largely abandoned. The Tuscahoma post office was in operation as late as 1873, and the voting precinct was continued there to a much later date. The Tuscahoma ferry was operating as late as December 2, 1882, as evidenced by the following quoted advertisement: "I will pay highest price for cotton and cotton seed at the warehouse near Tuscahoma ferry. Ferriage free to all bringing cotton and cotton seed to warehouse. Walter Crump."

Since Girault was such an important figure in the development of the town of Tuscahoma it is of interest to note that he, like so many other of the early land speculators, eventually lost most of his land. Perhaps his greatest business mistake was in subscribing to a large number of shares of stock in the Mississippi Union Bank. On May 23, 1839, he subscribed for 2155 shares of the stock at one hundred dollars per share. The involved assuming an obligation of two hundred fifteen thousand five hundred dollars, which indebtedness was secured by a deed of trust which Girault gave to the bank. Included in the instrument given to make possible the purchase of the bank stock were the following property items as set out in the deed of trust; nineteen hundred and sixty acres of land situated in several different locations; all of Bellevue plantation containing three hundred and sixty acres; an undivided half interest in thirteen hundred and fifty eight acres of land in two locations known as Black Creek and White Place tracts; and firty nine Negro slaves whose ages and work qualifications are listed. After a short, illfated operation the bank failed and when those people who had purchased stock were unable to pay for their stock purchases, the men in charge of the liquidation of the assets of the bank began to forclose on the many deeds of trust given to the bank. Girault was one of those who lost much property in this process. One of the last land transactions relative to property in Tuscahoma will indicate falling land value in the town; the need of Girault for ready cash, and the somewhat ambitious plan for the town. In January 1836 Girault sold to James N. Bryne, Louis T. Harman, and Charles Briggs of New Orleans and Charles A. Lacont of Natchez, thirty six lots in the town of Tuscahoma for a consideration of two thousand four hundred and fifty dollars. These lots were located in twenty different blocks. Since these blocks were the same as town squares, we learn that there were at least twenty squares in the original plan of the town. It is probable that there were squares in which none of the lots listed in the above mentioned transaction were located. Since the sale of these lots took place in 1836 when the town was still a place of some importance we may assume that Girault was in dire financial straights at this time.

We have little, or no, information relative to the people who made up the stockholders and residents of the town. Samuel B. Marsh was a lawyer who practiced in the courts of Yalobousha county and speculated in land. He was probably not a resident of Tuscahoma. William Huntly was an employee of the land office at Chocchuma who married a daughter of John Smith, one of the Elliott Station Indian missionaries. John Miller was one of the Trustees of the Spring Hill Methodist church to whom James Marble conveyed eight and a fraction acres of land in the year 1835.

Troy

The town of Troy, which in the early years of its existence, was expected to contend with Grenada as the chief town of the area, was the optimistic project of one of the most brilliant of the many young men who left their native states and came into Mississippi during the early years of the nineteenth century. They came to engage all branches of endeavor which would give them an opportunity to share in the prosperity of the new state. Robert J. Walker, the founder of the town of Troy, was a native of the state of Pennsylvania. He was graduated from the state university at the age of sixteen years. He studied law and was a practicing attorney at the age of twenty years. At the age of twenty two years he controlled the Democratic state convention of Pennsylvania to the extent that he was able to get that convention to endorse Andrew Jackson as a presidential nominee. In 1826, at the age of twenty five years, he came to Mississippi and began the practice of law at Natchez. In Natchez he became acquainted with Samuel Gwin and W. H. Gwin, two brothers who led the Jackson forces in Mississippi. United States Senator Poindexter had quarreled with President Jackson over federal patronage in Mississippi, Jackson being inclined to appoint friends from Tennessee to the better positions, while Poindexter insisted that these offices should go to Mississippians. Walker was known to be a very close friend of the President, so the Gwin brothers and other prominent men who helped lead the Jackson forces in Mississippi, looked upon this brilliant young lawyer as the logical person to run against Poindexter for re-election. Having broken with Jackson, Poindexter made the race for re-election as a Whig candidate. Walker received the support of the many Jackson supporters in the state and was elected in 1834 as United States Senator instead of Poindexter. He was re-elected in 1841 over his opponent, the brilliant Mississippi orator S. S. Prentiss. While serving in the Senate Walker became a very close friend of Tennessee Congressman James K. Polk and was very active in the campaign which resulted in the election of Polk to the Presidency. It is very probable that it was through the influence and advice of Walker that Congressman Polk had bought up some of the land opened up for settlement by the Treaty of Dancing Rabbit Creek. Polk's Mississippi land was located about three miles southwest of Coffeeville. In 1844 Polk appointed Walker to his cabinet as Secretary of the Treasury. In this capacity Walker financed the war with Mexico which came during Polk's term as President. Later, President Pierce appointed Walker Ambassador to China, which position he resigned after a brief tenure. His last public service was when President Buchanan appointed him Territorial Governor of Kansas. Mississippi hostorians have failed to recognize the powerful influence which this strange, brilliant, eccentric man exerted in Mississippi from the time he came to Mississippi in 1836 until he left the state in 1844 to accept a position in Polk's cabinet. A contemporary describes Walker in this manner: " a mere whipped of a man slooping and diminutive with a whezy voice and expressionless face." His wife, who stuck by him through both good and ill fortune, was a grandaughter of Benjamin Franklin.

Walker was probably the most extensive land speculator of the period, acquiring large areas of public land in Louisiana, Mississippi and Wisconsin. In 1833 and 1834 Walker bought, either individually or in partnership with Thomas Barnard, over nine thousand acres of land in that area which is now located in Grenada county. He paid from seventy five cents to a dollar and a quarter per acre for this land. At the land office at Chocchuma he, along with a large number of other land speculators, paid down one third of the purchase price of the land to James A. Girault, Receiver of Public Monies, and then had seven years time in which to pay the balance due on the land.

Of course these speculators expected to sell off the land, pay off their debt to the government land office, and still have a tidy fortune left from their land speculations. An indication of this optimism is a power of attorney given by Walker and Bernard to Thomas Ives on January 29, 1836, less than three years after Walker had secured his Mississippi land. By this instrument Ives was given the right to sell any land which Walker and Bernard had in the counties of Carroll, Tallahatchie and Yalobousha, for cash or credit to responsible people. No land was to be sold for less than six dollars per acre. Cash received from the sale of the land was to be deposited with the Receiver of Public Monies at Chocchuma to the credit of Walker and Bernard. Land not sold for cash was to be sold for one third of the purchase price paid at the time of the purchase, and the balance payable on notes due in one and two years after the sale. These notes were to be payable at the Planter's Bank of Natchez. It would seem that Walker and Bernard hoped to sell enough land for cash to settle their obligations to the Federal Land Office, and derive their profit from the notes which were payable at their home town bank.

Because of his friendship with Samuel Gwin, in charge of the Land Office at Chocchuma, and W. H. Gwin United States Marshall for the Northern District of Mississippi, Walker purchased much of the best located land in the counties mentioned above. He entered land about, or in the vicinity, of practically every town or village springing up in the area. Ironically enough, it was an action of his friend Andrew Jackson, which ruined Walker's chance of becoming wealthy through land speculation, and caused him to lose most of the land which he had purchased. Jackson had destroyed the Bank of the United States. As a result, much currency issued by state banks was in circulation. This provided easy credit and encouraged speculation. Jackson, in 1836, endeavored to lessen this speculation by issuing his "Specie Circular." This was a directive to government land offices not to receive any kind of money except gold or silver in payment of public lands. Since there was not much gold or silver in circulation, land speculators still owing the land office two thirds of the purchase price of the lands could not obtain sufficient specie to pay off their obligations to the land office, and many of them including Walker, lost about everything they had, and still were burdened with debt which most of them were never able to pay off.

Having been able to get in on the ground floor, so to speak, in the matter of purchasing so much land in 1833, Walker conceived the idea of founding a town, just as other men were founding towns at Pittsburg and Tullahoma. So Walker had a part of the east quarter of Section thirty three, Township twenty three, Range four east, land which he and Bernard owned, surveyed and platted for a town to be called Troy. The town was located on a bluff above the Yalobousha. Today the only evidence which is visible to indicate the former existence of a town on the location is the ruins of a few building foundations, and under-water snags of former pier piles occasionally noticed at low water stages of the river. For a few brief years Troy was a prosperous business center for a few energetic business firms which capitalized upon the busy river traffic carried on by small river steamers and keelboats. A wealthy class of large plantation owners lived in the vicinity of Troy and, because of the almost impassable state of most of the early county roads, it was advantageous for these people to take their cotton for shipment to Troy, and to receive their plantation supplies there. The swamps north of the Yalobousha river made it more difficult for people north of the river to haul their cotton to Grenada than to get it a greater distance to Troy over better roads. There were no swamps to cross to get to Troy and, for the people north of the river, no ferry charges to cross the river since Troy was on the north side. Much cotton from the vicinity of Coffeeville went to Troy. President James Polk shipped his cotton by way of Troy. Some of the leading families residing on plantations in the vicinity of Troy were the Leighs, Powells, Talberts, Bakers, Minters and Townes.

The plan of the town was rather ambitious, more than two hundred lots being marked off and ready for sale in 1834. On October 23, 1834, just about a year later than the beginning of the two little towns of Pittsburg and Tullahoma, just a few miles up the river, Robert J. Walker appointed Angus Chisholm and William Minter "my true and lawful attorney in fact for me and in my name, place and state, to sell, convey, transfer and convey with full warranty all my right, title and interest in and to the town of Troy and the adjacent land, being the South East Quarter of Section 33, Township 23, Range 4 East." We may accept this date as the beginning of the town, since this was the first time lots were to be sold. Since Walker in 1834 was engaged in his campaign for the United States Senate, he must of necessity depend upon others to conduct the business of the actual development of his town. If Chisholm and Minter were not already in business at the place at the time when they were empowered to begin the sale of lots, they were in business soon thereafter, trading under the firm name of Chisholm & Minter. They evidently did a large credit business since we find many deeds of trust given by different individuals to the firm to secure credit, or to satisfy the firm for some previously contracted debt. For instance, Morelan Myrick gave a deed of trust to the firm on 80 acres of land, one cow, one calf, and one sorrel horse; this instrument was dated June 20, 1836. In June of the same year, a man by the name of Pressley, gave the firm a deed of trust on eighty acres of land to secure his debt to Chisholm and Minter. In August 1837 Moses Wells gave a deed of trust on lots 77 and 78 in Troy to secure an indebtedness due Chisholm and Minter, and also a note in favor of Angus C. Chisholm and William Minter, Agents for Troy Town Company. In January of 1838, Wells gave a warranty deed to the firm because of default in payment of the above mentioned debt. There are many more similar transactions but these few will give some idea of the extensive credit extended by the firm of Chisholm and Minter. As will be shown later this liberality relative to credit, secured largely by deeds of trust on land, proved fatal to the firm when the money panic of 1837 hit with full force. Evidently there was another business firm in the town which was extending credit on deeds of trust on land. On January 21, 1837, in an instrument dated Troy, Mississippi, John Kirkpatrick, in consideration of $1000 and cancellation of a debt of $5000, conveyed to S. McMullen & Company "all of Block 7 in the town of Troy, said block containing eight acres." Among those owning lots in the little town were Isaac Brunner, Allen Gattis, William Ross, D. B. Magnard, W. M. Minter, James Minter, Thomas W. Beall, George W. Topp, D. B. Mann, L. C. Gillespie, R. Hammer, W. H. Hammer, J. Holloman, R. L. Jones and Thomas G. Bowles.

Although Troy for a few years was a place of some importance, it is doubtful if it ever was as large a town as some of the claims made by some of the older citizens of the town as they related traditions of the past to succeeding generations. It probably never had more than three hundred inhabitants. It is also improbable that, as some have maintained, Troy was a serious rival to the town of Grenada until the construction of the Mississippi Central Railroad through Grenada delt a deathblow to the prosperity of Troy. As a matter of fact, Troy had become a ghost town some ten years before the railroad reached Grenada. It is very probable that the union of the two small Yalobousha river towns of Pittsburg and Tullahoma to form Grenada was the beginning of the end of the development of Troy. Dr. Isom who came to the future site of Grenada in 1832 as a representative of a St. Louis trading company and from that point fitted out a trading expedition to go trading into the Chickasaw country, states that when he came back into the area in 1838 he found the town in a bad state of deterioration, with only a few occupied houses remaining.

The few years following the Panic of 1837 evidently took its toll of the business formerly enjoyed by the town. The beginning of the end is probably indicated by the following excerpt from an instrument which indicates the failure of the firm of Chisholm and Minter, and the assignment of their property to a trustee who was to liquidate their holdings in an attempt to settle their debts. In a document recorded on June 7, 1841, we find the following excerpt:

> "James Minter, G. R. Morris and A. C. Chisholm, formerly merchants doing business under the firm and site of Minter Morris & Company grant to William Minter for a consideration of five dollars, all our right, title and interest in and to the following described land and lots situate, lying and being in the county and state aforesaid to-wit: Two twelfths of the Troy tract of land to-wit: The south east quarter of Section 33, Township 23, Range 4 east, and also two eights of a twenty acre tract of land on which the warehouse in the town of Troy now stands, and also the following town lots in the town of Troy, to-wit: Numbers 57, 58, 57, 177, 138, 139, 14, 39, 43, 72, 77, 78, 75, 87, 106, and also all the interest in and to the goods, wares, merchandise, notes, book accounts, belonging to or in any way pertaining to us as merchants trading under the name of Minter Morris & Company as aforesaid, and also the notes and accounts of Chisholm and Minter and G. R. Morris. Now the object of this conveyance and assignment is that the said William Minter is bound for us and liable as our security in the sum of twenty seven thousand eight hundred and twenty dollars as follows, to-wit: Five thousand three hundred and ten dollars to William M. Beal of New Orleans; two thousand dollars to Crutech & Company of Philadelphia, all said sums are now in judgement in the District Court of the United States, and the further sum of four thousand two hundred dollars to the Commercial Bank of Manchester, and seven thousand to the Agricultural Bank of Natchez, these last named two debts are not in judgement in the Circuit Court of Yalobousha County; and thirteen hundred dollars to Joseph Collins, this claim not sued on but now due; and perhaps some other debts now not recollected--William Minter to liquidate the property and to pay the overplus, if any, to the grantors."

This document not only indicates the magnitude of the firm failure, but is also indicative of the ease with which business men obtained credit from banks and business firms as widely separated as Philadelphia, New Orleans and Natchez. In 1844, about the time that Robert J. Walker went to his cabinet position in Washington, L. R. Steward, Yalobousha County Sheriff, began the sale of lots in Troy for failure to pay taxes on the same. It is probable that the date January 9, 1845, may be selected as the end of Troy as a town for on that date the sheriff sold one hundred lots belonging to Robert J. Walker for the high bid by M. L. Maynard of two dollars and thirty cents. This sale marks the end of Walker's dream of a fortune to be made in land speculation and town development. There must have been some activity at Troy for a year or so following this sale since we find on record a deed of trust, dated February 6, 1847, by which John Kirkpatrick gave William Minter, acting for William Clark, the right to sell, in case of default in payment of a stipulated obligation, certain property in the twon of Troy, said sale to take place "before the tavern door of Thomas G. Bowles."

It would seem that the departure from Mississippi of Walker, a successful politician, but a financially ruined land speculator, co-incided very closely with the end of Troy as a place of importance as a commercial center, although because of its location at the intersection of several important roads, and the continued ferry service for people wanting to cross to the south side of the river, many people continued to pass through the town site. It was connected by roads to Charleston, Coffeeville, Grenada, Hardy, on the north side of the river. On the south side of the river roads led to Tuscahoma and to an intersection with the Grenada-Greenwood road. The importance of the ferry is indicated by one of the last important land transactions connected with the town:

> "Troy, Mississippi, December 13, 1845. James Minter (surviving partner of the late firm of Chisholm & Minter of Troy) appoints Thomas A. Beall agent in fact to sell or dispose and control in any way all the interest that we have in a certain parcle of land known as the Troy Ferry Lot Block, running from the ferry as it now stands on the Yalobousha river up the said river to the old mill and bound on the west by section line back to the river."

Graysport

Graysport was settled during the early years of the Choctaw Cession. It came to be a place of considerable importance, and continued so long after the towns of Chocchuma, Troy and Tuscahoma became extinct. It was located at what was then considered the head of navigation on the Yalobousha river. Some of the early settlers came into the region and settled before the sale of Indian lands began. Under the pre-emption provision of the Federal Government these settlers were allowed to purchase the land on which they had settled after the public land sales began. A considerable number of the people who lived in the vicinity of the town also obtained their land by pre-emption.

The original entry book shows that the land on which the town was located, the south east quarter of section thirty six, township twenty three, range six east, was a float reservation of Ray Murdock, who sold his reservation to Thomas I. Porter of the state of Tennessee. In a power of attorney, given by Thomas I. Porter to Thomas C. Porter, the last named individual was authorized to settle any difficulties which had arisen over the fact that some other men were claiming the same land, on the basis of the pre-emption provision. On Nobember 23, 1837, Porter sold this land, for a consideration of three thousand five hundred dollars, to John Williams, Hilliary Talbert, David Mabry, John B. Pass, Nathinael S. Neal, and Allen Gillispie. Since the price paid for this quarter section was a great deal more than other similar tracts of land were bringing, it is very probable that these men who bought the land had already begun a town on the spot and expected to pre-empt the land. Since a "float" or "floating claim" as they were sometimes called, had priority over a pre-emption claim, it was necessary for the purchasers to protect their interests by paying the high price for the land. A float claim allowed the owner to locate his claim anywhere in the cession, while a pre-emption claim could be perfected only if the desired land had not been located as a float. Much of the land in the Yalobousha river bottoms just west of Graysport had been obtained by pre-emption. Among those obtaining land by this method were Nathaniel Ingram, James Weir, A. Chapman, Jesse L. Verhine, Robert Williams, William and Lewis Southery, Richard Koonce, Robert E. Chamley, Berry B. Tillhon, E. Blair and Richard Tillman.

It would seem that John Williams was the person who thought that he would get the quarter section by pre-emption since on April 6, 1836, he conveyed to David Mabry, for a consideration of two hundred fifty dollars, "an undivided half interest in the south east quarter of Section thirty six, township 23, range six east." This transaction occured over a year before Porter sold the same area to the several individuals who paid him the purchase price of three thousand five hundred dollars. Since both John Williams and David Mabry were members of the group making the purchase it is very probable that Williams and Mabry were the "persons unknown" mentioned in Porter's power of attorney who were claiming the land. On December 10, 1836, David Mabry sold to the firm of Liard and Neal, a one sixteenth interest in the same land, for a consideration of one hundred twenty five dollars. All the men involved in these transactions were interested in the transaction with Porter by which they cleared their title to their interest in the land. From these several transactions we may date the beginning of the town of Graysport as about 1836 or 1837. In 1841 Allen Gillespie sold to John Williams, for a consideration of one thousand dollars "all my right and interest in the east half of the south east quarter of section 36, township 23, range 6 east commonly known as the town of Graysport." This is the first transaction of record in which the name of the town is given. On March 22, 1850, David Mabry sold to Hilliard Talbert his one eighth and one sixteenth interest in the town.

The rather ambitious plan for the town provided for two wards known as north and south wards, which were separated by Monroe street. The streets in the north ward were Bluff, Congress, Jefferson, Madison, and Monroe. In the south ward there were five streets, Pine, Broad, Sycamore, Cypress and Cane. One hundred fourteen lots were laid off in the north ward and one hundred eight in the south ward. Among those owning lots in the town at some time were Henry Trussell, James S. Trussell, J. L. Obannon, B. F. Johnson, John A. Murray, J. E. Evans, E. Newberger, O. H. Perry, J. B. and A. E. Pass, the firm of Campbell and Aldridge, and E. G. Harris. On April 13, 1858, John J. Gage and wife Elizabeth sold to Harris seventeen lots in the town for a consideration of eighteen hundred dollars. This transaction would seem to indicate the decreasing importance of Graysport as a trade center. Lots in Graysport continued to be sold at a much later date, but the sale price reflected the decreasing importance of the town. For instance, in 1861 James Weir and wife sold to Eli C. Spears for a consideration of fourteen hundred dollars three lots, one of them being described as "the ferry lot." Because of the considerable sum paid for these lots we presume that the transaction included a ferry located adjacent to the ferry lot. We do know that Spears did operate a ferry at Graysport as late as 1875. After the organization of Grenada county in 1870, some citizens of Graysport petitioned the Board of Supervisors to buy this ferry and make it a public ferry, but the board rejected the request. In 1869 O. H. Perry sold Spears four lots for a consideration of sixty dollars.

Graysport was named for a man by the name of Gray who owned the west one half of the south east quarter of the section on which Graysport was located. During the early years keel boats, and perhaps small river steamers, came up the river as far as the town. It was an important cotton shipping point during the early years of its existence. The early town had a Baptist and a Presbyterian church. They also had a nice school building with an eight months school supported, very largely, by the citizens of the town. There was a race track near the town and saloons. J. Obannon continued to sell liquor in the town until well after the establishment of Grenada county. The town was surrounded by a number of prosperous plantations, and the early merchants did considerable business. The importance of Graysport as a cotton shipping point is indicated by the numerous loans made to farmers and merchants in Graysport and vicinity by commission merchants and cotton factors in the city of New Orleans, who wished to induce the people receiving loans to let the New Orleans firms handle their cotton. These commission merchants took deeds of trust on land, livestock and growing crops, and in addition, required the people who borrowed the money to agree to let them handle the sale of their cotton. Two of the New Orleans firms operating in this manner as late as 1870 were J. Chaffee & Brother, and J. Williams & Son. An example of such a loan is the deed of trust, given in 1870 by L. C. Lee to secure a loan of several thousand dollars from J. Chaffee & Brother, in which instrument Lee gives as security for the loan, a deed of trust on certain lands outside the village of Graysport and "on my residence in Graysport and lots 22 and 23 in the same town, as well as the growing crops on one hundred fifty acres of cotton and about the same number of acres of other crops, as well as a dozen head of horses and the oxen now used on my plantation." Perhaps it is an indication of the harsh financial demands of the early post-Civil War years, that a large planter would have to mortgage everything he had in order to get money to produce his next crop. It is very likely that these New Orleans firms had local agents in places such as Graysport and Grenada. From transactions taking place between the firm of Bodenheimer & Parker, which seems to have begun operations in Graysport, and later moved to Grenada, and J. Chaffee & Brother, we are led to believe that the first named firm acted as agent for the second named firm, in Graysport and Grenada. There are recorded some deeds of trust on lands in the vicinity of Graysport in which L. Newberger is named as Trustee in deeds of trust made out in favor of certain commission merchants in New Orleans. Evidently Newberger was an early merchant in Graysport. The W. P. A. Source Book on Grenada County has an excerpt from a letter, written by Mrs. L. E. Evans of Memphis, in which she writes, relative to the merchants of Graysport: "The few merchants seemed to do a thriving business, as they soon accumilated enough money to move to larger business places. Mr. Newberger, at the close of the Civil War, moved to Louisville, Kentucky to educate his children."

The men refered to in this letter was Leopold Newberger, an immigrant boy from Bavaria. He was set up in business by an uncle who gave him a few dollars to buy supplies needed to become a "back-peddler," that is, a person who wandered over the country roads with a small supply of varied merchandise to sell to the people living in areas remote from trading centers, either by distance or impassable roads. This Newberger became a man of considerable wealth. He was responsible for the establishment of the Newberger Cotton Company, which in the years following the Civil War was domiciled at Coffeeville with agents in Oakland, Hardy, Grenada, Graysport, and other places. Newberger & Company is reported by the Grenada Sentinel of February 1892 to have handled twenty seven thousand bales of cotton during the cotton buying season of 1891-1892. The company in Coffeeville did business as general merchants as well as cotton buyers. Other early business firms in the town were one run by Mrs. McCaslin who seems to have been operating a dry-goods establishment. In the letter from Mrs. Evans from which an excerpt has previously been given: "A. J. McCaslin of Grenada is a grandson of one of the first settlers and a very fine character, Mrs. McCaslin. She ran the town's fashions for more than fifty years." Another firm was that of Parker Brothers.

A letter published by the Grenada Sentinel and dated February 11, 1882, will indicate the continuation of Graysport as a trading center; the identification of two business firms still doing business in that town on that date, and transportation difficulties of the period: "We are expecting a visit soon from a large size craft, a flatboat now at Grenada sails for this point tomorrow morning, as we learned today. The boat is laden with corn, meat, meal, and other necessary supplies purchased by our enterprising merchants Messers. Parker and J. Walters & Son. The boat, I believe is owned by Captain Perkins, and will probably get a full load of cotton on its downward trip, as the road between here and Grenada is almost impassable with a loaded wagon. This opportunity to move their cotton and bring supplies should be hailed with delight by our farmers along the Yalobousha." Although for a quarter of a century Grenada had been a railroad shipping point for Grenada and adjacent counties, people were still using more primitive methods of getting their supplies from, and their produce to, Grenada.

Among the early settlers in and about Graysport not already mentioned were Dr. L. M. Mays who was family physician to many families of the area, Captain G. F. Ingram who was born in South Carolina. In 1851 he married

Rebecca D. Perry who came to the vicinity of Graysport with her father Zadoc Perry. John C. James came from Watauga county, Alabama, first to Shelby County Tennessee, and then to settle on Horsepen Creek at a point about three miles Southeast of Graysport. Dr. William T. Willis was born in Orange county Virginia but moved with his family into Alabama. In 1832, before the public sale of Choctaw lands began, he settled in the wilderness near the area which later was to become the town of Graysport. Dr. Willis was a graduate of both the Jefferson and Philadelphia Medical Colleges, but upon locating in Mississippi he did little or no medical practice. He became engaged in clearing and cultivating the rich lands upon which he had settled. Nicholus and Sarah Majet came to the vicinity of the Graysport in 1836. He was the descendant of a French Huguenot family of North Carolina. Major Jack Williams came from South Carolina to Mississippi and settled in the area where Graysport was soon to be located. He arrived in May 1835, just about the time the little town had its first beginnings. He assisted in opening the road from Graysport to Grenada. It is said he was a planter, trader and riverboat man. Oliver H. Perry came with his father Zadoc Perry to the Graysport area in 1842. His son, J. C. Perry was a businessman at Graysport and later became Circuit and Chancery Clerk of Grenada county. John B. Pass, heretofore mentioned as one of the men who bought the town site of Graysport from Thomas I. Porter, came to Grenada county in 1832. He evidently first settled at, or in the vicinity, of the future town of Graysport. Afterwards he moved to Grenada and built the first brick building in that town. He engaged in the mercantile business for some-time, and then moved to the farming lands which he owned, and became a successful planter. He owned much land and many slaves. His son W. N. Pass became vice-president of the Merchant's Bank in Grenada, and a director of the Grenada Ice Factory. In the year 1838 William Conly, James S. Gordon, Joseph Ligon, William W. Smith, Joseph Lamon and James Weir owned land in the vicinity of Graysport.

From the early years of its establishment, Graysport seems to have been the center of a very prosperous farming community. The effects of the Civil War and the ensuing period of reconstruction had a demoralizing influence on that prosperity in this, as well as most other communities and towns in the area. One evidence of the harsh financial circumstances of the period is the sale, on August 20, 1866, of five lots in Graysport, by B. F. Johnson to John T. Parker for a consideration of four hundred fifty dollars. Another and a more forceful indication of the financial distress of the time, is the record of thirty two hundred acres of land, largely in the vicinity of Graysport, which Leopold Newberger purchased at various tax sales, for the small total sum of twenty three dollars and sixty cents. It is possible that much of this land may have been redeemed at a later date by their former owners, although Newberger still possessed a considerable acreage of this land at the time of his death. The tax sales under which he purchased this land were held in 1864 and 1868.

Although Graysport was a declining town by the time the hard post-Civil War years took their toll, it continued as a place of some importance for many years to come. In 1888 a newspaper article in the GRENADA SENTINEL gives this description of the town: "It is one of the oldest towns in the state, once an incorporated town, and, at one time, as many as four keelboats could be seen anchored here, and as many as four thousand bales of cotton in her warehouses. Much horse-racing, gambling and drinking was carried on. The town has no lawyers but two doctors, Dr. Tilman and Dr. Mays, and the following business firms: Parker Bros., Ingram & Willis, James Trussell, Walters & Son, Rayburn Bros. and Keeton & Smith." The construction of the Grenada Reservoir was the final blow in the extinction of the little town, the town site and much of the adjacent farming lands becoming a part of the land acquired by the Federal Government for the reservoir project.

Chapter III

TRANSPORTATION

The Choctaw Indians spent most of their time in villages established throughout the area which they controlled until the Treaty of Dancing Rabbit Creek resulted in most of these Indians giving up their lands and migrating west. Since they were social-minded, they visited from one village to another. They frequently gathered together to go on big hunts, and on occasion, assembled to defend against, or make war on other tribes. Because of these several needs for communication between the Choctaw villages, paths had been established between the centers of Indian population. These paths, which were mere trails, and not adapted to wheel traffic, served the Indians for a long time, but were not of much use to the white settlers who came into the area after the land was opened up for settlement.

The only north and south road of any importance which ran through the area which became Grenada County was the Rankin-Memphis road. This road had been extablished some years before the signing of the Treaty of Dancing Rabbit Creek. Its primary purpose was to give a route by which the people of South and Central Mississippi could cross the Choctaw country and reach Memphis and other Tennessee towns. When the North Mississippi Choctaw lands were made available for purchase by white settlers, this road was the chief route by which settlers from South and Central Mississippi reached the new area. We have been able, by a study of the field notes of D. W. Connely who surveyed the western part of the area which eventually became Grenada county, to establish the approximate location of the Rankin-Memphis road. It came into that part of Carroll County, which is now a part of Grenada county, in the eastern portion of Township 21, Range Two East. In a general way it followed the range of hills just east of the rich delta section of the area. It ran almost due north for a portion of its course across Carroll county, but as it reached the vicinity of the area where the village of LeFlore is now located, it began to bear northeast to a point about two miles south of the town of Chocchuma. At this point the field notes state that it crossed the Rankin-Elliott road. This cross road extended from this point, by way of the place sometimes known as "Duncan's Crossing" to the Elliott Indian Station which was located just a short distance south of the present town of Holcomb. The Memphis-Rankin road then began to bear more to the east, passing near the area where Holcomb is now located and on to the vicinity of Dubard, where Connely notes that the road crossed the farm land of Chief Turnbull. This point was the eastern boundary of the survey made by Connely and the man who surveyed the area on to the east did a much less adequate job in his field notes. He does not note the location of the roads which he crossed in his survey. The route might be lost were it not for the fact that a deed given to Hardy Perry, a half-breed Indian, helps us relocate the road. In that deed Perry received a deed to the land about the place of his residence, which land is described in the deed as being located "on the Rankin-Memphis road about six miles north of the Yalobousha River." By a check of the land records we find that Perry's reservation was in the Riverdale community, a little northwest of Grenada. In Connely's field notes he had mentioned crossing the Rankin-Memphis Road at a point which we discovered to be in the vicinity of Oxberry. Evidently, after reaching the vicinity of Perry's place, the road bore to the northwest passing through that part of Tallahatchie county which is now a part of Grenada county. This would place the road very near to the place where, in 1834, George W. Martin established the Auverigine Plantation. Mr. Martin had been a staff officer with General Jackson in the battle of New Orleans, and was a lifelong friend and supporter of the General in his political battles. He was the grandfather of the late W. B. Hoff who for many years was a prominent businessman and constant booster of Grenada. Mr. Hoffa's mother, the daughter of Mr. Martin, was born on the plantation mentioned above. From the vicinity of Oxberry the Memphis-Rankin road continued on into the area which is still a part of Tallahatchie county. Oxberry is located on the land reserved for Chief Oxberry and his children. The chief had been one of the interpreters who assisted the land agents at Chocchuma. The only other road mentioned in the field notes was the Elliott-Mayhew road. After the Elliott Indian Mission had been established at Elliott, men from that station went across the country to set up another station somewhat north of the present city of Starkville, so we presume that they established some kind of passable road between these two Indian stations.

We do not have much information relative to the manner of establishing roads in the area after white settlers came to it. We do have an early record relative to the marking out of a road from Parsalia, located on the Yocona River in the northeastern part of Tallahatchie county, to Tuscahoma on the Yalobousha River. Another early road was marked out from Charleston to the ferry at Chocchuma which road, after intersectin the Rankin-Memphis road a little south of Chocchuma, extended on to Carrolton. It was not until after the founding of the towns of Pittsburg and Tullahoma that any passable road was established through the eastern part of the area. Early settlers who came down the Natchez Trace and turned off that route near Houston reported the trails westward as almost impassable.

As the several towns of the area were founded and developed, roads were marked out between them. The people of the area which now comprises Grenada county had to go to four different countyseats to transact business. Those in the northwestern part of the present county of Grenada went to Charleston for this type of business; those in the southwestern part of the county went to Carrollton; those in the extreme southeastern part of the county went to Greensboro, and those in the remainder of the county went to Coffeeville. Of course these above mentioned towns were county seats of those four counties out of which Grenada County was created. Roads were marked out from the northwestern part of the county to Charleston; from the southwestern part to Carrollton; from the southeastern part to Greensboro, and from the central and northeastern parts of the county to Coffeeville. We do not have any authenic records of the establishment of most of these roads. The Yalobousha County Minutes of the Board of Supervisors were lost in a fire, so we have no official record of the establishment of much of the early road system of the area which is not Grenada county. Since Grenada county was not created until 1870, the Minutes of the Board of Supervisors does not record the time and manner of the establishment of the county roads, but does indicate the existence and names of the several roads, in those parts of the minutes which give the names of the men appointed as "Road Overseers." Overseers were named to supervise the maintenance of the following designated roads: Grenada-Graysport; Grenada-Houston; Grenada-Providence; Grenada-Pittsbore; Center Road branching off the Grenada Providence Road at a point four miles east of Grenada; Grenada-Duck Hill; Grenada-Coffeeville; Graysport-Torrance; Grenada-Carrollton; Grenada-Hardy Station; Grenada-Troy; Grenada-Greenwood; Charleston-Carrollton; Grenada-Greensbore; Troy-Charleston; and Tuscahoma-Grenada. It is probable that at the time of the creation of Grenada county these roads were about in the same locations and the same miserable condition as they had been during the early years of their establishment. They were supposed to be maintained by the people living along the various specified sections of the roads. The county did maintain bridges and ferries, but otherwise spent no public funds on road maintenace. This condition was to continue for a quarter of a century after the creation of the county before the supervisors began to let road maintenance be bid in by private contractors. This was a little improvement, but it was not until well in the twentieth century that the roads were graded and covered with gravel. It was still later that some of the roads were paved.

These county roads served, in a measure, to enable the people of the various towns and communities to go from their homes to the other localities in the area. They also served, during several months of the year, to allow farmers to take their produce to markets in the trading centers, and to take home necessary supplies purchased in those trade centers. During the heavy rains of the winter months this transportation over the county roads became very difficult and at times, almost impossible. The merchants in the trading centers who bought farm produce, and supplied the farmers with necessary supplies, needed a better system of transportation than these crude dirt roads. This transportation to the outside world was supplied first by water transprtation, and later by railroad transportation.

The Yalobousha River--Early Economic Lifeline

Living as we do, in an age of rapid and efficient transportation, it is hard for us to envision the transportation difficulties faced by the early settlers of this area. Lacking all modern facilities such as railroads, well-developed highway systems, and speedy transportation by motorized vehicles, the early settlers had to depend upon un-improved, and at times, impassable trails which were called roads, and upon uncertain water transportation. Today, as we look at the Yalobousha River, shallow and filled with snags and sandbars, it seems a very unlikely channel of commerce, but in the early years of the settlement and development of our area, it was an economic lifeline connecting the settlers with the outside world. An indication of its early importance is the fact that the early towns of the area--Chocchuma, Troy, Tuscahoma, Pittsburg, Tullahoma and Graysport--were located on the river. Because of a watershed, much of which contained heavy vegetation, much falling rain was absorbed to a considerable extent, resulting in a more gradual flow of this water into the tributaries of the Yalobousha river. This resulted in a more even level of water in the river channel than we have today, but even so, any heavy river traffic had to be confined to a few months in the winter and spring when heavy rains maintained a sufficient depth of channel to bear heavy traffic. During these months the agricultural products sold in the markets of the outside world went down-stream on the river while the up-stream boat trips carried cargoes to stock the shelves of the river-town merchants. During these early years small steam-boats, keelboats and even flatboats were engaged in Yalobousha river traffic. Some early steamers made the long trip from Grenada to Vicksburg on the Mississippi river, but the keel boats and flatboats, having only manual motive power while going up-stream, confined their trips to the shorter run to Williams Landing on the Yazoo River. This was a transfer point where goods were exchanged by the larger Yazoo river boats, and the smaller Yalobousha river boats. It was located near where Greenwood was later established. The keel boats and flatboats had a comparatively easy trip down-stream, but on the return trip upstream had to use long poles to push their craft up-stream, or to attach ropes to the boat and walk along the banks towing the vessel. This was not conducive to heavy loads being carried up-stream by craft of this sort. For a quarter of a century the Yalobousha bore most of the commerce of the region situated along its banks, and even later, it made a considerable contribution to certain types of transportation. When better methods of transportation began to divert most of the long haul commerce from the river, it continued to serve short haul traffic to Grenada from communities down and up the river during the winter months when impassable roads made it almost impossible for those people to get their cotton and other agricultrual products to market by use of the county roads.

So far as we know, the first boats, other than small craft used by Indians and itinerate white traders, to come up the Yalobousha River were the keel boats used by Nat. Howard and Thomas Isom. Although they did not make the journey together, both tied up their boats in the vicinity of the plant of the Mississippi Cotton Seed Products Company. At that time the site was covered with a cane-break. Later it was to become a part of the town of Pittsburg. Howard set up a tent here and began trading with the Indians. Isom took his goods overland to the territory occupied by the Chickasaw Indians. They came up the river in the spring of 1832, over a year before the sale of the Choctaw Lands began at Chocchuma. We have no information as to the first steamboat to reach this area. The second steamboat to reach the vicinity came after the establishment of the two little towns of Pittsburg and Tullahoma. Its arrival was announced by the PITTSBURG BULLETIN in its issue of December 10, 1835: "Our town was visited on Saturday last, by the steamboat RICHMOND, Capt. Savage. This is the first steam boat which has arrived here this season, and the second that has ever penetrated so far up the Yalobousha as Pittsburg, but surely two experiments are sufficient to test the practicability of navigating the river by steam. The Captain of the RICHMOND informs us, that between this place and Tuscahoma, there are fewer obstructions to steam boat navigation, with the exception of projecting trees, than below the latter place, and that with a small expenditure the navigation of the river to that point might be rendered excellent. With this fact staring them in the face, will not the citizens of Grenada, Pittsburg and Troy unite their efforts for the accomplishment of an enterprise so beneficial to those towns and their vicinities, as would be the improvement of the navigation of the Yalobousha?" Steam boat activity on the river increased from an occasional visit such as the one described above, to the regular schedules runs up and down the stream. We don't know how early regular schedules were established, but do have information to the effect that such a schedule existed in 1842. On January 22, 1842, the WEEKLY REGISTER carried the following advertisement: "YALOBOUSHA PACKET-The new light draught, staunch built steamer YAZOO PLANTER, S. M. Hall, Master, has now commenced her regular trips, and will continue to run as a Weekly Packet, during the season between Williams Landing and Grenada. For freight or passage, having very excellent accomodations, cabin all in state rooms." Steam boats did not oust keel boats as a means of river transportation. On January 29, 1842, the WEEKLY REGISTER carried the following advertisement: "Just arrived the new and splendid Keel Boat HENRY CLAY. From Maysville, Ky., with a full cargo of produce consisting of the following articles, Viz.; Four, best quality, best rectivied whiskey, Bulk Pork, Lard, Bourbon Whiskey, five years old, assorted stoneware, cheese, wooden ware, small lots of medicine suitable for families, Window Glass large sizes, blue and black ink, Tin Ware, Books, Cog., Brandy, Pipes, Ploughs, Cigars, good quality chairs, Beef in bbls., a few barrels of best Ale, Salt in bbls., and various other articles which will be sold low for cash. The planters and citizens are invited to call and examine them. I will also take freight for New Orleans on low terms with privilige of re-shipping at Williams Landing." The above quoted avertisement is interesting, not only as it contributes information relative to Yalobousha River transportation, but also as an indication of the kind of goods in demand in Grenada nine years after the first white settlers came into the area. Bourbon whiskey and cigars were not usually found in pioneer settlements so soon after their establishment.

As the river began to get low during the late spring, river traffic gradually lessened, and did not pick up until the fall rains caused the river to rise to a satisfactory level. During the dull summer months the boat owners repaired their craft, and solicited business for the fall and winter season. On June 4, 1842, the WEEKLY REGISTER carried the following advertisement: "To Planters: The undersigned will run their good and substantial Keel-Boat 'NORTH STAR' between this place and Williams Landing the ensuing season, and will be ready to take COTTON, or other Freight, and give Bills of Laden through to New Orleans as soon as the river rises." River boats were owned by local residents of Grenada, and engaged in competition with boats not locally owned. Some of the local boat owners were in the business merely for the money to be earned, but we learn that other citizens banded together to build or purchase boats in order that they might give enough competition to other owners to keep rates from becoming exorbitant. We learn that in 1840, three prominent local citizens were involved in a boat trade. William O. Bryan sold to A. C. Baine and George P. Morton a one-half interest in "the Keel-Boat MONROE, and the Flat-Boat S. S. PRENTISS."

Since most all cotton produced was shipped by river, the problem of storage of bales of cotton, ginned before there was enough water in the river to justify navigation of the river, was a problem which was met by rough sheds called cotton sheds. At one time one of these cotton sheds was located on the lot at the intersection of Depot and Doak streets on which is located what is known as the Roane Building. It is probable that this shed was constructed after the traffic on the river ceased to be of importance, since during the hey-day of the river traffic it was more convenient to have the cotton sheds located on the banks of the river. On September 24, 1842, one of the owners of such a cotton shed solicited business in the following advertisement carried by the WEEKLY REGISTER: "Having procured a good Cotton Shed, lately occupied by Col. Morton, and put it in first rate order for the reception and preservation of Cotton, we are prepared to Store any Freight which may be consigned to our care, and will preserve it in good condition Free of Charge for storage, if shipped this season on our boats--if shipped on any other, the charge being at the usual rate. We will take cotton through to New Orleans at the lowest customary prices." The advertisement indicated that A. White and J. D. Jackson were agents for the owners of the enterprise. No indication is given as to the location of the above-mentioned shed, but it was probably on the river. We do have positive information relative to the location of cotton sheds on the banks of the river. This information is derived from an advertisement inserted in the WEEKLY REGISTER on November 5, 1842. In this advertisement George W. Lake informs the public: "Freight Storage: I have a cotton shed on each side of the river; and planters and others who may wish to haul cotton to this place can have their cotton stored on either side of the river at customary rates. I have also two good Keel-Boats, 'HENRY CLAY' and "NEPTUNE' that will run between this place and Williams Landing through the ensuing season, and freight cotton and merchandise at customary rates." In the early fall of 1842, the river traffic was in full swing. On October 7 of that year, the following news item was printed in a local paper: "Something New: The Keel Boat NORTH STATE started in gallant trim from our wharf on Thursday last with a load of cotton for New Orleans and a market. Capt. E. Kerwin had the honor of commanding the first boat that ever decended the Yalobousha in the month of October." As late as March 11, 1843, the river was still navigable. On that date the newspaper HERALD ran the following news item: "The river is still in good boating order. Most of the cotton had been carried off and the boats are all returning with rich cargoes to our merchants and others. By the way, our friend Munford has some of the finest apples ever brought to this place only $1.75 per bbl. Oats, Potatoes, Flour, Onions etc. are plenty in town, and low, for cash." On May 27, 1843, THE HERALD had an editiorial relative to the prospect for increased river navigation: "The experiences of the last ten years have demonstrated the practicability of navigating the YALOBOUSHA RIVER from Williams Landing to this place, with STEAM BOATS from four to five months during the business season of the year, with as much regularity and certainty, and with much more rapidity, and less than half the expense, than it is now done with Keel Boats. Then why not have a regular packet between this place and Yazoo? Why do not planters & merchants of this vicinity unite together as one man and encourage the construction of a Steamboat especially adapted to their wants? The saving to the county in down and up freights in a single season would be greater than the outlay of capital necessary to effect so desireable an object. We are glad to perceive that the public mind is already directed to this subject by our enterprising fellow-citizen, W. W. Munford, whose proposition to raise one hundred hands for ten days in the month of August (a season when the planters are generally at leisure) to remove obstructions on the banks of the river from this place to the mouth of the river. We understand that Maj. Munford, if properly encouraged, will have a regular Steamboat Packet from this place to Williams Landing the next freighting season." The editorial writer states that the greatest obstacle to a united front among business leaders to encourage the establishment of a regular steam river packet, would probably be the opposition of the owners of Keel Boats who had rather large financial investments in these boats. The editorial continued in the following words: "Some of our most enterprising merchants have withdrawn a portion of their capital from their regular business and invested in Keel Boats in order to prevent exorbitant rates in the transportation of their own freight."

Captain Munford must have succeeded in receiving the necessary encouragement to justify his project since on July 27, 1844, the paper HARRY OF THE WEST reports: "We are glad to learn that Capt. Munford has a Steam-Boat now building at Cincinnati expressly for this river, and will be in the Yazoo in October ready for the first rise to come up to Grenada. There are still some little funds yet on hand, and there are several who subscribed last year, both in labor and money, that have not yet paid. Capt. Munford intends commencing work again on the river in the first part of August, and is desirous that all who intend to help him, should come forward with their labor or money next month." From the above quoted news item it appears that a number of interested people had joined hands with Captain Munford in the project to clear out obstructions to river navigation. On August 17, 1844, the above named newspaper gives a progress report: "THE RIVER: we understand that the little company under the direction of Maj. Munford has proceeded as far as Troy, sweeping the river clean as they go. It shows what a little perseverance will do, and how easy the Yalobousha might be put in such order as to become an invaluable auxiliary in the prosperity of this part of the country. Let us all then put our shoulders to the wheel; Now is the time."

On December 14, 1844, the same paper proudly tells of the successful termination of the efforts to make the river safe for steam boat navigation: "The fine Steam Boat ENTERPRISE, Munford Master, arrived here on Thursday last. The ENTERPRISE carries 800 bales of cotton and was built expressly for the navigation of the Yalobousha river from this place. Captain Munford deserves great credit for his spirited efforts to improve our river and to put in trade so fine a boat. We hope that he will be liberally patronized and amply rewarded for his efforts. The ENTERPRISE left Tuesday on her downward trip." On January 18, 1845, the editor boasts of the speedy river transportation now available to the people of Grenada and vicinity: "Arrived on Sunday last, the Steam Boat ENTERPRISE, Capt. Munford, 18 hours from the mouth of the river. This is the quickest trip we believe that has ever been made. She brought freight to sundry merchants of this palce, but as they don't advertise we shall not name who they were. She may be expected to make trips weekly as long as the water is sufficient; of which there is an abundance, and more at this time falling." On November 15, of that same year, the editor was concerned about the lack of water in the river channel: "The Yazoo River is so low at this time that our merchants cannot procure their goods; some are waggoning from Memphis, some from Yazoo City. Our Majestic Yalobousha is many feet below low water mark; but no danger of starving yet--wild ducks, squirrels, fish and rabbits are in abundance."

It is probable that Yalobousha River traffic followed the uncertain pattern given above until the arrival of railroads to Grenada. After that date, river traffic practically ceased, with the exception of some shorthaul Keel Boat runs up and down the Yalobousha and Schooner river, to carry supplies and bring to Grenada cotton for the benefit of planters who lived near the rivers, and who had difficulty in making trips to and from town over the roads which were usually almost impassable for any considerable load during the winter months. There were also spasmodic attempts made to run cargo to the Yazoo River, which continued to serve as an important channel of commerce. These attempts were made in protest to rates sometimes charged by the railroads on freight shipments.

In 1879 the Grenada County Board of Supervisors made a feeble attempt to improve the river channel. They passed the following quoted order: "Ordered by any money in the County Treasury not otherwise appropriated for the purpose of cleaning out the Yalobousha River in the County of Grenada, and that Dr. William Mcswine, Capt. R. H. Turner, and Capt. R. N. Hall, be and are hereby appointed a Committee to authorize the drawing of the said money when the work is done, or as it is being done." A report in the GRENADA SENTINEL, published in February, 1882, may indicate that this effort on the part of the Supervisors to clear part of the river from obstructions, was made in behalf of the short-haul Keel Boat traffic on the river. That report in the form of a letter written from Graysport reads: "We are expecting a visit soon from a large size craft, a flatboat now in Grenada, sails for this place tomorrow morning, as we learned today. The boat is laden with corn, meal and other necessary supplies purchased by our enterprising merchants Messers. Parker and J. Walters & Son. The boat, I believe, is owned by Captain Perkings, and will probably get a full load of cotton on its downward trip, as the roads between here and Grenada are almost impassable with a loaded wagon. This opportunity to move their cotton and bring supplies should be hailed with delight by the farmers abong the Yalobousha." Another account of the influence which the bad winter roads had on short-haul traffic on the river was given by the GRENADA SENTINEL on February 25, 1882: "The Keel Boats plying the Yalobousha river and the Schooner east of this place, came down last Sunday afternoon loaded with cotton. One of the boats takes freight up the Yalobousha River and the other up the Schooner, and we understand, both are doing a profitable business. The boats ought to be encouraged in their undertaking, as it saves our farmers a great deal of hauling over the bad roads. The boats on their return trip carried over two thousand dollars worth of goods purchased from two of our popular merchants."

In December, 1883, the GRENADA SENTINEL reports another venture at Steamboat navigation of the river: "The Steamboat J. H. Williams, recently purchased by the Grenada Oil & Compress Company to run between this point and Greenwood for the purpose of bringing cotton seed here, landed at our town on Wednesday the 19th inst., loaded with 1300 sacks of cottonseed. The boat is 92 feet long; 22 feet wide and one hundred tons burden." Evidently this attempt to bring delta cotton seed to the Grenada mill was not profitable, since the March 1, 1884, issue of the SENTINEL reports the boat as operating under a new owner: "The steamer J. H. Williams, Capt. Walter Crump Commanding, is now making regular semi-weekly trips between this place and Greenwood. The WILLIAMS was formerly owned, the Grenada Oil Mill, but is now the exclusive property of her Commander, and prepared to do a general freighting business between here and Greenwood. She makes connection at that place with packets for New Orleans and all intermediate points." In a late, and final report on the steamer, the SENTINEL passes on this information: "The steamer J. H. Williams has transported 488 bales of cotton during the cotton season on 1883-1884." This very samll use of the steamboat for the transportation of cotton probably put an end to this venture. At least, the newspaper had no further new items relative to it. In order to explain this continued effort to use the river as a transportation channel to Greenwood, we should remember that Grenada had no railroad connection with Greenwood until April, 1901.

Keeping in mind the fact that railroad connection had been made with Greenwood in the spring of 1901, we are a little surprised to find that some of the best businessmen of Grenada organized a company for the purpose of transporting freight to and from Greenwood by way of the river. On January 3, 1903, the GRENADA SENTINEL printed the following quoted news item: "Grenada Transportation Company was organized last Wednesday with the following officers: Joe Newburger, President; Robert Doak, Vice President; J. P. Broadstreet, Secretary; George W. Field, General Traffic Manager and Treasurer; Board of Directors: Joe Newburger, K. W. Hornsby, Robert Doak, D. L. Holcomb and E. L. Gerard. The steam tug MOLLIETTA has been purchased from J. W. Stipe and will tow as many as two barges...The promoters of this enterprise are determined that they will ply the waters of the Yalobousha for at least two years." Since the completion of the Illinois Central branch line to Parsons, thereby giving Grenada Rail connection with Greenwood, would seem to mitigate against the success of the river transportation venture, it would seem that this was a very foolish move on the part of hard-headed businessmen such as those mentioned above. We find the explanation of the cause for the venture in an out-of-town newspaper. In January, 1898, the CARROLLTON CONSERVATIVE printed the following quoted news item: "The citizens of Grenada held a meeting last week for the purpose of discussing propositions looking to the establishment of a steamboat line between Grenada and Yazoo City. This is a good move, and should they succeed no doubt would prove a great benefit to Grenada. The greatest object in opening the steamboat line is to secure a cheaper freight rate which will be a great saving to the people." It is rather ironical that the last service which the river rendered the community should have been its use as a threat against the monopolistic freight charges when the railroads had superseeded the river as the economic lifeline of the region.

Railroad Development in Grenada County

Railroad development in North Mississippi came at least a quarter of a century later than such development in South Mississippi. Until the removal of the Choctaw and Chickasaw Indians from the north part of the state there was little white settlement in the area. After the land was opened for purchase by white settlers, it would take almost twenty-five years for the economy of the region to justify the construction of railroad lines into the area. For this period of time Grenada and Grenada county would have to continue to look upon the Yalobousha River as the principle channel of transportation to and from outside points of importance. South Mississippi had been settled at an early date, and by the year 1831 some of the planters whose property was not located upon or near navigable streams, began to advocate construction of short railroad lines to transport their cotton to Mississippi River Ports. In 1831 Judge Edward McGehee and other planters of Wilkinson county organized, and had chartered, the Woodville & St. Francisville Railroad. This twenty nine mile railroad line was completed just about the time the Federal Land Office began operation at Chocchuma. When the first settlers in this region were obtaining their land, the planters in Wilkinson county were shipping their cotton by rail to a Mississippi River port. In 1834, the year when the little towns of Pittsburg and Tullahoma were organized, a group of Natchez businessmen applied for a charter for the Natchez & Jackson Railroad, and actually constructed seven miles off the road in anticipation of the granting of the charter. By 1836, the year Pittsburg and Tullahoma united to form Grenada, three other proposed railroads had been chartered. They were the Vicksburg Commercial & Banking Company; the Grand Gulf and Port Gibson; and the Lake Washington & Deercreek. Although these roads were charted in different geographical locations they had two things in common: each line ran roughly in a east and west direction, connecting the interior of the state with the Mississippi River, and each had, as a part of its operation, a Banking House to finance railroad construction. The building constructed in Woodville to house the offices and banking business of the Woodville and St. Francisville Railroad is still standing. It was for many years the location of the town post office. The Grand Gulf & Port Gibson road was designed to connect the interior of Claiborne county with the then thriving river port of Grand Gulf which was an important river town until the 1850's. The Mississippi & Alabama road, chartered in 1836 was organized for the purpose of linking the river port of Vicksburg with the country east in the direction of the new capital of the state which was just coming into being. In the early 1830's the L & N road, the only road of that period which proposed any extensive mileage, was being built across the south part of the state in the direction of New Orleans. All the chartered lines were not constructed, but all of them, constructed or proposed, were intended to connect the interior of the state with the Mississippi River, which for many years thereafter would continue to be the main route of transportation for the commerce of a large portion of the nation.

This philosophy of considering railroads as merely feeder lines for the more important Mississippi River transportation system prevailed for a quarter of a century, and it was not until a few years before the outbreak of the Civil War, that railroad men were bold enough to begin thinking of establishing a north and south system which would challenge the river as the chief means of transportation of the traffic which was following the river in these directions. The first Mississippi railroad to begin construction of a line which was not constructed to feed traffic to the Mississippi River, was the New Orleans, Jackson & Great Northern. Early in the 1850's this road began construction, working north from New Orleans in the direction of Jackson. By 1856 it had completed its line north to Canton, Mississippi. One hundred and eighteen miles of this road was in Mississippi. This was the first serious railroad threat to the dominant position which the Mississippi River had held in attracting to its waters the commerce of the south part of the state. Just a little after the above mentioned railroad began construction of its line, the Mississippi Central Railroad began construction of 187 miles of rail line from Canton, Mississippi to Jackson, Tennessee. This line reached Grenada in 1860. When it reached Jackson, Tennessee, a little later, the three hundred and sixty-five miles of the two roads, offering convenient and rapid means of transportation, was a serious blow to the river transportation of the time. The arrival of the Mississippi Central line in Grenada changed the mode of life in the area. The cotton warehouses were moved from the river bank to the railroad line. The people who had formerly gathered to watch the arrival or departure of small river steamers and keel boats now went to the railroad station to watch the arrival and departure of the trains. The Mississippi & Tennessee Railroad was organized to connect the Mississippi Central line with the city of Memphis. This last named road was organized and constructed by a different group of men than those who had built the Mississippi Central, and for a considerable period of time, was independent of that line. The Mississippi & Tennessee line covered a distance of approximately one hundred miles. The charter stipulated a capital stock of $825,455. Two hundred and fifty thousand dollars of this stock was subscribed by the city of Memphis, which was anxious to attract to its cotton offices and merchants, trade which was now going south along the railroad. The remaining $575,455 of stock was subscribed by planters and other businessmen along the railroad line. The Line had been chartered by a Mississippi Legislative Act of October 16, 1852. On December 5, 1853, the Tennessee Legislature approved the charter which had been issued by the Mississippi Legislature, so the line was thereby authorised to do business in both Mississippi and Tennessee. The officers of the line were authorized by the Legislature to issue $125,000 in script to help finance the construction of the road. Some of the individuals who subscribed for stock in the Mississippi and Tennessee Railroad were: Dr. Henry Dockery, T. W. White and Gerneral C. N. Robinson of DeSoto County; Colonel F. L. White, Donald White and C. F. Vance of Panola County; and Joyn G. Brady, Samuel Garner and Nathaniel Howard of the town of Grenada. All of the above named stockholders were railroad directors. The Directors elected F. M. White as President of the Railroad; C. F. Vance, Secretary & Treasurer; and Minor Merriweather as Chief Engineer. In 1854 a contract was let for the grading of fifty miles of the road-bed. The one hundred miles road was completed early in 1861, shortly before the outbreak of the Civil War. Early in the year 1862 marked the last trip of a train over the whole distance from Memphis to Grenada until late in 1865. During this period military action of the Federal and Confederate forces caused much of the line to be unusable.

The Mississippi Central Railroad was financed by stock subscription, script, of the road in the amount of $300,000, and about two million dollars derived from the sale of bonds. We have very little information relative to the men who organized and constructed the Mississippi Central Line. Perhaps they weren't in control of the line long enough for any of them to become well known. Soon after the outbreak of the Civil War the Confederate government took over control of the southern railroads. When the Mississippi Central was returned to its officers after the war it was in such bad physical and financial shape that the original owners found it advisable to sell the line. The state Legislature tried to help the road during the last days of the war by providing that an indebtedness of a million and a half dollars could be paid off in depreciated Confederate currency, but this action was eventually declared unconstitutional when it was subjected to judicial review. The impoverished condition of the Southern states made it impossible for many of the railroads to pay off indebtedness contracted in the more prosperous years before the war, and to meet the expense of repairing the very extensive damage done to the roads by the contending military forces. In 1871 Colonel H. S. McComb of Wilmington, Deleware organized a syndicate which linked up the New Orleans, Jackson and Great Northern road with the Mississippi Central. Both of these roads had been built by Southern capital but had been obtained by Northern interests during the period of financial hardship suffered by the Southern states just after the close of the war. Although each of these roads continued to operate as separate entities, they were made part of an organization called the Chicago, St. Louis & New Orleans line. The ultimate objective of this organization was to link Chicago with New Orleans by a consolidation of and extension of existing lines. It would take some years to achieve this objective. When the Northern capitalists secured the possession of the Mississippi Central, it was indebted in the amount of $1,350,000 for mortgage bonds issued in 1854; for $1,279,000 in bonds advanced by the state of Tennessee authorized to do so by a legislative act entitled "An act to establish a system of internal improvement in the state of Tennessee," and $2,000,000 in mortgage bonds issued to Jacob Ryer, Daniel Raverl and William Sharkey, trustees for the capitalists who had bought the bonds. Soon after acquiring the road, eight million dollars in mortgage bonds were issued by the road for the purpose of "paying off existing bonded indebtedness and to extend the Mississippi Central Line to the left bank of the Ohio River opposite the southern terminus of the Illinois Central so as to make a contiguous line of railroad from its southern terminus at Canton to the Ohio." A little later the Mississippi Central and New Orleans, Jackson and Great Northern lines were leased to the Illinois Central, thereby placing under the control of the last named road a rail system reaching from Chicago to New Orleans.

For a few years after the end of the war, the Mississippi & Tennessee Line continued a precarious independent existence. It had been hard hit by the ravages of war. The road had been badly damaged except for a stretch between Grenada and the Tallahatchie River over which stretch some attempt was made to run trains during the war years. In a report made in late 1865, the Superintendent of the line gives an account of the condition of the road. "We are operating thirty miles off the road. The remaining seventy miles of the road is a mere wreck of a railroad, bridges destroyed, trestle work and culverts rotted by time and disuse, depots, water tanks and station houses destroyed, crossties rotted, track torn up, embankments reduced to a mere skeleton with barely enough rolling stock to make up one train." In October, 1874, McComb purchased a controlling interest in the road, but allowed it to remain in the hands of the officials who had been in charge previous to this purchase. It remained in their control until after the death of McComb in 1881. After his death his executors sold his interest in the road to the railroad promoter Harriman, who subsequently transfered his stock to the Illinois Central System. Soon thereafter, the minority stockholders sold out their interest in the road. During the period when McComb controlled the road E. C. Walthal, a Grenada attorney and war hero, acted as the legal agent for the road. The line was sold for $1,000,000 of which $470,000 went to the widow of McComb, and the remainder going to the other stockholders. In announcing the sale THE GRENADA SENTINEL commented: "This hundred miles of railroad had long been regarded and cherished as pecularly the outcome of Mississippi enterprise and capital. Built, orginally by farmers living along the line, nine tenths of whom are dead, and as many bankrupt in estate, it always has had a claim upon the sympathy as well as the patronage of the people between here and Memphis. The connection of Colonel F. M. White, its original and present President, has been one unbroken link between it and the people, and as long as he stood at the head of it, it was recognized as a Mississippi Corporation." The Mississippi Central road had suffered similar, but not as extensive damage. At the time of the close of the war, passengers were transported between Oxford and Holly Springs by hand car, and at Grenada, they had to be ferried across the Yalobousha River, the railroad bridge over that stream having been destroyed.

    The years following the Civil War was a period of feverish activity in railroad promotion and construction. The great trans-continental lines were in process of construction and many shorter lines were proposed, and some constructed. Although Grenada county had suffered severe financial reverses because of the war, it is indicative of the general interest in the construction of new railroad mileage that one of the first acts of the Supervisors of the newly created county of Grenada was to consider the advisability of the county subscribing to stock of the Grenada, Houston and Eastern Railroad. This proposed railroad seems to have been an ambitious plan by citizens of the city and county of Grenada to construct a feeder line through the area east of Grenada in order to bring the trade of that area to Grenada where the line would connect up with the Mississippi Central and the Mississippi & Tennessee lines. The proposed railroad was incorporated by the Mississippi Legislature in 1859. The men named in the act as incorporators were R. D. Crowder, G. W. Lake, B. C. Adams, J. J. Gage, A. S. Ross, Nathaniel Howard, J. L. Davis, P. Tillman, John B. Ross and R. Richardson, all described as being citizens of Yalobousha county. The proposed route was to be from Grenada, through Pittsboro and Houston to the Alabama line. Capital stock was not to exceed six million dollars. Thirteen directors were to be appointed, and shareholders were to be allowed to work out the price of their shares by use of their slaves and teams in construction work. The outbreak of the Civil War occured before any construction was started.

    The Grenada, Houston and Eastern was not the first railroad incorporated by the citizens of the area in and about Grenada. On May 13, 1837, a little over a year after the union of Pittsburg and Tullahoma, the State Legislature issued an act of corporation of the Grenada Railroad Company with an authorized capital stock of $800,000. The length of the proposed road was to be thirty five miles, extending from "Grenada, on the Yalobousha River, to Douglass, on the Yazoo River in Carroll County." James Smith, J. T. Talbert, J. A. Turatt, Uriah Tyson, A. C. Campbell, R. S. Bryley, and E. Luter were named commissioners of the proposed road. Just as the Civil War prevented construction of the Grenada, Houston and Eastern Railroad, the Panic of 1837 ruined any chance of construction of the proposed Grenada Railroad.

    Within six years after the end of the Civil War, promoters were again busy in an endeavor to finance the Grenada, Houston and Eastern Railroad. In 1860 just before the outbreak of the war, the Mississippi Legislature had passed an act entitled "An Act to Aid In The Construction Of The Grenada, Houston and Eastern Railroad." It would seem that this act authorized counties and towns along the proposed route to subscribe for stock in the proposed railroad. In August of 1871, just a few months after the creation of the county of Grenada, the Grenada County Board of Supervisors received a petition, signed by more than twenty five citizens of the county, requesting that the Board order an election to determine if the county should issue bonds in the amount of $100,000 to buy one thousand shares of stock in the Vicksburg & Grenada Railroad Company and in the Grenada, Houston and Eastern Railroad company. So far as we have been able to determine, there was, at the time the petition was received by the Board of Supervisors, no actual connection between the two railroads, although later developments seem to indicate that through a later ammendment to the original charter of the Grenada, Houston & Eastern Railroad, there was a consolidation of the two lines under the title The Vicksburg, Grenada and Nashville Railroad. In their petition the citizens cited the authority of the county to subscribe to the stock as being contained in the afore-mentioned "An Act To Aid In The Construction Of The Grenada, Houston and Eastern Railroad." The question as to whether the county was authorized by the act to subscribe for stock in a railroad by any other name later became a bitterly contested court issue.

The petition proposed that the stock subscription, if approved by a two thirds majority of the qualified voters of the county, should be paid off in eight installments, which installments should begin to bear interest from January 1, 1873. The Board set up an election to be held in the month of August, 1871, and the resulting election provided the necessary majority vote to authorize the Board of Supervisors to issue bonds to purchase the railroad stock. Although the Board was authorized to purchase stock up to the amount of $100,000 in the two railroads, we have been unable to find any record of any stock having been purchased from the Vicksburg & Railroad Company. The Board did issue $50,000 in bonds to pay for stock in the Grenada, Houston & Eastern Railroad. In court litigation which was to result in later, questions arose relative to the obligation of the county to the $50,000 authorized, but not used, for stock subscription in the Vicksburg & Grenada Railroad Company.

In its July, 1872 meeting the Supervisors levied a "special railroad tax" of seven-eighths of one percent on each dollar of county assessment of property, and ear-marked this levy to pay off the bonds issued to cover purchase of the railroad stock. On August 6, of the same year General W. F. Tucker, President of the Vicksburg & Nashville Railroad, issued a citation on the Board of Supervisors, requesting that the Supervisors deliver to him the bonds which had been authorized to purchase the railroad stock. It would seem that in the time elapsing between the election authorizing the bonds and their delivery in payment of the stock, the proposed Vicksburg & Grenada and Grenada, Houston & Eastern lines had been consolidated into a more ambitious project to build a line from Vicksburg to Nashville. We find that the Supervisors were disturbed relative to their obligation to deliver bonds intended for the Grenada, Houston & Eastern Line, to the line now called the Vicksburg & Nashville Railroad. Their doubts must have been resolved since we find that, in their October 1872 meeting, they decided to deliver the bonds to the Vicksburg & Nashville Railroad Company. In May 1874 bond cupons in the amount of $22,320 were cancelled by the County Treasurer, and this amount made available to the Supervisors for partial payment on the railroad stock. In the same meeting in which this sum became available to the Board of Supervisors, E. T. Fisher, an attorney and owner of considerable real estate in the county, entered a protest against the collection a special tax levied to pay off the railroad stock subscription. His contention was that the stock subscription was illegal on the ground that the Vicksburg & Nashville Railroad Company had never been chartered by the state legislature, but was operating under the 1871 ammendment to the charter of the Grenada, Houston & Eastern Railroad Company. The Board overruled Fisher's objection, but in December of the same year, the Supervisors suspended collection of the special railroad tax levy.

In March, 1875, a large number of influential citizens of the town and county of Grenada, including such men as Oscar Bledsoe, John C. Stokes, John Moore, J. R. Baker and R. J. Pass, secured an order from the Circuit Court providing for a temporary suspension of the collection of the special tax. It is possible that the action of these citizens was for the purpose of justifying the earlier action of the Supervisors suspending the collection of the tax. This legal relief was only temporary. In December of the same year the Circuit Court, hearing the case on its merits, ruled in favor of the legality of the bond issue and the special tax. In its judgement the Court ruled that the county was obligated to the Railroad Company in the amount of $42,000. It is not clear from the Minutes of the Board of Supervisors, which has been the source of our information relative to the litigation, if the court determined that the county was obligated only for the $50,000 stock subscription to the Grenada, Houston & Eastern Railroad Company or if the county was also obligated for the stock subscription authorized by the election for purchase of stock in the Vicksburg & Grenada line. If the $42,000 obligation set up by the Court was only for the obligation to the Grenada, Houston, & Eastern Railroad Company, this would seem to indicate that the county paid off only $8,000 on its stock purchase, whereas we know that the County Treasurer had cancelled bonds and made available $22,320 for payment of stock at least a year before the court verdict. If this amount had been paid to the railroad company, and there was still an obligation of $42,000 due on railroad stock subscription, this would indicate that the county had an original obligation of $64,320 for the railroad stock, which obligation was considerably greater than the stock subscription of $50,000, to the Grenada, Houston & Eastern Railroad, and less than the $100,000 authorized for stock subscription in the Vicksburg & Grenada and the Grenada, Houston & Eastern Railroad companies. Of course, there could have been some interest due on the $50,000 stock purchase, but interest due on unpaid bonds would not likely amount to $14,320.

During the time between the issue of the bonds and the court litigation, the bonds had come into the hands of A. R. Houston of Aberdeen. It was the demand of Houston for past due installment payment which set up the suit which resulted in the judgement against the county. The lower court verdict resulted in a series of appeals, both to state and Federal courts. Evidently the court procedure was a long drawn out affair. In the minutes of the Board of Supervisors of May, 1879, four years after the first court judgement against Grenada county, we find the following notation: "The Board met at the call of the President for the purpose of employing counsel to represent the county in a suit against the county for the collection of railroad bonds against the county." In this meeting the Supervisors adopted the following order: "Ordered that W. H. Powell, President of the Board, go at once to Coffeeville and employ the firm of Golloday & Freeman, and Mays, of the firm of Lamar, Mays and Branham of Oxford, and if the said Powell should find it necessary to go to Oxford, he is ordered to do so, for the purpose of defending the said suit." The name Mays, in connection with the Oxford law firm, should have been spelled Mayes, since he was a member of the Oxford firm. The upshot of the litigation was that a judgement of $85,000 against the county was sustained by the Federal Court. If the county had made a payment of $22,320 when the County Treasurer turned this amount of railroad tax to the Supervisors in 1874, this sustained judgement of an $85,000 obligation still due by the county would seem to indicate that the county was held obligated for the stock subscription authorized for the Vicksburg & Grenada Railroad Company as well as for the stock subscription in the Grenada, Houston & Eastern Railroad Company. To make the subject still more confusing we find that a compromise was finally worked out between the litigants, whereby the county agreed to pay the bondholders three installments of $20,000 each in full payment of their obligation to the bondholders. Of course the proposed Vicksburg & Nashville Railroad was never constructed, and the people of the county learned that there was a vast difference between proposed railroads and their actual construction. They paid dearly for that lesson. Although there was still much activity on the part of promoters seeking to promote railroad lines to link the eastern part of the state with the I. C. Railroad system, Grenada citizens, having once had their hands seared in such promotion refused to become excited at the optimistic plans of promoters of such proposed railroads. From a local newspaper we learn that in 1885 a group of promoters of a proposed Artesia, Starkville, & Grenada Railroad Company, came to Grenada in the interest of their project and received a very cool reception. When the Georgia & Pacific Railraod proposed an extension of its line east and west across the state it seems that Grenada made no effort to bring that road through Grenada. The railroad company did construct such a line by way of Winona to Greenville on the Mississippi River. The extension later came to be called The Southern Railroad and remained for many years as an affiliate of the Georgia Pacific Railroad, which system through its various affiliates had direct rail connection betweeen Richmond, Virginia and Greenville, Mississippi. The connection of Winona by rail with the area east of that town, and to the west in the rich delta terrirory, was a blow to Grenada which had no direct rail connection with those areas. Winona began to draw much trade from those areas which Grenada had hoped to make a part of its trade area.

The Yazoo & Mississippi Valley Railroad was another line interested in tapping the rich resources of the delta area. We have been unable to determine when its first construction began but from a mortgage recorded in the office of the Chancery Clerk of Grenada County we learn that some time before December 1887, the date of the recording of the mortgage, that line is described as extending from its junction with the Chicago, St. Louis & New Orleans Railroad in Hinds County, Mississippi, by way of Yazoo City, Tchula and Greenwood to its terminus at Parsons, Mississippi, a town in the western part of Grenada County. The description also noted that the line had an extension from Tchula through Lexington to Durant. The total mileage was stated as 140.36 miles. The mortgage was for the prupose of obtaining $2,800,000 to be used for the purpose of consolidating and paying off previous loans and for extending its line to a northern junction with the Chicago, St. Louis & New Orleans line. This last named line had been leased by the Illinois Central system. In their endeavor to tap the resources of the delta area, the officials of the Y. & M. V. system had routed their road as far west as Yazoo City, and then made a curve to the right bringing the road to Parsons which was only about fifteen miles west of Grenada. Thus in 1887, Grenada lacked only a short distance of rail connection with the delta area. The railroad officials considered Grenada and Batesville as the most logical points for the junction with the I. C. system. By 1890 the I. C. system had gained control of the Y. & M. V. system. It was the general opinion that the railroad officials were delaying construction of the line to effect the northern junction with the regular I. C. line in acticipation of the people of Grenada and Batesville offering inducements for the construction of the line into their particular localities. In August of 1890 J. W. Buchanan, Editor of the Grenada Sentinel, called the attention of citizens of the city and county of Grenada to the importance of the construction of the line from Parsons to Grenada. In a later editorial the same editor printed an excerpt from a Greenwood paper pluging Greenwood as a fine cotton market and giving as an example of the popularity of the cotton market in that city the fact that a farmer living "four miles west of Grenada" had carried his cotton to the Greenwood market. The editor of the Grenada paper stated that the Grenada county farmers lived four miles from Parsons rather than four miles from Grenada and explained that it was much easier to go four miles to Parsons by wagon and the remainder of the distance to Greenwood by rail than it would have been going fifteen miles by wagon and the remainder of the distance to Greenwood by rail than it would have been going fifteen miles by wagon to Grenada. Again the editor urged consideration of an attempt to have the lines completed to Grenada "Provided the I. C. Branch from Parsons to Greenwood could be leased from the I. C. System." This editorial sounds as if the editor was urging the people of the town and county to get back into the railroad business. A little later he writes that the I. C. System might go ahead to complete the line if the people of Grenada and Grenada county would "be generous in the matter of right of way." We assume that by this statement he felt that the people over whose land the proposed extension might be routed might make a free gift of the right of way across their property. If the proposed extention were to be taken to Batesville it would have the advantage of traversing a longer stretch of delta land, but if it should be extended to Grenada, there would be the advantage of a considerably shorter distance necessary to effect the junction with the I. C. System. There was an additional advantage to the juction at Grenada, which arose from the fact that a junction in that town would give the branch line direct connection with the branch of the I. C. System which ran north to Jackson, Tennessee, and also with the I. C. Line which went to Memphis. The choice of a route for the extension was hanging in the balance as late as April 18, 1892, when on that date the Sentinel published a news item to the effect that J. C. Mann, Chief Engineer for the I. C. System had arrived in Grenada to begin the survey of a route of the proposed extension from Parsons to both Grenada and Batesville, the most advantageous route to be determined by the results of the survey. It would be eight years before the railroad company announced its decision relative to the route selected.

During this period of indecision and uncertainty relative to the possible extension of the line from Parsons to Grenada, there was a revival of interest in the construction of a railraod along the route originally selected by the defunct Grenada, Houston & Eastern Railroad Company. In 1895, just about twenty-four years after the ill-fated Grenada, Houston & Eastern Railraod Company began promotion of the road, and about fifteen years after the county of Grenada had been held liable for its subscription of stock in that railroad venture, two men, H. L. Underwood and Judge J. W. Buchanan arrived in Grenada to try to induce the citizens of that town to contribute to the construction of a railroad called the Nashville & Mississippi Delta Railroad, which company, as a beginning of its ambitious project, comtemplated construction of a road between Nettleton and Grenada by way of Houston and Calhoun City. The overall plan comtemplated an extension of this line to Nashville. The promoters claimed they had financial backing to construct the road, provided the towns and citizens of the country areas, through which the line would run, would provide right of way and forty thousand acres of land, or the equalivent value of such land. They announced to the committee of Grenada people who met with them, that the citizens of the towns of Nettleton, Houston, Calhoun City, and the citizens of the counties in which these towns were located had already pledged thirty thousand acres of land to the project. They were requesting that the citizens of Grenada and Grenada County pledge the remaining ten thousand acres, or money equivalient. Realizing that the three counties of Grenada, Calhoun and Chickasaw had invested a total of three hundred thousand dollars in the Grenada, Houston and Eastern Railraod Company without receiving any benefit in the way or railroad construction, their proposal to the citizens of Grenada and that area was that deeds to the ten thousand acres required of Grenada citizens should be placed in escrow with the Chancery Clerk of Grenada County and not delivered to the railroad company until the proposed railroad line was "constructed, equiped and in operation." It is assumed that the same proposal had been made to the other towns and counties involved.

Max Ginsburger, William C. McLean, Alex Allison and Judge A. T. Roane were appointed to a committee to sound out the people of Grenada and Vicinity on the proposal. A mass meeting of citizens was called and considerable interest was inciated in the project. For some reason, possibly because of the previous bad experience with the former railroad project, the people of Grenada never carried through on the project. Eventually the company did construct a portion of the proposed line from Calhoun City to Houston, but failed in its proposed construction of the longer line visualized in the original plan. The short line between Calhoun City and Houston operated for a period of twenty five years or more before operation was discontinued. Their venture ended the original dream of a railroad line connecting Grenada with the county in the direction of the Alabama state line.

With the failure of this railroad to connect with Grenada there was increased interest in the completion of the line from Parsons to Grenada. If Grenada could not have a line which tapped the resources of the country east of Grenada, it seemed imperative that such a connection should be made with the fertile area west of Grenada. For five years the Illinois Central System delayed announcing a decision relative to which route it would take from Parsons to effect its junction with the main line of the system. On April 21, 1900, the Grenada Sentinel released the following news item: "W. G. Sloan, Assistant Engineer of the Illinois Central has arrived in Grenada for the purpose of constructing the railroad line from Parsons to Grenada, the road to be completed in October or November of this year." The predicted completion date was overly optimistic since it was not until April 20, 1891, that the editor of the Sentinel was able to announce that the last spike has been driven and that the road was ready to announce a schedule of trains operating between Grenada and Tchula by way of Greenwood. Thus, seventy four years ago, the era of railroad construction in Grenada county ended. The next several decades would be a period of struggle to build a system of dirt, gravel and paved roads which would make it possible for the people of the county to take full advantage of the railroad facilities which had already been provided.

Chapter IV

EARLY EDUCATIONAL DEVELOPMENT IN GRENADA AND VICINITY

As the American frontier gradually moved westward, the settlers who made up the western movement took with them a realization of the need for education. The development of schools in a newly settled area was, of necessity, a slow process. Homes had to be built, land cleared, and crops planted and harvested. In a new land these practical affairs of frontier life has priority over educational and cultural needs and desires. Children old enough to go to school were needed at home to aid their parents in the laborious process of carving out new homes, communities and towns. Available teachers were few in number, and prospective pupils for proposed schools were widely scattered. As a result of these conditions many of the children of frontier areas received little or no education. That area of the Third Choctaw Cession, which was to become Grenada and Grenada County, had to go thru the same slow process of educational development which other frontier areas experienced. In 1833 when settlers began to buy land in the vicinity of Grenada, there was little state wide provision for public schools. Indeed, there was little real provision for public schools until after the close of the Civil War. During the early years of the establishment of the towns of Pittsburg and Tullahoma; their consolidation into the town of Grenada; and the subsequent development of Grenada into a major trading center for the region which included several adjacent counties, there developed three kinds of schools. Public, or state supported schools, were called "poor schools." They were so called because only the poorer people were willing to enroll their children in these schools. They deserved the name "poor schools" because of the quality of instruction provided in the short three to four months school terms. In many places parents who lived at too great distance from this first class of schools to make attendance by their children practical, or because they wanted a better type of schools, organized what were called Subscription Schools. A number of parents would band together to employ a teacher and provide a place for the school which would run for as long a term as the parents felt advisable. Frequently a minister would be the teacher of such a school. These schools had no permanent existence nor location, their continued existence and location depending on the whims and needs of the parents, and the availability of a teacher.

To meet the needs of more affluent parents, in more thickly populated areas, there developed a tuition type school usually designated as a "private school." It was in schools of this kind that most of the better educated people of our section began their education in the years before Mississippi began to develop a worthwhile education system. Two of these private schools had been established as early as 1838. At that date William Duncan was conducting a Girl's High School and G. W. Mitchell had established a Boy's High School. It is probable that these two schools existed for a very short time since in 1839 the Mississippi Legislature incorporated by legislature action The Grenada Male and Female Academies. The first principal of the Grenada Female Academy was the same William Duncan who had started the Girl's High School while the principal of the Grenada Male Academy was B. J. Mendon. He explained the purpose of his school in the following words: "A thorough systematic course of instruction shall be given to every member of the school, both in the English and in the classical department. Scholars can be fitted to enter any college or pursue any of the branches usually taught at College." There seems to have been some objection to advanced education for girls. This objection is evidenced by a letter published in the February 25th edition of the local newspaper, The Grenadian. The following excerpt is taken from that letter. "A wise parent will not send his daughter to a modern boarding school to learn frivolous accomplishments, and make romantic friendships, and have her head filled with the fashions and beaus before any principles for the guidance of her conduct of life or any distinct ideas of what constitutes rational happiness have been conveyed to her. Certain it is that the love of home and the habits of domestic confidence must pervaid female education or merely being married will never make a woman fond of domestic pleasures or capable of discharging domestic duties. It is strange that men of sense, learning, and knowledge of the world can believe that a weak-minded, sentimental, frivolous young lady whose whole heart is devoted to dress, amusements and husband hunting, will make a kind, judicious and submissive wife. Such apparently gentle girls are as wives the most unreasonable beings in existence. Men will not believe until they find by conjugal experience that a pretty, soft-spoken sentimental young creature whose deepest learning is a few french phrases, and a few tunes on the piano, can exhibit passions as violent as Queen Elizabeth, or as obstinate as Madam De Steal." Evidently the opinion of the letter writer was not shared by many parents of the area since we find the following statement from the principal of the girl school: "Gratified with the success of the labors of the past, the Principal would beg leave to assure the parents and guardians of the young ladies of this town and surrounding country, that no exertions shall be wanting to place this Institution on a footing with the best of the South." Both of these academies must have been built and maintained by the efforts of a considerable number of the leading citizens of the town and country. The Board of Trustees of the Female school had Col. G. K. Morton as President, and the following named trustees: Major J. Y. Bayliss, E. P. Stratton, Col. N. Howard, John Smith, and William Lake. All of these men, except Bayliss, have been identified in previous chapters of this series. As an indication of the reputation of the Female Academy an advertisement by the school published in the Weekly Register on December 10, 1842, read as follows: "References may be made to the following gentlemen as patrons of the school: Dr. Snider, Dr. Gillespie, Major Whitaker, Col. Morton, Capt. Smith, Col. Howard, Maj. Bullock, A. C. Baine, Col. Abbot, Dr. Wright, and Messrs. Sims, Choate, Berry, Coffman, Stevens, Neal, I. Melton, J. Melton, M. Melton, Haden, Gill, Taylor and Hunley. Most of these names, found in other chapters of this series have been identified as men of influence in the area.

The First Trustees of Grenada Male Academy have not been identified, but we do learn that in 1841 the following men served as trustees of the school: Thomas B. Ives, Michael Melton, J. T. Talbert, John M. Chaote, A. C. Baine, Jacob Snyder, and T. P. Davidson. We are unable to determine just how long these schools operated but we do know that they were still in operation in 1849. On that date Daniel R. Russell, acting as a Commissioner of the Chancery Court to carry out a decree of that Court in a suit instituted by the President and Trustees of Grenada Male and Female Academy against George K. Martin, ordered the sale of thirteen hundred and sixty acres of land belonging to Martin. Evidently the defendant in the suit was indebted to the school. At the public sale of this land to satisfy the judgement of the court in favor of the schools, the President and Trustees of the two schools bought in the land. We have no information as to how Martin became indebted to the schools. The transaction indicates that one man was President of both schools at the time the suit was instituted. It is possible that the same men may have been serving as trustees for both schools. In 1852 and 1853 most of this land was sold by the schools to Sam W. Land and A. S. Brown. In the year 1853 it seems that each school had a "President" of its own, since we find that "W. H. Whiteside, President of Grenada Male Academy and A. Howard President of Grenada Female Academy," conveyed part of Lot number 190 and all of lot number 191, located in the East Ward of Grenada, to Joseph Collins for a consideration of two thousand one hundred and seventy five dollars. These lots comprise the area on which the North Mississippi Retirement Home is now located. The presumption is, although we have no definite proof to that effect, that the Male and Female Academies were located on these lots. This transaction is the last record we have of any activity of the two schools. It is possible that the schools were not located on these lots, but certainly there is no available evidence to indicate that they continued in existence after the last named transaction.

Although we have found no indication that the Male Academy was suffering from competion with other schools, it is very probable that the Female Academy was having serious competition from two church schools which had been established in Grenada. These were not the first church schools to be established in Grenada. Early in the existence of Grenada the people of the Presbyterian church, under the direction of their minister, established a school in a building located on College street. This building had once been the Union Hotel operated by John Smith. Mr. Holly was the minister who acted as principal of the school. The Baptist people opened a Baptist Institute under a minister by the name of Webb. The location of the building in which this school was taught is unknown. In all probability these schools were elementary in nature and could not have been serious competition for the Male and Female Academies. In 1850 the Methodist people of Grenada erected a new church, and the old building was used as a school. It was enlarged to cover almost a block and must have been of flimsy construction--a newspaper report in the late 1880's describes it as "that old rookery Bascomb's Academy." The school was a project of the Methodist people and was named Bascomb's Academy in honor of a Methodist Bishop of that name. S. W. Moore was the first President of the school which printed probably the first school paper ever published in Grenada when it published the Bascomb Gem.

The Baptist people, not to be outdone, organized the Yalobousha Female Institute. The first record we have of the establishment of such a school is a deed by which James Sims and his wife Harriett Sims deeded to Lewis Aldridge, President of the Board of Trustees of Yalobousha Female College, lot number 140 in the west ward of Grenada and also several lots in the block just south of lot 140. This south lot had been the site of the old Union Hotel, and the Presbyterian school. These two lots remained in the possession of the school until 1857 when Aldridge, still President of the Institute, conveyed them to R. D. Crowder for a consideration of two thousand dollars. It seems that the Baptist used the old Union Hotel building to house their infant school while they were constructing a fine building in another location. Their brief occupancy of the building probably resulted in the change of the name by which the street, originally called Pittsburg street, came now to be called College street. Late in the same year when the location in the West Ward had been purchased, a four-story building, costing about fifty thousand dollars, had been erected in the East Ward of Grenada, in the area just south of the North Mississippi Retirement Home. Many of the people still living in this vicinity will recall that building as one of the dormatories of the now defunct Grenada College.

Since both Bascomb's Academy and Yalobousha Female Institute (or College), as it was called by both names, claimed to doing work on both high school and college level, they could have become serious competators of the Grenada Female Academy. So far as the Male Academy is concerned, the only local competition which it could have had and that was probably not too serious, was a school established by the Masonic Order and called the Masonic Academy. It was later known as Brick Academy, leading to the presumption that it was constructed of brick. In 1856 Green Crowder sold to the Masonic Order all of lot number 25 and the north half of lot number 26. The Masonic Academy was located on these lots. There was some confusion, either in lot numbers or description, but the lots conveyed to the Masons was that area where the Lizzie Horn Elementary Building is now located. In 1879 the Masonic Order sold this property, including the building, to the members of the Episcopal Church, and for a brief time some of the Rectors of that church supervised a school there.

The new Yalobousha Female Institute had been constructed on lot number 1, of the Snider Survey. For some reason the school did not fulfill the expectations of those who had invested in the beautiful new buildings. At some undetermined date the name of the College was changed to Emma Mercer Institute, in honor of Mrs. Mercer who gave an endowment to the college. Since the new name was used in 1868 and since both the Bascomb's Academy and the Yalobousha Female Institute had been closed during the Civil War years, it is possible that Mrs. Mercer advanced enough money to get the college in operation and was honored by having the name changed. The new name and the endowments were not sufficient to make the college a going proposition. Shortly after the reopening of the school under its new name it ceased operation, and the indications are that the property was bought up by a group of Grenada citizens who were desirous of having the school continue operation. Evidently the name was changed to Grenada Female College. This is indicated by a transaction described in the following words: "Deed by Grenada Female College to David D. Moore of lot one in Snider Survey the Grenada Female College having succeeded to all the rights of the individual stockholders and subscribers in the purchase of the said lot." The stockholders and subscribers mentioned may possibly have been promoters of the Baptist College, but more likely were Grenada citizens endeavoring to keep the school going. The so-called deed was, in reality, a lease for a three year term of the defunct college property. Although the initials of Mr. Moore were not the same as those given for the Moore who had headed Bascomb's Seminary, it is very probable that the Moore who leased the college property was the same Moore who had been head of the Bascomb's Seminary. The lease was made out in 1875 and Moore attempted to run a private school. Evidently the project was not a success, since we can find no record of a renewal of the lease arrangement.

It seems that George Ragsdale had become President of the college some time after the lease had been made to Moore. We find that, in a suit instituted against "G. S. Ragsdale, President of Grenada Female College." John Stokes was given a judgement against the college to satisfy a loan of eight thousand dollars which he had made to the college. The property was sold at public auction sometime in 1883. Mr. and Mrs. H. C. Timberlake bid in the property for sum of seventeen hundred dollars. In July of 1883 the Timberlakes deeded the property to R. P. Lake, G. W. Jones, George Lake, and W. S. Lake. The consideration involved was sixty five hundred dollars, a very small price for the college property but represented a good profit to the Timberlakes. On the same day on which the men named above acquired the property, they deeded it to the Trustees of Grenada District High School of the North Mississippi Conference of the Methodist Episcopal Church. The four men who issued the deed to the church organization became trustees of the District High School along with two other trustees, one from Yalobousha County and one from Lafayette County. The deed given to the Church Conference stipulated that the Conference was to pay four thousand dollars for the property in annual instalments, said notes to bear eight per cent interest. Thus this Methodist school, which was to play such a large part in the educational development of Grenada and North Mississippi, began its existence as it ended it--burdened with debt.

J. T. Newell, Methodist minister stationed at Grenada, became head of the District High School, which began operation soon after the Church Conference had obtained the property. In 1884 the Trustees of the Grenada District High School transfered the property to the Trustees of Grenada Collegiate Institute. Mr. Newell continued as head of the school which now began offering some college courses in addition to the high school courses first offered. The school had three divisions: The Primary Department--small boys and girls; the Female Department--young ladies; and the Male Department--boys and young men. Tuition rates were set up in the following manner: Primary two dollars per month; Academic three dollars per month; Collegiate four dollars per month; Music five dollars per month and Board fifteen dollars per month. The college had dormitory space for sixty students. A large per-centage of the student body was made up of day students who lived, or boarded, in Grenada or vicinity. After a few years the name of the school was changed again to Grenada College. For many years it continued to serve the area as a Senior College, but financial difficulties which had beset the institution from its beginning continued to harass the college officials, so that, in later years they attempted to reduce expenses by changing to a junior college. This move was not successful, and in the year 1936 the Church Conference liquidated the property and transfered any assets remaining to Millsaps College. The establishment of Delta State at Cleveland, and state supported junior colleges at strategic points in the area from whence the Methodist institution had drawn its students, contributed to the decline of the school.

Bascomb's Female Academy which has been mentioned here-to-fore, at one time had a faculty comprised of the following teachers: Rev. A. J. Edgerton, Principal; C. M. Lawton, Clara George, Olivia P. Sudley and Sarah W. Hutchings. We have mentioned the existence of the Masonic Academy. We know little about this school except that its first Principal was W. E. Beck, and that the school had a very brief existence as a school operated by the Masonic order. During the period in which the above named school operated, the people unable to pay the tuition charges of the different private and denominational schools were sending their children to a rather poor system of town and county elementary schools. These schools ran very brief terms of three to four months per year. Before the Civil War period the state contributed very little to public education, and any public schools which operated were financed very largely by counties and towns. During the post-war period the state began to make a larger contribution to public education, but for several decades this increased support was very inadequate, and private schools continued to flourish from the patronage of well-to-do people, while the children of less-well-to-do parents continued to obtain very inadequate educational training. In order to bridge the gap between people wealthy enough to send their children to the better private schools, and those less affluent parents who were willing to make a sacrifice to obtain better educational training for their children than that offered by the public schools; educated ladies living in the town, set up schools, usually in their homes, where for very small tuition charges they taught primary, and sometimes, higher elementary grades. Two of these teachers were Mrs. P. J. Dudley and Mrs. M. M. Ransom. At various times these two ladies are found on the faculty lists of the public school. Another of the ladies teaching one of these schools in her home was Mrs. Franklin E. Plummer, wife of the man who was instrumental in the establishment of the town of Pittsburg. Mrs. Plummer was conducting a school in her home when a tornado struck Grenada in 1846, and she and several of her pupils were killed.

In 1884 John J. Gage Jr., who at times taught in the public schools, announced the establishment of Grenada Normal School, he was to act as Principal and was to be assisted by Mrs. P. S. Dudley, Miss Mary Guage and Miss Kate College. The school was to be domiciled in the Parish School Building. Since the Episcopal Church had bought the Masonic Academy bulding in 1879, we assume that the Parish School Building in which the Normal School was to begin, was the Masonic Academy Building. Gage advertised that the completion of the courses offered by his school would entitle the student to a first grade teaching certificate. The new school seems not to have prospered, since a little later Gage transfered his school to Slate Springs in Calhoun County. In 1883, Gage had served as Principal of the Grenada Free (Public) School. In the same year when John Gage Jr. was serving as Principal of the Grenada Free School, Dr. John J. Gage Sr. was acting as part-time Grenada County Superintendent of Education. His was a part time job, for which he received a very small salary. At that time, and for a number of years thereafter, the position was appointive rather than elective. Dr. Gage reported that the total amount of school money received from all sources for schools in the county was six thousand and ninety six dollars. County white teachers were paid twelve hundred thirty dollars and eighty three cents to instruct six hundred and thirty seven white children, while negro teachers were paid five thousand two hundred fifty seven dollars and twenty cents to instruct twenty one hundred and twenty negro children.

Dr. Gage received two hundred dollars as his salary for the year. He reported that sixty county schools had run for four months, while the Grenada City Schools ran for seven months.

In 1885 George E. Critz came from Starkville to Grenada to set up a school for boys, to be domiciled in the Brick Academy (the old Masonic Academy Building). After one year as director of this private school for boys Mr. Critz became Principal of the Grenada Public School. As assistants he had Mrs. M. C. Ayres, Mrs. M. H. Ransom and Miss Mattie Ballard. At the time, the Board of Trustees of the City school was composed of the following men: S. S. Fairfield, R. T. Latling Jr., Alex Davis, Robert Brown and G. G. Leonard. Mr. Fairfield was a native of New Hampshire who moved to the Natchez District of Mississippi. While there he taught school for a time at Woodville, Mississippi. He came to Grenada in 1854. When the threat of secession from the Federal Government arose, he announced that he was a union man. Regardless of his opposition to secession, when the war broke out he became a member of a local militia unit, composed of boys and men either too young or too old for active service in the Regular Confederate Military Establishment. During the war years he and his wife conducted some type of school in Grenada. R. T. Latting, Jr. was an outstanding business man of the town, serving as manager of a cottonseed oil mill, and being interested in other projects, such as an ice factory and a local telephone company. G. W. Leonard was a colored merchant who operated a grocery store on Green Street. We have no information relative to the other two Board Members. It is significant of the disturbed conditions of the time, that there should have served as Members of the Board of Trustees a white republican and a colored one, in a town and county which had long been a stronghold of the Democratic Party.

For some reason Mr. Critz either resigned, or failed of re-election, and was replaced by a Mr. Christian who had been an employee of the Railroad Express Company before resigning that position to become Principal of the Grenada School. A prominent Grenada County citizen, now deceased, who had an opportunity to know Mr. Christian, describes him in this manner: "He was an awesome and fearful being; long and awkward in his walk, making me think of the seven-league boots. He wore a long-tailed coat and broad hat; his mustache was almost as long as a walrus' tusks, and he carried a big silver watch with a heavy chain, which he twisted with his fingers as he spoke. He often applied the rod." At the time when the above described gentleman became Principal of the school it was housed in the old building which had been called the Masonic Academy. Evidently the city had already purchased the property since just a short time later the city erected a new building on the lot. Mr. W. E. Boushe, whose description of Mr. Christian I have quoted, has this description of the school and school building: "There were one hundred pupils; desks were crude and homemade, three pupils sitting to the desk. The shotgun building, first made for a Masonic Lodge, consisted of four rooms, three downstairs and one upstairs. Two strange arrangements were the facts that the youngest children were taught in the upper room and had to go upstairs that were almost as steep as a ladder; all children, in going to their rooms, had to pass through a room in which the coal was stored, which kept all rooms dirty. A large part of Grenada children, even small boys and girls, went to the College; some went to Private Schools; some did not go at all. An unsightly ditch ran diagonally across the school-yard, in which several Negro cabins stood. A high fence was across the back yard of the building; here the girls played. A single plank was the sidewalk to the street in front of the school, and a square surface-well furnished water. Once that gave out and we were forced to cross line street to Judge Wilkins' home for water."

Under the direction of the members of the Board of Trustees, or with their permission, Mr. Christian set up rules and regulations regarding school attendance, and pupil conduct. One of the regulations provided that absence of a certain number of days from school, without reasonable cause for such absence, would be grounds for suspension of a pupil from school. Exercise of that regulation started off the Principal on a brief and stormy tenure. When some boys were suspended from school because of such absence, the suspension created considerable ill will against Mr. Christian, as well as a division of opinion on the part of the patrons of the public school; some of them commending, and others condemning the Principal. Those who supported Mr. Christian felt that the School Board did not back him up when people began to raise a fuss over the suspension of the boys. From the issue of the Grenada Sentinel printed on July 16, 1887, we quote the following statement relative to the school session just finished-the session in which Mr. Christian suspended the boys: "The Free (White) School opened with an attendance of sixty. Mr. G. W. Christian Principal, assisted by Mrs. M. C. Ayrea and Mrs. M. M. Ransom." At this time Grenada was a town with a population of about three thousand. Although a considerable number of the inhabitants of Grenada then, as now, were colored, it is indicative of the lack of interest in public education, that there were only sixty white children in average daily attendance for the school year of 1886-1887.

Some of the people who patronized the public school felt that the School Trustees were not too much sold on the importance of the public school. In a letter to the Editor of the Grenada Sentinel, one indignant patron brought out the charge that one member of the Board had no child in school; another was sending his children to private schools and a third member was financially able to do so, while the poorer people of the town were compelled to put up with the sorry public school which the town provided. Evidently a number of Private Schools were still in existence in Grenada at the time. Most of them were either Primary or Elementary in their instructional fields. Some women were still running such schools in their homes. For instance there appeared in the local newspaper on August 17, 1887, an advertisement in which Mrs. Dudley notified the public of the opening date of her "Mixed School." The term "mixed" refered to sex, rather than to race. This was the same Mrs. Dudley who had previously been a member of the faculty of the public school. The inadequacy of the Public School System was commented on by J. W. Buchanan, Editor of the Grenada Sentinel, in this manner: Before the war this town held high rank as an educational point. Since, it has fallen, until it has almost reached the freezing point. Our forces are so divided that a school is to be found on almost every corner, without fame, almost without name or even local habitation. We would not be considered as in the least reflecting upon any of the worthy ladies who have the solitary and arderous, and perhaps profitless task of conducting them. We are now advocating the public and not private interests, and would say that here in Grenada, with ananimity and concentrated purpose we might build up a free school that would be much more than an honor, a postive blessing to Grenada." This editorial was written in 1882. A little later we find the same editor advocating the purchase, by the city, of the property of the defunct Grenada Female College, which property would be used by the public school. It will be recalled that, a little later, the Timberlakes bought this property, at public auction, for the small sum of seventeen hundred dollars. Unfortunately, the editorial had no immediate effect, and the city lost the opportunity to obtain, at a very small price, property which would have been adequate for a good public school. Within less than seven years, the city was to spend a great deal more than this price to construct a new school building less adequate than the College building would have been. Although the reputation of the Grenada Public School System was nothing to bragg about, the establishment of the Methodist District High School did enhance the educational standing of the city. This School had some boarding facilities, and also attracted many day students from the town. People who lived in communities where school facilities were poor began to move to Grenada to give their children the opportunity to attend the Methodist District High School. In the January 20, 1884, issue of the Grenada Sentinel we find the following news item: "Rev. S. M. Thames, Judge A. T. Roane, Dr. J. M. Williams, W. B. Saunders and others have moved to Grenada to take advantage of the District High School." Within five years of the appearance of this news item, the Judge became a member of the Board of Trustees of the Grenada City Schools.

Demand for better school facilities at last moved the Board of Aldermen to set up a special election by which the citizens of the town should have the opportunity to vote on a bond issue of fifteen thousand dollars which, if approved by a majority of the voters, would be used for the purpose of purchasing lots and building two school buildings; one for the White children and one for the Colored children. The resulting vote was one hundred and seventy five favoring the bond issue and only six votes against the proposal. This election held on July 7, 1888, reflects a definite change of attitude relative to public education from that time, just a few years before, when a similar bond proposal had been decisively defeated. Indicative of the prevailing thought of the time relative to the importance of education of white and colored children, contracts were let for the construction of a brick school building for the white children, and a wood building for the colored children. The old Masonic Academy building was in a bad state of repairs, and the Board did not want to spend money on repairs on the old building when a new building was under construction. Anticipating a rapid pace of construction which would have the new building ready for use by January 1, 1889, the School Board decided to defer the beginning of the white school until that date. As the fall season passed, and the construction of the new building did not progress as rapidly as had been anticipated, the Board reconsidered its decision, and repaired the old building to the extent that the school session could begin either late in November or early in December.

The controversial Principal Christian had not been re-elected by the School Board, notwithstanding a petition signed by many school patrons and submitted to the Board. Hoping to avert dissention among the school patrons, Mr. Christian had tendered his resignation. The School Board then inserted the following quoted advertisement in the Grenada Sentinel: "Teachers Wanted- One Principal, and Two Assistants for the Grenada White School. Apply to A. T. Roane, Secretary of the Board of Trustees of Grenada Public Schools." Even after the insertion of this advertisement, there was considerable pressure, led by J. W. Buchanan, Editor of the Sentinel, exerted on the School Board to force the re-election of Mr. Christian. As an inducement for the rehiring of the Principal, his friends got him to agree to accept the position at a salary of seventy five dollars per month instead of the salary of one hundred dollars per month which the Board proposed to pay a new Principal. The Board remained firm on their refusal to re-elect Mr. Christian, and began to interview men seeking the Principalship. After several meetings in which applicants were interviewed, the Board elected H. J. Phillips, who came from a small town in Tennessee. We do not know the average attendance for the bob-tailed session in the old building while the new building was being completed, but with the beginning of the first school session in the new building in the Fall of 1889, about one hundred children were enrolled. Mr. Buchanan, still rankling from his failure to pressure the Board into re-electing Mr. Christian as Principal, seemed happy to report in his newspaper that the attendance in the new building under the supervision of the new Principal was less than half the attendance which Mr. Christian had the previous school session. After the school session had run for a short time the paper reported that the attendance in the new school building had reached one hundred and seventy eight. This rapid increase in enrollment seems to indicate an easing of the tensions resulting from the unfortunate disagreement relative to the selection of a Principal.

The date 1889 marks the beginning of an effective Grenada Public School System which gradually developed into one of the better school systems of the state-a position which it has continued to maintain. Because of the superior advantages of the City School System, a number of small county taxing districts which maintained schools began, one by one, to request permission to send their children to the City Schools on a tuition basis. The new school building mentioned above was a two story building constructed on part of the area on which the present Lizzie Horn Elementary Building is located. It had a combination auditorum study hall located in the upper story of the building, with classrooms on both stories. This building, which had two four room wings added to it in 1906, continued to house both Elementary and High School grades until the present John Rundle High School Building was constructed in 1922. Some of the local taxing districts which began to send their students to the city schools were Fairgrounds, Mitchell, Tie Plant, Elliott, Brooks, Kirkman and Wolfe-Hardy. At the time of the completion of the Lizzie Horn Elementary Building all of these districts, with the exception of Wolfe-Hardy, were sending both elementary and high school students to Grenada. When the completion of the Lizzie Horn Elementary Building was acomplished, that school, which had been sending only its high school students to Grenada, abandoned its elementary school and sent all its school children to the Grenada School. Since all of these county taxing districts had their assessed property valuation set by the county, and their school mileage set by their trustees, it presented a rather complex administrative problem for the County Superintendent of Education. Finally, the people of several districts got together and consolidated their several districts into a single district called the Grenada Consolidated District. This district included all the central part of the county with the exception of the part which lay within the boundaries of the city of Grenada. This District had, by this time, been designated as Grenada Municipal Separate School District. The term "sparate" indicated a new type of school which had no direct connection with the county school system. Although the above mentioned taxing districts had been sending their white children to the City Schools on a tuition basis, no such provision had been made for colored children of these districts. They attended small, mostly one teacher schools, and had no transportation provided them, as it was provided white children. After the consolidation of the several county taxing districts into the Grenada Consolidated District, that district maintained no schools for white children but continued to operate elementary schools for the colored children of the district. No provision had, at first, been made to give the colored students a chance to attend a public high school. The only way a colored student, living in the county could obtain a high school education in the county, was to pay tuition to attend the City Colored School and provide his own transportation. Some boarded in town. Soon after the Grenada Consolidated District was constructed, that district began to pay the tuition of such colored students who could manage to get transportation into town. This condition prevailed until 1954, when both City and County began building new facilities. A new Colored High School was constructed by the city, which enabled the school to provide facilities for all colored high school students in the county. About this time, under new school legislation enacted by the State Legislature, all existing school districts were abolished, and a new system of schools organized. The new school legislation provided for financial help from the state to aid in creating new school facilities, with emphasis being placed on the equalization of school facilities for white and colored children. Under this Program, or in anticipation of it, the County had constructed adequate colored school buildings at Holcomb and Tie Plant. These schools were designed to house the colored elementary children of the county, all colored high school continuing to attend the Grenada City Colored High School. Before the school reorganization mentioned above was effected, The Holcomb Consolidated District in the Western part of the county maintained a twelve grade white school until about a year before the consolidation of all county schools into a County Unit System. At that time, the members of the Holcomb School Board requested that the City School take their High School students on a tuition basis. In the Eastern Part of the County The Gore Springs Consolidated School District maintained a twelve Grade School, which continued until after the school reorganization was effected.

After this was done, the Gore Springs High School students were sent to the Grenada High School, and the elementary students continued in the school at Gore Springs until the completion of the Jones Road Elementary School, after which they were sent to that school. The county continued to maintain the white elementary school at Holcomb. Both these twelve grade schools had resulted from the consolidation of a number of smaller schools. Neither district had any provision for colored twelve grade schools in their districts. In fact, most if not all, of the colored elementary schools in these districts were financed very largely by the county. The arrangement explained above continued until the Spring of 1965 when, by agreement of the two school systems, the limits of The Grenada Municipal Separate School District was extended to include the whole county.

From the opening of the new school building in 1889 down to the present time, a period of about seventy seven years, sixteen men have served as head of the white schools of the Grenada School System. Some of the earlier school heads were called Principals, and had supervision over only the white schools. Later they came to be called Superintendents, and were given charge of both white and colored schools. The first thirteen of these men served a total of thirty one years, while the last three, one of whom is still serving, cover a period of forty five years of service.

H. J. Phillips was the first of these men, followed in order by S. A. Morrison, E. L. Bowman, J. A. Granberry, J. N. Powers, J. M. Hubbard, J. H. Woodward, R. H. Hester, V. G. McKie, S. Claude Hall, A. B. Campbell, Clinton Bigham, A. S. McLendon, John Rundle, J. C. Hathorn and the present Superintendent F. G. Wilborn. Mr. Morrison became an attorney in Grenada after retiring from the school superintency; J. B. Powers became State Superintendent of Education and then the Chancellor of the University of Mississippi; A. B. Campbell became a very successful Jackson businessman, and served a term as President of the United States Chamber of Commerce; S. Claude Hall continued in school work, by becoming a member of the staff of State Normal School at Hattiesburg, which school has now become the University of Southern Mississippi.

The early Grenada City Colored Schools were even more inadequate than the white schools. Well-to-do white parents could send their children to private schools existing in the town, but the economic situation of the colored people was such that there were too few colored parents able to pay tuition to a colored private school to justify the establishment of such a school. If the colored people were to have any local educational opportunity for their children it would, of necessity, have to come from the public schools. For a long time two colored teachers struggled to look out for the educational needs of the colored children of the city. Then, when the new colored school was constructed in 1889, a new era began to dawn for the colored school children of the community. Gus Henderson, educated at Alcorn Agricultural and Mechanical College, was made Principal of the Colored School. He and his two assistants began the long process of building an improved Colored School. Although the White School was operating to cover both elementary and high school grades, the Colored School operated for a time as an elementary school. Gradually, as the scholastic achievement of the colored children justified the action, extra grades were added to the elementary school program until about 1930, the Colored School consisted of twelve grades.

We have little information about county schools, white or colored, before the year 1870. Before this date there was little state aid available to assist counties in supporting public schools. There was no such thing as a real, effective public school system. Regardless of the ills brought to the people of Mississippi as an aftermath of the Civil War and Congressional Reconstruction, we must admit that both Grenada County and the beginning of a statewide public Education System are the children of the Reconstruction Period. The Legislature which met at Jackson in the year 1870 was largely made up of members of the Republican Party; many of the members were colored men. Governor Alcorn had been elected by the Republican vote, causing many of the white men of Mississippi to look upon him as a traitor to his fellow white Mississippians. Even so it was this Legislative session which created Grenada County and which passed a Legislative Act in 1871 entitled "An Act By The State Legislature Regulating The Organization, Supervision, and Maintenance Of A Uniform System Of Public Education For The State Of Mississippi." By that act, some state money was made available for the so-called "Common School" which schools were set up and operated, at first, very largely on the scant funds supplied by the State. It is probable that the State Funds were distributed on a per capita basis as we know they later came to be distributed. After the Organization of Grenada County in 1870, little was done about education until after the passage of the 1871 Legislative Act quoted above. The County began operation of public schools under the above act by establishing five school districts, these districts coinciding with the five Supervisor Districts. School Directors were provided for each of these districts. The first Directors were appointed by the Board of Supervisors. The first supervisors had also been appointed. After the first term of the Supervisors and the School Directors had been completed, both the Supervisors and School Directors became elective.

On Friday August 5, 1871, the Board of Supervisors appointed Hilliard Hames and J. R. Rosamond School Directors to serve three years; William Bell and A. H. Graves to serve two years, and Ralph Coffman and W. H. Powell to serve one year. Each of the first four directors named were to serve the schools of his own Supervisor's District. Coffman and Powell were both residents of District One which included the City of Grenada. The presumption is that Powell was appointed to represent the people of the District outside of town, while Coffman, a merchant doing business in Grenada, was appointed to represent the people living in the city. Since each Director was supposed to look after the schools of his district, Powell could look out for the county schools in District One while Coffman could look out after the state interest in the City Schools. This assumption is more or less confirmed by the fact that at the expiration of the one year terms of the two District One Directors, only one was elected thereafter. By this time the City Schools had established their independent existence, and the needed no city representation relative to the direction of the schools in the rest of District One. The city schools received their pre-rata share of the state money sent to Grenada County. The County School Directors were required to visit all schools, white and colored in their School Districts, and received three dollars pay for each day in which they engaged in this visitation. The Directors were required to submit estimates of the money needed to run the schools of their District. This estimate was presented to the Board of Supervisors for approval. In 1871 the Director of District One estimated that it would take seven hundred and twenty one dollars to run the schools of his District-this amount included four hundred seven dollars for teacher's salaries, and the rest for rental and repairs of school buildings and contingencies. The Director of District Two estimated that he would need twenty one hundred dollars, nineteen hundred and forty dollars of this amount for teacher's salaries, and the rest for school house espenses. District Three Director estimated his need at eleven hundred and twenty dollars, nine hundred and twenty dollars of which were ear-marked for teachers salaries and the rest for "School House Expenses." This probably was a catchall item to cover, rent, repairs and supplies such as crayon, etc. District Four required the same amount as District Three, and made the same division of funds between teachers salaries and School House Expense. The Director of District Five estimated that he needed sixteen hundred fifty seven dollars and fifty cents. Of this amount fourteen hundred and forty dollars were to take care of teacher's salaries. The rest was to be divided between "Schoolhouse and Contingent Expense." The fact that District One, the most populous District in the county, had the smallest estimate of District School Expense, is a further indication that the city schools were taking part of a large segment of the school population of the District, and that the school population of District One outside the city boundaries, did not contain as large number of children of school age as would be found in the other Districts. The largest estimate of District school expenses, coming from District Two, is no surprise. That District contained the area of the county in which the Yalobousha River towns of Chocchuma and Tuscahoma had been located. Although these two towns were practically extinct by this time, populous communities had grown up on the fertile land in that area of the county, and since none of this school population was included in an incorporated town having a school of its own, all the school children had to be educated in the schools of the District.

State support for the common schools was raised by a four mill state levy on property. This is indicated by an order of the Board of Supervisors which is quoted hereafter: "Ordered by the Board that the County Treasurer be and is hereby authorized to use and to pay over to the Treasurer of the City of Grenada the sum of one dollar and eighty cents for each educable child within the corporate limits of the said City out of funds now in his hands from the State four mill Tax, or such proportion thereof as the city may be entitled to under the statute in such case made and provided, and that the recipt of the Treasurer of the City to the County Treasurer shall be a valid voucher for said payment in his settlement with the Board." The spelling, pronunciation and capitalization found in the order is just as it was recorded. It is clear enough, however, to indicate that the state funds were paid to the county on a per capita basis, and that the Board of Supervisors distributed to the City Government of Grenada its rightfuly share of the State School Tax. Realizing the inadequacy of the state support of common schools, the Districts began to supplement state school money by local tax levies. In the year of 1871 District One had a school levy of three and one fourth mills; District Two levied five and three fourths mills; Districts Three, Four and Five set their levies at six mills. The assessed valuation of the property in the several school districts is not now available, so we do not know just how much money these several tax levies brought into the school districts which made the levies. We do have information that in 1878 the assessed value of real and personal property in the county had reached one million three hundred thousand dollars. Using this valuation, the millage levies set by the several county school districts would have brought in about thirty two hundred dollars. The returns in 1871 could not have been more than this amount, and was probably considerably less. We have not determined just when the City of Grenada began to impose a local school tax, but we find that in 1878 a school eax of three mills was being collected from city taxpayers. The assessed valuation of the property in the city was five hundred thousand four hundred and sixty seven dollars. The school tax collected that year for local school purposes was fifteen hundred one dollars and six cents. Both the city and county schools received some extra school money from the license fees charged by city and county authorities for the operation of saloons. Such licenses had been issued to individuals in villages of Hardy, Graysport, Elliott, and possibly to individuals in other areas of the county. Several saloons were operating in the city of Grenada. We get some idea of the money which these saloon licenses provided for school purposes from an argument advanced by those persons who were fighting to defeat the prohibition forces in an election proposing the outlawing of saloons in the city of Grenada under the local option law existing at the time. Grenada had permitted saloons since the very beginning of the establishment of the two small towns which united to form Grenada. In 1886, those citizens favoring abolition of saloons in the town finally got the town authorities to set up an election to determine the will of the town citizens relative to the issue. There were two newspapers in the town; one was controled by the prohibitionists, and the other by those favoring retention of saloons. The following editorial was published by the paper which supported retention of saloons in the city: "It costs $1,014.57 to run the free schools of Grenada town for four months.

The tax paid by the people is $195.00 which, with $222.00 of poll tax we have $597.57 which is about half way the required sum. Now where is the deficit to come from when the saloons are closed? This is a serious question to every poor man who had children to educate and we prepare them in advance, not to kill the goose that lays the golden egg." If the figures used in the editorial were correct, they tend tio indicate two things; that license fees from the saloons were financing the city public schools to the extent of approximately five hundred dollars; and that the school millage, which had once been three mills, had been reduced since the school session of 1878.

The county schools were also running on a very limited budget. Fifteen months after county was organized the county was paying S. Riley two hundred and ninety five dollars for services as County Superintendent for service through August 10, 1871. On the same date William Pierce was allowed ninety five dollars for similar service. We assume that one man had been appointed for a short term, and the other for a longer term. On July 2, 1872, J. J. Williams received one hundred and ninety dollars for service in the same capacity. In 1873, the Board of Supervisors allowed A. C. Snider sixty two dollars and fifty cents as rental of a house, in the town of Grenada, used as a school for county pupils. This item indicated the prevailing practice, during the early years of the operation of the county school system, to rent rather than build school buildings. The practice was to establish county schools close to the homes of a number of school children. It is quite probable that a considerable number of county school children lived in the area around the city limits, and that a house in the city was the point most convenient to a majority of the children. It must be remembered that the county, still in the grip of the economic depression resulting from the Civil War and the consequent period of reconstruction, could well have decided that its economic situation would not justify building substantial school buildings, and that it would be better to rent buildings for school purposes until such time as the county was able to build substantial school buildings. To those people who think that Negro education entirely disregarded the following order, passed by the Board of Supervisors, will be reveiling: "Moved and passed that one hundred dollars out of the common school fund be paid to H. R. Revels, Presidents of Alcorn University to pay for clothes and board of Edward Muffett in the said institution, holding a free school fee scholarship therein for the year of 1874." The Alcorn University mentioned in the Board order later came to be known as Alcorn Agricultural And Mechanical College. It was a Negro school named to honor Governor Alcorn who served a term as governor during the Reconstruction Period. The college was located near Rodney, which had been the center of a very prosperous plantation economy in the years before the outbreak of the Civil War. The College was located on the spot, and in fact, used some of the surviving buildings of Oakland College, which had been a pre-war educational center for the white people of that area. It was from Oakland College that Smith Daniel graduated in 1846. He built the magnificent house known as Winsdor, the ruined corinthian columns of which are still standing to-day, to attest to the opulent life of some of Mississippi's pre-war planters. Hiram R. Revels, President of the Alcorn Agricultural and Mechanical College, was a negro leader during the reconstruction period who served a term as United States Senator from Mississippi. He was succeeded in that office by Governor Alcorn, and became President of the College mentioned above. It is indicative of the great change, brought about in Mississippi by the Civil War and Congressional Reconstruction that, within twenty five years after Oakland College was a center of culture for class of wealthy white planters, a Grenada County Negro should have been a student in some of the buildings of the older college.

As an indication of the financial insecurity of the schools of Grenada County in the year 1888, we quote the following order passed by the Board of Supervisors in April of the same year: "In view of the fact that the county school funds are being rapidly exhausted and a number of the public schools not being taught to this term, the Board hereby orders that the salaries of the teachers in the county for the year 1888, commencing at this date, be fixed as follows: First Grade Teachers twenty five dollars per month, Second Grade Teachers twenty dollars per month and Third Grade teachers fifteen dollars per month, and that the County Superintendent be requested to use his descretion in aid of this purpose." It should be noted that the designation of the teachers as First, Second and Third Grade Teachers did not have reference to the grades taught, but to the type license held by the teachers. The problem of selection of proper textbooks for public schools, and their high cost, is not a new one, but one which existed in 1884, as evidenced by the action of the Board of Supervisors on March 3, 1884, when they accepted the recommendation of the County Superintendent of Education relative to the books to be used by the county schools. The recommendation was accepted on the basis of a proposal by the publishers, to furnish books at two thirds the established retail price of the books, or one half the retail price in exchange for the old books. This shrewd bargining on the part of the Board of Supervisors was probably highly appreciated by the parents of school children in the county. At this time, of course, school books had to be purchased by the parents of the school children.

The County Superintendent reported the receipt in the School Fund of two hundred and thirty five dollars from the sale of whiskey licenses in the county. This probably encouraged the Superintendent to request an allowance of ten dollars per month to be used for rental of an office from which conduct of the county schools would be carried on. At the time, the County was still using an old store building as the Courthouse, and there was a serious lack of space for County Officials. The Board approved the allowance over the protest and negative vote, of James H. Miller, President of the Board. He insisted that his reasons for his negative vote be included in the Minutes of the Board. They were expressed in the following words: (1) Because the law does not authorize us to make such a provision; (2) Because the Superintendent of Public Education is amply paid for his services and to procure for himself an office; (3) Because the people are poor and crushed by taxation; (4) Because there are several important offices in this county such as Treasurer, Assessor and Coroner all of whom have no offices provided for them, and an order by this Board to provide an office for the Superintendent would open the door for them all, even to the Justice of the Peace. Therefore I enter my protest in justice to the people of Grenada County." In view of the alleged serious condition of county school finances, it seems strange that the school fund had accumulated a surplus, as indicated by the following order of the Board of Supervisors in August, 1874: "The County Treasurer is hereby authorized to convert into United States Currency the school funds of the County now invested in State Warrants or bonds, at not less than eighty cents on the dollar and for as much more than eighty cents on the dollar as he is able, and to report his action to the Board." This would seem to indicate thrift on the part of the School Officials, as well as the depressed value of State warrants and bonds. Financial conditions relative to school funds must have improved somewhat in the next two years, for we find that in the October, 1876 meeting of the Supervisors, they passed the following order: "On motion of the Board and with the consent of the County Superintendent of Education the maximum salary per month for teachers shall be thirty five dollars per month."

Once, an old Negro preacher trying to encourage his people made this plea "Judge us not by the heights which we have attained, but by the depths from which we have arisen." When we are inclined to discount the educational attainment which has been accomplished through the years down to the present time, we would do well to note "the depths from which we have arisen."

Chapter V

HENRETTE SIMS LIFTS A CLOUD FROM TITLE TO LOTS IN EAST HALF OF SECTION SEVEN

The Treaty of Dancing Rabbit Creek had three provisions by which Indians belonging to the Choctaw Nation, and desiring to obtain title to blocks of the Indian lands, could obtain legal title to such lands. The first provision was made by a section of the treaty in which a number of Indians, and one white man, were specifically granted the right to select certain acreage anywhere in the area of the land ceded by the Choctaw Nation. These were called "float reservations." These reservations could be occupied by the persons for whom the reservations had been made, or they could be sold, without restriction to any person who made a deal to purchase them. The second provision was a general one and came under "The Cultivation Article" of the treaty. Under this provision any Indian who had occupied and made any considerable improvement on a tract of land before the signing of the treaty, could select the allotment of land due him and his children under the third provision, which was general in nature, and have that land located so as to include the land which he had improved. As head of a family an Indian was entitled to a section of land; his children over ten years of age a half section, and children under the age of ten, a quarter section. The only difference in the second and third provisions were, that under the second provision the Indian could select the location of his land, and had the right to dispose of it, if he so desired, and give legal title to it. Indians claiming reservation under the third provision would have their land located for them, and would have to remain in Mississippi five years before they could obtain legal title to the land. Since most of the tribe had decided to go west with the rest of the Choctaw Nation, very few Indians obtained title to land under the third provision. Indians claiming title under the first two provisions were relatively few, and, since they could give a good title to any purchaser of their property, land speculators sought them out, and some of them sold their lands. John Donly, only white man given land under the treaty, and Peggy Tryhan, illiterate Indian woman, and mother of two children identified in the Treaty of Dancing Rabbit Creek and "the fatherless children" of Peggy Tryhan, are examples of holders of "float" claims who sold these claims to white men. James Oxberry and Chief Turnbull, are representative of owners of float claims who located and lived on these reservations.

John Donly lived in Nashville, Tennessee, and seems to have had no desire to locate and live on the section of land to which he was entitled by the treaty. The treaty states that it was the desire of the Indians that he be given this land since he had for a long time been the mailrider through their country and since he had "Indian grandchildren." For an undisclosed amount, Donly sold his reservation claim to another resident of Nashville, Henry R. W. Hill by name. Through his agent, William M. Gwin, Hill sold this reservation to Hiram Runnels and John Watt. The land involved was Section eight, township twenty two, range five east, which was to become the section in which Tullahoma was to be located. There was never any suspicion that there was anything illegal in these transactions, so there was no desposition on the part of anyone to challange the legality of the title which was obtained by the Proprietors of the Town of Tullahoma. On the other hand, there seems to have been a feeling that there was something fraudulent in the disposition of the four hundred and sixty seven acres of land reserved for Peggy Tryhan and her two children. Three hundred and twenty acres of this land was located in Section seven, Township twenty two north, range five east. The remaining one hundred forty seven acres was located in Holmes County. It is well to note that the entire acreage was reserved for Peggy and her two children, without anything to indicate that this land was to be held other than in common by the mother and her sons. On July 29, 1833, almost two months before the public sale of lands was to begin, Franklin E. Plummer purchased from Peggy the three hundred and twenty acres which had been reserved for her and her children in the East Half of Section Seven. It is also probable that he also purchased the land located in Holmes County, but we have not confirmed this. Unfortunately, the transaction by which Peggy sold her reservation to Plummer is not on record, the Original Entry Book merely indicating that the above mentioned half section was a float reservation for Peggy Tryhan. We do not know what price was paid by Plummer for this land, but it is a matter of record that Samuel Gwin, Registrar of the Land Office at Chocchuma, felt that there was fraud in the manner in which the land was obtained. On August 26, 1835, Samuel Gwin in a letter to the Commissioner of the Federal Land Office made this statement: "Under the eighth paragraph of the Treaty of Dancing Rabbit Creek, there is a reservation in favor of Peggy Tryhan and her two fatherless children, and Delihah and her five fatherless children, to be located under the direction of the President of the United States. The following lands have been reserved from sale." He then describes the location of the land reserved for these two Indian women and their children. He then mentions the half section reserved for Peggy and her children, describing it not only by its half section nomenclature, but also as Lots one, six, seven, eight, nine, fourteen and fifteen. Sections divided by the Yalobousha were usually identified by lot numbers as well as in the usual manner of description. The lot numbers covered all the land in the East Half of Section Seven. Mr. Gwin continues his letter; "These lots are believed to have been reserved for the children of Peggy Tryhan; for Governor Runnels purchased the claim if I mistake not." (He was mistaken since Runnels had bought Section Eight.) Mr. Gwin continues: "It has been represented that frauds have been practiced on these orphans by a person having himself appointed their guardian; ordering the land to be sold, and he becoming purchaser for little or nothing." Plummer was the purchaser of the land, and while Gwin seemed to think that Runnels was the guilty person, the implication is very clear that purchaser of the land was guilty of fraud. Of course if Peggy had been given an individual reservation, she could have sold the land to anyone without question as to the legality of the sale, but the question bothering Gwin was whether she had the right to sell the land reserved in common for her and her children. The question as to whether Plummer did, in reality, become Guardian of the sons of Peggy, and as such, purchased the land for himself, or, if he merely bought the reservation without considering the rights of the sons will probably never be answered, but, within a few years after the establishment of the twon of Pittsburg on part of the land included in the purchase, the question would become a serious one to the people owning lots in that part of Grenada which had once been lots in the town of Pittsburg. The undue haste in which Plummer seemed to dispose of his title to the land might indicate that he knew of the suspicion directed at his acquisition of the land, and felt that it would be a good idea to unload the land on others. In eighteen hundred thirty four he sold all his right in the property to two partnerships and one individual. They became the Proprietors of the Town Company of Pittsburg. Later, when one of the firms defaulted in some part of their obligation to Plummer, he again became a fourth owner of the property. For some unexplained reason, neither Plummer nor the Proprietors of the Town Company of Pittsburg ever bothered to apply for a government patent to the land involved. For about three years there was a brisk sale of lots in the new town. Homes were erected and business houses established. As the financial panic, beginning in 1837, became more severe the sale of lots by the Town Company slowed down, and soon lots were beginning to be sold for taxes. Many unsold lots belonging to the Town Company were sold in this way. During the height of the tax sales another menace to lot owners in the little town appeared in the form of a deed recorded in 1845 which purported to be a conveyance by Jerry Tryhan to L. P. Edington of his interest in the half section of land on which Pittsburg was located. The alleged conveyance was dated as of June 15, 1845, and for a consideration of two hundred dollars conveyed to Edington the half section on which Pittsburg had been located some ten years earlier. This transaction would seem to indicate that there was still some suspicion relative to the legality of the transaction by which Plummer came into possession of the land. It is improbable that Jerry Tryhan, and illiterate Indian, initiated this action. It is possible that Edington felt that the deed given by Jerry Tryhan would cast a shadow of title on the property, and that he might be able to use the threat to force the owners of lots to buy quit claim titles from him. If this was his motive, it did not result in the desired end. There is no record of Edington ever giving either warranty or quit claim titles to any of the lots in the town.

Evidently the action of Jerry Tryhan in seeming to assume that he had a legal right to part, or all, of the East Half of Section Seven caused concern among some of the property owners in Pittsburg. The first action taken to protect property in the town of Pittsburg against the threat imposed by the transaction between Jerry Tryhan and Edington was taken by a woman who, at the time of her first action, does not seem to have been an individual property owner, but whose husband and father were considerable property owners in and about the town of Pittsburg. On November 11, 1845, just about six months after the date of the transaction between Jerry Tryhan and Edington, Jerry Tryhan gave a deed to Henrette Sims to the same property to which he had given a previous deed to Edington. This time the consideration was one hundred fifteen dollars. Thus, within six months time, Jerry Tryhan makes two conflicting sales of land which his mother had sold to Franklin E. Plummer thirteen years before. At first it would seem that Mrs. Sims had made a bad purchase, since the deed given to Edington preceded the deed given to her. But she seems to have had a long range plan to put her claim in a preferred position. On May 21, 1846, for a consideration of five hundred dollars Peggy and Jerry Tryhan made a joint conveyance of the land in question to Mrs. Sims. Thus two members of the Tryhan family made another conveyance of the land in question. There was still another part involved in original title to the land. James A. Tryhan, unlike his mother and brother, had not remained in Mississippi, but had gone with the Choctaws to the western Indian reservation. He seems to have been a little better trader than his mother and brother, since we find that on April 27, 1846, he had conveyed to Mrs. Sims, for a consideration of five hundred dollars his interest in the East Half of Section Seven as well as his interest in the one hundred forty seven acres of land reserved for the Tryhans in Holmes County. In three transactions with Mrs. Sims, one by Jerry alone, another by Jerry and his mother jointly, and another by James and his wife Sarah, the Tryhans realized eight hundred and fifteen dollars to relinquish whatever claim which they may have had in the land in question. Of course, in addition to this sum, Jerry had received two hundred dollars from Edington. As matters now stood, Edington had only a deed from Jerry, while Mrs. Sims had a conflicting deed from Jerry Tryhan and ten undisputed deeds from Peggy Tryhan and her son Jerry. Perhaps this shrewd action on the part of Mrs. Sims convinced Edington that he had been out-maneuvered. This may explain why there is no record of any conveyance made by him of property involved in these several transactions.

On January 5, 1845, just ten days before Jerry Tryhan gave the deed to Edington, there was a tax sale of lots in the town of Pittsburg. At that sale, Thomas B. Ives, acting as agent for Charles Price, bought in one hundred and twelve lots in the old town of Pittsburg, now a part of the town of Grenada. Most of the lots had been owned by the Town Company, and many of them were located in that part of the old town north of Cherry Street, although a number of the lots were located fronting the old town square. The total sum paid for these tax titles was thirty nine dollars and forty cents. We wonder if the members of the Pittsburg Town Company realized that there was a possible defect in their title, and by allowing the lots to be sold for taxes, hoped to erase the cloud on their title and then redeem the lots later. If this was their intention, things did not work out that way. On December 10, 1846, just about a year after Mrs. Sims had secured the three deeds from the Tryhans, Price, acting thru his agent Ives, sold his tax titles to the one hundred twelve lots to Mrs. Sims for a consideration of fifty five dollars. There was another tax sale of lots which brings to light another strange maneuver on the part of Mrs. Sims. On April 17, 1847, she purchased at the tax sale twenty four lots for a consideration of one dollar and sixty eight cents. So far as we are able to ascertain, these were the first individual lots acquired by Mrs. Sims. The strange part of the transaction is that the deed given Mrs. Sims by the sheriff described the tax defaulting owner of the twenty four lots as Peggy Tryhan. Mrs. Sims already had the three deeds from the Tryhans conveying the whole half section. Why were the lots sold listed as the property of Peggy Tryhan when there is no record of her ever having had title to any individual lots? We can only speculate as to the reason. It is possible that Mrs. Sims still feared litigation by Edington and had alleged ownership of these lots as being in Peggy, and hoped in this way to make out a stronger title to property which she already owned if her deeds from the Tryhans to the half section of land gave her a valid title to the property involved.

Mrs. Sims did not cease in her endeavor to make certain that the cloud of title was removed from the property which she was acquiring. She contacted the Government Land Office relative to obtaining patent to the half section of land. On March 27, 1847, we find the following notation from a letter to the United States Secretary of War, under whose general direction the Indian treaty had been made and Indian lands disposed of: "Respectfully submitted to the Secretary of War with the recommendation that the sale from James A. Tryhan, as within indicated be approved by the President of the United States. Office of Indian Affairs, W. Middill." Then comes the next action; "respectfully laid before the President of the United States for the approval recommended by the Commissioner of Indian Affairs." This notation has the following statement: "Approved August 2, 1847, James K. Polk." The Original Entry Books shows that the patent to the land involved was issued to Mrs. Sims in 1851. It would seem from the statement of the Commissioner of Indian Affairs that it was only after the deed from James Tryhan was submitted to him that he was willing to recommend that the patent be issued to Mrs. Sims. This leads to the supposition that the Commissioner had decided that it was necessary to have the deeds from all the Tryhans before he would recommend issuance of the patent. This in turn, seems conclusive evidence that Peggy Tryhan did not have the right to make an individual conveyance of the property to Franklin Plummer, and that in fact, the original transaction was fraudulent. By December 20, 1850, it must have become evident that Mrs. Sims would eventually receive a patent on the land, since on that date A. Bew deeded to Mrs. Sims the one hundred twelve lots which he had purchased at the tax sale. Since he had paid only fifty dollars for the tax titles, and received five hundred dollars from Mrs. Sims as the consideration of the transaction with her, he made a profit on his deal, but sold the lots for much less than their real worth. The financial panic was nearing its end, and property values were beginning to recover something of their former values. During the waning years of this depression Mrs. Sims continued to buy up lots at tax sales, and some by individual transactions with owners, until by 1855 she had become owner of a majority of the lots in that ward of Grenada which had been the original site of Pittsburg.

We should like to know the motives which impelled Mrs. Sims to engage in these various transactions, but can only speculate as to those motives. Her father, John Smith, one of the members of the staff of the Elliott Indian Mission, and an early settler in Pittsburg; her husband James Sims, merchant, and also an early settler in Pittsburg, and William Huntly, former member of the staff at the Chocchuma Land Office, and husband of her Mrs. Sims' sister Maria, all were owners of considerable real estate in the old town of Pittsburg. Was she acting at their direction, and for their benefit, in trying to remove the cloud of title from their rather extensive land holdings in the half section involved? Was she trying to clear the title of her relatives, and intending to sell quit claim deeds to other property owners? Did the threat of defective title cause so many lot owners to allow their property to sell for taxes? Did the fact that John Smith, father of Mrs. Sims, was a member of the Proprietors of the Town Company of Pittsburg, and a fourth owner of the original town property of the town of Pittsburg, have anything to do with her transactions? John Smith was the owner of considerable land in and around Grenada. Did his daughter fear that if Edington's deed from Jerry Tryhan proved legal that her father, as a member of the Town Company, would become responsible to the people who had bought defective titles from the Company? These are questions which probably will never be answered, but they present an interesting side light upon early land transaction in and about the area in which Pittsburg had been established.

Chapter VI

Organization of Grenada County

The people living in that area of the Third Choctaw Land Cession, which eventually became Grenada county had to transact their county seat business in four different county seats. These county seats were Charleston in Tallahatchie county; Carrollton in Carroll county; Coffeeville in Yalobousha county and Greensboro in Choctaw county. Of course the county seat in which they transacted their business depended upon the geographic locations of the residents. Early roads were frequently almost impassable at certain stages of the year. High water made ferry crossings dangerous and undependable. Many of the residents had to go considerable distances in order to reach their county seat. Because of these conditions it was always advantageous for the people to have county seats located in the towns which were their most convenient trade centers. After the union of Pittsburg and Tullohoma to form Grenada, that town rapidly outgrew the other towns of the area, both in population, and as an advantageous trade center. Because of its strategic location on the Yalobousha river, the main route of early transportation, people from a wide area brought their cotton to Grenada and purchased their supplies there. Many of those people would take several days to make the journey, camping out along the way. The present area of Futheyville was much used as a camping gound when these people reached Grenada. Within nine years of the incorporation of Grenada, and possibly even earlier, the people of the area about Grenada began agitation for the establishment of a new county with Grenada as the county seat. The first written record which is available relative to this agitation is found in the March 29th, 1845, issue of the newspaper HARRY OF THE WEST. From that paper we quote the following excerpt: "We are glad to hear that people are beginning to talk about making this a county seat. It is the center of business for this part of the country, and most earnestly desired by the surrounding country......notwithstanding the depressed state of our great staple our town continues to grow rapidly; several new storehouses are being prepared and there are not enough dwellings for the demand. There are at present several dwellings with two families in them, and we know not where they are to be accomodated." Presumably the incomplete phrase "most ernestly desired by the surrounding country" referred to their desire to have Grenada a county seat. Of course the words "our great staple" had reference to cotton which had already become the basis of the economy of the area.

On February 8th, 1845, the newspaper mentioned heretofore published a petition by residents of certain areas of Tallahatchie, Carroll, Yalobousha and Choctaw counties which petition is quoted hereafter. "To The Honorable Senate and House of Representatives of the General Assembly of Mississippi: The undersigned, at present citizens of the respective counties attached to our names, respectfully represent, that for many years we have labored under many difficulties in consequence of the great distance at which the seat of Justice is held from our respective places of abode. That frequently, in the inclement seasons of the year, we are not able to surmount the many difficulties that lie between us and the Court House. That the section of country of which Grenada is the center, is very densely populated and probably affords one third of the business now done in the courts at Carrollton and Coffeeville, That there is no person living within the bounds of the lines we propose but could return each night to his home, thereby saving an expense, that bears extremely heavy on the agricultural part of the community. That the proposed lines will enclose a constitutional limit both of miles and numbers. That it will leave the respective counties in a much better shape and far more convenient for all purposes than at present. That most of the new county will be taken from the south of Yalobousha, and that the citizens have paid their part to the completion of the public buildings. That the town of Grenada is the great center of all

71

our trade, the head of navigation of the Yalobousha river, and from its beautiful and healthy situation must ever be the principal depot for the great staple of our country for a great distance around us."

"The frequent journeys that we now have to make in our business with the different courts, and court clerks, are a serious inconvenience, and attended with a serious expense. We feel that the favor we ask is due to us in our peculiar situation, as it will in no way interfere with the convenience, or prosperity of our neighboring counties." The petition goes on to set the limits of the proposed county which would be oblong in shape, six townships long and three wide. Under this proposal the greater area to be included would come from Yalobousha and Carroll counties, with only small areas from Tallahatchie and Choctaw. After describing the area proposed as the new county the petition goes on to mention other disadvantages of the existing county seat arrangements: "The undersigned would further represent that the small pittance now allowed witnesses and jurors by no means pay the tavern expenses, and that repeated instances have occured when from high water, persons have been unable to reach the seats of justice in time, during the sessions of the courts, their cases have been continued or trials have been terminated in the absolute perversion of justice and oppression of the unfortunate suitor. The undersigned are willing to take on themselves all the trouble and expense incident to the operation, and feeling that as it can injure no one, and benefit the country about Grenada, we indulge a fond hope that as a matter of right this petition by speedily acted on and granted."

"And should your honorable body grant our petition we would also request that a law should be passed forbidding any tax to be laid on the citizens of the New County for the building of a Court House to exceed $1000 for the term of seven years, from the passage of the act, and as in duty bound will every pray."

From this petition it would seem that the people most dis-satisfied with the existing location of county seats were those who had to cross the Tallahatchie River to go to Charleston and those who would have to cross the same river to go to Coffeeville. Since the petition states that the people of the proposed new county have paid their share for public buildings it would seem that the public buildings of the four county seats had probably been paid for. The petition for a legislative act to prevent the levying of any considerable tax to build public buildings in the county probably was reflected in the attitude of the people relative to building an adequate Court House when Grenada county was finally organized.

The petition for a new county came at an unfortunate time so far as state politics were concerned. The rapid settlement of white settlers in the recent Choctaw and Chickasaw Land Cessions toppled the balance of power which the South Mississippi counties had controlled since the admission of Mississippi as a state in the Federal Union. Natchez, once the seat of political power in state politics, was resentful that the common people were wrestling the leadership, once held by their aristocratic section. There was a bitter controversy over the location of the University of Mississippi; the northern legislative members favoring Oxford, and the southern members wanting to locate the University in the costal town of Mississippi City. Although in 1846 congressional districts were established in Mississippi, in 1845 the four Mississippi congressmen were still elected from the state at large, resulting in the northern counties of the state, because of their rapid population increase, having a greater voice in the selection of the congressmen from Mississippi. With all these differences of opinion it is not surprising that the South Mississippi legislative representatives were not sympathetic to the creation of a new county in North Mississippi and that the North Mississippi members should have had so many irons in the fire that they did not consider the time opportune to raise the issue of the creation of a new county. The conditions heretofore related may or may not have had a decisive effect on consideration of the petition for the creation of the new county, but the fact remains that the petition was rejected by the legislature, and the people of the area signing the petition were going to have to wait a quarter of a century before they would finally succeed in their desire to have a new county with the county seat at Grenada. The Mexican War; the growing threat posed by the abolitionists of the north directed at abolition of slavery; and the fight for political power by the Democratic and Whig parties probably served to take the minds of the disturbed people off the desirability of a new county and county seat.

When Mississippi seceded from the Union the area about Grenada was still a part of Yalobousha county, and it continued so during the Civil War years and on into the post-war years. It is ironical that Governor Alcorn, considered by many Mississippians of the time as a "Scalawag" and a "Black and Tan" legislature made up very largely of negro and white republicans, should have been the political set-up under which Grenada county was finally created. On the ninth of May, 1870, the Legislature passed an act creating the county of Grenada so, forty years after the Treaty of Dancing Rabbit Creek, and thirty four years after the town of Grenada had been formed thru the union of Pittsburg and Tullahoma, a new county was created to bear the name of Grenada, and to have, as its county seat, the town of the same name.

The Legislative act creating the county provided that Governor Alcorn should appoint five men to comprise the first Board of Supervisors of the new county. These men were to be selected from the county at large, but they were directed to divide the county into five supervisor districts so that succeeding Board members should be elected, one from each district, by the qualified electors thereof. The Governor evidently made his appointments soon after the passage of the act creating the county, since the first minutes of the Board of Supervisors meeting is dated May 30, 1870. The Board Members attending this meeting were J. D. Leflore, John L. Milton, F. P. Ingram, Andrew Davis and Freeland Townes. The meeting was held in the office of Dr. John L. Milton which office was located up-stairs over the Lake Brothers Store. The Board organized by electing Leflore President of the Board with Dr. Milton selected as Secretary. The Board Minutes indicate that the second meeting of the Board was held "in the office of the Chancery Clerk in the town of Grenada." This notation raises an interesting question. The county had been created less than a month; no elections had been held for county officers as yet, and no Court House Provided, yet there was "a Chancery Clerk's office" in the town of Grenada. We wonder if, because of the difficulties set forth in the petition for the creation of a new county in 1845, Yalobousha county had established a second Chancery Clerk's office in Grenada, just as today that county has such offices both at Coffeeville and Water Valley.

That first Board of Supervisors was faced with many pressing problems. The county had to be divided into Supervisors Districts; voting precincts had to be located; some sort of facilities had to be provided for courts and county officials offices; taxes for the current year had to be pro-rated between the New County and the counties from which it was created on the assessed value of the land of the New County; and provision had to be made for a transcript of the Deeds Records relative to the lands of the new county. It was also necessary that Overseers be appointed to supervise the upkeep of the county roads. At the time the county was created, and for many years thereafter, all able-bodied men were liable for a certain number of days work on the county roads. These men, or substitutes they were allowed to provide, were supposed to work the roads under the direction of the Overseers appointed by the Board. The appointment of these overseers was the first order of business of the Board in its August meeting. Meeting on the First Monday in that month the Board proceeded to appoint the following men as overseers: John P. Nowell,

C. L. Hardemna, J. G. Gibbs, William Bosworth, J. D. Vance, J. Mayhew, W. O. Rayburn, A. W. Thomas, William DuBard, Wesley Beard, A. J. Simpson, William Dvaidson, R. Kendrick, John Richardson, James Williams, B. J. Rook, Edward Lamb, J. C. James, B. P. Williams, George Crowder, H. G. Taylor, J. R. Coffman, R. C. Weir, George Davis, J. D. Crawford Richardson, Samuel Edom, Chance Edmonds, W. H. Aldridge, J. J. Jennins, Henry C. Townes, J. A. Marten, Ales Krwin, James B. Lacock, William Townes, C. C. Peete, William Turner, W. B. Smith, J. Hightower, Thomas Koon, J. B. Heath, James Loving, William Winter, R. L. Jones, W. M. Holly, George Wright and Thomas Flippen. Some of these men were appointed at the August meeting and others at meetings following soon thereafter. Each of the overseers was given a designated stretch of road, usually in the vicinity of his home or place of business. The descriptions of the stretch of road for which they were responsible were usually similar to the following quoted description: "E. S. Fisher, Overseer of that section of the road beginning at his place and terminating at William Winter's place." All of the men appointed to this task were responsible men, many of whom still have descendents in the county today. At least one of them, Samuel Edom, was a Negro. It is possible that there may have been other Negroes appointed as overseers. From the appointment of these overseers to certain county roads we are able to ascertain that, at the time of the establishment of the county the following named roads had been laid off and were part of the county road system: Grenada-Graysport; Grenada-Houston; Graysport-Pittsbore; Grenada-Providence; Center Road, branching off the Grenada-Providence road at a point about four miles east of Grenada; Grenada-Duck Hill; Grenada-Carrollton; Grenada-Coffeeville; Graysport-Torrence; Grenada-Hardy Station; Grenada-Troy; Grenada-Greenwood; Chareston-Carrollton, by way of Chocchuma Ferry; Troy-Charleston and Tuscahoma-Grenada. It is possible that there were other roads not mentioned in the above given list, but the roads mentioned made up the main travelled roads of the county. One problem relative to the establishment and maintenance of roads in the county hinged about the necessity for some of the roads to cross the Yalobousha river and other streams within the county. At the time of the establishment of the county there was a toll bridge at Graysport, with ferries located at Chocchuma, Tuscahoma, Troy and two, the Upper and Lower Ferries at Grenada. Within a year or so other ferries in the vicinity of Grenada were authorized by the Board which set the prices charged for ferriage by the various operators. The upper, or Sherman Ferry, had once belonged to the Proprietors of the Town of Tullahoma, and the Lower Ferry to the Proprietors of the Town of Pittsburg. The right to operate these two ferries had been leased by the town proprietors. John Balfour is the earliest man of record who operated one of these ferries. There were ferries over the Bogue Creek. Another big task of the new Supervisors was the building and maintenance of bridges over the lesser streams of the county.

Public schools in Mississippi really began to develop after the Civil War. Evidence of their beginning in Grenada county is found in the action of the Board of Supervisors in 1870, by which the Board appointed the following named six men as School Directors: Hillsford Hames, J. R. Rosamond, William Bell, A. H. Graves. Ralph Coffman and W. H. Powell. The first four men were appointed for terms of two years and the last two for one year terms. After the expiration of the terms of the appointed Trustees all appointed from the county at large, there was to be one trustee from each Supervisor's District. It is probable that six men were appointed to what was ultimately to become a five man board, and since the one year term men were from the district in which Grenada was located, it was intended that, upon the expiration of the one year terms, District one was to select a single director. Evidently the other four men with two year terms must have been selected from the other four districts although they were nominally choosen from the county at large.

The first indication that we have, from the Minutes of the Board of Supervisors, that a county Sheriff had been selected is a notation in the minutes of the Board meeting in September 1870. That reference reads as follows: "L. French having been elected Sheriff, and J. B. Townsend, Clerk, met with the Board." It seems strange that previous Minutes of the Board have no reference to an election being called, but if the term "elected" was used in the proper sense, the use of such a term would seem to rule out the possibility that these officials had been appointed either by the Governor or the Board of Supervisors.

On August 4, 1870, the Supervisors purchased a building which was to serve as a Court House for a period of a little over thirteen years. On this date the Board accepted the offer of A. S. Brown to sell to the county a store house located on lot number sixty seven. This was the lot on the north side of the square just east of the present Grenada Theater building. The consideration involved was three thousand dollars, evidenced by three notes payable on February first, 1871, 1872 and 1873. The last two notes were to bear interest at the rate of six per cent. This purchase also included "one little back office as described in the deed." In addition to the building purchased, the Board also rented two rooms, one on the first floor and one on the second floor, of a store building owned by W. M. Hankins. The rental was for a term of twelve months at a stipulated price of eight dollars per month. It would seem that, from the very beginning, the facilities purchased by the Board were inadequate for all county business. In 1874 the following order was passed by the Board; "Inasmuch as both the Circuit and Chancery Courts will convene on the second Monday of September, it is hereby ordered that the room presently occupied by the Chancery Clerk of the said county in the town of Grenada may be used at the said term of the Chancery Court." It would seem that the Chancery Clerk was not lotcated in the building purchased by the county but at some other place, possibly the same location where the Board of Supervisors held its second meeting. Another indication of the inadequacy of the County Court House is the fact that several of the county officers were required to provide their own office space. This is indicated by the request, made in 1874, by the County Superintendent of Education that he be allowed ten dollars per month for office rental, and by the objection of one Supervisor to the order of the Board allowing such rental. His objection was as follows: "1. Because the law does not authorize us to make such provision; 2. Because the Superintendent of Public Instruction is amply paid for his services and to procure for himself an office; 3. Because the people are poor and crushed by taxation; 4. Because there are several important offices in the county such as Treasurer and Coronor all of whom have no offices provided for them, and an order by the Board to provide an office for the Superintendent would open the door for them all, even to the Justice of the Peace. I enter my protest in justice to the people of Grenada County." Lack of space for all county functions and contention resulting from this lack, is indicated by the following notation in the minutes of the Board of Supervisors, said notation being dated May 4, 1875: "Whereas it appearing that L. French, Sheriff, having selected a room for the use of the Board of Supervisors at the May term thereof 1875, the Court House being occupied, the Circuit Court being in session, and the Board preferring to occupy the Chancery Clerk's office, and he having refused to open said Supervisors Court at said Clerk's office as required by law, it is therefore ordered that W. T. Tiller be and he is hereby, in accordance with Section 314, Revised Code 1871, designated and appointed to discharge the duties of said Sheriff by attendance upon said court during its May term 1875, the said W. T. Tiller appearing and taking the oath of office as required by law." This appointment was, of course, for one specific purpose, and we find that at the next meeting of the Board Sheriff French was back at his customary duty of opening the Board meeting. The location of the jury room is revealed by the following allowance by the Board of Trustees: "Ordered that whereas J. S. Ladd being the lowest bidder for repairing and fitting up the Jury Room in the rear of R. Doak's storehouse, that said contract be and is hereby awarded to him, and having the same as to the expense of operation."

Evidently, there were many requests by various groups for the use of the Court House for their meetings and there may have been some opposition on the part of the custodian of that building to the use of the building by some of these groups. This possibility is indicated by the following order to the Board: "Ordered that the Sheriff of the county be, and hereby is required, not to withhold the key of the Court House upon application of any respectable and responsible citizen when the fact shall be made known to him that it is contemplated to be used by any respectable religious denomination provided in so doing, that the interest of the county and offices the same shall not be molested thereby." In October, 1878, the Board of Supervisors abandoned, for one meeting, the use of the Court House as is indicated by the following notation in the Minutes of the Board: "The Board met at Bew School House, the place of meeting being designated by the President of the said Board by reason of yellow fever being in the Court House." On at least one occasion the Circuit Court convened in the building of the Grenada Collegiate Institute "because of the intense heat in the regular court room."

There were probably good reasons for the new county's delay in providing adequate court house facilites, but the need for expanded facilities was so apparent that the people were beginning to become impatient with the long delay. Editor Buchanan of the Grenada Sentinel published, on June 30, 1883, thirteen years after organization of the county, an editoral in which he made the following statement: "The time has come for the Board of Supervisors to take some action twoard building a Court House. This matter has been deferred so long, and has become such a plain, practical necessity that the Board can hsitate no longer." In a subsequent issue of his paper the editor is a little more emphatic: "Just now is time to talk of building a Court House. The present one is a disgrace, not only as to ornamental architecture, but is a reflection upon the good will of our citizens. The people really do not intend to kill, by suffocation, the Court, the juries nor the officers, but if they do not do something better than punish them in this large stew kettle these learned bodies will begin to think that there is a secret murder in roasting live men in discharge of official duty, and an action will be against the county for premeditated murder. Will not some of our leading citizens attend the meeting of our Supervisors and see if they can not stir up the officials to the humane and christian purpose of building a new Court House in order to save the lives of those who have to remain in the present one during Circuit Court?" We don't know if this editorial prompting moved the Board, or if they had already contemplated some action relative to a new building, but we find that on July 3, 1883, the Board purchased from W. C. McLean and others the following described fractional lots in the town of Grenada: "Thirteen feet off the north side of lot number eighty one; the south one half and the north half of lot number eighty." This is the property on which the present now Court House is located. On September 15, 1883, the Board let a contract to George S. Covert of Meridian, Mississippi, to construct a new Court House. The contract price was seventeen thousand five hundred and seventy five dollars. This new building was destined to serve the county for three quarters of a century. Although some additions were made to the building, the original building, along with the additions, served the county as the seat of justice until it was demolished to make way for the construction of the present building.

It seems rather strange to us today to learn that during the thirteen year period when the county tolerated all the inconvenience and inadequacies of the three thousand dollar storehouse used as a Court House, the Board of Supervisors spent more money on jails than it was to spend on the Court House contracted for in 1883. On January 4, 1871, the Board of Supervisors purchased from Robert Hightower lot number 37 and part of lot number 44, both in East Ward, for a consideration of five hundred dollars. These lots were on the corner of Main and Front streets. The present box factory is situated on this property. The purpose of this purchase was to obtain a location for a jail.

In September 1870 James Ladd had been given a contract to construct a jail building according to plans and specifications on file, said building not to exceed sixteen thousand dollars in cost. John Moore, Robert Mullin, and L. French were appointed as commissioners to supervise the erection of the building and each of them was paid twenty five dollars for this service. John Moore was an architect and builder who erected several of the most pretentious of the early homes in Grenada. Robert Mullen was a successful business man and outstanding civic leader who began his business career in the old town of Troy, and, as that town began to decline, moved his business interests to Grenada. L. French was the first Sheriff of Grenada County. Soon after the purchase of the jail lot, J. L. Payne was paid five dollars to survey the lot. On December 6, 1871, Ladd announced completion of the building. The Board inspected the building and then authorized warrants to complete payment on the contract. Evidently the county was using part of the jail before it was completed, since in August of 1871, because of a rumor that prisoners in the jail were ill-treated, the President of the Board of Supervisors made an inspection of the building, talked with prisoners, and reported that the rumor was without foundation in fact. The only complaint on the part of the prisoners was that, when wind blew from a certain direction, some rain fell into their cells. In the report the Board President gave prisoner A. W. Wood as the source of much of his information. In this manner Mr. Wood became the first county prisoner of record. On September 7, 1871, the jailor, F. P. Ingram, was authorized by the Board to contract for digging a well in the jailyard, the well "to be walled with brick and cemented, and the cost not to exceed one dollar fifty cents per foot." For some reason, not set out in the Board Minutes, the new jail was soon in need of repairs. On April 14, 1873, the Board contracted with John Moore to repair the jail according to plans and specifications on file. He was allowed five hundred dollars for this purpose. It would seem that the Board was much concerned relative to the comfort of the county prisoners since on January 11, 1875, the jailer was authorized to spend as much as eighty dollars "for stoves or other heating apparatus in the descretion of the jailor to make prisoners confined in the county jail comfortable."

This first jail served the county for a period of approximately thirty years. On January 4, 1892, the Board of Supervisors made a trade with Bertha McLean by which they deeded the jail property to her, and she deeded to the Board lot number sixty four. On May 7, 1904, a contract was let to Dobson & Bynum of Montgomery, Alabama, to construct a jail bulding on lot number sixty four. The contract price was twelve thousand four hundred dollars. It seems that this second jail building, built at less cost than the first one, was a much better building since it was used for half a century, being abandoned when the present jail building was completed.

The men who had the responsibility of organizing a new county in the difficult post-war reconstruction period deserve much credit for the manner in which they discharged their duties. In a period of extreme financial hardship and political turmoil, they managed to provide physical facilities for county government; to set up a county educational system; to provide for upkeep of the county roads and to establish ferries and regulate the ferry charges for existing and newly authorized ferries. The passage of almost a hundred years since they began their work, and the present prosperous condition of the county they created, bears testimony to the fact that they discharged their responsibilities with faith, courage and sound judgment.

Chapter VII

Grenada During Civil War Years

The twenty eight years elapsing between the beginning of the Indian land sales in the the area, which was later to become Grenada County and the outbreak of the Civil War had been fruitful ones for the inhabitants of the area. Destructive fires and a devastating tornado had not broken the spirit of the people of the town of Grenada. Financial hardship brought on by the financial panic, beginning in 1837 and continuing for almost seven years, had been hard on the people, and the purchase by many people of the area of stock in the Mississippi Union bank brought about many foreclosures of property in the area. In 1861 the people had overcome these circumstances and had established a prosperous economy, built for the most part, on Negro slavery and cotton production. Large plantations had been carved out of the rich lands; a number of fine plantation homes erected; schools and churches provided; and railroad connection established with the important trade centers of Memphis and New Orleans. Those small farmers who did not aspire to become great plantation owners had, by the application of their own labor with perhaps the help of a small number of slaves, established small self-sufficient farms which, because of their rich, new soil, returned a comfortable living to those who worked the soil. Among the people there also existed a number of independent individuals who had no desire to own slaves to help them in their farming operations. These various classes of people were typical of the people of Mississippi who, by the time of the outbreak of the war, had so prospered on the new lands that the per capita income of Mississippi ranked fifth in the nation. Grenada and vicinity, from the date of first settlement to the outbreak of the war, had shared in the heyday of the influence and the prosperity of the so-called "Cotton Kingdom."

Although no major battles were fought in Grenada or vicinity, the town was destined, because of railroad facilities and geographic location, to become a strategic point about which hinged many military movements. When Mississippi seceded from the Union on January 9, 1861, no one knew if there would be peace or war. Governor Pettus was uncertain relative to organization of state military forces. As yet, there was no Confederate Government. Mississippi claimed to be an independent state with both the responsibility and the right to organize such a force. At the suggestion of the Secession Convention the Governor called for eight thousand volunteers to serve in state forces for a period of twelve months. These forces were to compose four brigades. Jefferson Davis was made Major General of the forces, with Brigadier Generals Alcorn, Van Dorn, Clark and West commanding the different brigades. Over one hundred companies had been organized throughout the states, and these companies were divided among the several brigades. Soon after the organization of this state Military force Jefferson Davis was selected as the Provisional President of the newly organized Confederate Government and left Mississippi to report to that government at Montgomery, Alabama. Ruben Davis was appointed Major General in his stead. Shortly after this state force was organized, Governor Pettus received an urgent appeal from the Confederate authorities to trun over the state military force to the Confederate army authorities.

Among the companies organized in Grenada and vicinity for this first state military force were the Grenada Rifles, Yalobousha Rifles, The Carroll County Rifles and The Carroll Guards. Major General Davis ordered the four brigades to report to Corinth, Mississippi, where he turned them over to Confederate authorities. The Grenada Rifles, having been a part of that first state force, reported to Corinth and became Company G of the Fifteenth Mississippi Regiment, called by many observers, "The Fighting Fifteenth." As organized the comapny had the following named officers: W. S. Statham, Captain; E. R. Armistead, Lst. Lieutenant; I. H. Ayres, 2nd Lieutenant; and W. L. Grim,

3rd Lieutenant. There were eighty two privates and several non-commission officers in the company. The Confederate concentration at Corinth was for the purpose of providing additional soldiers for General Albert Sidney Johnston, who was in charge of the Confederate defenses extending from Columbus, Kentucky to the Cumberland Gap near the border of Virginia and Tennessee. Some of the other comapnies organized near Grenada were included in the troops sent to Corinth, and became a part of the 15th Regiment. This regiment was sent from Corinth to Union City, Tennessee. After the regiment went into Confederate service, Captain Statham was elected Colonel of the regiment, and Dr. John J. Gage was made Captain of Company G. Colonel Statham wrote, before being made Colonel of the Regiment, a letter to W. H. Brown, Mississippi Adjutant General relative to the condition of Company G. "With a full complement of non-comcission officers and eighty seven privates. We have ninety six Mississippi rifles, Sabre Bayonets with Cartridge Boxes, Knap Sacks, Belts, Cap Boxes, Canteens, adn Haver Sacks, all of which the company furnished themselves. The state furnished us with four tents, the company furnishing themselves with thirteen additional tents, making in all seventeen tents. I further state that I will furnish to this office a true list of the names of all the members of the company at an early day. I further report that we will be ready by Monday next to march." Since this report was made to the Mississippi official, it would seem that this letter was written before the unit was turned over to the Confederate Army, and before it became a part of the Fifteenth Mississippi Regiment. It indicates the very serious shortage of military supplies available to State Forces, since most of the men armed and equipped themselves. We wonder about the term: "Mississippi Rifles." There had been a bill proposed in the Mississippi Legislature by which State troops would be armed with double-barrel shotguns. It is conceivable that all members of the Grenada Company could have supplied themselves with shotguns, but for them all to have provided themselves with rifles would have been more difficult, although there were rifles in use at the time, and the original name of the company Grenada Rifles indicates that the company intended to be a rifle unit.

The Fifteenth Mississippi Regiment became one of the crack regiments of the Western Army. It fought in most of the major battles of the Western Theater of the war. Some of those battles were: Fishing Creek, Laurel Bridge, Bakers Creek, Corinth, Peach Tree Creek, Franklin and battles taking place as General Sherman drove the Confederate Army from Northern Georgia to Atlanta. During the battle of Fishers Creek Brigade Commander General Zollicoffer was killed, and Colonel Statham assumed command of the Brigade. Later he was given a commission as a Brigadier General. He lost his life in a battle near Vicksburg, Mississippi. In the Battle of Shiloh the 15th Mississippi lost, killed, wounded or took prisoner 234 out of 500 men engaged. In the fierce battle of Franklin during the Nashville Campaign the Regiment lost about half its number. The most severe loss of life sustained by soldiers from Grenada and vicinity came from the Grenada Company serving with the 15th Mississippi.

After the shifting of the original state forces to the Confederate army Governor Pettus became alarmed at the undefended state of Mississippi and western Tennessee, and the southern Part of Western Kentucky. With all state forces from Mississippi engaged with The Army of Tennessee under General Albert Sidney Johnston, it was feared that General Johnston's very much extended defense line from the Mississippi River to the Cumberland Gap might give way on the western part of the line, and open up Western Tennessee and Mississippi to Federal invasion. The Legislature authorized the enlistment of ten thousand volunteers in a state force, which would be enlisted for sixty days service in the State of Kentucky. Corinth and Grenada were selected as the points of rendezvous for these troops earmarked for service in Kentucky. General Alcorn at Grenada organized a force of 2,500 men, while General Davis had about the same number at Corinth. General Johnston, in dire straights for re-enforcements, requested that these Mississippi State troops be sent to aid him. He ordered General Alcorn to send his Grenada assembly of soldiers to join General Polk at Union City, Kentucky, while Davis was directed to take his troops from Corinth to General Johnston at Bowling Green, Kentucky. This second contingent of Mississippi State troops diverted to the Confederate Army took place in early Fall of 1861.

It is probable that it was with this second contingent of State troops that a second Grenada Company went into action. This unit which we know to have been inducted into Federal Service on November 6, 1861, was Stanford's Battery. The commissioned officers were Captain T. J. Stanford, First Lieutenant Hugh McSwine, Second Lieutenant Dr. J. Harden, Third Lieutenant Dr. T. R. Trotter, who later became surgeon of the 15th Mississippi. This artillery unit of eleven officers and 70 privates was sent to General Polk (probably with the other soldiers sent by Alcorn to Polk) and was stationed at Columbus, Kentucky, the extreme western point of General Johnston's defensive line. The fact that this unit fought pretty much in the same battles as the 15th Mississippi, and the further fact that this unit fought pretty much in the same battles as the 15th Mississippi, and the further fact that one of their officers was made surgeon for the 15th, inclines us to believe that, at some point in its service, this artillery unit became connected with the 15th Regiment. In its original makeup after going into Federal service the 15th was composed of the following units which while in state service were enlisted under these company names: Water Valley Rifles, Grenada Rifles, Wigfall Rifles, Choctaw Grays, McClung Rifles, Winona Stars, Longstreet Rifles, and Quitman Rifles. It will be seen that the regiment was largely composed of soldiers from the North Central part of Mississippi. With Colonel Statham from Grenada and Lt. Colonel Walthall from Coffeeville, the Regiment had both ranking officers from Yalobousha County. Stanford's Battery participated in the Battle of Shiloh, and General Polk had this commendation for the conduct of the battery in that battle: "One company artillery-that of Captain Stanford, from Mississippi, from the scarcity of ammunition had never before heard the fire of their guns, yet from that facility which distinguishes our Southern people under the inspiration of the cause which animates them, they fought with steadiness and gallantry of well trained troops." Captain Stanford was to die in the battles around Northern Georgia, and Second Lieutenant Harden on some other hard fought field. In a diary kept by George W. Jones much of the activity is related by the writer who was a member of the battery. Just before his death Stanford had been promoted, and his death cast a pall of gloom over the detachment. Many citizens of Grenada and vicinity had enlisted in other companies, and rendered distinguished service to the Confederacy, but since they were distributed through so many different units we have only fragmentary information relative to them. Later we shall list some of these men.

With their able-bodied men away in the Confederate army, and with the war still far away from Grenada, the city and county had to rely on a local organization of old men and young boys for local defense. One man prominent in this local organization was Judge Fairfield. This man was a native of New England who came to the Natchez area of Mississippi and served for a time as a teacher in the town of Woodville a few miles south of Natchez. He studied law, and came to Grenada about 1850. He opposed secession but, when Mississippi seceded from the union, he cast his lot with his adopted state. As the Confederate High Command shifted troops to points of danger such as Baton Rouge, Vicksburg, Jackson, Meridian and other places, Grenada became an important communication center. Located at the junction of the Mississippi & Tennessee and the Mississippi Central Railroads, soldiers could be entrained at Grenada for the defense of Memphis, or by the Mississippi Central could be sent to points of danger as far north as Jackson, Tennessee. Since the Mississippi Central raod stretched all the way to New Orleans, troops going south from Grenada on this road could be transferred to the railroad line running to Vicksburg and Meridian. A large supply of rolling stock was kept available in Grenada for such troop movements. Because of its location as a strategic communication center Grenada was host to many of the dashing leaders of the Confederate military forces. Among those military leaders who were in Grenada from time to time were two of the outstanding cavalry leaders of the Condederacy. General Van Dorn, one of these leaders was a West Point trained officer and General N. B. Forrest, the other outstanding cavalry leader, was a self-trained soldier and probably the most feared calvary leader operating in the Western Theater of the war. General Pemberton, Commander of Confederat forces in Mississippi, from time to time made Grenada his headquarters. As General Grant attempted to go down the Mississippi Central Railroad to get in the rear of the Vicksburg defenses, Pemberton, after being forced from his defenses along the Tallahatchie River, established his second line of defense along the Yalobousha River. It was from his Grenada headquarters that he planned, with Lt. Colonel Griffith and General Van Dorn, the successful raid against Grant's supply depot at Holly Springs which raid forced Grant to give up his attempt to force his way down the Mississippi Central Railroad. General Loring, who was to defend Fort Pemberton against an attempt of Federal gunboats to get in behind Yazoo City by coming thru Yazoo Pass and then down the Coldwater and Tallahatchie rivers, was frequently operating from Grenada. Generals Chalmers and Fetherstone operated in and out of Grenada. During the early years of the war General Sterling Price had headquarters for his army in Grenada, and Jefferson Davis, President of the Confederate States visited General Price at his Grenada Headquarters.

After the fall of Vicksburg it became apparent that the concentration of eighty locomotives and about two hundred railroad cars, in and near Grenada, could still be used to transport soldiers and supplies in that part of Mississippi not under Federal control. A drive was soon started by way of Holly Springs, Oxford, Water Valley and Coffeeville to reach, and capture Grenada, in order to make possible the destruction of this railroad rolling stock. Grenada was weakly defended because of lack of sufficient troops and the Federal drive succeeded, resulting in the destruction of most of the rolling stock available to the Mississippi Central and the Mississippi & Tennessee railroads. This phase of operations in and around Grenada had been very adequately covered by J. B. Perry in his paper YANKEE INVAIDERS CAPTURE GRENADA. At a later date during the closing months of the war, small forces of Federal troops occupied Grenada from time to time.

While the people living in Grenada were experiencing the raids by Federal soldiers, the able-bodied men of the town and community were scattered over the entire Confederacy. Although some units from the area fought in Virginia, most of the soldiers who went out from Grenada were in the Confederate forces which fought in the western theater of the war. A good account of the activities of these units is given in a series of articles entitled "OLD SOLDIER'S DIARY." This diary was kept by George W. Jones who was a member of Stanford's Battery. Mr. Jones related many details concerning the military service of Stanford's Battery. He writes: "November 6, 1861, Mustered into the Confederate Army by Lt. Lanier of the regular army at the Old Fair Grounds. Marched to the Mississippi Central Railroad and were loaded on flat cars which carried us to Columbus, Kentucky. Arrived at Columbus a day or so after the Battle of Belmont, just across the river from Columbus. Saw the awful toll of that battle in which our boys whipped General Grant. Spent several days clearing a camp and fallen trees. Built snug cabins, there being twenty eight in all." Good things came every day or so from Grenada. Turkey, ham, and all manner of other " goodies." Soon ordered to Union City. Columbus evacuated by the Confederates. At Union City guns loaded on cars of the Mobile & Ohio train and shipped to Shiloh. Battery members march across country to the same point. On arrival at Corinth the guns were delivered to us. April 2, 1862, - ordered to cook three days rations. I am beginning to feel pretty weak about the knees. I can almost smell powder in the air.

April 3- ordered to march with five days rations. April 5 - we are moving in line of battle caustiously and slowly. I have the shakes badly. Well I am not alone-in fact, we all look like shaking quakers. Scared? Oh no, only old fashioned rigor. We have several bow-legged in line, and you ought to see their knees knocking together. Well, when the battle is on I reckon we will be there-in the thickest of the fray, as our battery is looked upon as one of the best in the army. I do pray that our Heavenly Father will shield and protect every one of us. April 6 - by three o'clock this morning we had our horses all harnessed and hitched up. We are waiting orders to take our position in line. Day is now breaking. Volley after volley we can hear all along our front by our skirmishers. At 5:30 A. M. our lines and columns were in motion for our front. We are now with Cheatham's Division and formed in three lines of battle. Our troops in front are advancing steadily, followed in perfect order by us. The Yankees are contesting every inch of ground. They are struggling hard to hold their encampments. At 7 o'clock our battery was brought into action. Bang! Bang! Zip! Zip! go the minnie balls. Down I go-boys dodging the big ones-12 pounds shells are flying thick and fast over us and about us. We were ordered to silence a battery of nine pieces that had our range just in our front. Before we could fire a gun a shell blew up one of our ammunition chests; another cut off the splinter bar of the third detachemnt; another almost cut our wheel rider (Bewen) into. He was killed instantly. Wm. Jones (nephew of Judge Fisher) had his right arm shot off. Oh, how I wish that I were a dwarf instead of a sixfooter. My hair, good heavens, is standing on end like the quills of a porcupine. Silence that battery is the command from Cheatham, and we did silence it; for we opened with our six guns and an awful artillery duel was kept up for some minutes (seemed like an hour to me). Finally, we succeded in silencing the battery. Our infantry support made a charge about this time and the battery was taken. With our well directed fire we disabled every piece save one.

I am writing this little sketch in my diary about 6:00 P. M. If my handwriting is not readable you can blame the Yankees, not me-they are lying dead and wounded all around us. Victory! Victory! But, oh, if we could have followed it up. What a pity that Gen. A. S. Johnston was killed. If he had not received that fatal wound, Grant and his army would have been either all killed, drowned in the Tennessee river, or taken prisoners. After our artillery duel we had them on the run - a perfect stampeed. We drove them before us until our battery was near the river banks.

Monday, April 8 Gen. Beauregard took command after Gen. Johnston was killed. We have just heard that Gen. Buell has come up with 30,000 fresh troops. We have none. At early dawn heavy and rapid fire of musketry and the constant booming of cannon told us that the bloody contest of yesterday would be renewed. We fell into position at once. Our boys stood bravely at their post. About noon the battle raged furiously on our part of the line. The loud peals of artillery fairly shook the earth with incessant roar, while the more deadly clang of musketry rolled, in peal after peal, across the woods. Never, never, do I wish to be in such a hot place again, but we are fighting for our homes, our mothers, and our loved ones. In the thickest of the fight, our support gave way, but only for a short time. A most furious and fearful charge was made upon our battery by a Yankee Brigade. On they came. We were pouring it into them by well directed and rapid firing. They were falling thick and fast. Lewis Matlock (no. three at my gun) was shot in the head and killed instantly. He died with a smile on his face. Lee McMillam and myself laid him aside and resumed firing. About the time when the Yankees were in thirty yards of us, having no support, we were ordered to fall back by Gen. Breckenridge, who came dashing up. Our guns being disabled and most of our horses killed or wounded, we were ordered by Captain Stanford to fall back the best way we could. I called to friend Laycock to come on, but poor fellow -the Yankees got him. I do hope that they will not mistreat him; he is one of my best friends. In about twenty minutes we re-captured our guns and managed, by securing a lot of mules to get them off the field. April 8, we are now falling back to Corinth. The roads are in awful condition, mud in some places being knee-deep. I was so sick today, if it had not been for Ben Duncan and Pitt MCall I would have been left on the wayside for the Yankees or the buzzards. April 9 - back in Corinth. After being forced out of Corinth, Statford's Battery was with a part of the Confederate Army which marched across central Alabama to join Confederate troops being massed near Chattanooga for the purpose of defending that important rail center from an impending attack by General Grant's Federal Army. Mr. Jones tells us something of that march. "Retreating from Corinth, April 10, 1862, received orders to send away all extra baggage. We are now living on blackberries. June 29, we are now paying $1.75 a piece for chickens, other things being in proportion. Our battalion made up of Stanford's and Eldridge's batteries. Through Tupelo, Aberdeen, Columbus and Tuscaloosa." The Battery went to North Georgia, and soon to the area in and around Chattanooga. As things developed, the battle for the possession of that city was delayed by a bold attempt by General Bragg, who had succeeded to command of the Confederate Army of the West, to throw the Federals off balance by making a drive thru Tennessee and Kentucky in order to threaten the Ohio River city of Louisville. Stanford's Battery was ordered from the vicinity of Chattanooga to go with the main army as it drove up the invasion route into Kentucky.

Mr. Jones relates some of the events of this invasion: "August 14, 1862, left Chattanooga this morning, crossed Walfon's ridge and came to Pikesville, Tenn." For several days the battery marched and counter-marched, as Bragg endeavored to get his army in position to make a determined push against the forces of General Buell. On Sept. 8, 1862, Mr. Jones related with pride an honor which had come to the battery: "Received orders to have SHILOH inscribed on our flag." Later, he indicates the purpose of the invasion: "Bragg and Buell racing for Louisville. We passed through Bardstown, Kentucky. Large whiskey storehouses at this place, and a large Catholic School." Later Mr. Jones relates the part which his unit played in the battle of Perryville-a battle which should have assured the success of the invasion, but did not do so because of indecision on the part of General Bragg: "Wed. Oct. 8, 1862. Battle of Perryville. Relieved Carnes' Tennessee Battery. The Yankees had perfect range on us. Had one of our ammunition chests to explode. Pitt McCall and Charles Boycoft killed and several wounded before we could fire a gun. We opened fire on a twelve pound battery. We kept up a constant cannonading for two hours and finally silenced tha battery. Our infantry at this time made a furious charge and captured the battery. In the afternoon we were ordered still further to the right and opened an enviable fire on the Yankees. They had a strong position behind a stone fence. Our line of support was about two hundred yards from them. Both lines were in full view of us. It was a grand sight. Our boys, it seems, could not go further, Yankees having advantage of position, they were pouring into each other a deadly fire. Oh, how anxious we were to do something to relieve our men. We waved our flags to the front: Gardee's Corps recognized it and we opened a terrific fire with double charges down the Yankee lines. Our well directed shells threw them in great confusion. As we ceased firing our noble boys gave a Confederate Yell and charged the stone fence. What few Yankees that were left stampeeded. It was a grand sight to see the flashing of guns and bursting of shells. At this point a solid twelve pounder struck the ground in about two feet of me and knocked me down. I thought I was killed, but soon found that I wasn't-only slightly demoralized. We were greatly out-ranged, but our boys did not hesitate to engage at any odds. Our force, so I am told, captured about twenty pieces of artillery, killed one General and wounded two, and captured nearly one thousand troops, as well as killing about five thousand. If we could only have a few fresh troops to follow up victory we could route Buell and take Louisville." Mr. Jones, as well as other soldiers in the lower rank of the army must have understood the purpose and importance of the battle. Mr. Jones writes: "Oct. 9, 1862, well the Battle of Perryville has been fought and won by us-can we follow up the victory? I am afraid not! The Yankees have the world to draw from. We have none." Having failed to take Louisville, the Confederate Army began to march in the general direction of Chattanooga. On October 27, 1862, Mr. Jones writes: "Thru the Cumberland Gap; no rations." This gap had been the eastern terminus of the defense line which Albert Sidney Johnston had tried to establish before the fall of Forts Henry and Donaldson. It was also the gap through which Daniel Boone had guided settlers into Kentucky. It seems that rations were not the only necessities in short supply for Mr. Jones writes: "Oct. 29th, Captain Stanford, W. B. May, Charles Roberts, and William Brooks detailed to go home after clothing, some of the boys being nearly naked. Hurrah for me-I was lucky to draw an overcoat this evening-well boys I am willing to divide these cold nights when on duty. Marched five and one half miles this afternoon and passed through Knoxville on our march." East Tennessee was the center of a great deal of Union support, and the soldiers of the Confederacy didn't get much consideration from most of the people of that area. This may have been one of the causes of the first real complaint which the diarist entered into his diary: "We have been resting our poor old worn-out bones today. I am sick enough to go to bed. Oh, My God, how long will this war last? It is alright when I am at myself, but when a fellow feels as I feel now it is enough to make him wish he were dead." Mr. Jones seems to have been sick enough for the medical officer in charge to decide that he needed rest. We find that a medical furlough was given the diarist, and he returned home by a very circuitous route: "To Chattanooga, Atlanta, Mobile, Meridian, Jackson, Jackson to Canton and from Canton to Grenada."

The Bragg invasion having failed, the Confederate Army which had attempted the invasion took position to defend Chattanooga. Stanford's Battery took part in the battles in and around that key city. On October 6, 1863, Mr. Jones writes: "We are now on Lookout Mountain, fired a few shells into Chattanooga." Federal forces had occupied the city and soon heavy battles would be fought for its possession. Mr. Jones continues: "We had orders to throw a few shells into a log house occupied by some Yankee sharpshooters. Our first shell blew up the house and stampeeded the Yanks; killing some of them. We had the exact range. Oct., 10th, President Jefferson Davis passed our lines at eleven - short rations but plenty of good water. Our Battery is now complete with new guns, cassions, and harness. It's now dark. Look out boys! Lie down! Here comes a lamppost. It exploded just over our heads, here they come thick and fast. Dodge the big ones boys so says General Cheatham." It seem that Stanford's Battery was not the only battery having the enemy range. On Jan. 23, 1864, Mr. Jones records the inlistment of a young recuit: "Little Ben Adams, son of Col. B. C. Adams, is now with us and has enlisted for the balance of the war. He helps us eat our grub and divides his blanket with us." A little later, Feb. 26, 1864, the diarist records the visit of another Grenadian to the camp of the battery-then at Kingston, Georgia. "Uncle Levin Lake arrived in camp this morning. He found us sitting around the campfire, some eating, others smoking etc. How delighted we were to see him. He is now giving us the news from home (my adopted home), had just handed me a long letter from the girl I left behind me. The Yanks made an attack on our works this afternoon. They fell back after a few of them were killed." In reference to Mr. Jones using the term "my adopted home" to Grenada, it may be well to explain that Mr. Levin Lake and older brothers came to Grenada from Maryland very early in the period when the first settlers were entering the area. As early as 1835 the brothers were in business in Tullahoma. Mr. Jones came to Grenada from Maryland a few years before the outbreak of the war, and made his home with his uncle Levin Lake. He had a brother who became Colonel of a South Carolina Regiment, but gave up that command in order that he might become a member of General N. B. Forrest's fabulous Cavalry Command. It was during the campaign around north Georgia that the diarist saw his brother for the first time since leaving home. The older brother visited the younger one as a detachment of Forrest's cavalry passed the camp of Stanford's Battery.

Furloughs were a welcome break in camp life. Mr. Jones indicates his pleasure at the granting of a furlough to him: "March 27, 1864, received a furlough today, all properly signed; came very near jumping out of my old brogans. Left on 7:30 train for Grenada. Got to Atlanta at 4 P. M. Went to a restaurant and paid $5.50 for two sausages, one small cup of coffee and a piece of bread. Arrived at Montgomery at 10 o'clock this evening. Put up at the Campbell House; paid for a single bed $5.00. Left Montgomery at 6 this afternoon on steamer SOUTHERN REPUBLIC. March 11th, reached Selma, Alabama about 6 this moring; left at 7 o'clock on railroad for Demopolis, Ala. Left on steamer ROBERT WILSON, for Columbus, Miss.; here met conveyance sent by our friends in Grenada." That notation indicates the demoralization of transportation facilities in the Confederacy; the depreciating value of Confederate currency, and also the probability of Mr. Jones having other Yalobousha county boys with him. His expression "our fiends in Grenada" in connection with the conveyance sent to Columbus, would seem to give rise to the assumption that the conveyance was not sent that distance for a single soldier.

By May 15th of the same year, gun-sergeant Jones was back with his unit at Resaca, Georgia. Joseph Johnson, supposed to be a defensive specialist, was now in charge of the Confederate army. General Sherman and his Federal Army were slowly driving toward Atlanta. Johnson would select a strong defensive position and wait for Sherman to make a frontal attach. But, instead of doing this, Sherman, having a numerical superiority of troops, kept outflanking the defensive positions, forcing Johnson to make another retreat and select another defensive position. It was into the growing dispute between President Davis and General Johnson, relative to the conduct of the campaign, that Jones came back to his unit which had been taking part in the defensive battles waged by Johnson. Soon after rejoining his campany he writes: "Resaca, Georgia, May 14th, in line of battle at 4 o'clock this afternoon we advanced and drove the Yanks over a rough, hilly country for about two miles-we surely had them on the run, but what can we do with only about 40,000 half-starved, ragged soldiers against 100,000 well equipped, well fed ones? We can get them on the run every time, but cannot follow up victory." The soldiers of the Confederacy were beginning to realize that they were, henceforth, to always face overwhelming forces of Federal soldiers in almost every engagement. They were beginning to become troubled relative to the outcome of the conflict. Then came a heavy blow to the company, which is related by Mr. Jones in these words: "Sunday, May 15th. It is now 4:30 P. M. Our dear Captain had just been killed by one of the sharpshooters; was shot in the head and died instantly. His place cannot be filled. Oh, what a brave, daring officer, and with it all a perfect gentleman. We loved him. We have laid away our Captain on the mountain side near Resaca." Lieutenant McCall assumed command of the battery and the unit soon engaged other battles. Mr. Jones writes: "May 25th, here they come. On, on, and on, they come with their banners flying and re-enforced with fresh troops. Quit yourselves like men says McCall, every man at his post. Down goes poor Dollar, shot in the head just as I was handing him a shell to put in the gun, and George McMillian shot in the leg poor fellow. Sergeant Jones he cries, I am shot what must I do? Go to the rear at once and get out of this hot place I said in an instant. Our number one, Ben Hill, is struck on the head. What shall we do, only two men at the gun, but Hill, brave fellow is he, will not leave his post. With blood running down his face he stands his ground, also Albert Lake, shot in the arm, stays until the Yankees are repulsed for the fifth time, and when a minnie ball struck me on the shoulder. I yelled at the top of my voice like a Commanchie Indian, charge boys, charge them and give them the grape."

Regardless of the fierce opposition by the out-numbered Confederate forces,

General Sherman was slowly and methodically driving the Confederate forces toward the key city of Atlanta. Mr. Jones relates a tragic occurance which came about during this withdrawal action by the Confederates. "Monday, June 13th. The enemies of our country are feeling their way slowly. They are skirmishing just to our right. Generals Johnson, Hardee and Polk have just passed us on their way to the outpost on Pine Mountain. While viewing the ground in front of our (Polk's) corps, General Polk was killed by a shot from a Yankee shell." General Johnson was relieved of command. General Hood, looked upon as a "fighting General", engaged the Federal army in a general engagement and lost possession of Atlanta. This defeat convinced Hood that he did not have enough troops to halt General Sherman's proposed "March to the Sea", so the Confederate commander moved most of his soldiers back toward Chattanooga in a vain attempt to so harass Sherman's line of communications that the Federal General would be forced to abandon the proposed movement. This ill-advised action by General Hood was the beginning of the end of Hood's army as an effective force to resist the Federal forces in the west. As Sherman was slowly driving Johnson in front of him, General N. B. Forrest had begged permission to use his force of hard fighting Cavalrymen to cut Sherman's line of communication, but he was refused permission. Now it was too late. The Mobile river was one of the last interior lines of transportation for the Confederate forces in Alabama. In order to keep open this avenue of transportation, Stanford's Battery was detached from General Cheatham's Division and their guns placed in a defensive position on the Mobile river. It was here that they began to hear sad news from Virginia. On April 29, 1865, Mr. Jones writes: "We have been camping here for several weeks. We feel very much discouraged. Have just heard that our noble Gen. R. E. Lee has surrendered with only 20,000 troops to Gen. Grant's tremendous army of 100,000 or more. We have just heard that in the interview between Lee and Grant that Lee remarked well, General Grant, I deem it due and proper, that I should be frank and candid at the very beginning of this interview. I am not willing to discuss any terms of surrender inconsistant with the honor of my brave men, and I am determined to maintain that to the last. How proud we are to learn that Grant accepted surrender on General Lee's terms. Well, of course, we feel that it is useless to continue the war any longer. But still, if our Generals think it best, we are willing to fight on until the last one of us bites the dust. May 1st. Surrender of General Lee and his brave boys confirmed; so notified today. We are now off for Cuba Station, 22 miles from Meridian. At this point we surrendered, not whipped, but over-powered. On the 149 men entered on the battery rouster from 1861 to 1865, over one half were killed or wounded in battle." On this note Mr. Jones ends his diary. When the diary was published in the Grenada Sentinel during the years of 1898 and 1899, Mr. Jones stated that, at the time of the publication of the diary, only twenty one members of the battery were still living.

    Unfortunately we have no diary to record the activities of the 15th Mississippi Regiment in which so many men of Grenada and of Yalobousha county fought during the war. All military historians are in agreement that it was one of the finest units in the Confederate Army of the West. For many years after the termination of the war this regiment held frequent reunions, most of which were held in Grenada.

    Before the Grenada Rifles left Grenada to become a part of the 15th Mississippi Regiment, Miss Mollie Granberry, daughter of the President of Yalobousha Female Institute, acting in behalf of some ladies of Grenada, presented to Captain Statham a flag to be used by the company. At some hard-fought battle in the invasion of Kentucky by the Confederate forces that flag was captured by a Federal unit. A number of years after the war, Mrs. B. S. Dudley, sister of General Statham, learned that the unit which captured the flag was the 10th Indiana Volunteer Infantry. She learned the name of the commanding officer of that unit. After considerable communication between Mrs. Dudley and the former commanding officer of the Federal unit, that officer obtained permission from the surviving members of the unit to return the captured flag to Mrs. Dudly, and through her to the surviving members of the Grenada Rifles. Thus, in 1890, a quarter of centry after the end of the civil conflict, hatred engendered by the Civil War had diminished to the extent that the Federal unit could make this gracious and generous gesture toward members of the defeated Southern military force.

Grenada survived the ravages of the war; the inconvenience of occoupation by Federal Troops for several years after the end of the war; and the hard years of reconstruction, as well as the ruined economy which faced the returning soldiers. Their slaves had been freed; their livestock impressed by the contending armies; and their farms and plantations greatly neglected for four years. Much property of impoverished people was sold for taxes, and it took a great deal of courage for a war-weary and defeated people to rebuild a new economy and a new way of life on the ruins of the past. To the credit of those people of that day, we may say that they met the test.

Chapter VIII

Reconstruction in Grenada and Yalobousha Counties

The immediate effect of the Civil War was to leave Mississippi, as well as the other Southern states, in political eclipse and economic ruin. These states had pledged and delivered to the Confederate Government most of their resources of manpower and wealth to be used in the struggle for southern independence. Mississippi had been very generous in her contributions to the government which was headed by one of her native sons. At the end of the war eighty thousand of her fine men were either buried in the cemeteries of every battlefield of the war, or so badly maimed as to be incapable of much physical activity. Her fields were barren; her railroad lines torn up and worn out, and neither recently freed slaves nor former slave owners knew how to adjust to the new relationship between former slaves and masters. There were plantations to be worked, and there were thousands of freed slaves to be absorbed into a new labor status. Many of the freed slaves, looking to the Freedman Bureau to feed, clothe and house them, refused to work under any inducements. Many of the former slave owners sought to re-employ slaves under conditions which was somewhat similar to peonage. Stringent laws called "Black Codes" were passed to try to place these former slaves under some sort of civil restraint. These "Black Codes" were to give radical members of Congress an excuse to pass harsh laws aimed at depriving the leading white people of political power, and by blanket enfranchisement of all adult Negroes, to shift political power from southern leaders to the Carpetbag and Scalawag led Negro majority which supported the radical Republican Party. Most southern white men were, at first, not allowed to vote if they had served the Confederate Government, or the seceeded state governments in any capacity during the war years. Before these men could vote again they would have to apply for, and receive, a pardons from the Federal Government. The effect of the enfranchisement of all the illiterate Negroes was just as disasterous to honest and efficient local and state government, as the Civil Rights Laws of 1965, which enfranchised illiterate Negroes in only southern states, will be to those states and counties where this enforced Federal registration has taken place.

The grief and sorrow resulting from the loss of relatives and friends who fell fighting for the "Lost Cause" was natural, and the passage of time would tend to heal the scars left by these tragic losses. Soliers who had fought to the last to sustain southern independence had respect for the fighting men of the Federal armies, and many of them had no bitter feelings which would not pass away in time. So the defeated soldiers returned home, defeated but not ashamed of the part which they had played in the tragedy of the civil war. They began to try to reconstruct the lives they had lived before the war, but the Congressional Reconstruction of the southern states by the vindictive Radical Republican majority in Congress inflicted new wounds, the scars of which would be generations in the healing. The war years had for the South their periods of glory, but the reconstruction years were years of bitterness and frustration for the southern white people.

Reconstruction in Grenada and Yalobousha counties pretty much followed the course of reconstruction in the other counties of Mississippi. Since Grenada county was not organized until 1870, the people of this county first experienced its effects while still a part of those counties from which the new county was to be created. A large part of the area which was to become Grenada county came from Yalobousha county. It seems necessary to discuss reconstruction of both Grenada and Yalobousha counties in order to give a representative description of the reconstruction imposed upon the people of the area which became Grenada county. In previous chapters of this work, most of the information given had been obtained from sources such as news-paper files, deed records, minutes of Board of Supervisors, and personal letters of the period covered. Because of the destruction of some of these sources in the fires which destroyed courthouses in Yalobousha county, and the fact that newspaper files available of papers printed in Grenada county do not begin until 1881, much of the factual material in this chapter must come from the memory of men and women who lived through the reconstruction period. The passage of time may have dimmed the memory of some of the people who related the incidents which will partly make up information given here-after, but we may be sure that most of the information is substantially correct. In 1912 there was printed in Vol. 12 of the Mississippi Historical Publications a very fine article on "Reconstruction in Grenada and Yalobousha Counties." Miss Julia Brown was the author of the article, and it is to her fine work that we are indebted for a considerable amount of the factual information given hereafter. Miss Brown names sixteen individuals who supplied her with information, nine of these individuals being residents of the town of Grenada. They were W. H. Winter, a longtime Legislative representative from Grenada county; Tom Garner, who at one time served as Marshall of Grenada; Dr. T. F., Brown physician and County Health Officer; Mrs. P. S. Dudly, longtime teacher in the private and public schools of Grenada, and the sister of General Statham; Mr. W. E. Smith, Grenada Jeweler; Dr. Hughes, a Grenada druggist, and Captain M. P. L. Stephens, about whom we have no information other than he was at one time a resident of Water Valley.

At the outbreak of the Civil War Yalobousha was a large county. It had a population of 16,952 of whom 9,531 were Negro slaves. The county seat was located at Coffeeville. In 1873 a second Judicial District was formed in the county with Water Valley being the site of the Courthouse for that District. In 1870, the county had a population 13,254. This considerable decrease in population resulted not only from the ravages of war and reconstruction, but also from the fact that part of the county had been taken away to help create Grenada and Calhoun counties. During the course of the war much property had been destroyed. All business houses in Water Valley except two or three had been burned by the invading Federal forces. At Grenada, when it was realized that it would be impossible to hold the town against approaching Federal soldiers, much rolling stock of the Mississippi Central and Memphis & Tennessee Railroads had been burned by the retreating Confederate forces. The end of the war found the two railroads in desperate financial circumstances.

The returning soldiers of Yalobousha county found that the local government was still in the hands of white men. All five members of the Board of Supervisors were leading citizens. This condition was to prevail for only a short time. The Civil Rights legislation mentioned above soon eliminated a majority of the white electorate, and enfranchised every resident male Negro who was of requisite age. These Negroes were, for the most part, illiterate, and were easily controlled by northern adventures and native renagades. Behind these leaders was the power of the Federal government, exercised part of the period by military governors, who were backed by garrisons of Federal soldiers stationed at strategic points. Grenada was one such point. An officer of the Freedman Bureau was also stationed at Grenada, and his organization was the source of much trouble for the white people of the area. Very early during the reconstruction period a Federal infantry force made up the Federal garrison at Grenada. In 1866 a company of cavalry was sent to Grenada. Because of the mobility of this unit it was used to go out to investigate trouble developing in any of the nearby towns and communities. During much of the time General Pennypacker was in command of the garrison, although General Rosecrans and Major Allen served brief periods as garrison Commander. General Pennypacker was sympathetic with the white people in their period of trial, and did everything he could to make the military occupation tolerable. Rosecrans was respected, but Allen was hated. Either as a measure to further humiliate the white people of the area, or because those in authority did not realize the reaction of the white people to their action, the Federal Authorities sent in a troop of Negro soldiers as part of the garrison. At first this force was under the command of a white officer, and during his tenure as unit commander, conditions were not too bad, but he was soon replaced by a Negro, Colonel Albert Floyd. He exercised very little restraint over his soldiers who delighted in insulting the inhabitants of the town. When these soldiers were on leave in town they would frequently line up, arm in arm, and walk down the sidewalks forcing all white people to go out into the street to avoid them. Any resistance offered to actions of the Federal soldiers and officials could be tried in military courts, and offenders imprisoned at the whim of such courts. These conditions brought on a near reign of terror in the town of Grenada and the area about Grenada. Although not a permanent citizen of Grenada, the Negro Colonel decided that he would vote in one of the elections being held in the town. He was told that he was not eligible but started in to vote despite the protest of the election official. Among the election officials, who were of course Republicans, was a Negro box guard. He evidently didn't like the overbearing Negro officer, and when Floyd attempted to go to the polls the guard ran him through the shoulder with a bayonet. It is reported that the Colonel never attempted to vote again so long as he was in Grenada, and that the Negro box guard was never punished.

When the Civil Rights Acts of 1866 became effective, the military governor of Mississippi revoked all office appointments which had been made, and ordered new elections for elective officials. With Carpetbaggers and Scalawag leaders and their responsive Negro majority making up the Republican party, that party came into control of state and local offices. Soon the majority of the Board of Supervisors of Yalobousha county was made up on Negroes. A Negro sheriff was elected. It was during this time that some respectable white men who had belonged to the Whig Party before the war decided that they had better become Democrats and aid the men of that party in their fight against the intolerable conditions prevailing at the time. Among the influential former Whigs who cast their lot with the Democrats were Judge Fisher, who was to become a judge of the Mississippi Supreme Court, and Dr. D. H. Staham, the father of deceased General Staham and of Mrs. P. S. Dudly. Judge Fairfield, a northern Whig who came to Grenada a few years before the outbreak of the war joined with the Republicans, and was appointed a Judge for one of the courts of the area. It seems that the Judge was a man of honor, and white citizens could obtain justice in his court. There seems to have been no considerable animosity directed toward him as was the case of other white men who affiliated with the Republican party. After a time, most of the adult white men regained the right to vote, but during the early years of overwhelming Negro registration the editor of the newspaper GRENADA VISITOR had this editorial comment: "The disgraceful exhibition of the utter trampling on all law, right and decency-known as registration in the city is still continued. More than half of the white citizens, fully qualified under the law, are turned away while every negro who applies is immediately accepted and registered. Naturalized citizens are not only required to produce their papers, but leave them with the registrars, with a very dim prospect of ever getting them back. Old citizens who have lived a quarter of a century, and who pay individually more taxes than the whole radical party in the state collectively, are turned away because they have, at some remote period of their lives, been school directors, or aldermen under city government and are suspected of having sympathized with the rebellion. But few naturalized citizens are registered on any terms except that of adherence to the Radicals. That virtue will purge all vices. Renagades who fought in the rebel ranks and deserted when the cause became desperate and joined the Radicals- even some who were punished by Butler and Banks for their rebellious excesses and who have the disqualification of having held Federal or State offices previous to the war are admitted to the honor (?) of registration without question."

When Grenada County was created in 1870, the Republican Party was still dominant in politics. The first officials were appointed by Governor Alcorn. Among his appointees were L. French, Sheriff and J. B. Townsend. French was considered a Scalawag. Townsend seems to have maintained the respect of the people regardless of his affiliation with the Republican Party. Green Dubard and Bill Davis were among the other white men who became affiliated with the Republicans.

Grenada and Yalobousha counties were fortunate in having outstanding white citizens who, as soon as they could qualify to vote under the new regulations, began a gradual and cautious movement to drain away some of the more respectable Negroes from the enticement offered by the corrupt leaders of the Republican party. The large body of Negro voters were enrolled in the Loyal League, an organization set up to use Negro voters to maintain political control of the counties. Because of fear of white retaliation, the names of those enrolled in the League was kept secret at first. The white people never knew which Negroes with whom they came in contact were members of the League. This information was obtained through the loyalty of two Negroes to their former masters. Bob ("Banjo") Dudley, had belonged to the Dudley family, and became a member of the Democratic Party, and a leader of the Negro Democrats. Austin Dudley who had been a slave of Captain B. S. Dudly, husband of Mrs. P. S. Dudly, was induced, probably with the encouragement of Banjo Dudly, to become a member of the Loyal League for the purpose of revealing the names of the members to his white friends. This information was to prove very valuable when, a little later, continued intolerable conditions resulted in white robed Ku Klux Klan members visiting obnoxious members of the League.

Although the activities of the Klan had its effect in breaking the hold of the Republicans on the Negro voters, the respect which many of the Negroes had for a number of outstanding white leaders was, perhaps, more effective in attracting Negro voters to the Democratic party. For a considerable period of time the carpetbagger William Price was the leader of the Negro voters. He had a number of qualifications for this position. He first came to Grenada as the chaplain of a Negro regiment. He was a preacher of great oratorical power, and he associated freely with the Negroes. These threee qualifications appealed to the illiterate Negro majority. Although not welcomed with open arms, Price was respected by the people of Grenada when he returned to the city after the termination of the Civil War. In some way he had come into the possession of a watch lost during the war by Colonel A. S. Pass who was a resident of Grenada. Price returned the watch to Colonel Pass, and this episode helped him gain a measure of acceptance by the white people of the area. Things looked so good for Price that he brought his whole family to Grenada. His two sons-in-law, Lincoln and Kelly became engaged in the same type of activity as that in which Price was engaged. After a time Price had his wife appointed as Postmaster at Grenada. He ran the office while Mrs. Price and her daughters engaged in the millinery business. Son-in-law Lincoln later became Chancery Clerk of the county. Things looked good for the members of the Price family for several years, but eventually the activity of Lincoln and Kelly in connection with the Loyal League became so notorious that they were visited by Klan members and advised to leave the city and state. They took this good advice and left Grenada to be followed soon by Price and his family. M. K. Mister was a Scalawag who later became Postmaster at Grenada. He was a native of the county and lived on a nearby plantation until he became Postmaster. It seems that his affiliation with the Republican Party was for the purpose of receiving Federal appointment and not adverse to the interests of the white people.

One of the Negro leaders in the struggle for political power was a mulatto by the name of Schurlock. He was the Federal patronage referee for the appointment of federal offices in the area. He was the reputed son of a white northern teacher who conducted schools in Yalobousha county in the period before the Civil War. Schurlock was aggressive and arrogant, but very popular with the

Negro voters. He was much in evidence at the various political speakings when candidates of the different parties were contending for votes. He usually had with him large numbers of Negroes who, at his instigation, heckled the speakers who were Democratic candidates for office. Once, at a speaking near Coffeeville, he moved up his mob to engage in this practice. He was met by Captain Roland W. Jones, who caught him by the collar of his shirt, pulled out a knife and told Shurlock "If you don't lead that mob away from this speaking I will cut your throat." Evidently Schurlock took this statement at face value, for he removed his followers from the site of the speaking. At one time Negro leaders moved a colony of about five hundred Negroes into the fringes of the town of Coffeeville with the stated intention of taking control of the local government of that town. This move was met by the town officials reestablishing the boundaries of the town so as to exclude most of the area in which the Negroes had settled. It was during this period of reconstruction that the Negroes were able, for a brief period, to elect a Negro Mayor of Grenada, and several members of the Board of Supervisors of Grenada County.

Other white leaders of Grenada County who were able to appeal to the Negroes were General E. C. Walthall, Major William Barksdale, Captain John Powell, James Crowder and R. H. Golloday. Major Barksdale had a considerable following, but did not pamper them. On one occasion, while speaking at a political rally he told them: "You negroes think that we'll let you smite us on one cheek and then turn and let you smite us on the other, but I tell you that we will have an eye for an eye and a tooth for a tooth." On another occasion, a political specking at Spring Lake, he spoke for the Democratic candidate while Roland Collins, a Negro leader and former slave of the Barksdale family, spoke for the Republican candidate. As an indication of the respect which the Negro leader had for his opposing speaker he made this statement during his speech: "Marse Billy I lernt you to walk and to talk. I lernt you to read. I lernt you to hoe corn and cotton, and Marse Billy you's do bes' man I nows." Some of the negro Democrats who stood by the white people were Ben Staham, John Golding, Bob Reed, John Cooly and Frank Mayhew. They were probably attracted to the party because of their admiration and affection for men like Major Barksdale. One very amusing incident occured at another speaking when Judge Fairfield and William Price were running for different offices on the Republican ticket. Although Fairfield, an old line Whig, had joined the Republican ranks he still maintained the respect and friendship of many of the white residents of the town. As the time for the speaking drew near, one of these friends offered the Judge a drink of whiskey. Other drinks followed and, in the spirit of good fellowship engendered by these drinks, the friend confided to the Judge that he had great respect for the Judge who was honest in following his political principles, but had nothing but contempt for his fellow Republican Price. Basking in the glow of the approval of his friend, and remembering that the friend had no respect for Farfield's fellow Republican Price, the Judge began his speech by stating his own qualifications for the office which he was seeking, but then said: "That fellow Price is the grandest rascal in the county." Price was surprised and crestfallen, but most of the white people agreed with the Judges' befuddled statement.

During the period of heated political rivalry between the negro and white voters there was a near riot in Grenada. On this occasion an election was being held in the store building then used as a courthouse. This building was located on the north-west corner of the lot just north of the city square. Some of the white leaders of the Republican Party, fearing that they would be outvoted in the election, lined up a large crowd of negroes and instructed them to crowd around the polls and prevent white voters from entering. Thirty or forty white men had brought guns with them to the polling place, but in the interest of peace, had been induced to store their guns in a nearby store building. In the vicinity of the courthouse was a small cannon, perhaps a relic of the Civil War, which was used to fire salutes on the fourth of July and other occasions of celebration when such action was deemed seemly. As the negroes came marching up Green street, some one shouted "fill the cannon with buckshot." Men nearby ran to the gun and began either serious or pretended activity in that regard. The head of the marching rank of negroes heard the order and saw the activity. They began a rearward movement which became a rout as they shouted to those in the rear ranks "they are loading the cannon with buckshot." At this juncture the men who had stored their guns in the store building ran into the building to reclaim their guns, probably with the intention of expediting the hasty withdrawl of the negroes. General E. C. Walthall, realizing that such action might precipitate a race war, had the door of the store closed and locked before the men could get back on the street. It should be said in defense of the newly freed, and mostly illiterate negroes that in most cases of similar trouble, the negroes were usually incited by some of their white leaders. Some of the negro leaders were men of more integrity and respectability than most of their white leaders. One of these better class negro leaders was a lawyer George W. Jones, not to be confused with George Washington Jones, nephew of Levin Lake, confederate soldier and Grenada Business man. In 1883, when the Republican Party still was strong, this negro lawyer was elected an Alderman from the West Ward of Grenada. He brought up some sort of a charge against a Mr. Ferguson who was serving as Street Commissioner. The Street Commissioner became angry and tendered his resignation. Angry at the accusation made against Ferguson, Max Ginsburg resigned his place as an alderman. In a subsequent meeting of the Board of Aldermen Ferguson was induced to withdraw his resignation, but some of the white people, angered at what they termed "the presumption of a negro in accusing a white man of misconduct", began a movement to induce Jones to leave town. In July, 1885 Jones announced that he had received an anonymous letter in which he was directed to leave town in four days and never return to the town. He refused to leave, and there is no record that he ever received any physical violence, but it is very probable that the incident, and the letter, ruined his political career as a member of the Board of Aldermen. In October of 1886 the GRENADA SENTINEL reported that Jones had been defeated for a seat as a member of the Board of Aldermen. These incidents are good proof that white political supremacy was not achieved in the first few years following the beginning of reconstruction. In fact such supremacy was not completely established until the adoption of the Mississippi Constitution of 1890, and its acceptance by the Federal Government. It is interesting to note that the one man most responsible for the acceptance of that constitution by the Federal Government was a Carroll County U. S. Senator, James Z. George.

Another erroneous belief held by many people is that, during the entire period of reconstruction, the political fight was between the Democrats and the Republicans. As a matter of fact, this was true only during the period from 1865 to 1875. By the time this ten year period had elapsed many of the negroes had become dissatisfied with the achievements of the Republican Party which they had been lead to believe would furnish each able-bodied negro with a mule and forty acres of land, and other evidences of the love of the Republican Party for the former slaves. The years of the next decade were years of political unrest and the formation of splinter parties which drew strength from the dissatisfied elements of both old parties. The Greenback Party attracted many dissatisfied voters, both white and colored. Various combinations of the Greenback with so called political independents became, from 1876 to 1885, a stronger rival of the Democrats than the discredited local Republican organization. The promises of the Greenback and Independent candidates became more attractive to negro voters than the unfulfilled promises of the Republicans. This desertion of the Republican party by many of the negroes was the beginning of the end of political control of local government by the combination of Carpetbaggers, Scalawags and Negroes. Some of the better negroes remained faithful to the Republican Party. One of these faithful few was E. E. Pettibone. He, so far as we have been able to learn, never sought public office for himself. For many years after the period of Republican control of local affairs in Grenada had passed Pettibone attended the National Conventions of the Party as a delegate from Mississippi. He was respected by his white contemporaries. Recovery of a measure of political control over local affairs did not entirely remove from the minds of the white people the possibility of racial trouble. This uneasy feeling is reflected by an editorial statement found in the June 23, 1883, issue of the GRENADA SENTINEL: "A dangerous colored society is in existence around Grenada, which is something on the order of the jesuitical order, each member swearing to stick by the other no matter what happens." This was a period when the politically illiterate negroes, feeling that they had the backing of the Federal Government, had the most extravagent ideas relative to their capacity to obtain everything which had been enjoyed by white men. The Grenada Sentinel of April 11, 1885, quotes the following statement made by a negro member of the Massachusetts Legislature: "If a notice should be placed over the gates of hell forbidding negroes to enter, we would not be satisfied until we got in." In the same paper appears an item without editorial comment: "Two negroes, convicted of the murder of a peddler, were taken away from the Sheriff and hanged on a persimmon tree just across the Bogue by a mob of seventy five men."

After a brief period under William L. Sharkey, appointed Provisional Governor by President Andrew Johnson, Governor B. C. Humphreys who was elected at the first election held after the termination of the war, was removed from office and Mississippi placed him under military control of the Federal Government. Humphreys had been a Brigadier General in the Confederate service, and the Legislature elected along with him made the mistake of passing some very strict laws governing the employment and conduct of the freed negroes. These two facts gave the Radicals in Congress the excuse which they sought to refuse to accept Mississippi representatives in the Federal Congress, and thereby refuse to accept the state back into the Union. For a period of over three years Mississippi was under the political and military control of a series of Federal Military officers. The first such official appointed was General E. O. C. Ord who in charge of the Fourth Military District of which Mississippi was a part. General Ord had his headquarters at Vicksburg. Next came General Alvan C. Gillem who had little sympathy with the excesses in the use of military power for political purposes. Because General Gillem would not go along with the Republican Radicals in overuling an election in which a state constitution, made to order to favor the Republicans and to perpetuate their hold on state government. General Gillem was removed and the obnoxious General Ames placed in charge. This was the darkest period of the long dark period of reconstruction.

Shortly before Ames was appointed Military Governor, Congress had declared vacant all civil offices in the state, thereby giving the new Military Governor the right to appoint almost two thousand men to these vacant offices. Greed for appointment to these positions caused some of the white men who had previously voted the Democratic ticket to change their allegiance to the Republican Party. Among those who deemed it expedient to change parties was James. L. Alcorn. In his case he was not abandoning his early political philosophy, but merely seeking a new political home. He had been a Whig before the war, but that party had, because of the rise of the Republican Party, and the almost total revision of Mississippi Whigs to the Democratic Party after the election of Lincoln, disappeared so far as to be of any significant political importance. Alcorn became affiliated with the Republican Party, and was elected Governor of Mississippi in the first valid election after Mississippi was re-admitted to the Union on February 17, 1870. The Republicans made a clean sweep of major state offices electing beside Governor Alcorn, General Ames and Hiram R. Revels as United States Senators from Mississippi. Ames was the hated fromer Military Governor, while Hiram Revels was a negro who later became President of Alcorn College which was established for negro students. In 1873, Alcorn who had been elected to the United States Senate before the end of his term as Governor, and Ames who had been elected to the Senate later than Alcorn, both resigned and came back to Mississippi to run for the office of Governor. Although both the Senators were members of the Republican Party, Ames was able to get the support of the Republican nominating Convention. Alcorn and his scalawag following bolted the party, and Alcorn ran as an independent. Since the Democrats distrusted Alcorn, they mostly refrained from voting, and Ames was elected, and ushered in the most corrupt period of reconstruction. In order to win the election, the carpetbaggers who worked with the negro Republican majority had to agree to have three negroes on the state ticket. These three, candidate for Lieutenant Governor A. K. Davis, candidate for Secretary of State Jim Hill, and candidate for State Superintendent of Education T. W. Cordosa, were elected to state office along with sixty four other negroes, most of whom were illiterate, to the State Legislature. Both Davis and Cordosa, by their conduct brought discredit on the whole administration. Their action was compounded by the thorough mess the negro members made as legislators. It is of interest to note that the negro Lieutenant Governor had once been a Grenada barber.

It was during this period of almost complete political control by the Republicans that the people of Grenada county were to be forced to stand aside and observe the corrupt regime of selfish white men and ignorant negroes ruining the economy of the area. Helpless at first, because of the iron grip of occupying military forces, there was born in the minds of the leading citizens the belief that they must use any sort of weapon to regain control over local affairs. Some of the methods used were not very nice; some were actually illegal, but all were deemed justified on the ground that the end would justify the means. As heretofore related, the ranks of the Loyal League had been infilterated, and the names of its members were available to those who wanted to influence these members. Different kinds of "influence" were used. At times a former master would approach some of the better class members of the League and reason with them to convince them that they were in the wrong Party: Sometimes members would be issued warnings relative to their conduct, and on a number of occasions, physical violence was resorted to. The formation and development of the Ku Klux Klan gave the white resistance group a very potent weapon against the superstitous negroes. Often a parade of white-sheeted klansmen was enough to put the fear of God into the heart of people, white and colored, who were out of line with the convictions of the better element of people in a community. A visit by the Klan was usually a warning, which might be followed by an order for a person to leave the community, and if these visits were not effective, physical violence was certain to follow. As long as the membership of the Klan was secret the local officials and Federal Military force could not move against the klansmen. If physical violence was to be resorted to, it was customary for the local klansmen to send out to request that members of some other out of town klan group should ride in to give the physical punishment. This, of course, lessened the possibility of some of the men being recognized.

The area unit of the Klan which was active in Grenada and Yalobousha counties from 1867 to 1875 was led by M. D. L. Stephens of Water Valley who was the "Grand Cyclop". Captain John Powell was the leader in Grenada. Hal Fisher, son of Judge Fisher, was the leader of the Tallahatchie county clan. The Judge and his son lived in that part of Tallahatchie County which became a part of Grenada county in 1870. James M. Taylor was leader at Coffeeville and W. H. Winter led the Pea Ridge den. Tom Garner who lived in Grenada during the reconstruction years, related that the Grenada den was organized by seven men in a bank located directly over a barber shop. This would have been either the Lake Brothers Bank or the N. C. Snider Bank. The only serious encounter between klansmen and negroes occured near Grenada when some white officers of the Loyal League were drilling a crowd of about five hundred negroes at a point near Grenada. Thirty Klansmen from Panola county rode down and fired upon the negro group killing two officers and wounding a number of the negroes.

In order to obtain the names of klansmen the Federal officials used the same infiltrating tactics which had been used earlier by the klansmen in order to obtain the names of the members of the Loyal League. Green Dubard is reported to have joined the klan and betrayed the members to the Federal officials. At Coffeeville Bud Green acted in a similar capacity to betray the klansmen of that den. Dubard seems to have escaped physical punishment by the men of the klan, probably because they were not certain that he had betrayed them, but Green was not so fortunate. He went to Jackson to give his information to Federal officials and, on his return to Coffeeville was assasinated. Someone connected with the Federal officials, whose name has never been revealed, tipped off the klan leaders, and many of them left the vicinity for a period. Hal Fisher left Mississippi and made his home in Texas. He remained there, becoming a judge of one of the courts of that state. Many years later his son, a prominent lawyer practicing his profession in Texas, made a visit to relatives living in the northwestern part of Grenada county.

The Klan served to make the negro leaders and their negro following more cautious in their political activities, but it took several years after that organization ceased activity before their political power was neutralized by increased registration of white voters, and bolder white measures to decrease the interest of negroes in participating in political activities. After a few years the enthusiasm of the Federal Government for feeding and housing a vast hoard of idle negroes began to diminish, and the idle negro adults began to realize that they were going to have to look to the white people to provide homes and employment. These employers put pressure on their employees to discourage active participation in politics. On election days men would ride up to the polls twirling ropes which had hangman nooses already tied. On nights before a large negro political rally, men would take an old blacksmith anvil and fill the recess in it with powder. When this was exploded near the meeting place it usually broke up the rally. Another method of discouraging negro voting was called "rushing the voter". When the negro came to the polls he would be greeted in a friendly manner by two white men standing near the door who, on the pretense of directing the voter to the proper place to vote, would take him by the arm, pass the poll box, and shove the potential voter out the back door. After this experience few of the voters thus treated would return for a second try. James Crowder and Crawford Staham were two of the most efficient "rushers" serving at the Grenada voting precinct. Despite all of these discouraging activities on the part of the white people, the continued threat of the use of the still large negro vote to the detriment of the good of the community, continued to harrass the minds of the white leaders until the adoption of the Mississippi Constitution of 1890 with its poll tax and educational provisions. Left alone, the negro interest in voting would have been relatively small, but unscrupulous white men, both native and newcomers, did not scruple to use the negro vote for their personal advantage.

An editorial in the Grenada Sentinel of October 29, 1881, is a good example of the appeal which was made to the negroes to realize that their best interest would be served by alignment with native whites. That editorial reads: "The colored men of Grenada county are not fools, and at this particular crisis, are not going to be gulled into a wicked opposition to the Democratic-Conservative party to gratify the wishes of a few men for the sake of office. These men, if elected could be of little service to them, and they know it. They are every year becoming sensible of their dependence on their white friends. They know that next year will be a hard year, and that hundreds of them will be severely pinched, even for the necessities of life. To whom can they look but to their white friends for support? Who will furnish the meat and bread they will need, but the very men they are called upon to vote against in the coming election? The white people of Grenada county are the best friends the colored people have, and are always willing to help the honest, industrious and respectful of their color. The white people own the bulk of the property of the county. They pay taxes to educate the colored people's children. They wish to see them thrifty, good citizens, and will give the helping hand at all times. Can it be possible the colored people will vote a ticket hostile to the interest of their white friends. They are not so blind to their own interests. We will not believe it. We shall see."

In the Democratic primary in 1881 the Grenada county Democrats had nominated Dr. William McSwine their candidate for the Legislature, and Captain R. N. Hall as candidate for the office of Sheriff. J. J. Williams had been the previous Democratic representative in the Legislature but lost out to Dr. McSwine in the primary. Mr. Williams was an employee of the Grenada Sentinel. The owner and publisher of the paper was a young man of twenty six years of age by the name of John W. Buckhahan who purchased the paper just three months before the Yellow Fever Epidemic of 1878. Being very busy in running the business end of the publishing business, young Buchanan had employed Williams and gave him the important sounding title of "Senior Editor". Buchanan was a staunch Democrat, and had no patience with any native white men who voted Republican or independent tickets. Williams, making the political philosophy of his employer his own editorial policy, wrote strongly worded condemnations of any native white men who did not support the Democratic ticket. After his primary defeat by Dr. McSwine he wrote, relative to his victorious opponent: "Our nominee for the legislature, Dr. William McSwine, is a man in whose honor and capacity, the people can trust. Having been here from boyhood, no man has a better social, and none a finer political record. We do not hesitate to say that the interests of the county will suffer no detriment by want of his watchfulness or lack of ability, and that he will be elected is a foregone conclusion. "Rally round the flag boys!"

In the next issue of the paper Williams printed his own announcement as an independent candidate for the Legislature. On the same ticket was M. K. Mister as a candidate for Sheriff. After stating his qualifications for the office Mr. Williams continued in this manner: "It is well known that the small pay of $400 for a legislative term would have been a wanton waste in his (McSmine's superabundant coffers, so far as his necessities were concerned, while in mine it would be a welcome treasure, enabling me to stem the desolate winter now portending, in feeding and clothing the dependent and little ones that nestle like fledging birds in my affections). For this sum I can pay the state and county in honest, intelligent labor, and thus feel the pride and dignity of a man who has earned his money by considerations of value. While this is not, and never should be a qualification for office, all other things being equal in men asking public favor, it should never be recklessly ignored." Upon the publication of this letter by Williams, Editor Buchahan dismissed the former as an employee of the Sentinel. This dismissal led to a dispute between the two men, Williams claiming that he had resigned, and Buchanan contending that Williams turned in his letter of resignation after he had been informed that he had been fired. Someone inquired of Williams why he had written such vigorous Democratic editorials if he believed in the platform of the Independent party and he answered "for five dollars a week". Buchahan retorted that if a man could be bought to go against his political principles for five dollars a week he would prove to be a bad risk as a member of the Legislature. Five dollars per week seems a very small sum, even in the hard times of those days, as pay for a newspaper man. This leads to the presumption that Williams was a parttime employee, probably just writing some of the editorials. After this episode the Sentinel listed Buchahan as editor, as well as owner and publisher. Buchahan's parting shot at Williams was to pring the letter which has been referred to above and to comment as follows: "If the above does not show Col. Williams to be the most utter inconsistent man on earth, what in the name of God does it show? Col., may the devil hereafter take a likening to you, for we can assure you that a large majority of the voters of Grenada county never will."

In this general election of 1881 the Democratic Party elected its state ticket of State Office candidates. The ticket was headed by Robert Lowery who took over the Governor's office in January of 1882. In Grenada county the Democratic candidates were victorious. Hall was elected Sheriff by a majority of 310, while Dr. McSwine won by a majority of 297. This victory for the Demcratic party completed the destruction of the Republican party as a factor in Mississippi politics for many years to come. That destruction had begun with the election of Governor Stone in 1876 in an election in which many of the Republican incumbents were defeated in their bid for re-election. Editor Buchahan was elated over the results of the election, and he expressed his feeling in these words: "Never was a style of organization more complete. Every county in the state was thoroughly canvassed, and the watchword was opposition to Democracy. Here the Greenbackers, the Independents, the Soreheads, and the old Radical himself, perhaps with the brow of Egypt, but certainly not Helen's beauty, met and mingled and kissed and swore to be true in opposition to Democracy. But, in the election of Tuesday last, this enemy, the unterrified Democracy met, as it has met in former years, the Radical hordes and scattered them like chaffe in the wind. We have met the enemy on the strongest ground they could take. We have come off conquerors. The field is fairly won. The State has escaped a second captivity". The happy editor could not foresee that less than eighty five years later his beloved State, along with sister states, would be re-fighting the same battle against a Federal Government as arbitrary as the one which fastened the first reconstruction on Mississippi.

Chapter IX

The Yellow Fever Epidemic of 1878

The Minutes of the Board of Supervisors of Grenada County show that on October 7, 1878, the following entry was made by the Clerk of the Board: "Because of Yellow fever at the Courthouse the Board met at the Bew Springs school house." This seems to be the earliest official public record which has reference to the most tragic period of the existence of Grenada. That period lasted a little over three months, and threatened to wipe out the majority of the people living in the stricken town. The period, of course, was the time which is known as the "The Yellow Fever Edidemic". The type of fever prevalent in Grenada during this period was of the most malignant form and no medical remedy seemed to be effective against the disease. In the course of the epidemic, about eighty per cent of the people who remained in the town after the outbreak of the fever contracted the disease. Accounts as to the number of deaths resulting from the epidemic vary, but none of the accounts attribute less than three hundred and sixty three deaths as the toll of the epidemic.

The disease struck without warning. The Minutes of the Board of Supervisors for the August meeting show no apprehension relative to an epidemic. In less than a week after the Board met the disease struck, resulting in panic, not only in Grenada, but in other towns up and down the railroad. Memphis, having experienced an epidemic a few years earlier, was very much concerned because of apprehension that the disease might spread to that city, and because, having experienced the devistating effects of a similar epidemic, the people of the city wanted to render aid to the stricken people of Grenada. We learn from various letters, receipts, vouchers for expenditures and orders for payment of services rendered the fever victims, which records were made available by Miss Robbie Doak, that August 9th was the date where it first became apparent that there were cases of fever in Grenada. The papers made available by Miss Doak were preserved by the Reverend McCracken, Rector of All Saints Episcopal Church. Mr. McCracken was a member of a "Sub-Relief Committee." We shall have occasion to discuss the work of this committee. The full fury of the epidemic had run its course by the end of October, but there were still some cases of the fever in November. So far as we have been able to ascertain, there is no record on the Minutes of the City Government relating to the outbreak and course of the epidemic. This is understandable when we realize that the town government was practically non existent during the epidemic. The Mayor, Dr. J. L. Milton, was one of the early victims of the disease. Other town officials, along with many other heads of families, left the town to seek some place of refuge for their families. The only possible town official referred to in the papers mentioned heretofore was Sam Ladd who served as Town Marshall during the epidemic. We are not certain if he was the elected Marshall, or if he was merely an appointee of the Relief Committee which had general direction of the relief efforts made to render assistance to the victims of the disease. We are inclined to believe that Mr. Ladd had been elected to his position, and that he was the only representative of the Town Government present during the early days of the epidemic. He had charge of hiring men to do police and "watch" duties, as well as of employing grave diggers. He turned in to the proper officials of the relief committee bills for at least thirty nine full days of grave digging, as well as other bills for shorter hours of service. These bills, or vouchers, were made out to a number of different men who received two dollars per day for their service.

The first case of the dread disease must have begun developing in late July, or very early in Auguest since rumors began to reach Memphis early in August about the presence of the disease in Grenada. The Memphis Board of Health sent Dr. R. F. Brown, Secretary of the Board, to Grenada to ascertain if the rumors were justified in fact. The Doctor reported back to Memphis that the fever did exist in Grenada, and that it was in its most malignant form. Dr. Brown reached Grenada August 9th, and it is possible that it was he who first identified the disease. It will be remembered that old accounts of the epidemic report that the first death from the disease occured on the same day that Dr. Brown came to Grenada. Help came pouring into the stricken town from various sources. The first help to arrive came from the Howard's Association. That association grew out of the organization of a group of young men in New Orleans who, in 1853, banded together to give help to people of that city who were suffering from yellow fever. The organization continued to grow, with its main objective being to give relief to victims of the fever which usually broke out at some place in each summer season. Relief to victims of such a terrible disease struck a responsive chord in the hearts of many generous people, not only in the South, where the disease was more prevalent, but throughout the whole nation. These people made such generous financial contributions to the Howard's Association that it was usually well supplied with funds and able to send immediate relief to stricken areas. The name of the association was chosen as a tribute to John Howard, the great English humanitarian. After the Epidemic, which Memphis suffered in 1867, a chapter of the Howard's was established in that city. It was from this chapter that immediate help came. On Sunday, August 11th, General W. G. Smith, Vice President of the Memphis chapter received the news of the outbreak of the fever in Grenada. He called together several members of the chapter and they decided that help should be sent at once. By seven o'clock P. M. of the same day experienced nurses had been assembled; equipment and supplies provided and a special train supplied by the Mississippi & Tennessee Railraod, stood ready to start for Grenada. Colonel B. P. Anderson, another officer of the Memphis branch of the Howard's Association, joined General Smith before the train left Memphis. The train arrived at Grenada about midnight. Both of these leaders were fated to contract the disease. Mr. Smith was returned to Memphis and eventually recovered. Col. Anderson died a few days after he went on duty in the stricken town.

The party from Memphis was housed for the night in the Chamberlain House, then the best hotel in Grenada. It was located just east of the present railroad station of the I. C. Railroad. It was located on railroad property, but was operated at the time by Dr. P. W. Peeples and J. C. Branum. The building had been erected by a Mr. Chamberlain who had a thirteen year lease from the railroad to operate the hotel, with the provision that, if services were unsatisfactory, the railroad company could terminate the lease by paying the value of the building. This lease had been transferred to the men who were operating the hotel at the time of the epidemic. The building had a waiting room for railroad passangers and a telegraph office. It is probable that it also had a ticket office. Since passengers had to transfer from the Mississippi Central (later the I. C.) trains to make connection with the Mississippi and Tennessee lines it was desirable that a hotel be established near the railroad. A similar hotel, operating under lease from the railroad existed for a long time at Holly Springs, where the Frisco Railroad intersects the I. C. Railroad. The Chamberlain House became the headquarters for the members of the relief party sent in from Memphis.

When the Memphis party reached Grenada, General Smith and Colonel Anderson conferred with a number of Grenada citizens at the hotel, and then went to the town square where they had another meeting with citizens. From these two conferences the Memphis leaders learned of the panic which existed among the people to the extent that most people, who were able to do so, had already left town, or were in the process of doing so. Many of these refugees were going to visit relatives in other parts of the state. Some of them went to the Gibbs Springs resort about a mile and one half southwest of town. This was a rustic summer resort which had a few cabins and a central cookhouse and dining hall. Others found a place of reguge on the Montevello plantation of Oscar Bledsoe which was located just west of the town of Grenada. Nurses were placed on duty the night they arrived, and the following day General Smith sent telegrams to New Orleans, Mobile and Memphis for doctors and nurses who had experience in attending yellow fever patients. The Howard Association Branches from these three cities sent twenty one nurses in answer to the call. Other organizations began to help. The Masonic order sent in four nurses and the Odd Fellows sent three. As the need for help of all kinds was made known to the nation, help in the form of money, equipment and supplies came from many parts of the country. A sum of money was sent from Liverpool, England. The Howard's of Mobile sent Dr. J. H. Beatty, and from New Orleans the Howard's sent Doctors W. R. Mandeville and H. A. Veasy, Dr. Ringold was the county health officer. Dr. Gillispie and Dr. Capmbell were two local doctors who joined Dr. Ringold and the out of town doctors in attending the yellow fever patients. It is possible that there were other local doctors serving but we have found no confirmation of the fact. From a communication which Rev. McCracken received relative to money being sent to care for the children of Dr. May it is possible that a doctor of that name may have served and lost his life during the course of the epidemic. We do know that both Dr. Ringold and Dr. Gillispie died of the disease. Among the papers preserved by Rev. McCracken there is, in beautiful handwriting a schedule of the assignment of the available doctors to specified sections of the town. This schedule, written on stationary of the Chamberlain House, made the following listed assignment of doctors: Dr. Beatty-All north and west of Dr. Hughes Residence. (We know that this man was a druggist, and it is possible that he was as M. D., although it was a frequent practice of the time to apply the courtesy title "Doctor" to druggists); Dr. Ringold-All south of General Wathall's and east of Main street; Dr. Veazie-All west of Line street between Dr. Hughes and the Baptist Church; Dr. Wallace-From Public Square East to the Railroad and north to the River; Dr. Warren Stowe-All between Line and Main streets; Dr. C. H. Stowe-All east of Main street between Depot street and the street south of the College. There were other doctors, including Dr. Mandville, serving during the epidemic but we do not know their assignments. The list given above was drawn up soon after the arrival of the relief train from Memphis, and may have been changed later. Rev. W. C. McCracken, Rector of All Saints Episcopal Church, evidently had considerable to do with the assignments set out above. In a letter to Rev. McCracken, dated March 12, 1881, during the course of a controversy between Rev. McCracken and members of the Relief Committee (John Powell, Robert Mullin and Judge Watson), relative to a misunderstanding which arose between the General Relief Committee and a Sub-Relief Committee composed of Rev. McCracken, A. Weigart and Dr. Campbell, Thomas J. Rogan who identifies himself as "Officer of the Howards Association 1878", Mr. Rogan writes: "It (the assignment of doctors) was done after the meeting on the square, held I believe, in a Dentist's office, in which we agreed on the plan of districts. Mr. Coan and I worked in our respective districts one day only. Col. Anderson was taken sick on the 18th of August; Mr. Coan a few days later. All the general visiting work done after that date was preformed by you solely and alone. I know it to be a fact that you walked over the town carrying baskets and bundles containing medicine for the sick for four consecutive days (possibly a week or more) before you were furnished a horse and buggy with which to continue your charitable and distinguished service. My services after the sickness of Anderson were confined exclusively to the office." From this letter we assume that the districts assigned doctors had volunteer helpers like Rev. McCracken who rendered services other than medical to the sick people of those districts.

Soon after the arrival of the Howard Association Relief Train the people still remaining in Grenada, by some method not on record, selected John Powell, Robert Mullin and Thomas Walton to act as a Relief Committee, which committee was to have general supervision of the several different types of relief which were being given to the people of the town. The first official record, now in existence, of any action on the part of that Committee is found in a letter from members of the Committee to General Smith and Col. Anderson (we do not know if the titles were military titles of officers in the Howard's Association, or merely the courtesy titles freely used at the time) in which it is stated that a rumor was prevalent that these two leaders might be re-called to Memphis. The letter contained an urgent plea that these two men remain in Grenada to direct the relief efforts of the Howards Association. The letter was dated August 15, 1878, and signed by John Powell and Robert Mullin. For some reason Judge Walton is not mentioned in any of the actions taken by the Relief Committee. In answer to this appeal the Two Howard Officers agreed to remain in Grenada, conditioned upon the full co-operation of the people of the town who were not afflicted with the fever. Three days after this agreement to remain in Grenada, Col. Anderson was down with the fever and dead within a few days; Gen. Smith soon fell a victim to the fever and rendered incapable of directing relief work. It is very probable that this unfortunate removal of the two leading officials in the Howards in Grenada, contributed, in large measure, to the unfortunate misunderstandings which were to arise between the members of the General Relief Committee and the Sub-Relief Committee. The Sub-Relief Committee was organized on September 9, 1878, about three weeks after the organization of the General Relief Committee. Rev. McCracken left this record of the organization meeting: "At a meeting of the convalesent citizens of Grenada to take action concerning the relief of their destitute fellow citizens the following resolution was offered and adopted. On motion of Rev. McCracken the President of the meeting, Col. Townsend, was requested to appoint a committee of three to act as a Sub. Committee in conjunction with the Relief Committee of Mullins and Powell. The President of the meeting appointed as said Sub-Committee W. McCracken, Doctor Campbell and A. S. Weigart." It will be noted that in its reference to the General Committee Mr. Watson is not named. Something, perhaps illness or death, seems to have prevented him from taking any active part in the relief efforts. Members of both committees were sincere men who wanted to serve their town. The fact that they were selected in such a time of stress is indicative of the regard in which they were held by their fellow citizens. John Powell was interested in several local businesses as well as being an important member of the New Orleans Cotton Firm of Chaffee & Powell. An honored Civil War soldier, he had recouped his war business lossess and was quite well-to-do at the time when he was selected on the Relief Committee. Robert Mullin, born in Belfast, Ireland, had come to this country as a young man. He settled briefly in Kentucky, and about 1835 came into Mississippi and went in business in the town of Troy. He prospered in his business, and just before the Civil War, he built a beautiful house on his plantation about four miles northwest of Grenada. That house is still in existence. The war ruined his dream of retiring from business and becoming a large scale planter. Returning from the war, he came to Grenada and re-entered business, and became prosperous again. Of the Sub-Relief Committee, we know Rev. McCracken to have been an energetic and compassionate, if somewhat contentious, pastor and friend to the people left destitute by the ravages of the epidemic. Dr. Campbell served as the director of the hospital which was set up in the County Court House, and which served both white and colored patients. The courthouse, at the time of the epidemic, was an old store building located just east of the present site of the Grenada Theater, which building had been purchased soon after Grenada became a county in 1870. A. S. Weigart was an old Union soldier who had come to Grenada in the years following the Civil War. He was a blacksmith by trade and a Republican in politics. He was appointed Post Master at Grenada in 1904.

The differences between the two committees arose over the proper method of expenditure of relief funds. In their endeavor to aid the suffering people in Grenada, people were in some confusion as to the proper agencies through which to channel their aid. The Howard Association of Memphis had made available generous financial relief which could be expended only by the approval of the General Relief Committee. This committee was supposed to adhere strictly to the Howard regulations as to how these funds could be expended. Since the General Relief Committee had been formed during the early days of the epidemic, before the distress of the people of Grenada had been widely publicised, very few people outside of Grenada knew about the existence of this committee. On the other hand, by the time the Sub-Relief Committee was organized, people all over the nation knew about the desperate situation in Grenada. Organization of the Sub-Relief Committee, with Rev. McCracken named as chairman, got nation-wide publicity. It was, therefore, a very natural occurence that much of the money and other forms of relief should have been directed to Mr. McCracken. The first evidence of a possible clash between the two committees came in an incident occuring at Torrence, a small railroad stop a few miles north of Grenada. Because of the epidemic, trains did not stop at Grenada, going through the town with all windows closed. Money and supplies sent by rail were unloaded at Torrence. Money came by mail and express. John Powell was in Torrence and learned that the express agent there had a sum of money directed to Rev. McCracken. Mr. Powell offered to take the money to Grenada. Before he had left Torrence the express agent received a telegram from Rev. McCracken which read as follows: "Please do not deliver any money or supplies sent to me except to me, or to persons authorized by me to receive the same." The agent then wrote Rev. McCracken as follows: "Dear Sir: Your telegram of the twenty first received and would say there has been none of the packages addressed to you individually delivered to any person. Captain Powell called upon me for some packages addressed to you as Chairman of the Sub-Relief Committee, saying that he was Chairman of the General Relief Committee and was going to Grenada and would take them in and turn them over. I did this thinking the money was needed and that Captain Powell was a responsible person and that it would be alright. After receiving your telegram I showed it to him, whereupon he returned the package to me saying that he did not want to cause any trouble about it. They are here now ready for delivery at any time you wish them. Hoping that this is satisfactory I remain yours respectfully, D. Ewing, Acting Agent."

The next disagreement came over the refusal of the General Relief Committee to approve some bills against Howard Association Relief funds for nursing services which had been sent in by the Sub-Relief Committee. In explanation of this failure to approve the bills a letter addressed to Rev. McCracken, and signed by John Powell and Robert Mullin, reads as follows: "In regard to the claim for nursing Mrs. Sherman we have to state that in the commencement of our work, it was agreed by Colonels Butler and Anderson (deceased) then directing, that no nurses were to be paid only on doctors certificates, and that the sick who are able, are to pay their own nurses. You can see that a great many claims will be pushing upon us and on that account we think it important to adhere for the present at least to instructions. When all are paid and there be money over, we can then get instructions again from proper authorities and pay all doubtful claims if it is advisable." The claim which caused this disagreement reads as follows: "This certifies that Henry Young (colored) nursed faithfully Mrs. Ed Sherman for twenty five days at $2.00 per day for twenty five days $50.00." It was signed by E. T. Sherman. The following notations were a part of the bill: "Dr. Gillispie attending physican dead, and we are unable to get his signature, and approved by Rev. McCracken. If Mr. John Powell advises payment I will pay. Signed: W. C. McCracken." It would seem that, among his other duties, Rev. McCracken had authority, after proper approval of the General Relief Committee, to make payment on all claims submitted. The Rector stated that the reason that he would not allow anyone other than himself, or his authorized representatives, to receive funds directed to him as Chairman of the Sub-Relief Committee, was that he was responsible for making a proper account of all such funds. So far as we have been able to determine the only records still existing relative to disbursment of relief funds are the rather voluminous files of received bills and letters to and from members of the Relief Committee. These receipted bills are for all sorts of things; food, medicine, nursing, tons of ice, coffins, police duty, night-watching, grave digging, telegraph charges and a host of other items.

Rev. McCracken not only had to keep up with all expenditures from the regular relief funds, but he was also entrusted with, and authorized to spend, funds provided by church and fraternal organizations for the benefit of their members who were sick or destitute. His responsibility for church funds is indicated by two letters to him from Bank officials of the N. O. Canal and Banking Company. One dated September seventh reads: "Yours of the 5th instance with checks amounting to $475.18 (four hundred and seventy five and 18 one hundredths dollars) which we will collect and place to credit of your church as directed. I trust you and your family will escape. Kind regards to your wife. My children are at Mississippi City, and all well." The second letter reads: "I am in receipt of your favor of the 4th instant enclosing two thousand dollars (2,000) currency which I put as directed to the credit of "All Saints Church". Enclosed I send you some blank checks. Rev. McCracken had considerable business with the Masonic Fraternity. Early in September he received the following letter from the Masonic Committee of Newport, Kentucky: "Dear Sir: Enclosed please find fifty dollars ($50.00) being an offering from the Masonic Fraternity of Newport, Kentucky to the afflicted sufferers of the South under your jurisdiction. Trusting that our mite, like the widow's, may do some good, and hoping to hear that it has reached its destination, I am yours respectfully, John J. Raipe, Chairman of Masonic Committee". In late September the Rector received a letter from the Secretary of the Grand Lodge of Mississippi which letter is quoted in part: "My Dear Sir and Brother: I am in receipt of your estemed favor of 25th, giving me the information that I wanted about the families of our brethren, Masons and Odd Fellows. I note your statement that 'so many leave as soon as they are strong enough, the call for help will come a little later'. Anticipating this I shall reserve funds for their benefit. To relieve the necessities of those within your reach, I send you $500.00 by today's express. Please hand Mrs. J. C. Ayres $200.00; reserve $100.00 for the care of Dr. May's children and expend it in their behalf as you may deem best, until they can further be provided for. If Brother Coffman's children are within reach expend $50.00 for them. I have sent Mrs. McCampbell $150.00, and will help the families of other ministers if you will let me know their necessities and how to reach them. I send $150.00 for your own use-having done the same for ministers in Port Gibson and Vicksburg. This calamity is especially hard on ministers, whose congregations are scattered or dead, and who have no resources. I fear that we are in for an epidemic here. Have had only two cases-both died. This morning one of my printers has black vomit." The letter is signed by J. L. Power amd mailed from Jackson, Mississippi.

While Rev. McCracken was dealing with financial matters connected with the epidemic A. J. Weigart was in charge of the commissary, located near the railroad station, in which food and other supplies had been accumulated through gifts and donations. It was from this place that tons of ice, ordered from a town in Illinois, was distributed to the fever victims. Vinegar was distributed as a possible disinfectant, and hundreds of paper bags, presumably for use as the victim reached the "black vomit" stage of the disease. This was also the distribution point for coffins for the dead. Mr. Weigart was a very busy man and needed much help as evidenced by numerous orders he signed for payment of people who worked with him. Dr. Campbell, the third member of the Sub-Relief Committee, was busy at the hospital which was filled to overflowing. He requisitioned beef, ice, various drugs, bedding, sheets and towels. There can be no doubt that the three members of the Sub-Relief Committee rendered inestimable service to the fever victims of the town, but, in their earnest efforts to render aid, they seem sometimes to have gone beyond the limits of their authority as set out by the General Relief Committee. The members of the General Relief Committee seem to have been overworked and, at times, sick of ills not connected with the yellow fever. A number of letters from John Powell to members of the Sub-Relief Committee indicate that he is unable to contact them in person because of being under the care of a physician. As indicated earlier, Judge Walton seems to have served only very briefly on the committee to which he had been appointed. The headquarters for the General Committee was Lake Brothers Store. Many letters written to the members of the Sub-Committee are dated from that store. Perhaps the lack of personal contact between the members of the two committees was largely responsible for the lack of close co-operation between them. About the middle of September Mr. Powell and Mr. Mullin wrote the members of the Sub-Committee suggesting that henceforth all unsettled claims be settled by the General Relief Committee, since, under existing conditions, there was a possibility that some of the bills might be paid more than once. Soon thereafter the Rev. McCracken tendered his resignation, and an accounting of his stewartship during the time he acted for the committee. A little later came a brief note from A. Weigart announcing his resignation. He gave neither reason, not justification of himself in any way. Dr. Campbell, so far as we can ascertain continued as the surviving member of the Sub-Committee. The worst of the epidemic had passed by the time these resignations occured. Perhaps the resigning members felt that there was no longer a need for their services. Rev. McCracken seems to have felt that he had been badly used, since as late as 1882, he was writing various individuals relative to his activities during the epidemic, and requesting that they confirm his own recollection relative to certain facts stated by Rev. McCracken in his letters to the individuals who received these letters from the Rector. Some of the letters confirmed some of the statements in the letters; other, in their desire to satisfy Rev. McCracken confirmed some statements made by the rector, which we know from other sources, to be incorrect, such inaccuracies probably being due to the confusion of the period of epidemic; other letters regretted that the writer was unable to confirm the Rector's statement. Mr. Rogan, the Howard Association official heretofore quoted, seems to have been very much in sympathy with Rev. McCracken, and knowing very little about the service of people not coming into direct contact with him, was ready to accept accusations against some of these people at their face value. In a letter written in 1882, about four years after the period of the epidemic, he makes this statement: "I do not remember ever having met Mr. Powell. Mr. Mullins I saw once or twice before he 'lit out for the tall timber', where he engaged in the laudable business of trying to embarrass men who were rendering some service to his fellow citizens, by writing notes and telegrams (specimen and copy enclosed) in which he appeared to be morbidly sensitive on the subject of money. Seemed to be afraid of any of the abundant means contributed by a charitable public would be expended for the purposes for which it was contributed, and pursued throughout the whole affair a kind of shuffling policy." This statement by Mr. Rogan does a great injustice to a man who contributed much to the relief efforts rendered to his fellow citizens. We know from a number of letters dated from Lake Brothers Store, and signed by Mr. Mullin, that both he and Mr. Powell spent considerable time in town during the epidemic. Since both these men were in general charge of relief matters in Grenada and vicinity, it was no doubt necessary for them to be in and out of town. At the time of the death of Mr. Mullin, several years after the end of the epidemic, the Grenada Sentinel printed an article relative to the fine services rendered by Mr. Mullin during the course of the epidemic. The account stated that, after Mr. Mullin's death a letter was found among his papers which evidently had been written during the early days of the epidemic. The letter which was printed stated, in substance, that the Relief Committee of Mullin, Powell and Watson, during the Yellow Fever Epidemic of 1878 had, without legal authority, used money from the Lake Brothers to take care of the sick and dying. All such use of money was correctly entered on the Lake Brothers Books. Mr. Mullins requested that if he should lose his life during the epidemic, Mr. Powell and Mr. Watson, if they survived, should not be condemned for the joint action of the Relief Committee, but that the citizens of Grenada who had benefited be reequested to make up the money. Fortunately relief funds soon came in whereby the Lake Brothers funds could be replaced. This letter does not bear out Mr. Rogans' statement that Mr. Mullin had fled town and that he was reluctant to spend available funds. In connection with the funds of Lake Brothers being used in this way, we should explain that at the time of the Epidemic the Lake Brothers had as a part of their business operations, a private bank which served the people of Grenada pretty much as incorporated banks now serve them. The only other bank in Grenada at the time was another private bank operated by N. C. Snider & Son. Both of these banks were to fail within six years after the end of the epidemic. Considerable loans secured by Deeds of Trust on lands, and mortgages on personal property and growing crops, overextended the credit of the banks during a period of bad crops and low prices. In 1883, a little over a year before Mr. Mullin died, the Rev. McCracken severed his connection with his church and at a last service was eulogized for his services during the epidemic. This action seemed to terminate a misunderstanding which must have caused serious concern to all parties concerned, and which would have been entirely forgotten except for the various letters and other papers so carefully preserved by Rev. McCracken.

A letter addressed to R. Mullin, Relief Committee, Torrence, Miss., and signed by J. P. Smith, Secretary H. A. would seem to indicate that Mr. Mullin and Mr. Powell spent considerable time at that place, evidently with the understanding and probable consent of the Howard Association. It will be remembered that since no trains stopped in Grenada to deliver mail and express, it was necessary for members of the Relief Committee to keep in close contact with the Post Office and Express Agent at Torrence. The letter dated, Memphis, Tennessee reads as follows: "Since Col. Anderson's death there is no member of our Association at Grenada. Messrs. Rogan and Coan were sent by us to assist there and are yet there and we are sending them all supplies ordered. You can rely on them. If you need money draw on us. Mr. S. P. Reid, Cashier of M. & P. Bank here, says there is sixty five hundred to your account subject to your draft. We will keep separate account of your expenses and receipts. You should have someone at Grenada to receive contributions sent there. If they were sent here we would keep your account separate."

With so many people dying daily, it became necessary for the Relief Committee to furnish coffins for people who left no surviving relatives able to pay for such expenses. In a letter to Rev. McCracken, Mr. Powell states that Mr. Mullen had made an agreement with a certain firm to furnish coffins at five dollars each. In order to explain the cheapness of such coffins Mr. Powell stated "Of course when it devolved upon our committee to furnish coffins and pay for them in such cases we could only furnish the cheapest, and treat all alike." This letter may have been written in connection with a bill which Mr. McCracken received from A. P. Saunders & Comapany on Sept. 16, 1878. The bill indicated that the company had furnished coffins and hearse service for ten different individuals. They were H. M. Jones, Dr. Ringold, Mrs. Ringold, W. V. Cole, Mrs. W. T. Cole, Mrs. Kettle, Mrs. Mary Huffington, Marion Huffington, Sallie Huffington, and Minnie Huffington. The total bill was for the sum of three hundred seventy five dollars. On two of the itemized statements a penciled note comments "Two much. $35.00." These items had a charge of fifty dollars. Two other items had this notation "Nothing to do with this". On December 10, 1878, almost three months after the date of the first bill, a bill was sent to Rev. McCracken, listing the same items by reducing the charge to $240. The company acknowledged payment by Rev. McCracken. He, before paying the bill, had written in as a part of the transaction: "It is understood that Rev. W. C. McCracken is responsible to A. P. Saunders &Co. for no other coffins ordered by him than the above list. Neither is said Rev. W. C. McCracken responsible for anything else ordered by him during the epidemic than above." It is possible that Rev. McCracken, not understanding the policy of the Relief

Committee, was ordering a better class of coffin for some people than for others, or it may be that the list which he paid for may have been from funds available fraternal or church sources which he could spend for members of families belonging to either his church, or one of the fraternal members. We have confirmed from other sources that most, if not all, the people whose names appeared on the list of coffins for which Rev. McCracken paid were members of his church.

Generally speaking, most of the people involved in the tragic period behaved in a creditable way. Of course there were a few who sought to take advantage of the situation to gain personal advantage, but these cases seem to have been small in comparison with the number of people who went all out to render relief to the fever victims. There were some complaints relative to the nurses sent in to help during the epidemic. It was charged that some of them drank to excess and were negligent in their attention to their patients. This may have been true on a few occasions, but we do know that many of the patients who recovered, and the relatives of patients who did not survive, wrote notes to the relief authorities commending the fine service rendered by various nurses. The pay of five dollars per day was rather small remuneration for nurses who were risking their lives to nurse the epidemic victims. With the daily task of burying the overnight victims reminding everyone of the uncertainity of life, Grenada must have been a gloomy place in which to live. The death of three hundred sixty three people in a period of about eighty five days was a tremendous shock for a town of the size of Grenada. Almost everyone in town had relatives and close friends who were victims of the epidemic. People who had never before thought it necessary to do so now began to make out wills. We will give short excerpts from two of the wills written during this period. The first, by William M. Redding, reads in part: "Last will and testament of William M. Redding - August 8, 1878; I, Wyatt Redding, being of sound mind but sick of yellow fever, do make the following bequests which are my last will and testament." The second will by W. W. Hall reads: "August 25, 1878. In view of the unprecidented fatality of the present epidemic of yellow fever, I deem it proper to make this, my last will and testament." But, despite the fear and anxiety of the time, some people continued to carry on their business. One evidence of this is a statement dated Oct. 18, 1878, sent by Gus Wolfe to Dr. J. H. Campbell. It will be remembered that Dr. Campbell was in charge of the hospital set up in the Courthouse. Mr. Wolfe sends a bill for four bottles of champagne at Two dollars per bottle; one bottle of whiskey at one dollar and fifty cents; and a single order of one bottle of champagne at two dollars. Total bill eleven dollars and fifty cents. This bill was approved by Dr. Campbell, and paid by the relief committee.

The Odd Fellows cemetery, and the old "Yellow Fever" cemetery east of the I. C. Railroad tracks are the last resting places for many of the yellow fever victims. Many of the colored victims were buried in a now abandoned cemetery north of Odd Fellows Cemetery. Although many of the victims were so humble and obscure that they were buried without any sort of permanent marker being erected to mark their resting place, many of the leading citizens of the town and community died during the epidemic, and many of them had lasting markers erected above their graves by relatives or friends. It is unfortunate that conditions were such that we have no record of the names of all the fever victims. Although the list must necessarily remain incomplete, the writer will list hereafter the names of yellow fever victims which names he has verified by grave markers, and from other sources. Dr. Ringold, County Health Officer, Dr. Gillispie, practicing physician; Dr. J. Milton, dentist whose office in 1870 served as the first meeting place of the Board of Supervisors (Dr. Milton being a member) when the county was created, and also as the place where on August 11, 1878, a meeting was held between Members of the Howards Association and Grenada Citizens to work out relief plans; Captain Saxton S. Angevihe, a well liked Civil War soldier; Oliver Perry Sanders, about whom we have no information; Boyd M. Doak, Father of Robert Doak who founded Doak

Hardware Company; Robert Stevenson whose grave marker has this bit of information: "Born in Airshire, Scotland"; Ralph Coffman, who began his business career in 1835 when he became associated with Joseph Coffman in a mercantile business in the town of Pittsburg. He soon bought out Joseph Coffman who moved to Arkansas. Ralph Coffman was a respected citizen and influential business man until the time of his death; Eliza S. Coffman, wife of Ralph died just four days before her husband; Rev. Hiram T. Haddick was the pastor of the Grenada Baptist Church. He was out of town when the epidemic broke out, but returned, against the advice of members of his church, to minister to the sick members of his flock until he became a victim of the deadly disease; Lida R. Hughes, probably the sister of Mrs. Ralph Coffman; Dr. William Wood Hall, who had written his will in anticipation of possible death during the epidemic, and whose tomb is marked with the tribute "Died at his post of duty"; Mary Koen Hall, wife of W. W. Hall; James G. Hall, one of the original members of the Baptist Church of Grenada, and one of the early pastors of the church. Mr. Hall earned his living from farming and other activities, and preached for no compensation; Harriet J. McLean, member of a prominent Grenada family which once owned much city property including the lot on which the present Grenada County Courthouse is located; J. S. Payne, about whom we have no information; Alice Walters, wife of an early editor of the GRENADA SENTINEL; wife and son of J. G. Stokes; Dr. W. E. Hughes, druggist, and possibly an M. D. of whom it is related on his tomb, "Died at his post of duty"; Mary Hughes, wife of Dr. Hughes; Jane, wife of W. E. Long, about whom we have no information; Clara Hart, wife of Dr. Jacob Snider who had died several years earlier. The Snider family first settled in Coffeeville and came to Grenada preceding the Civil War where they set up a private banking company; and finally there is the marker which simply states this to be the resting place of "Fenner Hugo, born in Germany, died of yellow fever in Grenada Miss. Sept. 1, 1878, age 51 years.

Although the epidemic was over by late fall of 1878, it had created an atmosphere of fear among the surviving population to the extent, that for several years after the epidemic of 1878, unusual precautions were taken to isolate Grenada from any area in which there was an outbreak of the fever. In 1897 a severe epidemic of the fever occurred in Ocean Springs, and Grenada County and City Officials began to take measures which they hoped would avert another epidemic in the area. One newspaper report of the time states: "Grenada is not at home to visitors at Present; call again". The Board of Supervisors passed an order making it a tresspass for any stranger to come into the county unless that stranger could produce proof of not having been in or near any fever infested area. In commending the Board for this action Editor J. W. Buchanan, of the GRENADA SENTINEL, observed: "If heroic efforts and a strict quaranteen will keep the 'dengue' fever from Grenada it will never get here."

Evidently people who had not experienced the horror of yellow fever could not understand the precautions taken by Grenada, which precautions included refusal to allow trains to discharge and take on passengers. This feeling was reflected in another comment in the GRENADA SENTINEL: "There are numerous cases of "sour grapes" reported of people who didn't want to stop at Grenada anyway. Again we have this report from the SENTINEL: "Unless the yellow fever news takes a decidedly more favorable turn for the better, it is more than likely that the Public Schools of Grenada will be temporarily suspended. The following report would seem to indicate that restrictions relative to trains discharging passengers had been slightly modified: "Mr. W. P. Ferguson and Mr. A. S. Bell are the inspecting officers for Grenada, and it takes a smooth one to escape their vigilance. They meet every train and examine all who get off here". Mr. Ferguson was to pay for his close attention to railroad passengers. A report came to Grenada of the death of a railroad conductor who had stopped off at Grenada. The cause of the death of the railroad employee was diagnosed as yellow fever. Mr. Ferguson and other individuals who had been around the railroad station, and had come in contact with the unfortunate conductor, were ordered to the quaranteen station two miles outside of Grenada to remain there for a period of ten days. Reported outbreaks of the fever in Oxford and Taylor led to an order by the Board of Aldermen that no members of a train crew were to leave trains at Grenada, and all trains passing through the corporate limits of Grenada should do so with all windows closed. Soon the State Board of Health ordered all railroad traffic stopped between Grenada and Holly Springs. Company K, a Grenada company of volunteers who had served in the Spanish-American war was being transported back home, and had to go into quaranteen near Elliott for a number of days. All approaches to town were guarded. The SENTINEL had the following observations: "All ministers of the city were detailed for guard duty last Monday and every one of them responded promptly", and "If you see numerous small holes punched in your mail it is an indication that the same has been fumigated." Another report by the above mentioned paper reads: "No sickness to speak of in Grenada except sudden rheumatic pains that strike a man when he sees his name posted for guard duty. While a number of Grenada's good citizens have taken to the woods during the yellow fever scare, most of them are women and children who were sent away by husbands and fathers who believe in taking no chances. Consequently there has been no noticeable decrease in population. Very different is the case at Jackson, the State Capital, for it presents the appearance of a deserted city. Mr. E. S. Wilson writes to his paper THE NEW ORLEANS PICAYUNE, that on a drive down the most prominent residential street in Jackson, at noon on Wednesday he did not see a single white face. All the residences are closed and left in charge of servants. A number of stores are also closed. Mr. A. C. Lee collected $77.00 for yellow fever sufferers at Biloxi. People in Hardy subscribe $19.50 for the same purpose." The SENTINEL also printed the following diagnosis of yellow fever: "First stage, chills and fever; second stage, dengue; third stage, suspicious ease; fourth stage, suspicion emphasixed; fifth stage, death from yellow fever." Perhaps this somewhat frivolous "diagnosis" indicated the frustration of a people who had painful memories of a disease which, at that time, was so mysterious that no one knew its cause or any effective remedy for it. The passage of time, and scientific research, have resulted in the discovery and the cause of the disease, and effective public health service has all but eradicated the disease in our country, so that most residents of present day Grenada have little idea of the devastating effect of the Epidemic of 1878. In order to give an idea of the great apprehension which the outbreak of the epidemic brought to the people of the community we quote hereafter the letter, already referred to, which Robert Mullin had written to General Walthall explaining the use of certain funds of the Lake Brothers Bank. This letter was written to be delivered to the General if both Powell and Mullin should fail to survive the epidemic. It was never delivered to General Walthall, and was found years later among the papers of Banker J. W. Griffis, son-in-law of Mr. Mullin. The letter reads: "Gen. E. C. Walthall: The chances are that we shall never meet again. When all things get quite I request that you will have the citizens hold us harmless in any private endorsments or guarantees that we (John Powell, Thomas Watson and myself) have given to receive money that was directed to other parties. You will see from Lake Brothers books that we have applied the funds correctly, but, in my opinion, not according to the law. Get the citizens to hold a meeting, examine our vouchers and, if paid out morally right, then have the citizens foot the bill. We had no time to act carefully. People dying, laborers and nurses coming for their pay every night, and everything in confusion. All of Gus Lake's family down; John Powell's brother sick, and all the writing and talking fell on Walton. His office is our headquarters. Powell and myself have been there as much as we could, but that not a great deal at first, so Walton had to receive and check money out without our presence, and I here say that Judge Walton deserves the everlasting thanks of all citizens of every class. He is entitled to more thanks than Powell and myself both, for he had a buggy and horse here and in six hours could have been out of danger, and I here request that in case of Powell's and my death that you will insist that the people shall show by their acts that they appreciate Walton's noble work. He has risked his life, given his money and name without limit. He, Powell and myself may all be dead when you get this, but I select you, from what I think is the right grit, to have us made whole for any outside liabilities that we may have laid ourselves liable for, and have the citizens pay it back so far as you see and think right. The masses will not look at this fairly, but I believe you will. We have kept receipts and vouchers so far, but should we all die there is no one to take hold and fill our places. All the best people are gone, sick or dead. The bank check we give will show what we paid out, and the book account will show what we have received. If Walton is taken off I cannot tell what to do for a man to write, and I have to do a great deal of talking and arranging, and as you know I am a poor scribe at best. If there is any deficiency in the account have the citizens to protect Walton whether he lives or dies, if you even let Powell and myself suffer. I sincerely believe that this will be right. If we all die anyone that gets possession of this letter will please hand it over to some good citizen that will act and carry out this request. If Walton lives I have no fears about the right thing being done. The chances are that none of us will live through. Later: Night, August 24, 1878, Judge Walton, poor fellow, is down. He had done his work up to this time nobly. Is very ill now, and is still trying to advise and assist, but his symptons are bad, and I fear he is gone. I want him to have all the credit that it is possible for us to give him, and it cannot be too much." This letter which, because of the survival of Mullins, was never delivered to General Walthall, was found in 1885, after the death of Mullins, and printed in the Grenada Sentinel. I think that one reason for Mr. Mullin's insistance on all due credit being given to Judge Walton was that the judge was not very popular with his fellow townsmen. He was one of those men who had been old line Whigs and who, after the destruction of that party, had joined the Republicans rather than the Democrats. Some of these men were rewarded with public office during the Reconstruction Era, and it is possible that Judge Walton had received such an appointment. In an issue of the Grenada Sentinel, published soon after their termination of the epidemic, Judge Walton is listed among the dead. Both Mullins and Powell survived to make personal explanation of their actions, but the letter of Mullins to General Walthall is the only written evidence which we have today of the heroic and unselfish service of Judge Walton. It also serves to answer the question raised earlier in this paper as to why Walton took no part in the controversy with Rector McCracken. His death, so early in the epidemic, left the burden of the General Relief Committee upon Mullin and Powell. An issue of the Grenada Sentinel published soon after the termination of the epidemic listed the following white people who died during the epidemic.

Mrs. Fields	Mrs. H. S. Derrick	Samuel Kendall
Harry Fields	Mrs. M. Huffington	Sammie Marshall
Thomas Fields	Miss S. Huffington	John P. Eason
Kattie Shephard	Miss M. Huffington	G. W. Campbell
Mrs. Wilson	Miss M. Lacock	Frank Mitchell
Mrs. Davidson	Miss Alice Lacock	Dr. Walfork
Mrs. Irene Bakewed	Miss Addie Bishop	Fred Finner
Mrs. Doak	Miss Belle Bishop	R. S. Bowles
Miss Lula Doak	Mrs. J. M. Bishop	Mrs. Scanlin
W. F. Beauchamp	Mrs. E. Shankle	Mrs. Dr. Ringold
J. W. Beauchamp	Pete Kirby	Mrs. McDonald
Mrs. McMillan	Mrs. Pete Kirby	Lunwig Hummel
Mr. McMillan	Mrs. McLean	Cawein S. Child
Mrs. L. French	Miss Lula McLean	Mr. Shaw
T. E. Peacock	De. C. Bristol	Mrs. Bailey
Miss Mammie Peacock	Miss Emma Bristol	Charles Yates
Mr. DeJarnett	M. Conley	Rev. Haddick
George Cromwell	Miss Kate Clark	Sallie DeJarnett

George Cromwell
John Cromwell
Miss Marie Mole
George W. Lake
Mrs. Lake
Miss Annie Lake
Delia Lake
Mrs. Sadler
Miss Rosa Sadler
Walter Sadler
John E. Sadler
Robert Sadler
A. W. Ayres
W. I. Ayres
Miss Jennie Ayres
Miss Lizzie Ayres
E. W. Hughes
Mrs. Hughes
Mrs. J. E. Hughes
Ralph Coffman
Mrs. Coffman
Charles Coffman
Mrs. Charles Coffman
Miss Kate Coffman
Price Carl
Miss Ella Carl
German Carpenter
Dr. J. R. Wilkins
Mrs. R. Irwin
Robert A. Young
Mrs. Young
Miss Lulla Kendrick
Bob Mayhew
S. S. Abgevine
Miss M. Angevine
Jacob Pottevent
Mrs. Pottevent
Miss M. Pottevent
Wyatt M. Redding
Tom R. Marshall
Miss Sallie Leidy
Mrs. Kettle and child
Charles Hall
Alex Rafalsky
Mrs. J. A. Morrison
Dr. Gillespie
R. A. Irwin
J. W. Knox
Thomas Powell
Dr. W. W. Hall
Mrs. W. W. Hall
Rev. J. G. Hall
Mrs. J. G. Hall
Mrs. J. C. Stokes
John Stokes
James Stokes
Judge J. C. Gray
Ed Gray
Mrs. Ingram
Eugene Ingram

Miss Florence Ingram
Prof. Welsh
Miss Sidney Welsh
M. Wile
Mr. Strang
Emanuel Wile
W. E. Eskridge
Eskridge child
Walter Eskridge
Fox Eskridge
Dr. W. B. May
Mrs. W. B. May
Dr. Hankins
Mrs. Hankins
Miss Fannie Peebles
Henry Ratalsky
O. B. Rollins
Ben Gage
Two children of Dr. Gage
Mrs. Hooks
B. M. Doak
David Hooks
James Benke
Scanlin child
William Chandler
R. A. Collins
Tom Irby
Dave Moore
Mr. River
Dr. J. L. Milton
John Morrow
Barry Rose
F. K. Hall
Hugh Goham
Sherman infant
Robert Stevenson
Harry Hart
T. P. Baines
John Thomas
H. M. Jones
Jos. A. Morrison
A. Gerard
Mrs. Alice Signaigo
Judge Tom Walton
Thomas Kendall
Samuel Flippin
Hugh R. Davis
S. L. Davis
Colly Davis
Mrs. I. S. Parker
Miss Jennie Satterfied
M. Friedman
Mrs. Smith
I. K. Wood
Rev. John McCampell
Samuel Marshall
Mrs. Cary
A. P. Sanders
Charles Weigert
Mrs. W. A. Belew

Frank Holly
Rev. J. K. Armstrong
Mrs. E. E. Vinson
Charles Newell
J. A. Williams
Tom Phillips
Dr. Ringold
Coleman Armstrong
Abb Garner
Mary Lacock
G. T. Coan
Sam Flippin
Willie Bea
Mrs. Howell
E. J. Eli
Ida Rosser
Mrs. Spence
Joseph Newell
Mrs. Beasley
Henry Burt
Robert Shankle

111

Chapter X

Grenada Experiences Banking Difficulties and Triumphs

In order to understand the banking situation in Grenada during the early years of its existance it becomes necessary for a brief review of the banking situation in the state and nation. The Bank of the United States was chartered in 1791, and became the fiscal agent of the young nation, and the depository of federal funds. It was re-chartered in 1816. At a time when there was an unusual demand for currency to be used in the purchase of the vast acreage of public land being placed on the market, the Bank, realizing the inflationary tendency of the land boom, became very conservative about granting loans for extensive land purchases and new business ventures. In 1819 there was a business panic in the country, resulting in many business failures and land foreclosures. The people who suffered most from this business depression blamed the panic on the conservative money policies of the Bank. On the other hand, the conservative Eastern businessmen claimed that the fiscal policies of the Bank led to inflation. The many state banks located in Southern and Western states, did not like the Bank of the United States because the well secured notes issued by this bank had the effect of driving out of general circulation the notes issued by the less secure state banks. So long as people could secure banknotes from the Bank of the United States they selected them in preference to the notes of the state banks.

The conservative policies of the Bank of the United States led to reckless banking policies on the part of the state banks. In order to supply the ever growing demand for currency to finance the speculative land boom, the state banks issued many notes without having sufficient specie to honor these notes if specie should be demanded. Because of the conditions described above, Mississippi, as well as other states, was flooded with a variety of bank notes issued by a number of state banks. This currency varied in value. Money from banks reputed to be in sound financial condition was accepted at face value. Notes on other banks were discounted, or even refused, depending upon the reputation of such banks for sound fiscal policies. Natchez was the banking center of Mississippi when the initial settlements were made in Pittsburg and Tullahoma. Under a provision of the Mississippi Constitution of 1832, the state had been authorized to own bank stock. It had purchased such stock in the Planters Bank which was domiciled in Natchez. The state investment in stock of that bank was, during the early years of the investment, a profitable one for the state. On several years the investment return was as much as two hundred thousand dollars. Another Natchez bank chartered by the Mississippi Legislature was the Agricultural Bank, also located in Natchez. These two banks drew business from a large area of the state. Many of the early business transactions involving land purchases in Grenada and vicinity, named one of these two banks as the agency for the payment and collection of deferred payments on land purchases.

President Jackson, being a son of the optimistic West and somewhat hostile to the business interests of the Eastern part of the country, became an enemy of the Bank of the United States. He listened to the complaints of his friends that the fiscal policies of the bank were placing an unnecessary brake on the development of the South and West. He also became convinced that the bank was discriminating against his political supporters. In some way, he learned that his political opponets Daniel Webster and Henry Clay had received retainers from the Bank. He knew that the bank charter would expire in 1836. He let it be known in no uncertain terms that he would oppose a re-chartering of that institution. In a message to Congress, in 1829, he expressed his opinion that the bank was un-constitutional. Clay and Webster, wishing to make a political issue of the bank question, approached Nicholas Biddle, President of the Bank, relative to applying for a re-charter in 1832, rather than waiting later.

Their argument was that it would be better to put over the project before more people could be more aroused against it. Against his better judgment Biddle was persuaded to make this early application for a re-chartering of his bank. The re-charter bill was approved by both houses of Congress. Jackson vetoed the bill, and the veto was sustained. Having achieved his purpose of preventing the re-charter of the bank, Jackson decided to destroy the influence of the bank during the remaining years of its existence. He removed federal deposits from the Bank of the United States and placed them in some state banks called "Pet Banks". This action on the part of the President had a twofold effect on the economy of the country, both harmful. It increased the amount of currency available for speculative purposes, and in a large measure, by diminishing the available sound currency of the Bank of the United States, it encouraged the expansion of the notes of state banks. In a very short time outstanding notes, issued by state banks, increased from forty eight million dollars to one hundred forty nine million dollars. This inflationary increase in un-sound money alarmed President Jackson who now realized that some kind of brake was needed on the rapid inflationary influence of this reckless issue of state bank notes. Since much of this issue of state bank notes was being used in land purchases, many of the purchases being of land secured by the Federal Government from various Indian tribes, the President decided that he could counteract the rapid inflation by requiring that land purchased from the Federal government must be paid for in specie-gold or silver or any other currency designated as legal tender by the Federal Government. In 1836 he issued the "Specie Circular" which put this policy in effect. The land speculators began to call upon the state banks to redeem their notes in specie so that the speculators might continue to buy public lands. This demand on the part of the speculators for specie alarmed many people holding these bank notes to the extent that they also sought to redeem their bank notes in specie. Most of the banks had to suspend specie payment in redemption of notes. This condition prevailed not only in the West and the South, but also in the East. Banks in New York, Boston, Baltimore, Philadelphia and other Eastern cities also suspended specie payment. The resulting Panic of 1837 was disasterous to the nation. Eighty per cent of the Eastern factories shut down operations. Many purchasers of public land who had made down payments on their purchases were unable to meet the deferred payments and thus lost the equity which they had in the lands purchased.

The bankers and politicans of Mississippi felt that something should be done to stabilize the currecny being used in the state. They conceived the idea of a strong bank which would serve Mississippi as once the Bank of the United States served the nation. The result of this thinking was the chartering of the Union Bank of Mississippi. The authorized capital stock of this bank was $15,500,000. A bill proposing that the state of Mississippi purchase 50,000 shares of the bank stock and issue state bonds in the amount of $5,000,000 to pay for the stock passed two different legislatures, as was then required for such state investments and the state thereby became a partner in the banking operation. The bonds were purchased by the Bank of the United States of Philadelphia, a new bank organized by Nicholas Biddle, and this bank unloaded the bonds very largely on English investors. Soon $5,000,000 in English silver and gold was loaded on an oceangoing steamer and unloaded in New Orleans. Here it was transferred to a river steamer which carried the specie to Vicksburg. From this point the shipment went to Jackson by a well-guarded wagon caravan. The bank had been chartered in 1837 and was authorized to begin operation as soon as it had ten percent of the capital stock in cash. A stock sale was begun. Planters were assured that if they became stock holders the bank would advance money on their cotton crops while the cotton was held in storage waiting for higher prices before sale was made. This was a very potent appeal to men who believed that the New Orleans banks and commission merchants were cheating them in interest rates and price paid for cotton. All over the state people, chiefly planters, began to purchase stock, paying little cash but giving mortgages on plantations, slaves, town lots and town buildings. Much of that stock was sold to men who lived in Grenada, or the area which is not in Grenada County. We have been able to trace 28 of these stock transactions by mortgages recorded on the county deeds records. These twenty eight individuals bought half a million dollars worth of stock, and gave mortgages on almost fifteen thousand acres of land and 152 slaves to secure the bank in payment of the stock. The largest purchases of stock was James A. Girault, although Sterling Harrison and A. Govan bought considerable stock. It is interesting to note that both Girault and Govan became financially embarassed soon thereafter, and neither ever entirely recovered from their reckless investment in bank stock and other unsuccessful ventures. Perhaps one reason that the stock found such a ready sale in the county was because two of the men appointed as Directors of the bank were men who were well known to Grenada people, because both of them were among the Proprietors of the Town Company of Tullohoma. They were Hiram G. Runnels and J. L. Irwin. Runnels was made President of the Board at a salary of ten thousand dollars per year.

Having set up the new bank in business, the Legislature attempted to discourage the reckless issue of bank notes by state banks by providing that any bank, not meeting its obligation to redeem notes in specie, when the demand was made for redemption, should have its charter suspended. In 1839, probably to replace some banks forced to close under the above mentioned legislative enactment, the State chartered new banks in Holly Springs, Vicksburg, Grenada, Port Gibson and Lexington, as well as two companies which also were engaged in banking. These two were the Hernando Railroad and Banking Company and the Vicksburg Water Works and Banking Company. So far as we have been able to ascertain, this was the first real bank to be established in Grenada, although it is very probable that some merchant of the town may have operated some sort of business in which money might be deposited and against which orders for payment of money might be made. Perhaps the bank chartered by the state might have some such beginning. We do know that, as early as 1838, there was an institution in Grenada known as "The Bank of Grenada". The local records indicating the existence of this bank are Deeds of Trust which recite in their body that these deeds are to be satisfied by the payment of specified sums of money at the Bank of Grenada.

The Mississippi Union Bank was a dismal failure. Bad banking judgment high overhead operating expense and depreciation of the value of property mortgaged and bank notes paid for stock forced the state to liquidate the bank. In a space of four years the bank was chartered, stock sold, loans made, much money advanced on cotton, and liquidation forced on it.

The state lost not only the capital invested in the bank but lost its financial standing for decades to come, because it repudiated the $5,000,000 dollars in state bonds on the ground that they were unconstitutional. Until comparatively recent times, this long-ago repudiation of just debts by the state caused Mississippi state securities to be very difficult to sell to foreign investors. Repudiation of the bonds became a political issue between the Whig and Democratic parties of the state. The Whigs, composed mostly of substantial planters and businessmen, favored paying off the bonds, while the Democrats were mostly in favor of repudiation. The state lost not only in honor and bond money in the bank failure, but also through accepting bank notes in payment of accounts due the state. The state auditor reported that the state lost $303,000 in notes issued by Brandon, Grenada and Mississippi Union Banks, and on the Natchez and Hernando Railroad companies, over $228,000 of which was on account of the Grenada and Brandon concerns". The state was in bad financial shape at this time. When Governor McNutt (under whose administration the bonds were sold) took office there was a treasury surplus of $279,613. This was in the year 1838. Four years later, at the time of the liquidation of the Mississippi Union Bank, there was in the state treasury 34¢ in cash and a lot of worthless bank notes, perhaps some from the Grenada and Brandon banks. The state also faced $8,000,000 in claims pressing for adjustment.

The banking and currency situation discussed above had a disasterous effect on the economy of Grenada and the trade area of the town. Much property was sold by the receivers of the assets of the Mississippi Union Bank in order to satisfy mortgages given on property in favor of the bank. During this period of the existence of the ill-fated Mississippi Union Bank, property values dropped drastically in the town of Grenada. Many of the lots sold for taxes. It was during the period that Harriet Sims acquired, by tax sales or purchases at very low prices, almost half of the lots in the West Ward of Grenada, formerly known as the town of Pittsburg. Much cotton had been deposited to the credit of the bank by planters who received $60.00 per bale advance, while the Bank held the cotton in storage in Liverpool, England, hoping for better prices. This cotton was sold along with the other assets of the Bank, the planters losing whatever difference that may have existed between their advance on the cotton and its ultimate selling price.

We know nothing about the banking business, if there was any, in Grenada from 1842 to just before the outbreak of the Civil War. If there were banks in the town we have no definite information to that effect. We do know from land records that considerable payments on deeds of trust were conducted through banks in other towns.

Just prior to the outbreak of the Civil War, N. C. Snider & Company set up a private bank in Grenada. His partner in the bank was W. A. Rayburn). Mr. Snider was born in Chambersburg, Pennsylvania in 1812, the son of Jacob Snider. Young Snider studied at St. Mary's College in Maryland, and in the law school of Washington College. In 1836, as so many other young lawyers had done, he journeyed to the new country opened up by Indian Land Cessions. He settled in Coffeeville in 1836, and began the practice of law there. He also became the agent for a New Orleans cotton firm. He remained here until he started his banking venture in Grenada as heretofore mentioned. Evidently his father joined him there, since there is a stone in the old or "yellow fever cemetery", which indicates that Jacob Snider was buried here sometime before the fever outbreak. We do not know how this private bank fared during the civil war years, but we do know that it functioned for at least twenty years after the end of the war. Its name was subsequently changed to The Banking House of N. C. Snider & Son. Shortly after the end of the Civil War, another private bank known as The Lake Brothers Bank was established. These two private banks served as the only local banking institutions for a period of about twenty years. These were difficult years for both bankers and businessmen. The people of the area were rebuilding upon the dead ashes of the prewar prosperity, and were fighting to regain political control from the carpet bag-scalaswa-negro regime, set up by the reconstruction acts of a radical congress. It was during the late years of this period that the town was swept by the yellow fever epidemic of 1878. On January 19, 1884, the Grenada Sentinel reported that the R. P. Lake Bank had failed, and that Mr. Lake had assigned all of his property to G. W. Jones for the benefit of creditors. Liabilities reported to be about $60,000 and assets nearly enough to pay off creditors if such assets could be liquidated at their real value. We assume that this bank was the successor of the Lake Brothers Bank established about twenty years earlier. After the failure of his bank R. P. Lake engaged in the insurance business, and became district manager for his company, having headquarters, first in Jackson, Mississippi, and then later in Memphis. We have no information as to the date of its establishemnt, evidently some time after the failure of the R. P. Lake Bank, but we do know that George Lake was running a bank of his own very soon after the failure of the other Lake Bank. On February 5, 1887, the following news item appeared in the Sentinel: "Mr. George Lake has moved his bank into his spacious two story building on the east side of the square, where he is fitted up with every convenience for the transaction of all business intrusted to him, and where he is better prepared than ever for the transaction of General Bank business. George Lake's Bank is known far and near, and is an institution in which people have implicit confidence, and that accounts for the immense business which he does". It would seem that the failure of the earlier Lake Bank had not destroyed the confidence of the people in the integrity and business ability of the Lakes.

About nine months after the failure of the R. P. Lake Bank, the business community of Grenada and vicinity was shocked by the announcement of the failure of N. C. Snider & Son, Bankers. The founder of this firm had died a few months before the announcement of the failure, and his son Jacob Snider was in charge of the bank at the time of its failure. Liabilities of the bank were listed as $85,728 while assets, consisting mostly of mortgages on crops, stock and lands, were estimated at about $70,000. If these two bank failures occurred, as they probably did, before George Lake had established his bank, it would mean that not only would the people of the area lose a portion of their deposits in the two banks, but would also be without the convenience of a local banking institution for some time.

Outside business concerns became interested in the possibility of coming into Grenada and establishing banking facilities in what was a good town with a large trade area about it. On November 15, 1884, the following news item appeared in the Sentinel" "Mr. C. W. Robinson, Cashier of the First National Bank of Meridian, is in town to take the pulse of the citizens relative to another bank". Unfortunately for the people of Grenada, there occurred another disaster which came a few months before the first bank failure and shortly before the second one. On August 23, 1884, the Grenada Sentinel came out with an issue which had the following quoted headlines: "GRENADA IN RUINS. THREE HUNDRED THOUSAND DOLLAR FIRE". The news article stated that the fire started in the S. H. Garner Furniture House and destroyed three fourths of the buildings around the square. There was also printed a note from B. C. Adams, Jr., Mayor of Grenada, that Grenada was not asking for any outside help because of the fire. It would seem to us today that the men who made up the business community of Grenada eighty two years ago must have been men of determination and courage. It took strong men to survive two bank failures and a disasterous fire within the space of nine months, and still be able to advise the outside world that they needed no outside help. From a news item printed in January 1885, it would seem that the R. P. Lake Bank and the Lake Bros. Bank were one and the same. That news item states that the assets of R. P. Lake and Lake Brothers had been sold for $15,500 for the benefit of creditors. It would seem that the optimistic estimates, as to the value of the assets of the failing bank, had been far in excess of the money realized from them.

In September 1885, The Bank of Grenada advertised for business. F. B. Nichols was President. We have not found the published charter of this bank and do not know the names of the stockholders but presume that the bank was organized by local business men since the President was a local buisnessman. The August 7, 1886, issue of the Grenada Sentinel gives the information that Ben Price, Cashier of the Bank of Oxford and Silas Owens of the same town, were in Grenada for the purpose of inducing local business interests to subscribe $10,000 in stock to help provide a capital of $40,000 with which to organize a new bank, to be called The Merchants Bank. The stipulated amount of stock to be subscribed by people of Grenada was purchased, and Mr. A. Beebe, a New York capitalist, made a large investment in the bank stock. Ben Price, Silas Owens, C. B. Howery and G. R. Hill, all of Oxford, bought shares of stock. Local subscribers to the bank stock were I. Wile & Company, W. N. Pass, Thomas Brothers, Doak & Laurence, W. C. McLean and John Powell. The bank organization was perfected September 13, 1866. In October of the same year the following officers were elected; President, Sam Laurence; Cashier, J. W. McLeod; Direcotrs,

Ben Price, B. F. Thomas, W. M. Pass, W. McLean and John Powell. As a temporary domicile the bank set up business in the jewelry store of W. E. Smith.

We have previously noted that a Bank of Grenada was advertising for business in later 1885, but no charter of that bank had been published. On April 3, 1886, the charter was published and R. W. Millsaps, George Lake and R. L. Prophet were listed as the men who had organized the bank. Since there is little evidence of any considerable business done by this Bank of Grenada, and since George Lake was in business the same year as the bank organization which was described in a previously quoted news article from the Grenada Sentinel, there is a very strong probability that the bank organized by the three men mentioned above became the George Lake Bank. The fact that in August 1886, there was an advertisement by the banking company of George Lake & Company would seem another indication that the George Lake Bank, the Bank of Grenada and the George Lake & Company Bank were just different phases of the bank run by George Lake.

On May 24, 1890, the Sentinel published the charter of a newly organized bank. It was called Grenada Bank. Early stockholders were J. W. Griffis, J. T. Thomas, George Lake, B. C. Adams, Jr., R. Horton, G. W. Jones, J. T. Parker, J. W. Buchanan, J. H. Barksdale, R. W. Mullen, D. B. Wiley, Edgar West, P. D. Witty, Walter Trotter, O. J. Moore, J. T. Lay, and T. H. Somerville. The list of stockholders, consisting of many of the most prominent business and professional men of the area inspired confidence in the new bank, which confidence was to be justified by the subsequent business career of the Bank. J. W. Griffis was elected President of the bank and J. T. Thomas became Cashier. Judge A. T. Roan was Vice-President and Byron Dudley Bookkeeper. Since the bank was originally organized, it has continued to grow, first as a local bank, and later as a chain of banks, under the name the Grenada Bank System, until today it is one of the strongest bank organizations in the state. Since George Lake was one of the stockholders in the new bank, and since we find no further references in the local paper to the existence of Lakes Bank, I think that we may presume that the organization of Grenada Bank pretty well coincided with the liquidation of the George Lake & Company Bank. Under the charter of Grenada Bank, the maximum capital stock was to be $200,000 with a paid in capital of $30,000 required before the bank could open for business.

On January 1890, the Sentinel had this comment relative to the Merchants Bank: "The Merchants Bank is one of the most solid institutions of the kind in the state". This statement was made a little more than three months before the organization of Grenada Bank. Evidently the competition furnished by the newly organized bank had its effect on the prosperity of the older bank. It is also probable that the Merchants Bank, in order to remain in competition, began to take doubtful security on loans made to people who borrowed money from the bank. This was a common fault of many of the earlier banking institutions of the state. Whatever reason, or combination of reasons, was responsible for the decline of the Merchants Bank, it soon became apparent that the bank was on shaky financial grounds. As these rumors spread, depositors began to withdraw their money, and soon the bank was faced with a shortage of liquid assets. On January 31, 1903, The Sentinel announced that the Merchants Bank had closed its doors and made an assignment of its assets for benefit of its depositors and other creditors. The newspaper states that the bank had been considered weak for some time, and that, in a circular letter, sent from the stockholders to depositors, the latter were informed that the action was taken because rumors regarding the financial condition of the bank had caused heavy withdrawals by depositors. B. C. Duncan was designated as the assignee. It was estimated that the liabilities of the institution amounted to about $88,000, while the assets were supposed to be worth $90,000. The capital stock of $60,000 was lost to the stockholders. There were about 350 depositors at the time the bank closed. It was hoped that when the assets had been liquidated the depositors would recover from 75 to 85 per cent of their deposits. At the time of the failure, A. C. Leigh was President of the bank, Robert Doak, Vice-President and J. W. McLeod, Cashier. J. H. Barksdale, D. L. Holcomb, J. Cuff and G. B. Jones were Directors. It should be noted that in none of the bank failures which occurred was there any evidence of embezzlement or dishonesty of any sort. The usual trouble was too much of the liquid assets of the banks invested in loans secured by crops, land and stock. Crops frequently were less than expected; stock died and depreciated in value; land values fluctuated; and eventually the bankung institutions had their vaults filled with paper of uncertain value and depleted cash balances.

The failure of the Merchants Bank did not discourage, in fact, it may have encouraged the establishment of another bank in Grenada. Less than two months after the Merchants Bank folded, the charter of Grenada Trust and Banking Company was published. J. W. Lee, A. S. Bell, A. Gerard, W. F. Martin, D. O. Semmes, G. W. Eatman and W. S. P. Doty were listed as incorporators. The capital stock was to be $15,000 and stock was to sell at $50.00 per share. The early organization of a bank, so soon after the failure of the Merchants Bank, and the small capitalization of the new bank, might lead one to believe that the new bank would not be able to compete with the older Grenada Bank. As a matter of fact, there was a general belief that the establishemnt of the new bank was not an adverse, or hostile move against the older bank, but was made with the consent and approval of the Grenada Bank. Many people felt that the failure of the Merchants Bank, leaving Grenada with only one bank, would certainly invite out-of-town capital to come into Grenada and establish another bank, while the chartering of the new Grenada Trust and Banking Company might prevent such a move on the part of outside capital. The men who incorporated this new bank were well-known local business and prefessional men. J. W. Lee was a Baptist minister who had become a man of some means. A. S. Bell was a lawyer and plantation owner who, on occasion, had served as Mayor of Grenada. A. Gerard had been a town official in various capacities. W. F. Martin was a large land owner. D. O. Semmes and G. W. Eatman were Grenada drug store owners. W. S. P. Doty was a lawyer who, at a later date served as Mayor of Grenada. On May 8, 1903, the following officers of the new bank were elected: W. F. Martin, President; J. B. Perry, Vice-President; H. J. Ray, Cashier; and W. F. Martin, A. S. Bell, A. Gerard, J. P. Broadstreet, J. W. Leigh, J. T. Thomas, R. H. Stokes, W. S. P. Doty and J. B. Perry as Directors. The fact that J. T. Thomas, Cashier of the Grenada Bank, was a director of the new bank seems an indication that the new and the old banks were on friendly terms. Although the Grenada Trust and Banking Company did not branch out into a chain of banks like the Grenada Bank, it has had a gradual, but substantial growth, since its organization. At this time (April 1967) it is considered one of the stronger individual banks of the state. The man who became Cashier of the Bank in 1903 has served the institution for sixty four years. Mr. Ray is still active as President of the bank. On March 29, 1904, the depositors of the defunct Merchants Bank received a payment of ten per cent of their deposits and in 1905 Mr. Duncan made a final payment to the depositors who, with this final payment, recovered seventy per cent of their deposits. This would seem to indicate that Mr. Duncan had done an excellent job in disposing of the assets of the bank.

In the year 1905 a bank was organized at Holcomb. The stockholders elected E. M. McShane of Greenwood as President, and L. L. Casey of Itta Bena Cashier. These two men, along with Dr. C. C. Moore, J. H. Brewer, R. D. Williams and R. A. McRee, served as directors. Eventually this bank, now no longer in existence, became a member of the Grenada Bank System. In 1907 an attempt was made to organize The First National Bank of Grenada, but this effort seems to have failed. In 1907 many banks of the state, because of a general financial uneasiness, limited bank withdrawls to one hundred dollars per day. Grenada Bank was one of the few banks which did not place this restriction on bank withdrawals. On January 18, 1908, the charter of incorporation of the

Citizens Savings Bank was published. Incorporators were M. B. Charles, W. E. Smith and Robert D. Talbert, all of Grenada. Capital stock was fixed at $30,000 and par value of stock at one hundred dollars. We have found no evidence of any activity on the part of this bank, so there is a possibility that its promoters were unable to raise sufficient capital to begin operation. In the same year the Bank of Commerce was organized. W. C. McLean was President and O. L. Kimbrough Cashier. Directors were J. H. Brown, W. C. McLean, S. T. Tatum, W. R. Baker, W. S. Van Owdell, Dr. C. C. Moore, Dr. B. S. Dudley and one other director whose name we do not have. This bank was destined to have a rather brief existence of fourteen years. There were several changes of bank officers and directors during these fourteen years. In 1910 the Bank of Commerce became one of the first banks in the state to come under the recently passed Guarantee Bank Law. In 1915 E. C. Neely became President of the bank with R. H. Wright as Cashier. In the same year the bank established a Xmas Club. In 1917 J. F. McRee was acting as Cashier. In 1917 E. C. Neely, A. M Carothers and J. T. Mason were listed as Directors. This frequent change of directors seemed to indicate that the bank was not having easy sailing, but an indication that another Grenada Bank was doing well was the court order for sale of shares of stock owned in the Grenada Trust & Banking Company. W. G. Eatman had died, and part of his estate consisted of five shares of stock in the last mentioned bank. The news report states that this stock, with a par value of one hundred dollars, sold at a price of two hundred eighty three dollars per share. In early September of 1918 E. C. Neely resigned as President of the Bank of Commerce to accept a position as the Cashier of the Bank of Schlater, and A. M. Carothers became President, with J. T. Mason and C. C. Provine listed as Directors. There were probably other Directors, but these men signed the annual published statement of the bank. In 1919 the annual statement of the bank lists E. L. Boteler as Cashier and J. T. Mason and G. R. Goza were Directors who signed the statement. In the 1920 statement, Mr. Boteler signs as Cashier and C. C. Provine and J. P. Meaders as Directors. Late in 1920 the Stockholders of the Bank of Commerce met and designated the year of 1920 as "A highly satisfactory year". At this date C. C. Provine was acting in the dual capacity of President and Cashier of the bank while E. L. Boteler was Assistant Cashier. Directors listed were E. L. James, J. H. Spence, G. R. Goza, J. P. Meaders and F. E. Gillon.

On February 17, 1922, the following news item appeared on the front page of the SENTINEL: "The Bank of Commerce closed its doors on Friday afternoon of last week under the order of the State Banking Department. Bank Examiner S. W. Wardlow of Grenada checked the affairs of the bank and represented the Banking Department in closing the bank. It had been generally thought that the Bank of Commerce had been in somewhat strained circumstances for two or three years. The adverse business conditions had hit the bank hard, and it had made some rather large advances on certain real estate upon which it was unable to realize. The Bank made a brave fight, and its management are to be commended for being able to weather the storm for so long. It is stated that the Bank had some obligations due certain New York Banks which matured the day of the closing. The stockholders got together, and it is understood that Mr. J. T. Thomas, President of the Grenada Bank, offered assistance in meeting the emergency. It looked, at one, time, as if the situation was going to be tied over. The State Guarantee Banking Law serves to assure the depositors that they will get their money, hence the closing of the bank's doors created no more comment in business circles than if some mercantile firm had come to embarrassment. Business moved right along, and nobody got nervous. The wise, and farseeing management of the other two banks which are as stable in a business way, as the Rock of Gibralter, serves to give business interests assurance. Of course sincere regret is felt at the Bank's collapse and general sympathy is expressed for the officers and the stockholders who have made such a brave fight against adverse odds".

For the past forty five years Grenada has been fortunate in having strong banks which have been able, in good times and bad, to meet their banking obligations, and during that period no local bank failures have come about to bring distress to our people. Of course the two existing banks have served for a longer period of time than the forty- four year period during which we have experienced no bank failures. In closing this article, I should like to contrast this story of banking in Grenada by quoting from a letter, written by General Andrew Jackson to George W. Martin of Grenada County. Martin was the maternal grandfatehr of the late W. B. Hoffa. He had served in the military forces of General Jackson, and, at one time, acted as Secretary to the General. In the Battle of New Orleans he served on the staff of General Coffee. He came into our area in 1833, and carved out a plantation called "Auverigne" in 1834. His daughter Elizaberh Donaldson Martin, born on the plantation in 1834, was a great neice of General Jackson. She was the mother of Mr. Hoffa. Mr. Martin had written the General, congratulating him on, at last, being able to give up the heavy responsibilities of the Presidency, and General Jackson's letter was in answer. We quote a porton of that letter: "My Dear Major ; Your kind letter of the 25th congratulating me on my return to the Hermitage has been received, and for your sentiments conveyed, and approbation of my official career, and good wishes for my happiness, in my retirement I sincerely thank you. I am truly thankful to a kind and overruling providence for preserving me through my arduous administration of the government, and permiting me to return to my peaceful home and enjoy my last few days in the bosom of my family, and with my neighbors and friends. I return with a peaceful conscience and review my public life with satisfaction, as I can with truth say that all my public acts were with an eye single to the public weal. My duties have been arduous. I had to contend against the whole aristocratic phalanx - the herculean power of the United States Bank, who by the paper credit system have formed the plan to make the laboring classes hewers of wood and drawers of water to these bankers, demagogues, speculators and gamblers, by a depreciated paper. These speculators, under the management of Mr. Biddle, and the Barings, and their influence over the whole corrupt system of banking, have caused the whole to stop payment of specie, with $30,000,000 of specie in their vaults, and in open violation of their charter, and every moral principle, to the great injury of the people and good government, expending their paper issue, depreciating it, and by their agents buying it up at 20, 30 or 50 percent discount from the people who have received it as specie, depriving the laborers of our country of one third or one half of the real value of their labor.

I am sorry that you did not receive Andrew's letter. He says that he wrote you, as I requested, enclosing you my note to Col. Walker, and his reply in reference to your appointment at Chocchuma, in the place of Mr. G. Col. Walker said at first that he would recommend you, but at last united with Mr. Claiborne and Mr. Gholston in recommending another, and as I knew Black was hostile to you, I would not hazard your nomination before the Senate. I am fearful that you have been puting too much confidence in the integrity of the Colonel, and his letter to Mr. Black will sometime pass over my mind and his large speculations and liabilities may have caused him to join the aristocracy, and become a paper credit system man........I was apprehensive from Col. Walker's course in the Senate on the subject of the Treasury Circular, that he was going over to the whigs, and wished to join them in deluging the country with paper to destroy our deposit banks. That circular secured the banks from the drain of specie for England and saved the country from ruin and entire bankruptcy. Still Col. Walker was opposed to it". The Mr. G. mentioned in Jackson's letter as the man appointed to the office desired by Mr. Martin was Samuel Gwin who became Registrar of the Chocchuma Land Office. The Col. Walker mentioned in the same letter was Robert J. Walker, United States Senator from Mississippi, and a very extensive land speculator.

Chapter XI

Founders and Builders of Grenada and Grenada County

The City and County of Grenada, as they exist today are, to a considerable extent, the reflected image of the energy, character and ambition of those early settlers who gave tone and direction to the religious, political and economic development of the area, thus establishing the foundations on which later arrivals built a city and a county. It is the purpose of this article to give available information relative to some of these pioneer settlers, as well as information relative to others who arrived later to build on the foundations erected by the earlier settlers. We shall confine our discussion to men and women who, during the first half century of the develpment of the region, were instrumental in shaping the destiny of the town and vicinity. There will be missing from our list many who probably deserve equal rank with some of those who will be mentioned, but this omission results from a lack of information rather than because of failure to recognized the important part they played in the development of the area. Some individuals, because of unique qualities of personality, leadership, political sagacity or economic shrewdness stand out above the crowd, and therefore find a place in the newspaper reports, legal documents and other written records of the time. Others, perhaps equally deserving a place in the history of the region, are all but forgotten because the nature of their activities were such as to gain no considerable contemporary notoriety.

The first white inhabitants whose lives had an impact on this area were members of the staff of the Elliot Indian Mission and School established in 1818 a little south of the present town of Holcomb. Mr. C. Kingsbury, leader of that group, seems to have made no contribution to the white community, leaving the area after the Treaty of Dancing Rabbit Creek; and subsequent removal of most of the Indians, caused his school and mission to be discontinued. Others of his staff choose to remain and become a part of the movement which, within a few years, would transform the newly opened region into a populous and prosperous community. Mr. and Mrs. Williams left the Indian Station and established the Wayside Inn at a Yalobousha River ferry crossing. This was the place where the town of Tuscahoma was to be located. John Smith and his wife Hannah went from the school to the little village of Pittsburg and began operation of the Union Hotel. Harriet Smith, daughter of Mr. and Mrs. John Smith, married James Sims, a merchant doing business in the town of Pittsburg. He later became Marshal of Grenada after the union of the two towns of Pittsburg and Tullahoma, and at a still later date became Postmaster of Grenada. His wife, Harriett by shrewd trading became a very extensive property owner in the town of Pittsburg. Mariah, another daughter of the Smiths, married William Huntly who was an employee of the Government Land Office at Chocchuma. Later they removed to Grenada and he became a considerable property owner; operated one of the ferry boats for a time and later established a cotton warehouse and mercantile established of the river.

While the Smiths and Williams were still living at the Indian Mission, a shrewd Yankee trader had already established a trading post in the area which was to become Pittsburg. In the fall of 1831 N. Howard was in Cincinnati, Ohio, fitting out a trading boat. He purchased a keel-boat, loaded it with merchandise and set out for the "Choctaw Country". He took his boat down the Ohio River, and then down the Mississippi until he reached a point near the present city of Helena, Arkansas. From this point he managed to float his boat into Moon Lake, and by way of Yazoo Pass he reached the Coldwater river. He followed this river till it merged with the Tallahatchie, and then down that stream to its juncture with the Yalobousha. He took his boat up this river and, in the spring of 1832, set up a trading post in a tent located about where the present Cottonseed Oil Mill now stands. This early trader was a descendent of John Howard who came over over in the Mayflower. He became a member of the First Board of Selectmen for Grenada. The establishment in the East Ward of Grenada. He became a stockholder in, and Director of, the Mississippi and Tennessee Railroad line which was constructed to link the Mississippi Central Railroad with railroad connections at Memphis, Tennessee. He continued as an important figure in Grenada life until his death in 1878.

Another early business man and community leader in the town of Pittsburg, and later in the town of Grenada, was Ralph Coffman. We have no information as to his home before coming to Mississippi. Our first information about him is his appearance as an associate in the business firm of J. Coffman & Company. This was a business located on the east side of the area first known as the Pittsburg town square. The business began operation about 1835. After about three years Joseph Coffman sold out to Ralph and moved to Missouri. Ralph Coffman was successful in business and became the owner of considerable property in the town. He engaged in many civic projects and seems to have done a large business with planters and farmers, selling them supplies on credit and collecting for the supplies in the fall after the cotton crop had been harvested. He was one of the early merchants who seems to have survived the financial depression of the 1840's and early 1850's. He continued in business until 1878 when both he and his wife died during the yellow fever epidemic of that year. Another early settler of Pittsburg was the well-loved Physician Dr. Allen Gillespie. Unfortunately we know little about him other than the fragmentary information which comes from land transactions and from traditions passed down by older generations of citizens. Land transactions indicate that Dr. Gillespie was not a man of wealth. Deeds of Trust on lots owned by him indicate that he, like many early physicans, did not accumulate enough wealth to enable him to be free from financial worry. There is a tradition that, when a question arose about a name for the town to be formed by the union of Pittsburg and Tullohoma, it was Dr. Gillespie who suggested the name Grenada. This story is related by the W. P. A. Source Book on Grenada County, but deeds record indicate that in late 1835, some months before the union of the two towns, the term Grenada was already being used for the Town of Tullahoma. Deeds written late in 1835 on lots in the original town of Tullohoma locate the lots in "Tullohoma, alias Grenada". A grave-stone still standing above his grave in Odd Fellows Cemetery bears the unique and touching inscription: "Dr. Allen Gillespie Born 1801 died 1869 erected to his memory by the citizens of Grenada and vicinity". Another early settler in the little town was Major Curtis Haywood Guy. He was born in Raleigh, North Carolina in the year 1809. He, with his wife, moved to Pittsburg in 1834. In 1835 the PITTSBURG BULLETIN had an advertisement in which it was announced that there would be held in his home in Pittsburg an organizational meeting to establish the Grenada Lodge of the Masonic order. Major Guy soon thereafter came into possession of a considerable acreage of land adjoining the west side of Pittsburg, part of which land later came into the possession of Col. Oscar Bledsoe, and which until recent years was known as "The Bledsoe Place". Later, Major Guy bought a large plantation near the present town of Holcomb. A crossroad area in that vicinity was known for a long time as Guy's Corner". It was at this place that the early private school known as the TUSCAHOMA ACADEMY was established. Another prominent, but rather vague character who lived in Pittsburg was G. W. Kendall. We know that he was a lawyer in partnership with another lawyer by the name of Finley. He not only practiced law, but did considerable speculation in land. He was Captain of an early military company organized in and about the two little rival towns. He was granted power of attorney by various individuals to act for absentee land owners in the sale of their lands. As was the practice of the time he endorsed the notes of various people engaged in speculative land ventures, and as a result of depreciating land values caused by the Panic of 1837, he became financially involved by the failure of some of the men whose notes he had endorsed. The last authenic information which we have of this early lawyer is to the effect that after moving to Jackson,

Mississippi, he granted a deed to a lot which he owned in Grenada. The date of that transaction was in 1842. Tradition, not authenticated, but seemingly well based indicates that in some way he became connected with Maximilian who, with French support, set up a brief Empire in Mexico and lost that empire when the support of French soldiers was withdrawn. Kendall is supposed to have held some sort of official position under the Maximilian reign.

At the time the men mentioned above were settling in Pittsburg, other men who were to have a decisive influence on the development of the area were settling in the rival town of Tullahoma. One of the earlier settlers must have been Larkin Cleveland. We know that when the Tullahoma Town Company held its first meeting in the town of Chocchuma in late 1833. Clevelnad was empowered by that Company to begin the sale of lots in the town which the company had organized. He was authorized to complete the survey of the town. He remained only a short time in the capacity and soon set up a mercantile establishemnt in the town. He continued as a citizen of the area for many years after the union of the two towns to form Grenada. An early hotel in the little town was operated by Major John Williams. In 1835 four brothers who came from Maryland were attracted to the raw, little frontier town of Tullahoma. They were Henry, William, George and Levin Lake. Three of the Lake Brothers had first established their business in the long extinct town of Hendersonville. It was in this village, in which Franklin L. Plummer, one on the men who were instrumental in the founding of Pittsburg, had an interest in that first meeting of the Board of Supervisors of Yalobousha County. There, in anticipation of the place being selected as the countyseat of Yalobousha County, several merchants and professional men were set up in business. Among those men and firms we have authenic information as to the presence of the following: Martin, Edwards & Company; Armour, Lake & Bridges; H. & W. Lake; McLain & Company; John H. McKinney, Alfred McCaslin and Thomas B. Ives. The Lakes soon transfered their operations to Tullahoma; John H. McKinney was one of the original Proprietors of the Town Company of Tullahoma, and Thomas B. Ives was very active in connection with the sale of lots in Pittsburg and in other areas in Yalobousha County. Levin Lake seems not to have been with the brothers at Hendersonville. Late in life he tells of his first sight of the town of Tullahoma. He relates that he came up the Yalobousha River on a keelboat owned by his brothers, arriving in the fall of 1835. Evidently the river had recently risen enough, because of fall rains, to make river navigation possible, since Mr. Lake tells of the great way in which the inhabitants of Tullahoma greeted the arrival of the keel-boat. He states that, having no cannon to fire a salute, the people placed powder charges in hollow logs which exploded with much noise when the powder was ignited. For over a hlaf century the Lakes were to be engaged in various business activities in Grenada. They had mercantile establishments, cotton warehouses, and a private banking institution. They also were engaged in river transportation on the Yalobousha river.

Dr. E. Cahn came from Philadelphia, Pennsylvania about 1835 to set up a mercantile establishment which did business in Grenada for over fifty years. During the late years of his life he lived in Philadelphia during the summer and in Grenada during the winter. He was the grandfather of the wife of Joseph Newburger who was the head of a company which did business in buying and storing cotton. He had outlets for his cotton in England and some of the countries of continental Europe. Mr. Newburger made many trips to these countries in the interest of his business. The first ferryman at Tullahoma was James Balfour. We know very little about him, but do know that he bought a number of valuable lots in Tullahoma and that his wife was probably the first person buried in the vicinity of the area which later became the Odd Fellows Cemetery. The inscription on her grave marker reads: "Sacred to the memory of Elizabeth Balfour, consort of Col. John Balfour, first settler of this town. Elizabeth was born February 17, 1807, and departed this life August 25, 1841". Since we have no evidence to the contrary may have been operating his ferry before the little rival towns were established. Another early settler in Grenada was John Moore who lived until July, 1891. The GRENADA SENTINEL OF July 18, of that year reported his death in these words: "A good old man passes away. John Moore 82, who settled in Grenada in 1835". In his younger days Mr. Moore was a considerable land owner in and about Grenada. He served as both architect and builder of several of the more pretentious pre-Civil War houses erected in Grenada. One of the fine examples of his skill is the house now owned by J. L. Townes. This house was constructed for a member of the Golloday family. In 1855 Mr. Moore bought a large lot on Margin street and constructed for his family a house very similar to the one which he had constructed for Mr. Golloday. The family lived in this house until the children were all grown. The house was later sold to Captain John Powell. Recently it belonged to Mrs. Bob Jackson. Moore was not only a builder of pretentious homes, but also engaged in all kinds of construction work. Records of the Boards of Supervisors for a period of years show frequent contracts awarded to this man to erect bridges over some of the minor streams of the county. He was also employed to make repairs on the county jail. He owned several town lots in both wards of Grenada, one of those lots being the one extending from College street east along Donkin street and including part of the area now covered by the Band Room of Grenada City Schools.

Albert Spooner Brown was another architect and builder who came to Grenada in 1835. He was a native of Tennessee. In 1829 he married in Nashville, and soon thereafter, moved to Natchez, Mississippi where he constructed some of the fine houses which were built during the boom years of slave and cotton prosperity. Like many other men in the older settlement of Natchez, he was attracted by the opportunity to move into a new area where Indian lands were being sold at low prices. He seems to have done more land speculating than construction work in Grenada, although it is quite probable that he constructed his own fine residence about which we will give some information later. Mr. Brown was one of the men who invested heavily in town lots in the town of Tullahoma. Unlike many of the other speculators of the period, he paid cash for his land purchases and was not caught in the financial bind that ruined many men who had bought largely on credit and were unable to pay off their debts after the Panic of 1837 struck in full force. Indeed, Brown was in a position to buy up much property which was sold under court judgements during this difficult period. He had several lots located at different points facing the town square of Tullahoma which, of course, came to be called the town square of Grenada. On one of these lots he erected a store building which, in the year 1870, he sold to the Board of Supervisors of the newly created county of Grenada to be used as a temporary courthouse. The purchase was made on credit, Mr. Brown receiving three promisory notes due in one, two and three years from the date of the purchase. This "temporary courthouse" was to serve the county for thirteen years. The first land purchase made by Mr. Brown was eighty acres bought from August Campbell. The land was situated in the southeast quarter of Section 17, Township 22, Range 5, East. On this land he built, with slave labor, a six room cottage in which he lived until 1849 when he built, near the same spot, the brick residence which recently belonged to Mrs. C. C. Provine. Considerable acreage was added to the original purchase, and the plantation was called Emerald Garden. Perhaps the name was derived from the several acres of flower garden which surrounded the house. In 1938 Mrs. John Cook Abernathy of Chicago, Illinois, gave the following information relative to A. S. Brown and the house on the plantation. She was the granddaughter of Mr. Brown. Her mother was first child born to the Browns in the new house, although the tenth child of the family. Mrs. Abernathy was born in the house in 1881. It has a fourteen foot "gallery" which extended the width of the house, there being two stories to the gallery. On each side of the main house were octagonal buildings twenty four feet across. One was joined to the house and served as a carriage house. The second story was enclosed in glass and was used as a hot house for delicate plants. Mrs. Abernathy was told by her grandmother that she had spent more than ten thousand dollars on rare plants. Financial ability to erect such an expensive house and to spend so freely on gardens and flowers indicate the measure in which Mr. Brown had continued to prosper since coming to Tullahoma fourteen years before he constructed the house. He was a friend of Jefferson Davis who persuaded Mr. Brown to send his eldest living son to the Military Academy at West Point. This son, William Brown, graduated from the Academy in 1860, entered the Confederate Army after the outbreak of the Civil War, and was promoted to Major before the end of the war. After the war, in an effort to rebuild his former secure financial status, Mr. Brown moved to Memphis and engaged in business there. He retained ownership of Emerald Garden and hoped to return to Grenada and live once more in the house. Before he could accomplish this he and his wife died in the Yellow Fever Epidemic which struck Memphis. In appreciation of his generosity in granting the Mississippi Central Railroad Company free right-of-way across his property at a time when some other land owners were trying to charge excessive prices for right of way across thier property, the railroad company placed a brass plate bearing the inscription "A. S. Brown" on their largest locomotive. During the early years of his residence in Grenada Mr. Brown was given power of attorney by a number of land owners to dispose of their property. In January 1882 Emerald Garden was advertised for sale: "Plantation for sale - Emerald Graden Place - the former residence of the late Col. A. S. Brown of Memphis. Containing 417 acres of bottom and plateau land about equally divided. All under fence and highly improved. Two story dwelling, office, carriage house, gin house, cabins and other necessary out houses. Flowers, shrubs, magnolias, evergreens, native forest trees and orchard. One of the loveliest places in the state-combining city and rural life-convenient to labor, good schools and churches. Possession given by the 1st of January. Terms: cheap for cash. Reasonable terms on time".

 A. C. Baine was a rather important contemporary of A. S. Brown. He never attained the wealth of his friend and associate Brown, but he was a participant in many of the real estate transactions taking place in Grenada and Grenada County. He was the first, and only lawyer, in the early town of Tullahoma, although other men of his profession came to Grenada after the union of the two towns of Tullahoma and Pittsburg. Mr. Baine acted as agent for many of the people who were making land sales in the town and county. He was rather active in purchasing lots for himself. He owned twelve lots in the East Ward of Grenada. These lots were not advantageously located and sold for rather low prices. Baine had political aspirations and became a candidate for District Attorney of the Judicial District in which Grenada was located. We do not know the outcome of this political campaign, but we do have information to the effect that Baine continued active in land transactions in the town and county for some years to come. Another early settler who played a conspicuous part in the development of the town and area was George W. Martin. He was a friend and supporter of President Andrew Jackson. It was probably through this friendship, that Martin was appointed Locating Agent for Indian lands sold at the Chocchuma Land Office. The duty of this agent was to locate claims made for land by Choctaw Indians who were claiming under either the "cultivation clause", the "float" provision, or the general reservation clause of the Treaty of Dancing Rabbit Creek. Under the first clause an Indian could make an immediate sale of his right; under the second clause the same right of immediate sale was also granted, but under the general provisions of the treaty, Indians had to remain in Mississippi for five years in order to perfect title to the land claimed by them. All these claims had to be located, either for the Indians, or for others who purchased land rights from the Indians. This was a task of considerable magnitude. It was, no doubt, Martin who located the land claims sold by Peggy Tryhan and John Donly. It would seem that, in the location of the land for Runnels & Watt which they had purchased from Henry Hill of Nashville, who had purchased from John Donly, Martin may have had personal interest in a good location, since he became a one tenth owner of the town of Tullahoma by a purchase made of Runnels and Watt.

Although they were not original settlers the brothers, Dr. Green Crowder and Ransom Crowder, were buying property in the area as early as 1836. They were born in North Carolina, but came to Grenada from Tennessee where they had resided for a number of years. They invested heavily in real estate in both the town of Grenada, and the areas which later came to be the counties of Grenada and Calhoun. Both of these men built pretentious homes a few miles east of Grenada. Together they owned several thousand acres of land and many slaves. Their houses were erected by slave labor. They operated a water mill along with their various other activities. A considerable portion of the present city of Grenada has been built on lands originally owned by these men who called their sub-divisions by their names. The Green W. Growder subdivision, or survey, in the southwestern part of Grenada, while the R. D. Crowder Survey is in the southeastern part of Grenada. Both of these men suffered severe financial losses as a result of the Civil War.

John R. Mitchell was another early settler in either Pittsburg or Tullahoma. He owned considerable property in Grenada and we note that he served as a juror in one of the earliest recorded trials in the Grenada City Court.

Most of the early settlers heretofore discussed settled in the towns of Pittsburg and Tullahoma, but others who made their contributions to the development of the area established and lived on farms and plantations then situated in Carroll, Choctaw, Tallahatchie and Yalobousha counties, which after 1870 became a part of Grenada county. Since Yalobousha county contributed a much larger acreage than any other county in the formation of Grenada county, we very naturally find that the settlers in Yalobousha county played a major role in the development of Grenada and Grenada County. In what is now the eastern part of Grenada County a considerable number of families came into the area before the land sales began at Chocchuma. They settled on desirable lands along the Yalobousha river, and later gained legal possession of the land under the provisions of the Premption act which allowed such settlers first right to purchase the land on which they had settled. Others in the area came in after the sale of land began at the Land Office. Dr. William T. Willis came into the area in 1832. He was born in Orange County Virginia, and came with his family to Alabama. From that state he came to, and settled on, land near Graysport. He was a graduate of both the medical colleges of Jefferson and Philadelphia. Although, for a time, he practiced medicine, his major interest was in farming the rich land which he pre-empted. He used slave labor to hew out boards and by 1835 had built the first plank house in that part of the county. Furniture for the house was brought across the country in covered wagons. As late as 1935 one of his decendents lived in the old house and had in use some of the furniture brought to the house by Dr. Willis. John C. James came with his family when they settled on Horsepen Creek, eighteen miles east of Grenada in the year 1833. He endured the hard frontier life of the period and at the time of his death had become a well-to-do planter. Captain G. F. Ingram also settled in the area near Graysport. He was born in Kershaw, South Carolina. In 1851 he married Rebecca D. Perry who, with her father Zadoc Perry, had left South Carolina to come to the little town of Graysport. Nicholous and Sarah Majet came to Grenada County in 1836. He was a decendent of a French Huguenot family which left France and went to North Carolina to escape the religious persecution then in effect in France. He became owner of about eight hundred acres of land, and in politics was an old line whig. Major Lewis C. Maget, who married a daughter of Captain N. B. Ingram, was the only surviving child of the above mentioned parents. Two early settlers who contributed in general to the development of the area, and in large measure to the religious foundation of the Baptist Church in the area were Francis Baker and James G. Hall. These men were representative of that early class of preachers who were servants of God by calling, but who were practical business men who made their living very largely by tilling the soil. Mr. Baker came to Grenada county in 1835 and settled on land near the town of Troy. He became the owner of the plantation known for many years as Mount Lore which property remained for many years in the control of his decendents. He was a Primative Baptist, and instrumental in establishing the Antioch Baptist church which was located near his home. Rev. James G. Hall and his wife Elizabeth were natives of North Carolina. They came to Grenada in 1837, and reared a large family here. Their first home was on a farm a few miles north of the town of Grenada. Rev. Hall was a moving spirit in the formation of the first Baptist church to be established in the town of Grenada. For a number of years he served as pastor of the church. He also preached at many of the nearby churches on occasion. His was a labor of love, and his preaching brought small financial return. Later Rev. Hall moved to Grenada and lived in a house, still in use today, located on South College Street. This good man and his wife died during the Yellow Fever Epidemic of 1878. Other members of his kindred were also victims of that epidemic. One son became a lawyer, served as a judge, and in 1888 was one of the speakers at the dedication of the Baptist Church building which had been erected on the lot west of the Post Office. The Evans building now occupies this lot. Living in the same general area of the county in which Baker and Hall lived was an Irish immigrant who was to become an important business and civil leader of the area. Robert Mullin was born in Belfast, Ireland. He came as a child to this country and, for a time, lived in Ohio with a sister. In 1829 he left the Ohio home of his sister and went to Kentucky. About nine years later he left that state and arrived in Mississippi in 1838. He located in the town of Troy. He went into the mercantile business, and soon became a buyer of much of the cotton which was brought to that place for sale. By 1850 he had become wealthy enough to purchase a 1200 acre plantation known as Evergreen. Here he erected a substantial brick residence which today is occupied by a decendent. The plantation acres are now in the possession of a number of individuals. Mr. Mullin's dream of living the life of a prosperous cotton farmer was rudely interupted by the outbreak of the Civil War. He suffered financial reverses as a result of the outcome of that war and, in order to recoup his financial position, he entered business in Grenada and became very successful in his new endeavor. When the Yellow Fever Epidemic struck Grenada in 1878 Mr. Mullin was one of three men selected by Grenada citizens to act as a Relief Committee which was to have general supervision of relief efforts in aid of those suffering from the effects of the Epidemic. John B. Pass came to the area in 1832. During the early years of his residence in the area he was a merchant. He erected the first brick store building in the little town of Grenada; he bought up a large acreage of land in the vicinity of Grenada; was the owner of many slaves; and later moved from town to a home on one of his plantations. He was known as Major Pass. His son, W. N. Pass was an influential business man in Grenada during the last quarter of the 19th century. He was Vice-President of the Merchants Bank of Grenada, and served as an officer of the Grenada Compress Company. He was a director of the Grenada Ice Factory.

N. C. Snider, Snider was born in Chambersburg, Pennsylvania, and came to Coffeeville in 1836. He had been educated at St. Mary's College. This school was located in Maryland. Later he studied law at Washington College. He began practice of his profession in Coffeeville, and also engaged in the cotton business, acting as the agent of a New Orleans firm which was interested in cotton produced in the Yalobousha county area. Some time before the Civil War Mr. Snider moved to Grenada to practice his profession, and to set up a private Banking House. This Bank survived the Civil War, the early years of Reconstruction, and the Yellow Fever Epidemic of 1878, only to become the victim of over-extended credit. In 1884 the son of Mr. Snider, who had become the head of the bank after the death of his father, made an assignment of the assets of the bank for the benefit of depositors and creditors. Michael D.

Talbert was one of the earliest settlers in the county. He came into the area before the sale of Indian land began. He was born in Edgeville District, South Carolina. His wife, Mary Cartledge, was also a native of South Carolina. They became the parents of ten children, seven boys and three girls. Their original home was a two story log house erected near the road which came to be known as the Troy-Memphis Road. This house was in use for one hundred thirty seven years. All seven of the Talbert boys became soliders in southern armies during the Civil War. Only one of the boys, James B. Talbert survived the war. He was wounded in the Battle of Shiloh and had no further participation in the war. Michael Talbert became rather wealthy. To a daughter who married Colonel Rhodes Baker, Mr. Talbert, in his will, bequeathed two thousand dollars in cash; a number of slaves; a number of oxen and mules, and enough household furniture to start a home of her own. Decendents of this family were long prominent in civic, business and religious affairs. A number of decendents of this family still reside in Grenada or vicinity.

Another early settler in the area around Troy was William Minter. He seems to have been a lay preacher. He assisted in the organization of the Grenada Baptist Church. When the Troy merchantile firm of Chisholm & Minter fell upon evil days and had to make assignments of their property for the benefit of their creditors, William Minter was the trusted person to whom the assignment was made. In that part of Grenada County which was once a part of Tallahatchie county, we find that James A. Girault was, perhaps, the most influential business figure of the area. We have mentioned him in our story of the founding of the town of Tuscahoma. Girault was a large land speculator, who lost much of his land during the depression which began in 1837. Girault was of French descent. He was reared in Natchez and began his business operations there. He married the daughter of William Dunbar, one of the wealthiest and most influential men of the Natchez area. Having good political connections, he received the appointment of "Receiver of Public Monies" at the Chocchuma Land Office. One of his daughters married James M. Duncan. Mr. Duncan's parents came from Virginia and settled in Green County Tennessee. His parents moved from Tennessee to Limestone County Alabama, and from there to Shelby County Tennessee. Mr. Duncan started business life as a merchant and continued in this line of work until 1840. In that year he came to Grenada to act as administrator of the estate of George Dillard. Having concluded this business, Mr. Duncan returned to Alabama, gathered together his three slaves and scattered personal possessions and set out for the Grenada area. In the latter part of 1840, he secured land near the old town of Chocchuma and began farming. He became, by the time of the Civil War, a rather large planter, owning 93 slaves and 2300 acres of excellent farming land. As an old man, he stated that he had made fifty two crops on his land. For a number of years, even up to the time of his death, he operated the Chocchuma Ferry. This was a so-called "free ferry". Ferries of this sort were financed by the county. Mr. Duncan received thirty-three dollars per month for the ferry service. Another influential planter of what is now the western part of Grenada county was John L. LeFlore. This man was the son of the Choctaw Chief, Greenwood LeFlore. His mother was a white woman, the daughter of John Donly, the man who carried the U. S. Mail along the Natchez Trace. The old Indian Chief gave to his son J. L. LeFlore over two thousand acres of valuable land located Southewast of the present place called LeFlore. Here he farmed and seemed to prosper in the years before the Civil War. When that war came on, the younger LeFlore favored secession, while he old Chief opposed the secession movement. The younger LeFlore became President of the first Board of Supervisors of Grenada County when this county was organized in 1870. Declining fortune during the reconstruction years resulted in him having some of his property sold under court orders in order to satisfy judgments obtained by creditors. He was buried in Odd Fellows Cemetery in the city of Grenada. Boyd Doak was born in Tennessee but moved with his father to a place near Canton. This place, known as Doak's Stand, served as the meeting place of the United States

Commissioners and representatives of the Choctaw Indians when the Treaty of Doak's Stand was negotiated in 1820. We have information that Boyd Doak helped his father move the Indians who left that area under the provisions of the treaty negotiated there. He moved to a place in the area of Pea Ridge in the early 1830's. Here was born Robert Doak, about whom we shall have more to relate as we begin to consider the contributions made by a later generation of men and women who built upon the foundations established by the early settlers. Boyd Doak joined a company of Mississippians who participated in the Mexican War. He died in 1878, possible a victim of the Yellow Fever Epidemic of that year.

Matthew K. Mister, Sr. came to the area in 1840. He was a merchant and planter. He was a staunch Union man, and during the Reconstruction period following the Civil War he was appointed Judge of the Chancery Court of Yalobousha County. His appointment came from the Federal General in charge of the occupation forces of the area. Later he was removed from this office by General Ames who was appointed Provisional Governor of Mississippi when the Radical Republican Majority in the Federal Congress declared all civil offices in the state government vacant. A son, bearing the same name as the elder Mister, later became Post Master at Grenada. Major Jack Williams came into the area about 1835. He was a planter, trader and river boat man. He assisted in opening up the road which led east from Grenada to Graysport. John Towne Leigh moved to Yalobousha County in 1835 and built a home which he called "The Mountains", about ten miles north of the town of Grenada. He came from Amelia County Virginia and with energy and vision, developed his lands until he became a man of considerable means. Although we have little information relative to the contributions made by pioneer women who came with their families into the area we know that these contributions must have been significant. Miss Carolina Lake, sister of the Lake brothers heretofore mentioned, was born in Maryland in 1822. She came to Grenada in 1835, probably on the same boat which brought her brother Levin to Grenada. She later married a man by the name of Williams. She lived until 1902. Another pioneer woman was Mrs. James Crump, mother of Walter Crump. They came to the area in 1835 and settled near Chocchuma. In her old age she related something of the hardship of the journey which brought them to Mississippi. When she arrived at Chocchuma that little town had, according to her account, five stores, five boarding houses and three hotels as well as a number of saloons. The large number of boarding houses and hotels found in such a small town can be accounted for by remembering that, at the time, Chocchuma was the center of feverish activity in land sales. Land speculators from many different areas were in the town and needed housing accomodations. Another pioneer woman who made her contribution to building the foundations of the community was Mrs. S. M. Correll. The only written evidence of her residence here was the advertisement which she inserted in the Grenada Bulletin of May 5, 1835. In this advertisement she announced the continance of a school which she had opened on April 25th of the same year. Another of these early school teachers was Mrs. John Yalmon who taught a school on the Mannie Plantation. Later this area became a part of Glenwild plantation. This school was organized in 1836 and was housed in a crude log house. Of course there were other men and women who were instrumental in building the foundations of Grenada and Grenada county, but lack of space and information make it impossible for us to give due credit to their contributions.

SOME OF THOSE WHO BUILT ON THE FOUNDATIONS

The foundations of the town and county were built in the first quarter of century of settlement, and this building was largely the work of those early settlers, a number of whom have been discussed. A new generation was to come on the scene after the Civil War, and build again on the foundations which had been partially destroyed by the ravages of the war. Of course some of the early settlers such as Ralph Coffman, John Moore and Robert Mullin lived on into the period after the war and continued to be effective in the rebuilding process, but decendents of the early settlers, along with people who came to the area later began to work along with these older men, and, during the last twenty five years of the 19th century, came to be leaders in the long process of restoring a war-ravaged area to something of its former prosperity. The men and women who will be mentioned hereafter will be those who made their contributions very largely in the last forty years of the century. Robert Doak was a second generation leader. He was born in 1838 in what is now Grenada County. He spent part of his boyhood years in Holly Springs. At the age of sixteen he went to Aberdeen where he learned the tinner trade. In 1861 he enlisted in the 11th Mississippi Regiment. At the battle of Gettysburg he was taken prisoner. He opened a tinner shop in Grenada in 1866. Soon he branched out into the hardware business. By the year 1891 he was the sixth largest hardware dealer in the state. Although Mr. Doak had at least two partners associated with him at different times, he was the sole owner of the business during the last years of his life. He was Vice-President of the Merchants Bank, and stockholder in and director of several industries formed in Grenada. Dr. William McSwine was the son of John McSwine who came from Virginia to Mississippi and settled in the area where Hardy is now located. Dr. McSwine began the practice of medicine in 1878. He served several terms in the State Legislature during some of the difficult Reconstruction years. His sister, Hester, married Captain J. J. Slack who was a prominent attorney in Grenada for many years. Leopol Newburger was born in Germany. He came to Philadelphia by ship, and to Grenada by stagecoach. He worked briefly with an uncle who was operating a plantation store. The uncle then gave him twenty dollars to invest in goods. He became a "back peddler" walking about the country with a small stock of merchandise which would appeal to housewives who had very few chances to visit the stores in the towns of the area. At this time the roads were almost impassable much of the time. Newburger prospered and began to invest his money in real estate. In the years following the Civil War he bought up a large acreage in and about Graysport. Much of this land was bought at foreclosure on tax sales. Later he moved his family to Louisville, Kentucjy to give his children better educational advantages. At a later date, in the last half of the 19th century, two other Jewish business men played an important role in the development of the area. One of these, Joseph Newburger, began his business career in Coffeeville where he and a brother operated a merchantile establishment and also engaged in cotton buying as did many of the other merchants of the period. The Newburger cotton interests soon branched out. The company soon had cotton buyers in as many as fifty different locations in the northern part of the state. Joseph Newburger moved to Grenada and made this town the headquarters for the firm. For a considerable period of time the Newburger Cotton Company was buying from twenty-five to thirty thousand bales of cotton each season. In conjunction with the purchase of cotton the firm became stockholders in a number of cotton compresses and storage warehouses. Joseph Newburger had outlets for his cotton in England and some of the countries where he had business contacts. In 1893 the Newburger Brothers had to suspend payment of their obligations and make an assignment of the assets of the company. In addition to buying much cotton for their European outlets they had bought for the company about 10,000 bales expecting a rise in the price of cotton. This rise did not materialize, and they had to sell the cotton on a declining market. Starting out again the company soon was able to recoup its losses and repay all its obligations not covered by the assignment which it had made to its creditors. A New England factory to which the company was indebted had gone out of business but stockholders of that company were searched out and payment made to them. Soon after the successful revival of the business Joseph Newburger moved to Memphis and made that city the headquarters for the firm, although he continued to have business interests in Grenada. He was instrumental in inducing the I. C. Railroad to build a railroad branch from Grenada to Parsons where the line connected with the old

Y. & M. V. Railroad which had been purchased by the I. C. System. At the time of his death in 1926 he left a sizable fortune. In his will he bequeathed twenty six thousand dollars to various churches, orphanages, youth associations, and homes of refuge. Although he was Jewish in faith, he made no distinction in favor of Jewish organizations, but contributed to Protestant and Catholic institutions as freely as he did to Jewish organizations. Another Jewish businessman was Max Ginsburger.

While a mere boy Max left his home in Louisville, Kentucky and came to Grenada and lived with his aunt, Mrs. Wile. He clerked in the store of I. Wile. He managed the store for a time and after the death of the founder of the firm he was associated with Sam Wile in a firm known as Ginsburger and Wile. Later he ran the business under the firm name of Max Ginsburger. He did a big business in furnishing supplies for farmers, and as a result of this credit business he had much capital invested in farming operations which capital was secured by Deeds of Trust on land and on crop mortgages. The records indicate that he seldom had to forclose on any of thse Deeds of Trust or crop mortgages. Mr. Ginsburger was active in many community projects and was a general favorite with both Jewish and Gentile people. When the Baptist Congregation began to raise money for a new church building he was one of the leaders of the fund drive committee. He was one of the men responsible for the organization of the Central Mississippi Fair which, for many years, was one of the outstanding organizations of its kind. Later it came to be called the North Mississippi Fair. Mr. Ginsburger continued in business until 1910 when he died after entering a St. Louis hospital for surgery.

Captain John Powell was one of the most influential post-war businessmen who lived and operated in Grenada. He was born in Virginia, moved with his mother to Alabama in 1831, and then to Grenada in 1836. He began his business career as a clerk in a store located in the town of Troy. In 1855 he became a member of the mercantile firm of Conley & Powell. This business was burned out in 1857, and Powell became Station Agent for the Mississippi Central Railroad. Later he served as Sheriff of the county, and for sixteen months was Treasurer of the Mississippi Central Railroad Company. When the Civil War broke out he enlisted in company H of the 15th Mississippi Regiment. After the termination of the Civil War he returned to Grenada and again engaged in mercantile business. He began buying cotton and soon thereafter became a partner of the New Orleans cotton commission firm of Chaffee & Powell. He became well-to-do, and was very generous in his financial support of various institutions including the Baptist Church of which he was a member. He donated the lot, now occupied by the Frank Evans Building, to the Grenada Baptist Church, and helped raise the funds to erect a church on the lot. He was one of the three members of the General Relief Committee which directed relief work in Grenada during the course of the Yellow Fever Epidemic of 1878. He bought from John Moore the old Moore home recently owned by Mrs. Bob Jackson. This home on Margin Street was built by John Moore who lived there until his children had grown up and left home. It came to be known as the Powell-Lea house. The Dubard family has long been identified with the history of Grenada County. As early as 1836 Philip and William Dubard were at Chocchuma for the purpose of purchasing land in the area of Grenada county in which members of this family have lived since 1836. There was also a William Dubard Jr. buying land about the same time. William M. Dubard, decendent of William and William Jr., Dubard, lived until comparatively recent times. In 1938 Mr. Dubard was one of three surviving Confederate Veterans then living in Grenada. Mr. Dubard who was a member of Company K., Third Mississippi Cavalry, had six brothers in Confederate service, all of whom had gone out with units formed in or about Grenada.

Jesse Clark and his wife Jane came into the Graysport area early and settled about three miles southwest of that village. In 1845 the youngest of seven children was born to the Clarks. He was given the name Adolphus Fillmore Clark. While he was still a small child the Hurricane of 1846 which created so much havoc in Grenada, struck the Clark home and completely demolished it. Mrs. Clark and little Adolphus Fillmore took refuge in the cellar and both survived without serious injury. When the house was rebuilt it was called The Hurricane. The family moved to the northeast part of what is now Grenada County, then a part of Yalobousha County, and were living here when the Civil War broke out. Three Clark boys, William, David and Thomas enlisted early in the war. Adolphus Fillmore enlisted as soon as he was eighteen years of age. For some unexplained reason he enlisted in Company D. of The First Mississippi Battalion of Sharpshooters, rather than in one of the several military units formed in the area of his home. He was still alive at the age of ninety three in the year 1938.

William and Thacker Winter were early settlers in the area near the present line between Grenada and Tallahatchie counties. They also owned land in that part of Grenada county which was once a part of Tallahatchie County. Old land records indicate that they came from Limestone County, Alabama. Thacker Winter bought land at the Chocchuma Land Office as early as November, 1833. William began to buy a little later. He was busy in late 1833 and early 1834 in establishing a government for Yalobousha County. The County was established and the first Board of Supervisors appointed December 23, 1833. On March 24, 1834, William Winter took his oath of office as a Supervisor of the newly created county. Thomas C. McMacken, William Metcalf, Dempsey H. Hicks and Robert Edington were the other Supervisors taking the oath of office. D. M. Rayborn took office as County Clerk, James H. Barfield as Sheriff and John Smith as Coroner. The first meeting of the Board was at the little village of Hendersonville, but the seat of county government was established at Coffeeville and the Board was soon meeting at that place. S. McCreles had built the first house on the site which was to become Coffeeville in 1830. He was evidently a "squatter" who later prempted the land on which his house was built.

Jesse Griffis who was born in South Carolina settled in Yalobousha County some years after the first settlers had come into the area. His son, John W. Griffis, began working with Robert Mullin. Later he worked for the Lake Brothers. He married the daughter of Mullin and established his own mercantile business in 1879. In 1890 he became President of Grenada Bank. Captain Gabriel P. Lake, a cousin of the four Lake Brothers who established their business firms in Tullahoma, came to the area some years after the arrival of his cousins, and worked for a time with his cousins. Later he moved to the area near Duck Hill. Oliver H. Perry came to Graysport with his father Zaddock Perry. His son J. C. Perry became a merchant at Graysport. He served Circuit Clerk of Grenada County. His son J. B. Perry was a prominent business man of Grenada until his death. Judge Fairfield was a native of New Hampshire. He came to the Natchez area and, for a time, taught school at Woodville. In 1858 he moved to Grenada. Although he opposed secession, he was loyal to his adopted state and served in a local military organization of old men and young boys which was designed for local defense during the Civil War years. He and his wife also ran a school during the war years.

John L. Scurr and his wife Lydia came to Yalobousha County in 1837. They were natives of North Carolina. Their home was erected near the extinct village of Torrance which was located a few miles north of Grenada. Adrian V. B. Thomas and his wife Mary moved in 1849 to a place on the Yalobousha River known as Whig Island. He owned much land and many slaves. James Tindall came to Yalobousha County in 1849. He owned land in the Gore Springs neighborhood. Besides farming, he was a lumberman who furnished the lumber for many of the buildings erected in the town of Grenada. Dr. G. W. Trimble came to Yalobousha County in 1852. He practiced his profession in the western part of what is now Grenada County. He moved to Grenada and became County Health Officer.

He became Surgeon for the I. C. Railroad. He also served a term as President of the State Medical Association. Robert H. Turner was the grandson of a man who was born on ship while on a voyage from Dublin, Ireland to South Carolina. He lived in the vicinity of the old town of Tuscahoma until 1890. He moved to Grenada and served as County Treasurer. Major John Williams came to Yalobousha County in 1833. He came from South Carolina. In 1838 he was living near Graysport. Samuel B. Marsh came to Yalobousha County about the time the land sales began at Chocchuma. He did extensive land speculation in that part of Tallahatchie County which later became a part of Grenada County. He was an attorney and there is on record a deed by which a father conveyed to Marsh a considerable acreage of land in consideration of Marsh defending two sons who were in jail at Coffeeville, charged with murder.

One of the most prominent post-Civil War residents of Grenada was E. C. Walthall. He was educated at the well known St. Thomas School of Holly Springs. He studied law and located at Coffeeville for the practice of his profession. He became Lt. Colonel of the 15th Mississippi Regiment, and before the war was over became a Major General. His Division acted at the rear-guard of the Confederate Army as it retreated from the disasterous battle of Franklin. After the war General Walthall moved to Grenada and began a law practice at this place. He was very successful in his practice and became chief legal officer for the Mississippi & Tennessee Railroad. Later he became a United States Senator from Mississippi. When his close friend and legal associate L. Q. C. Lamar, then United States Senator from Mississippi, was selected as a member of the Cabinet of President Cleveland, Walthall succeeded his friend as United States Senator and served until 1894.

John Gibbs was not one of the earliest settlers in the area of Grenada but was doing business in Grenada and vicinity a year or so after the union of Pittsburg and Tullahoma. In 1839 he bought the storehouse which had been occupied by the firm of Pryor & Howard in the old town of Pittsburg. He also bought a lot west of Pittsburg street and north of Cherry street at the intersection of these two streets. In 1839 he bought lot 34 of the Green W. Crowder Survey. On this lot, which was east of Commerce and north of Govan streets he erected a residence known as Shannon Grove. This name was the suggestion of his father who had lived on the river Shannon in Ireland. At the time this residence was erected it was situated in "Suburban Grenada" according to the newspaper reports of that period. Mr. Gibbs was engaged in much land speculation and, at times, became financially embarassed as promissory notes for lands became due. Perhaps it was this fact that caused his wife, M. M. Gibbs, to take advantage of a legislative act, passed by the Mississippi Legislature on February 28, 1846, which allowed a married woman to have control of their own property by having a schedule of thier possessions filed with the Chancery Clerk. On July 14, 1886, she filed such a schedule under "An act for the protection and preservation of the rights of married women". This was her reference to the recently passed legislative act. In this schedule she lists as her property five hundred and twenty acres of land, most of which was in the vicinity of Grenada. Part of the land which she listed was in Section 13, Township 22, Range 4 East on which was located a spring which later came to be the chief attraction of a health resort known as Gibbs Springs. The water was reputed to have medicinal properties which had a beneficial effect on people suffering with various disorders. This place was a point of refuge for some people who left Grenada during the Yellow Fever Edpidemic of 1878. Other property listed by Mrs. Gibbs was: "Lots 107 and 161 West Ward Grenada, and fifty feet off the south side of lot 104. One Negro man Richard, and one Negro man Ben about 28 years old; one Mulatto named Sallie about 20 years old and her child Harriett about two years old, and one Negro woman named Maria about twenty years old; one brown and black sorrel mare mule; one wagon and gear; three oxen, five cows, three calves and eight head of young cattle; one lot of hogs about thirty in number; three bedsteads with beds, and furniture, one clock, one bureau, two tables and twelve chairs, and one looking glass; one lot of books about one hundred volumes; one lot of glass and crockery ware and a small lot of silver; one lot of iron ware and stove; and one lot of arming utensils". It would seem that Mrs. Gibbs, by asserting her legal right to control this property was hedging against the speculative proclivities of her husband. This was wise, because, at a later date, it became necessary for Mr. Gibbs to sell off much of his land holdings to meet his financial obligations. During the later years of his life Mr. Gibbs spent considerable time and money in developing his health resort. He shipped to distant points and sold locally water from his resort. Mrs. M. M. Ransom who was an outstanding teacher, in both private and public schools of Grenada during the last quarter of the 19th century, was a daughter of James and Harriet Sims and the granddaughter of John and Hannah Smith. In her old age she made frequent visits to her daughter, Mrs. McCampbell, who lived on Popolar Street in Grenada. Mrs. McCampbell was the widow of Rev. John McCampbell, who died during the Yellow Fever Epidemic of 1878. At the time of the epidemic Rev. McCampbell was pastor of the Grenada Presbyterian Church.

In the post-Civil War years Grenada had many outstanding lawyers as members of its local bar. Judge E. T. Fisher was an early post-war member of the Mississippi Supreme Court. Later, Judge William C. McLean, who was born in a house standing on the site presently occupied by the Grenada County Courthouse, served for a time on the Supreme Court of the State. He was also a member of the Constitutional Convention which drew up the so-called "Constitution of 1890". This is the Constitution which, with ammendments adopted at various times, is still the organic law of the State - so far as the Federal Supreme Court will recognize the right of state to have any state organic law. Judge A. T. Roane came to Grenada from Calhoun County in order to obtain better educational opportunities for his children. He became a leading attorney judge, and a well-to-do business man. Judge Longstreet, a relative of L. Q. C. Lamar, was a strong member of the local bar for many years. Lawyers and law firms having professional cards in the local papers in 1881 were A. S. Pass, Slack & Longstreet, R. H. Golladay, B. C. Adams Jr., Fitzgerald & Whitfield, W. C. McLean, R. Horton and Thomas P. Gibbs.

During this same period Grenada must have been a good business town as would seem to be indicated by the long list of business firms advertising in the Grenada Sentinel in 1881. Those firms were J. M. Bishop watchmaker & jeweler, Leigh & Powell general merchants, Lake Brothers Bank, J. B. Lake Jr. cotton shed, Robert Doak hardware, E. Cahn drygoods, Chaffee & Powell cotton factors, Eugene Wolfe saloon, J. W. Griffis & Company drygoods, Sidney Kettle lock and gunsmith, W. E. Smith watchmaker and jeweler, J. E. Hughes druggist, Statham saloon and billiard hall, morning star saloon, Lacock & Garner furniture and coffins, Burnes, Dolittle & Company general plantation supplies, N. C. Snider's Banking House, W. N. Pass buggies, Huffington & Company drygoods, Charlie Stirle boot and shoe maker, W. I. Ingram groceries, John George saloon, W. C. McGee hardware, W. A. Belew hardware, Pryor & Mckie General Merchants, T. S. Parker druggist, Mrs. D. I. Lowensteen restaurant, W. G. Hamilton drygoods, L. G. Dubard & Company livery stable, F. R. Austine & Company general merchandise, A. W. Lake groceries, J. Cahn & Company drygoods, M. Cords groceries, W. P. Towles & Company druggists, George W. Jones general merchandise, Burns & Sons supply store, Fleece's Repair Shop, New Orleans Restaurant, E. F. Price Taylor, I. Wile & Company drygoods and Mrs. M. L. Powell, milliner.

These then, were the business and professional men who were instrumental in the long, hard task of rebuilding the economy of a town and county which had been devistated by the ravages of the Civil War with its aftermath of Reconstruction. Much credit is due to those hardy spirits who founded first a town, later a county, and developed both into a prosperous part of the pre-war South, but equal credit should be given to those men and women of a later period who rebuilt Grenada and vicinity upon the dead ashes of earlier prosperity. The Grenada Sentinel of Jan. 5, 1884, tells of the sturdy independence, thrift and perserverence of one of the men who struggled through the post Civil War years to support himself and his family: "Mr. G. W. Kendall, better known as "Uncle Wash" was born at Center, N. C. on the 25th of Oct. 1819. He moved to Mississippi and married on the 10th of September 1844, and in 1847 moved on the place where he now lives, six miles east of Grenada. During the year 1847 Mr. Kendall commenced the sale of butter and eggs. Since then he has been to Grenada every Saturday, not missing but two or three Saturdays, then he came on Fridays so that he would be at home the following day to attend to his christian duties. Since Jan., 1847, it has been 37 years, making 1934 days he has been in Grenada to sell butter and eggs. By dividing 1924 days by the number of days in a year, we find he as spent five years, three months and 9 days in Grenada. The average amount of butter and eggs sold on Saturday will amount to two dollars. Now multiply the number of Saturdays in Grenada by two dollars and we find that he has sold $3,848.00 worth of butter and eggs. It is six miles to "Uncle Wash's", making twelve miles he travels every Saturday. By multiplying 1924 visits to Grenada by 12 miles we find that he has gone the distance 23,088 miles. Subtract this number from the circumference of the earth and we find that he has to travel only 1912 miles before he will have gone the distance around the world, which will take him until March the 8th, 1887, to get home, making three years, three months and eight days he still has to spend on life's troubled sea before making the circumference of the earth. Now to the readers of "Uncle Wash's" history as stated above, I will say that this is but a small item in the worth man's history.

He has also raised a large family of children, one son and five or six daughters, all married and doing well, except two single daughters, who still remain with him to comfort him and their mother in their declining years. He has given all his children a good English education - over the average. His oldest single daughter has taken a high position as a teacher in our public schools. So now, you who want to go west, stop and consider "Uncle Wash's" history before you move, and take courage and see what can be accomplished in your beloved sunny South by perseverance, industry, and a close attention to your own business: living in peace and harmony with all good citizens, as this worthy man has lived; as can be testified by all his neighbors for 37 years past. So go on "Uncle Wash" and may kind providence extend your time to make the circuit of the globe at least once in a lifetime in selling butter and eggs, and when you take your departure from this earth, may you live on in eternity, on the river that flows with milk and honey. Last, but not least, this worthy man has lived and prospered independent of loans and mortgages.

This article was contributed by a neighbor, evidently a person who believed that, despite the ravages of civil strife and emancipation of Negro slaves, the South still offered opportunities for those who retained the independent spirit of the pioneer settlers of the area.

Chapter XII

Early Churches of Grenada and Vicinity

In any discussion of religious influence in that part of the Choctaw Cession of 1830 which eventually became Grenada County, we must remember that settlement of new areas west of the Appalachian Mountains did not follow the pattern set up by back-country New England and Middle Atlantic State settlers as they pushed inland from the established settlements on the coast. In New England, for instance, new settlements were not attempted until the existing settlements could no longer support their increasing population. When this occured, the surplus population had to obtain permission from the authorities of the existing settlement to move into the back country and establish a new settlement. When this movement took place the settlers, as a rule, went together, taking with them a minister, and frequently a teacher. Sometimes the minister served in the dual capacity of minister and teacher. On the other hand, the pioneers who settled the vast country west of the mountains usually came as individual families, or small groups of people closely allied by blood kinship or by former friendly association. They had to build homes and carve out farms as the first order of existence. Religious and educational organization usually came after, rather than with these pioneer settlers. In the early established little towns such as Pittsburg and Tullahoms (which later united to form the town of Grenada), saloons were built before churches. The earliest church on record in the area which was to become Grenada county was granted land on which to build a church in 1835, whereas as early as the summer of 1832 an enterprising merchant had set up a trading post in a tent on the banks of the Yalobousha River near the site of the present mill of the Mississippi Cotton Seed Products Company formerly known as the Grenada Oil Mill. Here he dispensed whiskey and other trade articles to itinerate traders operating the area, many of whom were "Squawmen" as evidenced by the many half-breed Indians having English sur-names. It was four years after the settlement of the two little neighboring towns on the Yalobousha before any religious organization purchased a town lot on which to erect a church building. During the intervals between the beginning of the towns and the erection of churches, a few itinerate preachers made occasional visits to the towns, officiating in marriages, funerals and in occasional religious meetings in the homes of some of the people, but no organized church existed during the first four years of the existence of the towns.

The first religious influence to be exerted in the area came not among the early white settlers, but through the establishemtn of the Elliot Mission School, which was established 1818 near the present town of Holcomb. Here, fifteen years before the area was opened for land purchase by white people, The Board of Commissioners for Foreign Missions, an inter-dominational project of the Congregation and Presbyterian churches of New England, established a school in which Indian children were taught domestic skills, elements of Agriculture, reading and writing, as well as being instructed in the Christian religion. This school ceased operation some time between 1830 and 1833, but had an indirect influence on early Christian religious observance among the early white settlers, as John Smith, one of the Elliot Missionaries, became one of the first settlers in Pittsburg, and frequently had religious services in the Union Hotel which he had established in the little town. His daughter Harriett, wife of merchant James Sims, sold for a substantial consideration, the lots on which the first, present Methodist church was located. It is known that before any regular church organization existed in either Pittsburg or Tullahoma there were occasional union services in a log store building located on the north-east corner of the lot at the inersection of Church and Third streets. This use of the building probably gave name to the street called Church.

So far as land records indicate, the first organized church group to be

deeded land as the location of a church building was the Spring Hill Methodist Church. On November 13, 1835, James Marble conveyed to John H. Hines, Isaac Taylor, Lewis Miller, and James Trotter as "TRUSTEES OF THE METHODIST EPISCOPAL CHURCH AT SPRING HILL MEETING HOUSE" a little more than eight acres of land. The wording of the deed would seem to indicate that meetings were already being held at the place preceeding the granting of the deed. At the time when the aforementioned deed was executed, Spring Hill was a rather important crossroad point. It was here that the Grenada-Carrollton road which passed through the area, had a road branching from it, which road branched again near the site of the present town of Holcomb, so as to reach the ferries existing at the two little towns of Chocchuma and Tuscahoma. A tavern was located at the crossroad point of Spring Hill, and taverns were located in the towns of Chocchuma and Tuscahoma. We have no written records to substantiate the tradition that Spring Hill had been a meeting place for the Methodist people for a year or more before the deed for the church lot was given, and that services were held under a rough arbor of tree branches. There seems to have been doubt in the minds of some people relative to the validity of the original deed given to the Church. On December 15, 1855, twenty years after the first deed was executed, Jacob Poitevent and his wife Mary granted a deed to William Dubard, Ables Eli, William H. Beck, Green W. Trimble and Henry Heath, all trustees of the Spring Hill Church, the same land which Marble had granted the church in the first deed. In an endeavor to determine why some one thought a second deed necessary, we checked the originial tract book and found that while James Marble is listed as purchaser of the land on which the church was located, he never obtained a government land patent to the land. Most early land purchases were made with a down payment and with several years to pay off the balance. If a purchaser defaulted in payment of the balance of the purchase price, the land reverted to the Federal Government. Of course if Marble had bought his land on the usual terms, he could give to the church only such title as he himself had in the land. Any sale made by him, and title granted, would be subject to the lien which the Federal Government had on the unpaid balance of the purchase price. Since Poitevent did purchase the land from the Federal government at a date later than the date of the deed granted by Marble, there seems little doubt that the original deed was defective because Marble never had legal title to the land. At this late date it is hard to realize the great contribution which the Spring Hill Church made to the religious life of the area. At this time, one hundred thirty one years after the date of the first deed transaction, the church still exists. Because of the shift of people from rural areas to towns and cities, the church does not now play as important a place in the religious life of the area as it once did, but it still has a place in the hearts of those who continue to look upon it as their place of worship, and of people now living in many different localities, who have loved ones and friends buried in the rather extensive cemetery located on the church lot.

    The first religious congregation to purchase a lot in Grenada was the First Presbyterian Church. We do not know when this church was organized, nor where it met before the erection of its first church building. On January 16, 1838, the "Proprietors of Grenada" conveyed to George K. Morton, John Moore, Nathaniel S. Neal, L. C. Caldwell, R. T. Briarly, U. Tyson, and E. P. Statton, Trustees of First Presbyterian Church of Grenada lot number one hundred thirteen. The consideration involved was one hundred thirty seven dollars and fifty cents. The lot, located east and north of the intersection of Line and Second streets, is the location of the present Presbyterian Church Building. Soon after the purchase of the lot the congregation began construction of a building which was to serve as their place of worship for a period of approximately sixty-two years. They erected a two-story frame building. The lower story was used for church purposes while the upper story was used as a meeting place for the Masonic Order. On January 5, 1900, The Grenada Sentinel reported that the Presbyterial Congregation had decided to erect a new church building which was to cost from "seven to ten thousand dollars". It was some time after this decision before any considerable progress was made relative to a new building. It is very probable that the delay arose from the need to accumulate money to pay for the new building. In the year 1903, the Sentinel carried an advertisement in which the church officials advised that they would receive bids on the old church building, said building to be demolished and materials removed from the church lot. In 1904, the same paper carried a news item that the new building, then in process of construction, was expected to cost sixteen thousand dollars. We note from newspaper items of the period that during the interval between the demolition of the old building and the completion of the new one, the congregation held services sometimes in the City Hall and sometimes in the City White School Building. Although the building must have been completed in 1904, we have not found any record of the actual date of completion. This building, with some renovations and additions has continued to serve the Presbyterian Congregation down to the present time.

The second sale of a lot in Grenada to a religious congregation came on September 4, 1838. By this transaction Hiram Coffee, Joseph McRaven, John and John A. Lane, John Shields, Samuel Puckett and John Smith "Proprietors of Grenada" conveyed lot two hundred forty two in the West Ward of Grenada to the following named Trustees of Grenada Baptist Church: John H. Baker, James G. Hall, John Pontivent, John G. Jones, Henry Allen, James Y. Blocker, Jeremiah T. Talbert, Charles R. Taylor and Howell Edmonds. The price paid for the lot was three hundred dollars cash. The men who sold the lot were owners of the old town of Pittsburg, and before the union of the two towns, did business under the title "Proprietors of the Town Company of Pittsburg". A few weeks before this transaction, a Baptist Congregation consisting of twelve members had been organized. In the interval between the organization of the congregation and the purchase of the lot, several new members had been received into the church. The lot purchased was the south half of lot 242, which lot is located north and east of the intersection of Margin and College streets. At the time of the sale College Street was known as Pittsburg street, and the deed lists the lot as fronting a certain number of feet on Pittsburg street. For some un-explained reason the Baptists never erected a building on this lot, though they seemed to have retained some sort of title to, or claim on the lot. In 1849 the church gave a quit claim title to James Slider for the sum of one dollars. In 1850 Slider sold this lot to E. F. Moody for the sum of one hundred fifty dollars. It seems strange that a lot which sold for three hundred dollars in 1838 became so useless, or worthless, to the church that eleven years after the church had purchased the property, that organization was willing to give a quit claim title to Slider for a trifling sum, and that, within one year, Slider was able to sell the lot for one hundred fifty dollars. It is possible that there may have been some sort of defect, or suspicion of defect of title relative to the lot.

On July 13, 1839, the Baptist Church purchased another lot. This time they obtained a lot in the original town of Tullahoma, now the East Ward of Grenada. Samuel Smith sold to Howell Edmonds, James, G. Hall, Henry Allen, John G. Jones, John C. Baker and Jeremian T. Talbert designated in the deed as "Trustees of the United Baptist Church of Grenada", the south one half of the one half lot 185. We wonder if any significance may be attached to the two terms "Trustees of Grenada Baptist Church" as written in the deed to the lot in the West Ward, and "Trustees of the United Baptist Church of Grenada". At the time there was a serious diversity of opinion among Baptist relative to foreign missions. We know that some Baptists in the county under the leadership of Francis Baker, were against stress on foreign missions and were called Primative, or Hardshell, Baptists. The Grenada Church, as it finally became established was a missionary church. It is possible that some sort of accord had been brought about between factions of the denomination, and the resulting church became known as the United Baptist Church. This may account for the abandonment of the first site purchased for a building, and the purchase so soon thereafter of another site in another ward of Grenada. This lot was rather expensive, the selling price being one thousand dollars. The Baptist Congregation began construction of a brick building on this site. Slow progress was made on the building, possibly because the Panic of 1837 had now hit the country with full force and money was very hard to come by. Before the building had been completed and occupied, a tornado which struck Grenada demolished the incompleted church building. This was a hard blow to the Baptist people, and it would be two decades or so before they would again attempt to build a pretentious church building. By another of those curious lot transactions the Church authorized Lott S. Humphrey, David Beck and George Donkin to act as commissioners for the church and, as such, to give a deed to Mrs. Grizzell Land, by which the church transfered its interest in its part of lot one hundred eighty five to Mrs. Land for a consideration of fifty dollars. Seven years earlier the church had paid one thousand dollars for the lot on which they had erected the ill-fated building which was demolished by the tornado. What had caused such a decrease in value of the lot? We do not know. It is possible that when the lot was purchased by the church there was already on it a building of some value, which building was torn down to make way for the brick church building. After the destruction of the church building there was nothing of value on the lot. Since the original price of one thousand dollars was a very high price for a small lot in the residential section of the city in the year 1839, it is conceivable that part of that price was for the value of an existing building as well as the lot.

No doubt feeling impoverished by their ill fortune with the tornado destruction, the church then bought another lot, and erected thereon a less pretentious building than the one first attempted. On July 13, 1847, the church purchased from John Duncan part of lot one hundred seventy three, for a consideration of one hundred dollars. The deed related that Duncan conveyed the lot to "Henry N. Bingham, treasurer of the Baptist Church of Grenada, for use and benefit of said church a part of lot one hundred seventy three, beginning at an ally on the south side of said lot and running north sixty eight feet six inches towards the Presbyterian Church, and east to the street which separates said lot from lots originally owned by the late Samuel Smith, and west to Line Street which divides the east and west wards of said town". A frame building on this lot served the Baptist church until 1888 when a new brick church was built on the corner lot north and west of the intersection of Second and Main streets. This lot is now occupied by the Frank Evans building. In the deed to the lot purchased in the west ward and never used for a church building, the Articles of faith of the church are set out and made a part of the deed, with the provision that should any of the church members depart from the faith as set out by the articles in the deed, the property should then be vested in any members of the church who continued true to the doctrines set out by Articles of faith found in the deed. In subsequent deeds to lots acquired by the church, no mention is made of these articles of faith.

The third church congregation to buy a lot in Grenada was the Methodist Episcopal Church. This purchase was made on July 9, 1839, when Proprietors of the Town Company which had developed the former town of Pittsburg, conveyed to John Gibbs, John A. King, James Sims, William Bush, William Lake and R. M. Spicer,

> "Trustees in trust -- for the uses and purpose hereafter mentioned--
> for and in consideration of three hundred dollars in hand paid at
> and upon sealing and delivery of these presents the receipt of which
> is hereby acknowledged, has given, granted, bargained, sold, released,
> confirmed and conveyed, and by these presents doth give, grant, bargain,
> sell, release, confirm, and convey the said party of the second part
> and their successors, trustees in trust for the uses and purposes
> hereafter mentioned the north half of the south half of Survey eight

south of the river, and in the west ward of said town of Grenada beginning 1.58 chains north of the south east corner of survey number eight, and runs thence north 1.58 chains to a stake thence west 3.11 chains, thence south 1.58 chains, thence 3.11 chains east, containing by estimate .49 of an acre of land, in trust that they shall erect or build thereon a house, or place of worship, for the use of the members of the Methodist Episcopal Church in the United States of America, according to the rules and dicipline which from time to time may be agreed upon by the ministers and preachers of the said church at their General Conference in the United States of America; and in further trust and confidence that they shall at all times whensoever hereafter present such ministers and preachers belonging to the said church as shall from time to time be duly authorized by the General Conference as the ministers and preachers of the said Methodist Episcopal Church or by the Annual Conference authorized by the said General Conference, to preach and expound God's holy word therin; and in further trust and confidence that as often as any one or more of the trustees herein before mentioned shall die or cease to be a member of the said church according to the rules and dicipline of the said church, then in such case it shall be the duty of the station minister authorized as aforesaid who shall have the pastural (sic) charge of the members of the said church to call a meeting of the remaining trustees as soon as convientiy may be, and when so met the minister or preacher shall proceed to nominate one or more persons to fill the place or places of him or them whose office or offices has or have been vacated as aforesaid, provided that the person or persons nominated shall have been one year a member or members of the said church immediately preceeding such nomination, and at least twenty one years of age; and the said trustees so assembled shall proceed to elect and by a majority vote appoint the person or persons so nominated to fill such vacancy or vancacies in order to keep the number of trustees forever; and in case of an even number of votes for and against the nomination, or nominations, the Station Minister or preacher shall have the casting vote-providing nevertheless that if the said trustees or any of their successors have advanced any sum of money, or any shall be responsible for any, sum or sums, of money on account of the said premises, and they the said trustees or successors be obliged to pay the said sum, or sums, of money, they or a majority of them shall be authorized the raise the said sum, or sums, of money by mortagage of the said premises after notice given to the pastor or preacher who has the oversight of the congregation attending divine service on the said premises, if the money due be not paid to the said trustees or their successors within one year after such notice is given, and if such a sale take place the said trustees or their successors in office after paying the debt and other expenses which are due from money arising from such sale shall deposit the remainder of the money produced by the sale in the hands of the Stewart, or Stewarts, of the society belonging to, or attending divine service, on said premises, which surplus of the proceeds of such sale so deposited in the hands of the said Stewart, or Stewarts, shall be at the disposal of the next annual Conference authorized as aforesaid, which said annual Conference shall deposit said money according to their best judgement for the use of the said society."

    The above quotation is given with the spelling and punctuation, or lack of punctuation, as best made out from the somewhat faded manuscript from which this copy has been made.

    The lot conveyed by this deed is located almost west of the Grenada County Library. It is interesting to note that two of the trustees named were also members of the Town Company which was selling the lot. They were James Sims and John A. Lane Assuming that the church was erected in the same year in which the deed was granted, this first Methodist Church served the congregation for a period of thirteen years. It is interesting to note that during this thirteen year period the Presbyterian, Methodist and Baptist Churches were almost within a baseball throw of each other. The Episcopal church, to be built later, as befitting its Church of England ancestry sat as a more dignified distance away. There is a tradition, which has long had credence among the members of the Grenada Methodist Church, that when a later church building was erected it was constructed on a lot donated by James Sims and his wife Harriet. There is no written evidence available that this tradition is true but, on the contrary, there is authenic evidence that the belief has no foundation in fact. In order to present this written evidence we quote the following excerpt from the deed by which Sims and his wife conveyed the block presently occupied by the Methodist church and Sunday School building: The deed from which we quote was dated September 17, 1850: The deed defines James Sims and Harriet Sims as Party of the First Part and William Lake. A. S. Brown, M. K. Mister, J. P. Mitchell, James Sims, George Lake, E. F. Gibbs, E. F. Moody, and J. P. Tarpley "Trustees in trust for the uses and purposes hereafter described". It also reads that the conveyance was made for consideration of five hundred dollars to them in hand paid. Of course this block conveyed to the church consisted of five lots which today are very valuable, but we must remember that when Mr. and Mrs. Sims sold the lots to the church, the Panic of 1837 still was in effect and money hard to come by. At this time many lots were being sold at tax sales. Mrs. Sims had bought in two of the lots conveyed to the church at a tax sale for the ridiculous price of two dollars and thirty four cents. We believe, although we have not been able to substantiate the fact, that Mrs. Sims obtained the remaining two lots conveyed to the church in a wholesale purchase of lots from A. Bew, by which she paid six hundred dollars for about fifty lots in the former town of Pittsburg. We may be sure that, whether she obtained these two lots from Bew, or from some other person or tax sale, she paid a very small price for the lots. Today such a sale of these lots would be a very generous gesture, but then it was a profitable real estate deal. With the purchase of this block of lots, and the erection of a church thereon, the old church lot and building were no longer needed by the Church. Soon after the erection of the new Methodist Church building, the trustees of that church conveyed the old church and church lot to an educational institution of the Methodist denomination known as Bascomb's Seminary. The institution was named in honor of a Methodist Bishop by the name of Bascomb. It advertised as an institution doing both high school and college work. For a number of years it was a competitor of the Yalobousha Female Institute which was established by the Baptist denomination. Neither of these two female schools were able to survive the ravages of the Civil War.

Probably the first Baptist Church to be established outside the town of Grenada was the Antioch Church. On February 16, 1839, Joseph and Moses Collins "in consideration of our desire to promote the worship of Almighty God and the love and affection we bear toward that branch of the regular ordained Baptist Church" granted to William Minter, Joel Hill, Michial Talbert, William Tullis, Macon Minter, Humphrey Hood and John Wilbourn, Trustees for the Baptist Church at Antioch an area of land located about one mile north east of the present village of Hardy. For a number of years this was one of the stronger county churches. Joseph Collins and his son Moses were extensive property owners. Some of their decendents still reside in the city and county of Grenada.

On November 25, 1850, a Baptist Church was established a mile or so northeast of the present Grenada Airport. Thomas P. Bowles and his wife Mary, for a consideration of one dollar, conveyed a ten acre square lot to Lewis Aldridge, Jesse Griffis, and Hillary Talbert, Trustees of Mr. Parin Missionary Baptist Church. It is probable that the church had been established before the deed of conveyance, since in the description of the land conveyed after the metes and bounds had been given we have the statement: "so as to contain the church building and grave yard". Lewis Aldridge later became President of the Yalobousha Female Institute. Griffis and Talbert were business men of considerable substance.

On December 25, 1850, a deed was granted to a Methodist Church which deed conveyed two acres of land located about seven miles east of Grenada to A. Rosamond, Jesse Verhine, William M. Beard, James M. Read and Levine P. Peacock," Trustees of the Methodist Episcopal Church". The consideration involved was one dollar. The name of the church is not stated in the deed. On July 8, 1852, Anderson C. Smith and his wife Ann in consideration of the love and affection which we have for the church granted a ten acre tract of land to "The Session of the Old School Presbyterian Church called Hope." This tract of land is three or four miles southwest of Grenada. We have no information as to just how active a church was located on the site, nor how long it continued as a place of worship.

The Episcopal Church was a relatively late comer to Grenada. The first written evidence of the existence, or proposed establishment of an Episcopal Church in Grenada, is a deed dated October 12, 1870, by which Thomas C. Buffington conveyed to Joseph Weatherly, R. S. Ringold, J. W. Bishop and John Powell "the vestry of Grace Chapel Parish" a fractional part of lot one hundred eighty five in the east ward of Grenada. This is the lot on which the present church and parish house are located. We do not have the date of the erection of the first church building, but we do know that it was replaced in 1877 by the existing building. Some time before the erection of this second church building the name of the Parish had been changed from Grace Parish to All Saints Parish. Like the Methodist and Baptist Congregations, the Episcopal people attempted to provide a school for their children. In the year 1879, the Church purchased the so-called Masonic Academy, or as it was sometimes called, The Brick Academy. This was a four room brick building which the Masonic order had erected on the lot now occupied by the Lizzie Horn Elementary School building. The Masons seem not to have been very successful in the educational endeavor. After the purchase of the building, the Episcopal people ran a parish school for several years. Usually, if not always, the Rector of the church served as principal of and teacher in, the school. The church has never been strong in point of number of members, but has had among its members many of the outstanding business men and civic leaders of Grenada.

On December 22, 1876, a deed was granted to a number of men who made up the trustees of a church which was to become and continue one of the strongest country churches in the area. By this transaction John S. King, for a consideration of ten dollars, conveyed to George W. Williams, T. B. Williamson, M. P. Burk, and A. Lucious as deacons of the Providence Baptist Church 16.7 acres of land located a mile or so southeast of the present community of Gore Springs. The extensive cemetery on the church grounds has gravestones which mark the graves of many of the prominent early settlers of the eastern part of the county. The names on the gravestones in the church cemetery seem to indicate there was a church before the date given above.

Since many of the pre-Civil War churches had galleries for the colored slaves, some people have the idea that the Negroes had no churches of their own. This is not true, although the number of Negro churches existing before the war were comparatively few in number. We know that one such church existed in Grenada a number of years before the outbreak of the war. On February 10, 1847, only thirteen years after the founding of the town of Pittsburg, James Sims, acting as administrator of the estate of Luther Granberry, deeded to Edward Moody, Edward G. Gibbs, Donald Robertson and James Robertson, "Trustees in trust for the uses and purposes hereafter mentioned the northeast corner

of the east half of northwest one fourth of Section eighteen, Township twenty two, Range five East, containing one acre, for the use of the colored (or black) members of the Methodist Episcopal Church South of the United States of America and in faith, trust and confidence that they shall at all times forever hereafter permit such ministers and preachers belonging to said church, as shall from time to time be duly authorized, to preach and expound God's Holy Word."
At the time of the conveyance the site was just outside the city limits but is now in the city and located near the Bus Station. We know that some of the trustees were white men, and it is probable that all of them were of the white race. At the time when the conveyance was made, slaves were not eligible to own property, and so far as we know, none of the men named as trustees were "free men of color", which was a term used to designate slaves who had become free men. We know that Sims was an influential member of the White Methodist Church, and it is possible that this new congregation of Methodists resulted from the desire of Negroes who once had attended the White Methodist Church, but who now wanted a church of their own.

The concern shown by white people relative to religious services for the Negroes did not die with the abolition of slavery resulting from the defeat of the Confederate States, but continued even during the reconstruction period when many of the freed slaves were arrogant and difficult to handle. An evidence of this post-war concern of white people for Negro church members is evidenced by a deed by which in 1870 George W. Ragedale conveyed town lot number 119 in the West Ward of Grenada to the colored people of the Baptist Church: "The said part of the first part for and in consideration of the welfare and prosperity of the Colored People of the Baptist Church do hereby grant the party of the second part full possession and privilige to lot one hundred nineteen, the same to continue as long as the part of the second part conducts themselves with good behavior and pays tax on said lot. Now if the party of the second part shall mis-behave in an unbecoming way or fail to pay taxes on said lot, or cease to use said lot for church purposes then this instrument shall be null and void, and said lot with all the appurtenances shall be at the control of the party of the first part." This lot is located on Water street a little south of the intersection of that street with Pearl street. From the wording of the deed I feel that we may presume that the congregation of the new church was to be made up of Negroes who at one time attended the White Baptist Church. We know that Mr. Ragsdale was a member of the White Baptist Church, and for a time was President of the Yalobousha Female Institute after that institution became known as Grenada Female College. When we read that part of the deed which cautions about "Mis-behaving in an unbecoming manner" we wonder what type of mis-behavior would be considered as becoming. Another post-Civil War Negro church to acquire a deed for a church lot was the Prospect Baptist Church. A. V. B. Thomas for a consideration of one dollar deeded a two acre lot to the Trustees of this church. This land is located southwest of Holcomb. On August 14, 1884, M. G. and Sally Dubard, for a consideration of one dollar, granted a lot seventy yeards by thirty five yards to "the trustees in trust of the African Methodist Episcopal Church in the United States. This lot was located in what is now known as the Sweethome neighborhood and lies several miles a little southwest of Grenada.

Because of its strategic location in North Mississippi Grenada became a center of much regional religious activity. Levin Lake, who came to the old town of Tullahoma in 1835, is authority for the information that in 1838, before the local Methodist Congregation had constructed a church building, there was a meeting in Grenada of a Methodist Conference which included churches from North East Alabama. This Conference held its sessions in the second story of a store building located on the north side of the Grenada town square. Because of distances to be traversed, and the primative methods of transportation, many of the delegates were late in arriving. This delayed the work of the Conference and caused the work of the Conference to last for two weeks.

Bishop Morris came five hundred miles from Ohio to preside over the sessions of the Conference. On at least two occasions Grenada was the meeting place of the Mississippi Baptist Convention.

Many of the early ministers of the different religious groups were men who received little compensation for their service. Most of them made their living by farming or by some other type of endeavor. James G. Hall, first minister of the Grenada Baptist Church had a farm a few miles north of Grenada, although at the time of his death during the Yellow Fever Epidemic of 1878, he was living in Grenada. He preached not only in the Grenada Church but also in other Baptist churches throughout the area when he was not in the pulpit of the Grenada church. Francis Baker was a primitive, or "hardshell", Baptist preacher who lived near the early town of Troy and served churches in that vicinity. He was instrumental in founding the Yalobousha Baptist Association, but later withdrew his churches from that association because the association believed very strongly in foreign missions. During the early years of religious activity in the town and area, people were much less tolerant in regard to members of denominations other than their own, and frequent newspaper controversy was carried on in the pages of the local newspaper relative to different points of religious belief. The most heated such controversy was carried on by Rev. McCracken, Rector of the Episcopal Church, and President Newell of the Methodist institution which began as a Methodist District High School and developed into Grenada College. Mr. Newell, had been the pastor of the local Methodist Church before assuming the responsibility of directing the Methodist educational institution.

The ministers of the town of Grenada deserve great credit for their faithful service to their flocks during the Yellow Fever Epidemic. So far as we have been able to ascertain none of them deserted their posts of duty. One of them, Rev. Hiram T. Haddick, pastor of the Baptist church, was out of town when the epidemic broke out but returned against the advise of some of his members. After a time he became ill and died a victim of the fever.

Early Churches

The Episcopal Rector, Rev. McCracken, survived the epidemic and was very busy in helping the people during the period when the disease was so prevalent. Rev. McCampbell, the Presbyterian minister died during the epidemic. There may have been other deaths among the ministers of the town, although we have no information to that effect. A Baptist minister who was not serving a Grenada church at the time he died during the epidemic period. He was the Rev. Armstrong, who had come to Grenada to head the College which would later come to be a Methodist institution. An editorial by the editor of the Grenada Sentinel soon after the end of the epidemic seems to point the finger of suspicion to some minister, or ministers, as not standing up to their responsibilities during the epidemic period. An excerpt from that editorial is quoted in the chapter of this work devoted to Newspapers and Newspaper Men.

One interesting incident in connection with a colored church occured just after the attempt on the part of some citizens of Grenada to prohibit the sale of whiskey within the corporate limits of the city. The Grenada Sentinel supported the cause of prohibition while the rival paper, The Grenada Gazette was controlled by the liquor interests. In the first election, held in 1888, the prohibition ordinance was defeated. The Rev. J. I. Garrett, who was minister of one of the colored churches of the town, became indignant because twenty five of his members voted against the prohibition ordinance and summarily expelled the offending members from the church. When the people who favored the continual sale of liquor in the city heard of this action they raised money to buy a lot and materials so that the expelled members could build a church of their own. We do not know if this action had any particular effect, but the fact remains that in another election, a few months later, the sale of liquor in the city was outlawed. While the saloons operated in the city, the money realized from the license fee charged the saloon operators was used for the purpose of public education. In an argument against the prohibition movement, the Grenada Gazette had the following quoted reference to the possible loss of school revenue: "It costs $1014.57 to run the free school of Grenada Town for four months." (Four months was the length of the term of the public school at that time.) "The school tax paid by the people is $195.00 which with $222.00 poll tax leaves $597.57 to be provided by some other source. Now where is the deficit to come from when the saloons are closed? This is a serious question to every poor man who has children to educate, and we prepare them in advance, not to kill the goose that lays the golden egg." It is of interest that just seventy eight years ago half or more of the four month public school term in Grenada was paid for by revenue derived from the license fees paid by saloons.

Chapter XIII

Grenada Newspapers and Newspaper Men

Living as we do in an age when Radio, Television and Daily Newspapers keep us well informed relative to contemporary events, and to a considerable extent, influence us in our political, religious, economic and social philosophies, it is hard for us to understand the influence which early small town newspapers exerted upon the minds of the people during the period when the town and county of Grenada were being settled and developed during their formative years. As a rule, the editors were fiercely partisan in their political beliefs, and some of the papers were established to promote political parties and political candidates. In the rough and tumble political struggles of those early years, editors were not always careful to avoid provoking retribution because of harsh, and sometimes untrue changes which they made against politicans and other individuals against whom they directed the influence of their papers. Difficulties over charges of this kind were not usually settled by suits in court, but by physical combat, including the use of firearms. In those days an editor had to be a man of courage and conviction if he was to make any considerable impression upon his subscribers. The better papers usually had good editorials, much local news, some stale national and international news, and considerable advertising.

In the sixty six years elapsing from the establishement of the first paper in the town of Pittsburg, to the year eighteen hundred ninety nine, papers were establihsed in the two little early towns or in the resulting town of Grenada. Most of these papers existed for rather short periods of time, and on more than one occasion, two or three little papers were competing for the support of the town and community. Some of these papers were established to advocate a particular cause, political party, or candidate, and they were discontinued when no longer needed for the purpose which brought about their establishment. Others found that the area would not support more than one paper and were forced to discontinue publication. We list below the names of the papers which were at one time published in Grenada, or in Pittsburg and Tullahoma. We give dates, not necessarly when the papers were established, but when they were known to be in business. Some will have the names of their editors or publishers. Others will just have the names of the papers and dates when they were known to be operating.

In all probability the Pittsburg Bulletin was the first paper printed in the area. We know that John J. Hamilton was publishing this paper in Pittsburg as early as 1834. We also know that in 1835, induced by some financial arrangement with certain men in Tullahoma, he moved his press to the last named town and began to publish his paper under the name The Tullahoma Bulletin. In 1839 The Southern Reporter was published in Grenada. It must have had a brief existence since there is no contemporary information relative to the progress of the paper nor the name of its publisher. The Grenada Herald was the name of a paper operating in 1842 and edited by J. J. Choate, Jr. This paper probably succeeded the Southern Reporter. Mr. Choate was opposed to the political philosophy of F. A. Tyler, editor of the Grenada Weekly Register, which paper was being published at the same time as the Herald. The two editors engaged in some rather hot political arguments. Choate changed the name of his paper to The Saturday Morning Herald, and later changed it again to The Morning Herald. An early paper which seems to have had little impact on the community was The Weekly Mississippian, edited by W. F. Hampton. This paper was in existence in 1837. A good example of a paper established to further the cause of a political party, or candidate, was the paper, Harry Of The West, which was being published in Grenada in 1844. This paper was established by supporters of the Whig Party which had as its presidential candidate Henry Clay who was called, by his fond admirers, Harry of the West.

The founding of the new paper, The Grenada Republican, about 1851, is indicative of the decline of the Whig Party and growth of the new-born Republican Party. The paper was published by Jacob Snider and G. W. Haynie. Mr. Snider is buried in the old cemetery across from the I. C. Railroad Station. The existence of a Grenada paper in 1859, called The Grenada Locomotive, probably has some connection with the arrival of railroad transportation. It was during the last months of this year that trains began to arrive in Grenada over the Mississippi Central Road, and passengers were transferring from that line to the Mississippi and Tennessee Line which gave access to Memphis. Another paper, established in 1861, choose a name indicative of the times. This paper was called Southern Motive, and no doubt sought to support the motive of the Southern States in their withdrawal from the Union. S. M. Hankins edited both the Grenada Locomotive, and The Southern Motive. It is possible that the last named paper succeeded the Grenada Locomotive. Another paper published in Grenada in 1861 was The Southern Rural Gentleman. It seems to have discontinued publication soon thereafter. Its editor was J. T. Davis. We don't know when it was established, but in 1864 the Tri-Weekly Rebel Picket was being published in Grenada. Its name would be supposed to appeal to those people who favored the Confederate cause.

Several new papers were attempted in the years following the close of the Civil War. In 1881 John C. Abbott was publishing a paper known as The New South. We know nothing of the policy of the paper, nor the political affiliation of its editor. In 1884 the Grenada Graphic was being published in Grenada. It soon failed and was followed by another new paper which began publication in 1885. This paper was called the Grenada Gazette and was edited by Walter Ladd. It was established about the time that the prohibition forces in the town were calling for an election to give the people an opportunity to vote on a proposed ordinance to prohibit the sale of liquor in the town of Grenada. The paper was against the proposed ordinace, leading many people to believe that it had been financed and controlled by the liquor interests. In 1896 J. M. Liddell established The Grenadian. It failed in a very short time. About this same period The Grenada News was established. Its purpose was: "To be published in the interest of Colored People". D. D. Sledge was the editor, and G. W. Leonard, a Colored merchant, was its business manager. Like the Grenada Gazette, it didn't last long, not obtaining sufficient support from the colored citizens. The Mississippi Baptist, journal of the Mississippi Baptist Convention, was published for a short time in Grenada, but later moved to Jackson.

We might well ask why so many newspapers attempting publication in Grenada, had to suspend publication. In the first place there was the usual hazzard any new publication faces in the way of competition, as well as the fact that some of the papers were established as the mouth-piece of some particular cause, and ceased operation as soon as that cause had been served. But, in all probability, the chief reason for these failures was the tough opposition offered by a paper which had been established in 1854. This paper was started by J. A. Signaigo. He continued in control of the paper until a short time before the Yellow Fever Epidemic of 1878. At his death the paper was sold by his wife to John W. Buchanan, a young man of twenty three years of age. He bought the paper less than six months before the outbreak of the epidemic of which Mrs. Signaigo was a victim. Mr. Buchanan was to publish this paper, known as the Grenada Sentinel, until his death in 1904. The young editor was not only able to survive many attempts of competitive papers to draw public support away from his paper, but also to become a well-to-do property owner. His newspaper contemporaries looked with envy and admiration upon the rarity of the newspaper game, an editor who managed to accumulate a modest competence. After the death of Mr. Buchanan, Mr. O. F. Lawrence was editor of the Sentinel until he was succeeded by his son Malcolm Lawrence. This editor lost his life in a tragic automobile accident and W. W. Whitaker then became editor of the Sentinel and continued in this capacity until April 1, 1937, when Rice Lawrence became editor for a brief period. After a time Frank Jones, owner editor of the Daily Star, acquired ownership of the Sentinel and on January 2, 1947, the name of his publication was changed from the Daily Star to The Daily Sentinel Star. That the Grenada Sentinel should have survived for a span of ninety three years during which period of years it had numerous competitive papers is pretty conclusive evidence that the publication was directed by men of integrity and ability. Many triumphs and tragedies were recorded by this paper. It told of the havoc created in the town by storms; great financial losses resulting from several disasterous fires which almost destroyed the business section of the town and the failure of two private banks which left the town without banking facilities. The paper must have carried much of the arguments which precipitated the Civil War, and of the training of the State troops ordered to Grenada during the early months after Mississippi had seceeded from the Union. It is probable that the paper recorded the arrival of the presses of the Memphis paper which was fleeing that city in anticipation of suppression by the invading Federal forces. Although silent and mute during the trying days and weeks of the Yellow Fever Epidemic, The Sentinel was the first paper to give information relative to the living and dead after the termination of that epidemic. The paper recorded the harshness of Federal Reconstruction, and the suffering of the people under Scalawag and Carpetbag Rule. The paper fought the good fight to help lift the control of state and local politics from evil white men and ignorant Negroes, and was priviliged to live to see the time when native white men were again in control of local affairs. It was not destined to live long enough to record the second reconstruction which began with a Supreme Court Decision of 1954.

Buchanan of the Sentinel

In November of the year 1878, Grenada was just beginning to emerge from the dark shadows of fear and sorrow brought by the tragic yellow fever epidemic which had raged in the town for two and one half months. Three hundred and forty three new graves in two cemeteries gave mute evidence of the disasterous effect of the epidemic. Many citizens who had fled the town to escape the disease had not yet returned, and many of those who had lived through the epidemic had been weakened by their fight against the effects of the fever which had not been fatal to them. Only those of the people who had remained in town during the course of the epidemic knew the full horror of the experience. Very few of the survivors had not lost some loved one, and all had lost many long-time friends. Their minds were conditioned to give grateful thanks to the various persons and agencies rendering aid. During the epidemic, and to be bitterly critical of some who, having positions of responsibility, forgot that responsibility and fled town.

Perhaps no one knew better the bitter experiences of the epidemic period and the behavior of the people, than a young newspaper man who, at the early age of twenty three years had, just fifteen months before, become owner of the GRENADA SENTINEL. On November 16, 1878, this young man published what must have been the first paper published after the epidemic had run its course. In an editorial relative to the conduct and duties of physicians and preachers during a period of trial such as the recent epidemic, he gave an early indication of the trenchant editoral pen which would make him respected by many and feared by some. We quote from this early editoral:

> "The physician may reach eminence in his ordinary practice, but it is only in times of fearful public calamity, like the period through we have just passed, that he has the opportunity of displaying all those great, but latent qualities, which trying circumstances can only develop. For a time the true physician may be overwhelmed by failure to arrest the progress of the plague, but true to his pro-

fession, true to his education, and true to his own noble nature, he stands firmly by the suffering people, exercising all the functions of skill and courage at his command, without the first thought of his own personal safety beyond the suggestions of prudence and necessity. So long as he stands with dignity and self-possession administering kindly to the relief of the distressed as best he can, there is still hope for the stricken multitude. Let him flee, however, and consternation, if not wild confusion, ensues. Be it said to the honor of the physicians, that few proved cowards in our recent troubles, and we presume, professionaly they will did by inanation, with the brand of fugitive from duty in the hour of peril stamped on their brow.

There is another calling whose obligations to society, in a time of peril, is equally important and none the less binding, though of a very different nature. We mean the Preacher. The bedside of the sick and dying is the chosen place of the Godly man, for exercising those ministrations which no other can lawfully do. His duty is to preach to the living, to be ready for war, pentilence and famine should they come by the intervention of Providence, or the violated laws of men or nature........To leave them under the demoralizing and crushing effects of the horrible plague, would betray a want of faith in his own teachings, a want of courage in the presence of danger he always affected, and a fear, which he ever concealed, of that very enemy now presenting his grim visage. The fireman who would flee when the bells were clanging, people shouting, and the flames roaring and leaping with fearful rapidity to the last retreat of some unfortunate being, whose only hope of rescue was the pluck and courage of some dauntless hero, would be forever dishonored. The Captain who would take to his boat, when his vessel was plunging before the tempest, and driving straight for the rocks that would shiver her timbers and consign scores of her trusting passengers to the tender mercies of the angry deep, could never again tread the quarterdeck of another ship but in disgrace. The keeper of a fortress, who would escape for safety, and leave the responsibility of defense in the hands of subordinates, when the guns of the enemy were tearing away the bastions and battlements, would be cashiered for cowardice. The Preacher, no matter of what church, who would leave his flock and people because of the terror of the pestilence, is far more guilty of a dereliction of duty than any of the above responsible officials. The butterfly floats upon the summer wind and sucks the nectar from the wayside flowers, but when the fierce blasts of winter come, his beariuful wings and erratic flight are seen on more. Thus, some of our holiday preachers when health and vigor spread quiet and contentment over the land, wandered admist the labyrinths of language to find terms severe enough to condemn the harlot, and when pestilence laden with shrouds and coffins stalked in, they left in haste for a safer place, while the polluted hand of society's exile administered to the sick. How truly she did it, in more cases than one, will be proclaimed in no bated breath from angel lungs on the great day of final reckoning. The death of the least significent of the brave who fell at their posts, faithful to their convictions, their teachings and example, is a broader and more imperishable seal to the Christian religion than all the sermons which our fugitive clergymen can proclaim, though they be permitted to live to the end of time, while those who stayed with their suffering people and survived, like Landrum, Marshall, Palmer, Elder and our own McCracken, will be Living epistles read of all men who in days of brightness preaches a religion which they practiced in the darkest hours that ever threw their dismal shadows over an afflicted people."

Although the young editor in the same issue of his paper listed at least five physicians who died at their post of duty during the epidemic, there must have been one or more who fled the town. He also lists two white and two negro preachers who died during the epidemic and one who survived, but there must have been some minister who did not live up to his obligations. The reference to "the polluted hand of society's exile" ministering to the sick had reference to the fact that one or more of the nurses brought in to nurse the sick during the course of the epidemic were supposed to be women of ill-repute. Evidently four of the ministers mentioned above must have served in other areas of fever pestilence, since the editor speaks of "our McCracken".

The young man who was responsbile for the above-quoted editorial was John W. Buchanan. During the first few years of his editorship he was known as the "Young Editor; later, as he matured in years and newspaper experience, he was generally known as Ole Buck", and during his years newspaper maturity, he was known by his fellow newspaper men as "Buchanan of the Sentinel". He was not a native of the South, nor of Mississippi, although he came to love the region and its people as much as any native-born citizen could have loved it. Mr. Buchanan was of Scotch Irish ancestry. His parents, Frances M. Buchanan and Ellen Malconsin, were both born in Ireland. They came to this country, and in 1846 were married in Brooklyn, New York. John W. Buchanan was born in that city in 1855. His parents moved to Woodville, Mississippi, shortly before the outbreak of the Civil War. Here, for the first few years of his residence in Mississippi, he became familiar with the atmosphere of the old South which had, as the basis of its economy, cotton produced by slave labor. The town of Woodville, and the county of Wilkinson were not a crude frontier region when the family of young Buchanan arrived there. The area had known something of French, Spanish and British civilizations. In 1798 Mississippi Territory was the southwestern corner of the American possessions. Here, in 1797, Adams was constructed as a Fort, a few miles west of the town of Woodville, and its guns overlooked the Mississippi River only a few short miles above the Spanish possession of West Florida. The importance of this fort was evidenced by a letter written by General James Wilkinson to C. C. Claiborne, Territorial Governor of Mississippi. An excerpt from that letter reads: "I hold this point to be the door to the whole western country, and while we keep it barred, we shall be able to secure and control the interion - a consideration paramount to all others and which would justify the abandonment of every inferior object." A little town grew up below the guns of the fort, and served as the first seat of justice for the newly created county of Wilkinson. In the year 1809 Woodville was founded, and in 1811 it was incorporated, and soon became the county seat. The town and county were already half a century old by the time the Buchanans arrived there from Brooklyn. It was a place of culture and refinement, somewhat akin to the atmosphere of Old Natchez, just a few miles to the north. It was an area of extensive plantations, and the accepted social customs of those areas which had been enriched by the bountiful crops from the relatively new and productive soil of the area. It produced a large number of important early political figures. The county furnished three early Governors of the state. They were George Poindexter, who later became a United States Senator, Gerard C. Brandon, and Abram M. Scott. Just a short distance east of the town of Woodville was the boyhood home of Jefferson Davis. The town was an educational center. As early as 1819 the Woodville Female Academy was in operation. Sligo Academy was established in 1821, and the Woodville Classical School for Boys in 1839.

It was in this atmosphere of wealth and culture that, just before the Civil War the young boy, John W. Buchanan, spent his formative years. He no doubt heard stories of the conduct of Federal soldiers when they invaded the section and burned the beautiful Bowling Green Plantation house just a mile or so outside town. He was probably old enough to remember the occasion when his father, less than six years away from his old home in Brookly, New York, left home after enlisting in Colonel Griffith's Arkansas Cavalry, to serve four years in that Confederate unit, and to die in 1864. As the boy grew older he witnessed harsh reconstruction of the conquered South by a vindicative Federal Congress. These early memories colored his thought and, more or less, shaped his political philosophy. He resented the actions of the radical Republicans, and could see no wrong in the Democratic Party.

At some unidentified time in early youth he began newspaper training in the Woodville Republican, which had been established late in 1823, and which has had a continuous existence from that date, and which is today the oldest paper in the state. We don't have information as to why he appeared on the scene in Grenada. The first authenic notice we have of his presence in the town is a deed recorded April 28, 1877, by which deed Mrs. Alice Signaigo, for a consideration of $1900 transfered the press and all other property of the Grenada Sentinel to John W. Buchanan. Mrs. Signaigo was to become a victim of the fever epidemic which struck less that fifteen months after the above mentioned transaction. This marks the beginning of a remarkable career which was to continue for almost thirty years. Editor Buchanan was a man of strong convictions, and, as is frequently the case with men of strong convictions, a man of strong prejudices. One such prejudice was against the reconstruction practices imposed upon the South. Four Buchanan uncles who had remained in the North, no doubt proud of the success of the young editor, became subscribers to the Sentinel. Soon the bitter criticism, which the editor made of the harsh reconstruction forced on the South by the Federal Congress, irritated the uncles who threatened to cancel their subscriptions to the Sentinel. This threat had no influence on the nephew. Mr. Buchanan's editorial policy was determined by no one other than himself. During the latter years of his career his paper had stade-wide recognition as one of the most forceful and outstanding papers in the state. His editorials were frequently re-printed in other papers. He felt free to criticize, or commend, as he saw fit. Local School, City, County and State Officials either basked in the glow of his commendation, or writhed under criticism. Often, in a single issue of his paper he would commend on action of such an official, and criticize another action. Occasionally he would come to the conclusion that he had been wrong in his attitude on some question, and then would champion the other side of the cause as vigorously as he had previously opposed it. One example of such a change of mind came on the prohibition of the sale of whiskey in the town of Grenada. Editor Buchanan made his paper available to all those people who wanted to either advocate or oppose the proposed move to outlaw the sale of liquor in the town, but his editorial policy was strong support for the passage of the prohibition ordinance. Another newspaper in the town had recently been established, and was supposed to have been financed by the whiskey crowd. This paper opposed the proposed restriction in the sale of liquor. When the election was held the whiskey element won out, and the sale of liquor continued within the town. Almost as soon as this election had been finished, Mr. Buchanan began, through editorials in his paper, to advocate another attempt to vote out the saloons in the town. In due time another election was held and, this time, the people of the town voted in the prohibition ordinance. As the months passed after the ordinance was put into effect, bootleggers began to operate in the town, and the officers either couldn't or wouldn't enforce the prohibition ordinacne. Within less than two years after the hard earned victory in padding the ordinance, the Editor of the Sentinel was commenting that conditions relative to the sale of liquor in Grenada were worse than had been the case before the prohibition ordinance went into effect.

The editor was very liberal with the several churches of the town in providing space in his paper for any sort of publicity they desired relative to regular servcies or the revival meetings which were very popular with most of the churches of that period. He made a practice of attending some of the services of all the churches, and frequently used his paper to comment on the services which he had attended. Usually these comments were favorable. During the early years of his ownership of the Sentinel, two of the ministers of the town got into an argument on the question of Apostolic Succession. The Rector of the Episcopal Church supported this doctrine, while the President of Grenada College, a Methodist preacher, discounted the doctrine. Each of the ministers. For several weeks the paper printed a series of letters to the editor in which these two ministers presented their views on the subject. The controversy became heated, and at last the editor became somewhat disgusted at the personalities in which the ministers indulged. He expressed his disproval of such tactics in the following quoted editorial: "As to the merits of the argument we leave to the judgement of their readers, but we do think that some of their personalities are unbecoming to ministers. The average editor would blush to make use of such language towards his brother contemporaries, and yet, an editor is usually regarded as a vicious being of low morals, while the minister is held up as an example. Unless our ministers can pursue a more even course of temper in their controversies they had better let them severely along. Precept is well enough, but people expect their ministers to mix a little example with it."

Another example of Mr. Buchanan's impatience with men who did not measure up to their pretentions was his dismissal of J. J. Williams as a part-time employee of the Sentinel. This dismissal, which came in 1881, early in the editorial career of the young editor, indicates the editor's firm belief that the success of the Democratic party in Mississippi was the only sure means of overcoming the reconstruction policies of the Federal Government, and his scorn for anyone who would desert the party for personal gain. Mr. Williams had served a term as a Democratic Party representative from Grenada to the state legislature. In the Democratic Parimary following his term of service in the Legislature Mr. Williams announced as a candidate for renomination by the democrats to the legislative seat. He was defeated in the primary, and shortly thereafter he announced as an independent candidate. At this time there was a fierce contest between the Republicans and the Democratic parties for control of state and county officers. The running of an independent candidate, formerly a democrat, would have the effect of splitting the democratic vote, mostly cast by white voters, between the regular democratic nominee and Mr. Williams, thus endangering the chance of the democrats to elect a democrat to the legislature. As soon as Mr. Williams announced for office as an independent, Mr. Buchanan informed him that his connection with the paper was terminated. After this, Mr. Williams wrote a note of formal resignation. In a news article in the Sentinel Mr. Buchanan gave his reason for the termination of the service of Mr. Williams. In the next issue of the paper Mr. Buchanan published the following quoted letter which he had received from Mr. Williams: "Mr. Buchanan: Believing that you did me an injustice (unintentionally of course) in your announcement of my dis-connection with the Sentinel, you will please publish the line which I wrote in reference to the same." Mr. Buchanan then printed the explanation which Mr. Williams had made to the public relative to the incident. "To The Public: Having become a candidate for the Legislature my connection with the Sentinel necessarily ceases." Then Mr. Buchanan makes the following comment: "It is immaterial to the public whether Col. Williams connection with the Sentinel terminated by resignation or dismissal. His own conscience must have whispered to him that the Sentinel would never be presented to the reader with the hand to shape its course and its policy, which was raised in opposition to the best interests and wellfare of the people of the county. (Mr. Williams had been allowed to write some political editorials - this was the meaning of the phrase, shape its course and its policy). But if the Colonel insists upon the public having the facts they are these: The first intimation the proprietor had of Col. Williams intention to break his faith and pledge was the request to publish his card of announcement, and the proprietor at once denounced his course and told him that his connection with the Sentinel ceased from that hour."

Grenada County, having been organized in 1870, was populated by people who had not yet recovered from the financial losses incurred by the war, and therefore the county was not in financial shape to build a pretentious courthouse. The county authorities rented a store building on the northwest corner of the Public Square to serve as a temporary courthouse. This building served this purpose for thirteen years. Almost as soon as he became connected with the Sentinel, Mr. Buchanan began advocating a new and adequate courthouse. From time to time he prodded the Supervisors because they were doing nothing, looking forward to erection of a new and adequate building. On more than one occasion the court room was so inadequate that the term of court would be held in the auditorium of the Methodist District High School, which school was the forerunner of the Methodist Grenada College established some years later. The building containing the auditorium had originally been constructed by the Baptist denomination for the Yalobousha Female institute, which institution folded up about the end of the Civil War. On June 30, 1883, Mr. Buchanan wrote: "The time has come for the Board of Supervisors to take some action toward building a courthouse. This matter had been deferred so long and has become such a plain, practical necessity that the Board can hesitate no longer." In a subsequent issue of his paper the editor is more emphatic and somewhat sarcastic: "Just now is time to talk of building a new courthouse. The present one is a disgrace, not only as to ornamental architecture, but is a reflection upon the good will of our citizens. The people really do not intend to kill, by suffocation, the Court, the juries nor the officers, but if they do not do something better than punish them in this large stew kettle these learned bodies will begin to think that there is a secret murder in roasting men alive in discharge of official duty, and an action will be against the county for premediated murder. Will not some of our leading citizens attend the meeting of our Supervisors and see if they can not stir up the officials to the humane and christian purpose of building a new court-house in order to save the lives of those who have to remain in the present one during Circuit Court?" About one month after the publication of the above quoted editorial, the Board of Supervisors purchased a lot on the west side of the square as the site for a contemplated new courthouse, and in September of the same year, the Board of Supervisors let a contract for a courthouse which was to serve Grenada County for more than sixty five years.

Space will not permit the inclusion of many other influential editorials written by Mr. Buchanan, but those heretofore given will serve as an example of his skill in advocating his civic and personal projects. He was an early advocate of a diversification of crops. He was convinced that the day of a purely cotton economy was over for the south. He was a kind of one man Chamber of Commerce in trying to build up an interest in some form of industry for the section, and in attempts to get local capital to invest in such proposed industrial establishments. The improvement of schools was one of his pet projects. He compared the low educational facilities of post-war Grenada with the much better facilities which had been provided before the war. As fire after fire devastated Grenada, which was then without any effective fire portection, he adminished the "City Fathers" that it was high time for them to make some provision for fire protection. He was one of the leading spirits in educating the people to the needs of the establishment of city water and sewage systems, and it was a proud day for him when his paper announced the completion of these projects. He also led in the movement to bring about the construction of a city power plant to produce electric power for local consumption. It was also his privilege to herald the establishment of a telephone system in the city. During the years of his editorship he saw Grenada transformed from a rather primative town with few public utilities into a modern town with modern facilities. He lived to see Grenada become known as the "City Beautiful", and to be one year selected by the State Board of Health as the cleanest town in the state. In almost every phase in this transformation, Mr. Buchanan of the Sentinel played a conspicious part. It would be difficult to overestimate the influence which the editor and his paper exerted over all phases of city and county affairs. Although there was only one paper published in Grenada when Mr. Buchanan took over the Sentinel, various other papers were established in Grenada from time to time, but were not able to meet the competition of the Sentinel, and one by one each new paper faded out of existence. On the other hand Mr. Buchanan was so successful in a business way that he began to buy up town property and, at the time of his death, was the owner of considerable real estate, chiefly in the town. He was elected Director of one of the Banks established in the town. One of his contemporaries remarked: "Ole Buck never runs for office, but always has a lot to say about who shall be elected to office."

By the year 1904 Editor Buchanan was the peak of his professional career. He was known, respected and admired by most of the newspaper men of the state. He was a familiar figure at state and national press conventions. He was that rare country newspaper who could mix with the editors of large national newspapers and feel at home with them, and have them accept him as a friend. But his health gave way. He continued his active career until about two weeks before his death. His last editorial was published on November 12, 1904. A presidential election had just been decided, and the Democratic nominee had lost to Teddy Roosevelt. This was a hard pill for Mr. Buchanan to take, but he attempted to face the defeat as best he could; the editorial which he wrote might be considered his swan song so far as his political convictions were concerned. He wrote: "Therefore, we of the South, who are unalterably opposed to his views on some questions, must make the best of the situation. We have done our duty as we saw it, and will continue to carry out our views along certain lines, regardless of who occupies the White House. The country is prosperous, the South particularly so; there is no use to worry. We will still move and have our being; still pursue the even tenor of our way. The South is prosperous and flourishing and will continue to so in spite of Roosevelt and Republicanism."

Two weeks after the printing of the last quoted editoral, the Sentinel came out with black bordered column lines and with this death notice in Grenada, on Saturday morning November 26, 1904, at half past five o'clock, John Walton Buchanan, editor and proprietor of The Sentinel, aged about forty nine years, after an illness of more than two weeks, of Brights Disease." Then followed an editorial comment by someone who had charge of the paper during the illness of the editor. This comment read: "For nearly thirty years Mr. Buchanan presided over the destinies of the Grenada Sentinel, and was one of the best known and most prominent members of the press of the state. Ever to be found upholding truth and justice, strong and forceful in his advocacy of all things for the betterment and advance of the state and of his people; fearless in his editorial capacity and tireless in his devotion to duty, he brought The Sentinel to the very front rank of Mississippi journalism. In his death the press loses a valuable member; the state a true and loyal citizen. His work is over; life's fitful voyage has ended. He has gone to that bourne from which no traveller returns. Peace be to his ashes. A widow and two daughters, two sisters, Mrs. Therrel, and Mrs. Richardson of Woodville; two brothers, William Buchanan of Starkville, and Robert Buchanan of Centerville, and many relatives are left to mourn his loss." In the December 3rd issue of The Sentinel appeared the following news local: "Mrs. Richardson, who has been in Grenada for several weeks at the bedside of her brother, the late J. W. Buchanan, left Saturday evening for Woodville, where she is serving as Postmistress."

The same issue of The Sentinel reprinted the following quoted editorial comments from some of Mr. Buchanan's newspaper friends. From the Jackson Daily News: "The News on Saturday conveyed the sad information of the death of Mr. J. W. Buchanan of The Grenada Sentinel. This information brought sadness to the News. The editor of this paper has long sustained friendly relations with the dead editor. He was blunt and bluff, but beneath his rough exterior there was a warm and loyal heart. As an editor he was courageous and fearless, doing his duty as he saw it. In his death the press of the state, and in fact, the South, has lost one of its noble members." From the Greenville Democrat: "Mr. John W. Buchanan for twenty five years the editor of the Grenada Sentinel, died at his home on Saturday, aged about forty eight years. Mr. Buchanan was one of the best known newspaper men in Mississippi, a strong man, a successful business man, true to his political convictions, and vigorous in advocating the right and denouncing the wrong. He was also one of the truest of friends, never forsaking the old for the new. He was a brother of Mr. W. H. Buchanan, for twenty years a citizen of Greenville and is therefore an uncle of Miss Jennie Buchanan connected with the Democrat. The death of Mr. Buchanan is a distince loss to the Mississippi Press". From the Clarion-Ledger: "Though young in years Mr. J. W. Buchanan, editor and proprietor of The Grenada Sentinel for the past quarter of a centruy, has always been known and referred to by his friends as "Old Buck", his peculiar styles - perhaps idiosycracies, which distinguished him as an individual, as well as an editor, from the others of his genus. Mr. Buchanan was born in Wilkinson County about 1856, and was therefore forty eight years of age at the time of his death, which occurred at his home in Grenada, a town with the upbuilding of which he had as much, or more to do perhaps than any other citizen thereof. It has been known to Mr. Buchanan's friends and intimates for some time that he was a victim of Brights disease. The last time he was in Jackson, or at least the last time the writer saw him, he stated that he was not long for this world, or words to that effect, but was as sociable and jovial, as lighthearted and gay as ever. He did not seem to dread, or fear, the end that he knew was near at hand, and when it was suggested that his condition was not as bad as he supposed, he declared positively that it was, and expressed a desire to retire from active business so that he might take better care of himself, and be spared to his family as long as possible. As indicated above, Mr. Buchanan was a peculiar genius. His likes and dislikes were as strong as those of any many in the state, and the beauty of his nature was that he had the courage of his convictions and never failed to call a spade, a spade, when he believed it to be one sure enough. This characteristic naturally made him enemies as well as friends but "Old Buck" pursued the even tenor of his way- fearing no man and rendering justice to all men - a tribute that can be paid few editorial writers of this day and generation. Requiescat in peace." From the Canton Picket: "Mr. Buchanan was a forceful writer, a practical and successful newspaper man, and one of the rare few of the profession who accumulated anything like affluence. He was a prominent member of the National Press Association, and numbered scores of friends all over the country. In his death The Sentinel loses an editor whose place will be hard to fill, and Grenada a loyal citizen." From the Summit Sentinel: "The editor of the Sentinel has known John Buchanan since he was a mere boy, and was well acquainted with his innate goodness of heart and nobleness of character. Although frank to a fault at times, he knew not what sophistry and policy meant. He was as true as steel to his friends, and his death, while a great loss to the state he loved so well, is deeply deplored by all who knew and admired him." From The Aberdeen Examiner: "The press of the state deplores the death of Mr. J. W. Buchanan, of The Grenada Sentinel. He succeeded Mr. Signaigo, the founder of the Journal, some twenty five years ago, and has for a number of years been regarded as one of the most prosperous and successful newspaper men in the state. He was a man of strong hates and affinities, and while his bold utterances frequently gave offense, few men had more friends and he was true to them." The Woodville Republican: "Mr. Buchanan was a native of Woodville where he spent his boyhood days, and learned the printer trade in the Republican Office. He move to Grenada and purchased The Sentinel which he owned for the past thirty years. He was a man who had the courage of his convictions; was an upholder of the truth and fearless in all his utterances on all questions upon which he was called to take sides. He was a loyal friend and ever ready to lend aid in their defence. As a result of his manly and fearless devotion to duty he gained for himself a position of high esteem with the people of the state, and his paper stands as one of the state's leading journals." From the Carrollton Conservative: "For several years the figure of J. W. Buchanan has been a familiar and prominent one in the business and political circles of Grenada. He came there in his young manhood and soon obtained control of The Sentinel, which at that time was the only newspaper in the county. His vigorous style as a writer, his independent individuality as a man, his success as a diligent man, marked him among the active, hustling business men of this section of the state. He never sought public office, but pursued the even tenor of his way, preferring success in his profession. He had many friends among the editors and correspondents is the state, all of whom had kind words for the deceased and kindly remembrances of their association with them. His death creates a vacuum in the editorial brotherhood that will be hard to fill. Peasce to his ashes."

Chapter XIV

Business and Industry

When the little towns of Pittsburg and Tullahoma were established American business and industry were just beginning to share the benefits of the socalled Industrial Revolution which changed manufacturing from small scale handiwork in the home, to large scale production in factories which were equipped with the improved tools of the mechanical age. The Revolutionary War and the War of 1812 had stimulated industrial development in the New England and the Middle Atlantic states, but the southern states which were to make up the socalled "cotton belt", or "cotton kingdom", did not become a part of this industralization, nor did the other states which were situated away from the ocean, and from the rivers which flowed down to the ocean from the eastern slopes of the Appalachian Mountain range. In these areas, remote from the manufacturing centers of the nation, there was very little industrial development. Although some Southern states such as Virginia, The Carolinas and Georgia had been long established before the Industrial Revolution, they had done very little in the way of establishing factories. The newer Southern states of the southwest had still less interest in industrial pursuits. All of these states made up what was sometimes termed an "Agricultural Kingdom", and to the more limited number of cotton producing states the term Cotton Kingdom was applied. Blacksmith shops were in demand, and found at almost every cross-raod. Men who could construct wagons and crude agricultural implements were found in many of the towns in these states. There was skilled labor to construct houses, and crude mills to produce lumber for such buildings, but industrial development, in its truest state, was non-existent. In the early years of the establishment of the towns in the Third Choctaw Cession no factory of importance existed in the entire area ceded by the Choctaw Nation. The smaller farmers and landowners had, of necessity, to know how to make and use homemade implements and other necessary objects required by frontier life. In this manner a group of artisans was developed who, by small scale operation, were able to supply some of the objects which less skilled neighbors were unable to construct. Some of the large slave owners coming into the region had trained slaves who were skilled in carpentry, masonry and other handicraft accomplishments. The more affluent settlers either brought with them, or sent back east for the beautiful furniture which was found in many of the pre-Civil War homes constructed in this area, but the furniture of the less affluent settlers was usually crude, home made, and frequently, uncomfortable.

Since the area occupied by the people living along the Yalobousha River was the most productive soil during the early years of settlement, the little river towns became the centers of trade coming to them from a rather extensive agricultural economy which had developed. As the early towns such as Chocchuma, Tuscahoma, Troy and Graysport began to decline as trade centers most of their business went to the town of Grenada, which had already been formed by the union of the two small towns of Pittsburg and Tullahoma. The merchants of the town were selling those goods most in demand by a people who were still in the pioneer period of their settlement. During the early years most of the goods sold were the actual necessities of life, such as cloth for clothing, groceries to supplement the food raised by the farmers and planters, medicines for man and beast, simple farming implements, and material for construction work. On a typical trip to town a farmer would go to the post office for his mail; to the general store to buy food items not produced on his farm, or to attempt to swap surplus farm produced food for these items, and to one of the several saloons for a drink, or for a bottle to take home with him. Once or twice a year he was likely to buy shoes and other items of clothing which his people at home were not able to manufacture. Many people still raised their sheep; and processed the wool to enable them to produce home-woven cloth. Most of the shoes used in these early settlements were made by local shoemakers and many of the clothes purchased were made by tailors who had set up shop in the small towns. The tailors business was mostly with men, since most of the clothing needs of women and girls were supplied by the work of female seamstresses, or by the sewing skill of the women in the homes of the town and county. This home production of clothing was not confined to the female apparel, but much of the clothing of men and boys was made in the homes. In many of the farm homes thread was spun and cloth woven to furnish the material from which the family clothing needs were supplied. An indication of the extensive production of homespun cloth in the area is the establishment of a carding factory in Grenada in 1840. The severe financial depression of that period is indicated by the fact that Mather Robinson, who built and operated this factory, accepted toll of wool in payment of his service. Mr. Robinson was one of the Grenada men who fought in the Mexican War and lost his life in that conflict. Jonathan Carl operated the first grist mill in Grenada. This first mill was operated by horsepower. He also had the first lathe in the community. Mr. Carl manufactured wagons, treadwheel gins, spinning wheels and looms. His son, Rius Carl, is reputed to have been the first white boy born in Grenada after the union of the two small towns to form Grenada.

With people coming into the area seeking new homes, and for other reasons, taverns were needed and soon established. We do not know which was the earliest tavern established in the area, but do know that one was in operation in Pittsburg as early as November 19, 1835. On that date the following advertisement appeared in the Pittsburg Bulletin: "John Smith, formerly of Elliot, respectfully informs his friends and the public generally, that he has opened a tavern in the town of Pittsburg, Yalobousha county, at the sign of the Union Hotel, on the south side of the public square, near the ferry, on the road leading to Carrollton, and half a mile from Belfor's Ferry in Tullahoma, on the road leading to Tuscahoma, Chocchuma, Leflore, Chula, and Manchester, where he will keep the best of grain and fodder, for horses and teams, and will furnish his house with the best provisions which the country affords." Mr. Smith, who had been one of the men connected with the Elliot Indian Mission, was well connected with the business life of the little town. One daughter, Harriet Smith, married James Sim, an early merchant in Pittsburg. He was later elected Marshall of Grenada with the specified duty of cleaning out the rowdy elements which came into the town on week-ends and defied local law officials. Later Sim served a term as Postmaster of Grenada. Another daugher married a Mr. Davidson who was partner in a mercantile establishment in Pittsburg. Still another daughter married William Huntley, who came to the area as a clerk in the land office at Chocchuma. At various times he was engaged in operating the "lower ferry" which was established by citizens of Pittsburg to counteract the advantage which Tullahoma had, because of the earlier establishment of a ferry which served the people of that town, and in operating a general merchandise establishment which was located near the Yalobousha river on a lot located west of Main street and north of the right of way of the ole "Peavine" railroad line. In the town of Tullahoma early taverns were operated by J. Williams and Mrs. Annie Parker.

One of the early business ventures by citizens of Grenada which necessitated co-operation on the part of several men was the building of a bridge across the Yalobousha river. On April 25, 1836, the Board of Police of Yalobousha County granted to a group of Pittsburg citizens a charter for the erection of a toll bridge across the Yalobousha river. This bridge was to have its southern terminus in the town of Pittsburg, thus giving that town an advantage over its neighbor to the east. Since the charter was granted such a short time before the union of the two towns, it is doubtful that it exerted much influence in this regard. The charter was to be in effect for ninety nine years. The stockholders were C. R. Morris, James Sims, Ralph Coffman, N. Howard, Allen Gillespie and J. T. Talbert. All the men, with the exception of Dr. Gillespie, were business men in Pittsburg. This must have been the bridge to which L. A. Duncan had reference when, in an article published in the Meridian Star in 1903, he tells of the arrival of his family in Grenada in the summer of 1838. He stated: "Pittsburg was noted for its high bridge across the Yalobousha River; but a steamboat, several years after, pulled it down."

In the 1840's, the editor of the local newspaper, Weekly Register, began advocating a program to supplement the agricultural economy of the region with industrial development. He argued that a stavemill and a shoe factory were feasible and desirable industries for the town of Grenada. He cited some of the advantages possessed by the area which would seem to indicate the probable success of the industries which he advocated. Some of the advantages as cited by the editor were the presence of a plentiful supply of hardwood timber; the abundant supply of hides of cattle, and the supply of cheap slave labor. During the same period a cabinet maker was in business in town as is evidenced by the following quoted advertisement in the Weekly Register: "The undersigned still continues the Cabinet business at his old stand in Grenada. He has reduced the price of all work done at his shop one third lower than the prices charged last year, which is as low as work can be done or furniture procured in Grenada; and he hopes by his attention to his business to merit a continuance of the patronage, heretofore so liberally bestowed. A. P. Dunaway." In the January 13, 1842, issue of the same paper there appeared an advertisement indicating the establishment of a firm which had as its purpose the handling of goods sent into Grenada and produce shipped out. It will be remembered that, at this time, the Yalobousha river was the chief avenue of heavy commerce. That advertisement reads as follows: "James McConnell and A. S. Brown have entered into a partnership, and have established a Commission, Receiving, and Forwarding House at Greenwood, Miss., on the Yazoo River, under the name and style of McConnell and Brown, and S. D. Brown at Grenada alone; and will keep constantly on hand, at both places, bagging, rope, and twine, and a general assortment of groceries and heavy goods, blankets, shoes, such as will suit the planter. They will also make liberal advances on cotton in hand, consigned to Messrs. Andrew and brothers, New Orleans, and will buy cotton at the highest market prices. A. S. Brown has also procured three first rate keel boats, in charge of the very best of managers, Messrs. White, Jackson and Duberry, which will ply through the boating season in the Yalobousha River, between Grenada and Greenwood. By this arrangement, the several firms will be able to transact their business with neatness and dispatch, and save the planter hundreds that he would otherwise lose, It is their intention to put every article that they have, or may have to sell, at the lowest prices; and they hope, by strict attention to business, to receive a reasonable patronage." This advertisement is the first Grenada documentary evidence we have of the existence of the town of Greenwood. In earlier referece to the place it was called Williams Landing. James McConnell had been an early purchaser of lots in Grenada. A. S. Brown, owner of the fine plantation Emerald Garden, has been discussed at length in another article in this series. George W. Lake was operating a grocery store in 1842. In an advertisement in the above mentioned newspaper he gives the prices at which he will sell his goods: "Bacon eight cents per pound; Bagging: Kentucky twenty eight cents per yard, Missouri the same price, German twenty five cents and India the same price. Bale Rope, Kentucky fourteen cents per pound; Manilla twenty five cents. Fresh butter twenty five cents per pound, candles; composition fifty cents per pound; Mould twenty five cents per pound, Sperm sixty two and one half cents per pound. Coffee, Havana, Green and Rio Java, sixteen to seventeen cents per pound. Cheese 18 cents per pound; Bar iron ten cents per pound; Molasses seventy five cents per gallon, Nails nine and one half cents per pound. Sperm oil twenty five cents per gallon; Pork four cents per pound; Powder fifty cents per pound; Sugar, Brown, ten cents per pound, Loaf twenty two cents per pound; Coarse Salt fifty cents per pound and Whiskey forty cents per gallon." In view of the prices which exist today on the above listed goods, it seems strange that a people who had to pay seventy five cents per gallon for molasses and fifty cents per pound for salt should have been able to purchase whiskey for forty cents per gallon.

Lumber was much in demand as a building material, so sawmills became the center of a great deal of activity. It is probable that most of the early mills were operated by water power. The Crowder brothers had such a mill east of Grenada. As the demand for lumber increased mills were established which were powered by steam. One large sawmill was established near Grenada by G. W. Ragsdale which supplied, for many years, the lumber needed by the builders of the community. When the Y. & M. V. Railroad extended its branch line to Parsons, some years before that line was extended to Grenada, Ragsdale established a large mill at that place. Mr. Ragsdale was an early settler in Grenada. As early as 1842 he was President of a school located in Grenada and known as Yalobousha Female Institute. He was a Baptist layman of considerable influnce. In 1866 he conveyed a lot to the "Colored Baptists" of Grenada, part of which lot is presently occupied by the Belle Flower Church. Another man engaged in extensive lumbering operations was G. W. Tindall. He lived in the eastern part of the county, and it was there that he had his timber lands and his mill. Records of the Board of Supervisors indicate that he furnished much lumber for the construction and repair of the many wood bridges which spanned the numberous small streams of the county.

Any sort of heavy industry was slow of development in the region. In the early days, before the arrival of rail road transportation facilities, when river transportation was confined to a few months each year, production of any sort of manufactured product was pretty well limited to supplying the local demand. Freight rates were so high and transportation so uncertain that it would have been too great a risk to try to manufacture goods to be shipped out from Grenada. After the arrival of railroads in Grenada the Civil War, and the resulting period of reconstruction, so ruined the financial resources of the region that no money was available for any considerable expenditure on factories or other industrial plants. One of the earliest manufacturing plants involving the investment of considerable money, and intended to process local products, was the Grenada Oil & Compress Company. The impetus which started the organization of this company came from a resident of Memphis. Mr. J. W. Caldwell came to Grenada in the summer of 1883 to spend some weeks at the rustic resort then known as Gibbs Springs. This resort was located about one and one half miles southwest of Grenada and the water from the adjacent spring was considered as being beneficial in treatment of various internal disorders. It is very probable that while Mr. Caldwell was in Grenada he was reading the Grenada Sentinel in which the editor, J. W. Buchanan, was advocating the establishment of industries in Grenada to balance the agricultural economy of the trade region. Mr. Buchanan had stressed the need of an oil mill which would process the large volume of seed which was then going to other points for processing. The editor stated that while Grenada prided itself on being the best cotton market in the area, the same could not be said, relative to cotton seed. Mr. Caldwell made a proposal by which he would take ten thousand dollars of stock in a cotton oil mill provided that local men would match time in the matter of stock subscription. He also stated that if this should be done, he would undertake to raise the monetary balance necessary to get the plant in operation. As a result of this offer The Grenada Oil & Compress Company was chartered on June 23, 1883. The incorporators were J. W. Caldwell, R. P. Lake, John D. Milburn, John Powell, and William-Mc-Swine. The charter provided that the company was authorized to begin operation as soon as thirty thousand dollars in stock had been subscribed. The charter stipulated that the purpose of the organization was to "Manufacture oil of any kind, and to gin cotton and to convert, reduce and manufacture cottonseed into any form or condition." The company began operation with the following named officers: R. P. Lake President, Sam Laurence Secretary and Treasurer, J. W. Caldwell, John D. Milburn and John Powell Directors. We have little information relative to Mr. Caldwell and Mr. Milburn, but the other officers were well known and respected Grenada business men. R. P. Lake was, at this time, head of the Lake Brothers Bank, which was to fail about one year later. Because of this failure Mr. Lake assigned all his property for benefit of the depositors of the bank, and it is probable that his oil mill stock was thus involved. We do know that shortly after the bank failure R. G. Latting, Jr. was designated as "President of Grenada Oil & Compress Company." After his business failure Mr. Lake began to sell all kinds of insurance, and soon became so successful in this business that he was made District Agent for his companies, being located first in Jackson, Mississippi, and later in Memphis, Tennessee. Sam Laurence later became a partner in the large hardware firm of Doak & Laurence. John Powell was a well-to-do business man who was interested in many kinds of business in Grenada. He was also a member of the firm of New Orleans Cotton Commission Merchants know as Chaffee & Powell. Perhaps the reason why Mr. Caldwell was interested in Grenada as a promising location for a cotton oil mill was because, as a member of the firm of J. W. Caldwell & Company, Grocers, Cotton Factors and Commission Merchants of Memphis, he knew of the importance of Grenada as a cotton market. It is possible that he may have known that other men were interested in the location of a mill in Grenada.

On May 2, 1883, a little less than two months before the Grenada Oil Mill & Compress company was chartered, H. Bates of Indianapolis had written J. K. Mister, Grenada Post Master, relative to the cotton seed situation in Grenada. He wanted to know if there was an oil mill in the town; if not, how close to Grenada was the nearest such mill; if Grenada people would be interested in an oil mill if none then existed in the town. Mr. Bates also wanted to know if there was enough cotton grown in the area to produce twelve to fifteen thousand bales of cotton, which production in the opinion of Mr. Bates, would be sufficient to justicy the establishment of a mill in Grenada. Mr. Mister answered the questions and then gave a sales pitch on the opportunities which existed in Grenada. He told Mr. Bates that there was no oil mill then in the town; that the nearest such mills to Grenada were Memphis 100 miles north; Jackson, Tennessee 150 miles north; Meridian 100 miles east and Yazoo City 100 miles south. He also informed Mr. Bates that in the previous cotton season Grenada had shipped in excess of eighteen thousand bales of cotton. He called attention to the fact that the Yalobousha River was high enough during the winter and spring season to justify cotton shipments on boats plying the river. He also stated that $6,000 had been appropriated to be used under the direction of the United States Engineers to clear the river of obstacles to naviagation. Having given this factual information Mr. Mister began his sales pitch: "We have been to a great extent governed by sentiment since 1865, but that sort of thing is rapidly disappearing and a business era setting in which, by the help of accumulated capital from abroad, is destined to make of this place a great manufacturing point and center of population. I am not an enthusiast but purely business, and state what I conceive to be a deliberate fact when I say that there is no town in Mississippi with more natural advantages for the manufacture of cotton in all its phases than exist in Grenada and its immediate vicinity." We do not know if Mr. Bates had any intention of establishing a mill in Grenada, but if he did, the organization of the Grenada Oil Mill and Compress before he could get organized probably prevented him from the erection of a mill in Grenada.

It would seem that the Grenada Oil Mill & Compress Company, because of the lact of local competition and the plentiful supply of seed available, would have prospered to the extent that it would soon be on a sound financial standing. But this was not to be the case. Throughout the life of the organization it was encumbered by debt. Perhaps the lack of men trained in the operation of such a mill mitigated against its success. None of the men who were first listed as stockholders and officers of the company had, so far as we can ascertain, any experience in operating an oil mill. Within a year of the beginning of the operation of the mill it lost both its President and its Secretary-Treasurer. We have already mentioned the apparent reason for Mr. Lake giving up the Presidency of the organization. In August of 1864, Sam Laurence re-

resigned from his position as Secretary-Treasurer of the mill in order to become a partner in the large hardware firm which came to be known as Doak & Laurence. On October 12, 1884, R. G. Latting, Jr., acting for the Grenada Oil & Compress Company gave a deed of trust to A. V. B. Thomas, acting for Robert Mullin, whereby the company, in order to secure a loan of $13,000 made by Robert Mullin gave a deed of trust on the following described property: "Lot 195 and part of lot 194 with oil mill and appurtenances, same being located in the East Ward of Grenada." These lots fronted on the I. C. Railroad tracks, and were located just a short distance south of the present railroad station. Again, on September 4, 1885, we find the company negotiating another loan. This time John Powell, now acting as President of the company, gave a deed of Trust on the property to secure a loan of $10,000 from the German Bank of Memphis. On April 3, 1886, the property of the mill was advertised for sale to satisfy the terms of the deed of trust in favor of Robert Mullin. The property was bought in by F. B. Nichols, brothers of a Boston promoter who was interested in cotton, and was represented in Grenada by C. L. Wilder. In 1887 another group of Grenada business men decided to try to operate the mill which they purchased from Mr. Nichols. The men and firms purchasing the property were: J. W. Griffis, W. N. Pass, W. B. Wolfe, C. L. Wilder, I. Wile & Company (which company was under the management of Max Ginsburger) and W. D. Dupree of Tennessee. The last named partner was the only one not a local Grenada business man. He was a member of a cotton firm, working in Grenada during the cotton buying season, but a resident of Jackson, Tennessee. One thing which had probably contributed to the financial troubles of the Grenada Oil Mill & Compress Company was the purchase of a steamer, the J. H. Williams, which was to be used to bring cotton seed from the delta area west of Grenada to the Grenada Oil Mill. It will be remembered that, at this time there was no direct railroad communciation between this area of the delta and Grenada. After a brief trial the boat was sold to Walter Crump, a merchant and cotton seed buyer then located at Tuscahoma. He later moved to Parsons when that place became the temporary terminal of the Y. & M. V. Railroad branch reaching out from Greenwood in the direction of Grenada. Although the property of the Grenada Oil & Compress Company had been sold to satisfy a deed of trust, as has been related here-to-fore, it is somewhat surprising to find that, in 1887, that company was advertising in the Grenada Sentinel that it was paying highest prices for cotton seed. It would seem that the men who bought the property under the deed of trust sale took over the Compress part of the operation and allowed the oil mill to continue operation under the original name. John Powell was now serving as President and R. G. Latting as Secretary-Treasurer. Perhaps the men who had obtained the Compress operation of the Grenada Oil & Compress Company worked in co-operation with the Boston capitalist, J. H. Nichols, who had purchased the oil mill and compress at the deed of trust sale, and then sold the property to the company of Grenada business men set forth above. As early as 1884 a movement began to construct an adequate warehouse and compress to handle the cotton of the area. At the time this movement began much of the cotton bought to Grenada was stored in two cotton sheds operated by local men, and one Alliance Cotton shed. This was a co-operative enterprise organized by the Farm Alliance people who were very active at this time. In September of 1884 J. B. Townsend, Mayor of Grenada, acting for the city, gave the Grenada Compress a ninety nine year lease on "that protion of Wood street south of Third street and running to the Illinois Central railroad track, and also that portion of Wood street north of Third street to the ally running east and west and crossing Wood street between Second and Third streets." Evidently this action made it possible for the compress company to consolidate its area by eliminating a little used public street which crossed the property of the compress company. The compress company received its machinery in late 1885. Mr. Wilder, the cotton buyer who had induced the Boston capitalist to become interested in the compress venture, managed the compress as long as Mr. Nichols maintained control. In 1887 he sold his interest in the compress to the same individuals to whom he had sold the property purchased from the Grenada Oil & Compress Company under the forced sale of the property of that company. The stock company formed by these men set up business under the firm name Grenada Compress and Storage Company. Max Ginsburger became President. W. N. Pass Vice-President, and J. W. Griffis Secretary-Treasurer. In the meantime the once defunct Grenada Oil Mill & Compress Company, still operating after some sort of agreement with the purchasers of the originial property of the company had a competitor. In 1887 we find these two short advertisements running in the Grenada Sentinel: "From this date the Grenada Oil Mill will pay ten cents per bushel for sound seed delivered at the mill" and "The Grenada Cotton Seed Oil Mill will give one ton of cotton seed meal for two tons of cotton seed delivered at the mill." It would seem that there were either two mills operating in Grenada at this time, or that one of the companies was representing some out of town mill which was in the local cotton seed market. We do know that at some time during these years, the Mississippi Cotton Oil Company operated in Grenada. It had been established by local capital, possible as the Grenada Cottonseed Oil Company but got into financial difficulties and had to call for outside help. It is entirely possible that with the advent of outside capital the name of the company was changed to the Mississippi Cotton Oil Company. It is probable that the company became a subsidiary of some larger and stronger company. This mill was operating in 1896 when it installed a generator to supply electric lights for the mill. This was three years before there was a generating plant providing electricity for the residents of Grenada.

The Editor of the Grenada Sentinel was very much pleased with the prospect of Grenada having an adequate compress and cotton storage warehouse as is indicated by the following quoted editorial: "The cotton compress is another one of those things which seem too large for our local uses, but it is another one of those industrial forces that is to send its influences to the manufacturers of the East and Europe. A load of one or of ten bales of cotton brought can soon be compressed to half the bulk in size for shipment by rail to any city in this country and then, if necessary, be transfered to an ocean steamer with but the detention of a few hours for Manchester, Harve or any other foreign city. This compress will introduce by investment between twenty and twenty five thousand dollars which goes to swell the financial strength of Grenada. To work this huge machinery, it will take a dozen or more intelligent, active agents and laborers to turn out seventy bales per hour ready for shipment. Mr. C. A. Wilder who knows all about its practical workings and use will employ it for all that it is worth for his own and the public interest." In 1887 Joseph Newburger bought a one eight interest in the compress. Newburger was a former resident of Coffeeville and a big operator as a cotton buyer. As his company increased both in financial standing, and in the area of operation, he came to Grenada and made this town the headquarters for the company. By the year 1892 there was a complete change in the officers of the compress company; Jeseph Newburger was President, B. C. Ducan Vice-President and A Mass Secretary-Treasurer. By this time Newburger was also part owner of a compress located in Winona.

Some of the leading business men of the city and county began to realize the fact that an economy, based principally on one crop, would not bring coninued prosperity to the area. For a number of years the editor of the Grenada Sentinel had been advocating the diversification of the agriculture of the region. He stressed the fact that the long grazing season of the area gave stock owners of Grenada county and Mississippi an advantage over stock owners in other parts of the country. The editor stressed the need for more cattle both beef and milch breeds. Evidently someone was able to convince the farmers of the area of the validity of this argument since, in 1889, a company was organized to be known as The Grenada Creamery, Cold Storage & Ice Company. It is not likely that such a company would have been organized if the farmers of the region had not owned sufficient dairy cattle to assure the new plant an adequate supply of milk. The published charter of the company listed capital stock at $30,000 nine thousand of which must be subscribed before any operation could begin. Robert Doak and W. N. Pass were officers of the company who were authorized to purchase machinery for the plant. On February 16, 1890, they bought a five ton ice machine. We have no record of the other equipment purchased for the new plant. Evidently the plant did not prosper, since three years after it began operation, the plant, which had been constructed at a cost of $18,000, was sold under a court judgement for the small sum of $6,580 plus accrued taxes. The men who got together to buy the plant were W. C. McLean, Robert Doak, W. N. Pass, Joseph Newburger, B. F. Thomas, F. N. Hartshorn and J. T. Thomas. It will be noted that two members of the new organization had been members of the original company. Misfortune seemed to plague the new venture which was destroyed by fire.

In 1889 The Grenada Tanning & Leather Manufacturing Company was established in Grenada. The company was chartered with a capital stock of $25,000, and was under the general management of V. Saltaemachie with P. C. Williams, former owner of the tannery which was purchased by the company, acting as foreman of the new and enlarged plant. The firm proposed to furnish leather for all manner of purposes, but its manufacturing centered chiefly on the production of saddles, horse collars and harness. The Grenada Gazette of November 29, 1889, gives an account of the business houses and industries-not by name but by number-which were operating at that time. He also mentioned some organizations. The report ran like this: "Grenada has three thousand citizens, 21 drygoods stores, 35 grocery stores, 3 first class resturants, 3 first class drug stores, 2 furniture stores, 3 jewelry stores, 2 dentists, 6 physicians, 9 lawyers, 5 regular licensed cotton buyers, 2 regular licensed cotton weighers, 1 life insurance office, 1 fire insurance office, 1 bank with a capital of $55,000, 3 white hotels, 1 colored hotel, 3 livery stables, 6 meat markets, 1 merchant tailor, 2 public schools, 1 collegate institute, 1 private school, 4 white churches, 4 colored churches, 1 compress, 1 oil mill, 1 tannery, 1 Central Fair Association, 1 Masonic Lodge, 1 Odd Fellow's Lodge, 2 sewing machine establishments, 1 photographer, 1 Alliance Cotton Shed, 2 private cotton sheds, 1 string band, 1 miliatry band, 1 fine court house, 1 fine opera house, 3 shoemakers, 1 of the best machininst and workers in metal in the state, and 1 wagon and carriage factory." The fact that there were so many mercantile establishments in the town would seem to indicate two things: Grenada was then the center of a much larger trade area than it serves today, and most of the businesses were modest ones rather than the larger type of business houses which we have today. The building of the extension of the Georgia Pacific Railroad from Columbus to Greenville by way of Eupora and Winona (a road now known as the Columbus & Greenville) drew much trade from Grenada which had earlier come to the town from Webster and Montgomery counties. Later the construction of hard surface public raods diverted much of the trade formerly coming to Grenada to points such as Memphis, Jackson and Greenwood.

On March 26, 1902, there was a land transaction which was the beginning of the establishemnt of an industry which would for many years be the largest employer of local labor. On that date S. T. Tatum and others sold several hundred acres of land to the Ayer & Lord Tie Company of Chicago, Illinois. On March 28 of the same year The Grenada Sentinel came out with the following quoted news item: "The Ayer & Lord Company of Chicago, Illinois will invest at $75,000 in their plant." The news articles also stated that the company had contracts to deliver 800,000 railroad ties per month, and had been doing an annual volume of business exceeding $10,000,000. Of course this had reference to parent company rather than the Grenada plant. The payroll of the Grenada plant was to run from six to eight thousand dollars per month, with from two hundred to three hundred men to be employed when the plant was in full operation. The sprawling plant was to cover about four hundred acres of land. The news article gave Judge J. C. Longstreet chief credit for the establishemnt of the plant in Grenada county. The area selected was about three and one half miles south of Grenada and the location of the plant came to be called Tie Plant. Construction of the plant began in 1903. On May 18 of that year the Company Superintendent of Construction, J. E. Willard, was on the job and soliciting bids for the construction work. Three buildings which would house the machinery and necessary working space were to be constructed. In addition to these buildings, another building was to be erected to serve as a boarding house, and several small tenement houses were also to be constructed. Irby & Whittaker, local brick masons, were awarded the contract for the brick work. This plant has continued operation down to the present time, although it now operated under the firm name of Koppers Company, Forest Products Division. This change in name came about by the consolidation of the Ayer & Lord Company which was chiefly engaged in preservation of wood products, with the Koopers Company which had a greater variety of industrial products. It would be hard to estimate just how much this company has contributed to the economy of the region. Although industrial companies employing many more people than the Tie Plant operation have located in Grenada, for many years the wages paid by the Tie Plant operation had a big impact on the economy of the area.

On May 9, 1903, the charter of the Grenada Oil Mill was published. That instrument listed as incorporators J. C. Perry, J. C. Longstreet, W. S. P. Doty and "such other persons who may become associated with them". The capital stock was not to be in excess of $50,000, nor less than $30,000, with the company having the authority to increase or decrease the amount "within the limits of the said sums". On the 16th of June in the same year the organization purchased lots 6, 7 and 8 in the West Ward of Grenada. The lots were purchased from W. M. Trussell for a consideration of $500. The mill was erected on this property and is still operating there today, although the passage of years and change in business methods have brought about change in the original firm name. It is presently operating under the firm name Mississippi Cotton Seed Products Company. In 1904 the organization decided to get into the brick manufacturing business. At the meeting which authorized this new venture the following named Directors were listed as being present: Dr. J. W. Sharp, D. O. Semmes, A. S. Bell, B. C. Adams, S. T. Tatum, James Cuff, Cowles Horton, J. C. Perry and J. B. Perry. At the time the Oil Mill Company began this new venture there were two plants already manufacturing brick. One was operated by O. F. Bledsoe and the other by J. A. Carl. The brick which the Oil Mill Company proposed to make were sand-lime brick which were made by a newly developed process. News items in local newspapers of the time mention trips made by J. B. Perry to several places where the new type brick was being manufactured. The new venture was not very satisfactory, and the company soon abandoned that part of their business. J. B. Perry Sr. began his connection with the company as a bookkeeper, was soon plant manager, and continued in that capacity for many years. His son J. B. Perry, Jr., succeeded him in this capacity. During the years of its operation this company has given employment to a considerable number of local people, many of them being negroes.

From time to time smaller manufacturing plants were established. Some were supposed to be temporary in nature and moved on as soon as they had exhausted the raw products from which the plants fashioned their product. Some of these companies were absorbed by, and became a part of, stronger organizations dealing in the same products, while others failed, frequently from a lack of capital necessary to tide them over temporary periods of business stagnation. One of these early twentieth century operations was a stave mill which was operated by K. W. Hornsby. The mill began operation in 1902, and had a capacity of 12,000 staves per day. Twelve to fifteen men were employed in the plant while seventy five to a hundred worked in the process of cutting the required timber and transporting it to the mill which was located on a site west of the present location of Highway 51 and just south of the Yalobousha river. In time the mill was acquired by the Dixie Hardware Speciality Company, which soon transferred the property to Anchor Sawmills Company.

This company transferred the property to J. B. and C. A. Perry who leased the property to the Boone Cooperaged Company. This company discontinued operation and, for a time, there was no activity about the plant. Today it is being operated by the Grenada Stave Company. A few years later an outside company came to Grenada and began the operation of a large sawmill, cutting mostly hardwood timber. From time to time it has been known as Gayosa Lumber Company, Belgrade Lumber Company, and is presently known as Memphis Hardwood Flooring Company. The Gayosa began operation by leasing the area where the Memphis Hardwood Flooring Company is now operating. The date was 1920, and a mill of some sort has operated there since that date. The different companies which have operated mills on this site have contributed materially to the economy of the region by offering employment for many people, and purchasing much timber from the landowners of the county. Another wood products company which operated briefly in Grenada was the Phoeonix Chair Company. In July, 1919, this company purchased sixteen acres of land from D. O. Semmes, B. S. Dudley and Mrs. Fannie Morrisson. This land was located in Section 17, Township 22, Range 5, just across the I. C. Railroad track. The purchase price was $3,000. Newspaper reports indicated that the firm would employ about seventy five men. The firm had its headquarters in Shebougan, Wisconson, and evidently the Grenada operation was just one of several plants which the parent company was operating. For some reason the operation in Grenada was not satisfactory. In February, 1924, the Phoeonix Company sold its holdings to the L. E. Glass Furniture Company. The sale price was $10,000 and the property transfered included the lot which had been purchased for $3,000; the buildings which had been erected; 700 feet of railroad track into the Phoenix property; 2500 feet of tramway, all the machinery of the plant including boilers, engine, sawmill, drills, as well as teams and vehicles used in transporting material to the mill. Included among the vehicles were two eight-wheel logging wagons - a vehicle much used in southern Mississippi but infrequently found in North Mississippi. The sale of such a large amount of property for such a small price would indicate that the Phoenix company was in serious financial difficulties. So far as we have been able to ascertain the company which purchased the property did not continue operation.

There were probably other small industries which we have overlooked, but after Grenada had built its oil mills, its compresses, and the Ayer & Lord Company had established its wood preserving plant at Tie Plant, any other major industries would be over a quarter of a century in arriving. Local capital, aided by some outside assistance, had accomplished about all the industrialization possible under existing financail conditions. The early years of World War One just about ruined the price of cotton, since the German Submarine blocade of England and the continent of Europe made delivery of cotton to those countries almost impossible. Then came the entrance of the United States into that conflict when all the resources of this country were mobilized in the American war effort. With the entrance of the United States into that war the demand for cotton and other agricultural products increased rapidly. Prices rose, and much capital, which otherwise might have been available, went into the purchase of high priced farm land. Shortly after the war overproduction brought about a drop in the price of agricultural prices, and before too many years came the great financial depression which brought about general stagnation in business. Powerful labor unions began to put the squeeze on the manufacturing industries of the North and Northeast, and some of those industries began to look toward regions which had adequate labor potential, and where there was little union activity. Under the leadership of Governor White the state introduced the Balance Agriculture with Industry program. Under this program it became possible for municipalities and other political units to issue bonds for the construction of industrial plants. These forces were the impetus which brought about the rather extensive industralization in Grenada and other towns and cities in the state of Mississippi.

This movement in Grenada began on a rather modest scale. J. A. and L.

L. Goodman who controled the Real Silk Hosery Mill, Incorporated, of Indianapolis, were among the industralists who began to look toward the South as the possible location of part of their operations. W. B. Hoffa, great booster of Grenada, was instrumental in interesting the Goodmans in the possibility of the establishment of a factory in Grenada. A bond issue of $32,000 was proposed and approved by the voters of Grenada. The bonds were validated on June 10, 1937, and the first unit of a plant was constructed. At the time the people termed this little factory "The Hosery Mill', since its product was silk hosery. For many years the operation was termed Grenada Industries, and then became affiliated with and known as the Grenada Division of U. W. Industries. From a rather small beginning this industry expanded rapidly and became Grenada"s first major industry, a position which it still retains. This rapid expansion has made necessary several other bond issues to provide additional housing for the industry. Under the provisions the contract between the City and the Industry, the buildings are rented to the industry for an amount which enables the city to pay interest on, and retire the bonds, without any tax funds being used for that purpose. This same financial arrangement also is a part of the agreement between the city and the Binswanger Company. Beginning with a few employees this hosery mill operation today employees hundreds of men and women and has had a great impact on the economy, not only of Grenada and Grenada County, but upon that of some of the adjoining counties from which a considerable number of employees commute to work in the plant.

In 1946 Grenada officials began the process of making application to State Agricultural and Industrial Board (the organization which has to approve any bond issue proposal coming under the Balance Agriculture with Industry Act) for permission to issue $75,000 in bonds for the purpose of constructing a building to house a unit of the Binswanger Glass Company. The election was set up for April 13, 1946, and resulted unaminous approval of the proposal, the vote being six hundred nine to six for and none against the proposal. This overwhelming approval of the bond issue reflected the general satisfaction of the people with the way in which the hosery mill operation was being conducted. Having seen the effects which a sound, well conducted industry had upon the community, the people were ready to encourage more industrialization. Like the Grenada Industries operation, the Binswanger plant needed more housing which was supplied by the proceeds of a subsequent bond issue. Although this plant is a comparatively small operation which employees fewer highly skilled workers than some of the other local industries, it has had a helpful effect on the economy of the area.

Another indication of the general satisfaction of the community in the method of attracting industry to the area by issuing bonds for the purpose of constructing buildings to house industries was the result of the election held to determine if the voters of District One of Grenada County would approve a $1, 075,000 bond issue for the construction of a building to house a plant proposed by McQuay Inc., a Wisconson Corporation which was contemplating expansion. By a vote of 1664 to 27 the voters approved the bond issue. This election which occured on July 24, 1954, brought to the area a plant which has had a rapid growth, and which now has a large number of skilled employees. The plant which is located a few miles south of Grenada, manufactures heating and refrigeration coils. It, like the other major industries locating in the community, has contribute materially to the economy of the area.

The most recent large industry to locate in the Grenada area is the plant of Lyon, Incorporated. Unlike the other major industries which have come into the area, this company did not request that any bonds be issued for land acquisition and construction of a plant building. The plant was constructed on a 7.9 acres lot which was purchased from the heirs of the Weeks Estate. The location of this lot is in Section 5 and 6, Township 22 N., Range 5 E. It is just a short distance north of the city of Grenada. The company which produces metal products such as wheel covers, had increased its labor force. The nature of its work is such that it can give employment to a considerable number of semi-skilled workers. It is rapidly assuming a place of considerable importance in the economic development of the area. The gradual industrial development of Grenada was, to some extent, fostered by several different organizations of business men which were operative from time to time. The first of these of which we have any information was the Board of Trade which was organized in September of the year 1893. Dr. J. W. Young was elected President; J. W. Buchanan Secretary and J. T. Thomas Treasurer. Charter members of the organization were J. W. Griffis, J. T. Thomas, O. L. Kimbrough, Samuel Wile, J. E. Hughes, J. C. Perry, M. G. Dubard, George W. Jones, Judge Roane, W. T. Burns, J. B. Snider, J. W. McLeod, Sam Newburger, A. Gerard, H. E. Cahn, C. W. Melton, W. B. Baine, J. W. Young, J. W. Buchanan and J. J. Williams. Initial membership fee was two dollars with dues of fifty cents per month. Evidently this organization became inactive because on January 25, 1904, the Business League was organized.

J. W. Lee, Pastor of Central Baptist Church, was selected as a delegate to represent the Grenada Organization at a state wide meeting to be held at Jackson. We know that this organization was active in Grenada as late as 1911. We do not know how long after that date it continued to function. If it continued in operation after that date, the service which it rendered must have been less than satisfactory, since we find that in 1921 a Grenada County Chamber of Commerce was organized to do the type of work which has been the function of the Board of Trade. The Chamber of Commerce has had its ups and downs; its periods of considerable activity and periods of relative inactivity; its triumphs of accomplishment and its times of disappointment when it has failed to put over some desired project. At the period of this writing (1967) the organization is functioning efficiently, and effectively. Much of the industrial development of the area can be traced directly to the efforts of this organization.

Chapter XV

The Advent of Utilities, Public and Private

Living as we do today in an era when public and private utilities are taken for granted, it is difficult for us to conceive of a time when such utilities were practically non existent in Grenada. Soon after the establishemnt of the town of Tullahoma a well, either dug or drilled, was provided for the convenience of the citizens of the town. This well was located on the public square of the town. This well continued to serve the general public for many years. We do not know when it was abandoned, but do have information that it was in use as late as the year 1885. This information comes from a news item in a local paper stating that there were three public wells in Grenada; one located in the western part of town; another in the eastern part of the area, and another on the public square. It is probable that the people of the eastern and western parts of Grenada did not all depend upon the public wells. Some of the people obtained water from wells bored, or cisterns constructed, upon their residential lots. There were no sanitary and storm sewers for many years after the beginning of Grenada. Falling rain water ran freely, following the natural drainage courses which emptied in either the Yalobousha river or the Bogue. Animal owners had the responsibility of removing the carcass of any animal belonging to them, which chanced to die within the city limits. Most of the homes had outdoor toilet facilities. An early attempt was made to provide some street lights, but this provision consisted of a number of oil-burning lamps located at strategic points in the town. Some early settlers complained that the lamps served only to guide the people in the direction they were supposed to go, but did not give them enough light to keep them from falling into the mud-puddles found in the streets and on the plank sidewalks which had spaces of earth between the boards. It was well into the year 1880 before any reasonably satisfactory system of street lights was constructed.

Today, we would consider the loss of any of our public utilities a very serious defect in our usual way of life, but for many years the early citizens of the community did not enjoy the conveniences which we have come to consider necessities of urban life. Perhaps the one utility which we have today which was most urgently needed by the earlier citizens of Grenada was an adequate water supply and distributing system. Their concern about an adequate water supply arose not only from a desire to have available water at their homes, but from their constant apprehension of disasterous fires which could not be controlled without an adequate supply of water. By sad experience those citizens knew just how much destruction of property could result from uncontrolled fires. There must have been fires destroying some of the early flimsy, wood houses from the very beginning of the two little towns of Pittsburg and Tullahoma, but it seems that it was not unitl 1855 that the people of Grenada were brought to realize the full fury of an uncontrolled fire which could destroy large sections of the town. A fire which occured that year and which threatened the whole town, destroyed about half of the existing buildings. This fire was a paralizing blow to a town which had not entirely recovered from the effects of the Tornado of 1846 which destroyed 112 houses, and killed and wounded many inhabitants of the town. Soon after the fire of 1855 the governing authorities of the town adopted an ordinance requiring all future buildings erected around the square to be of brick or stone. As the years passed, and the supply of water continued inadequate to make any considerable headway against fires, destructive fires continued to occur. Some of the fires which were detected soon enough were either extinguished, or prevented from spreading to other buildings, but there continued to be fires which ravaged individual buildings and larger sections of the town.

On August 23, 1884, there occurred a fire which destroyed three fourths of the business houses of Grenada. The fire started in the Furniture House of S. H. Garner and destroyed most of the buildings around the square. The Grenada Sentinel came out with scare headlines: "GRENADA IN RUINS". There could not have been a worse moment for a disaster of this magnitude. Two private banks, which had the only banking facilities in the town, had failed earlier in the year, bringing financial hardship to the under-insured business men of the town. Friendly people from neighboring towns expressed sympathy and offered help. It is indicative of the courage and fortitude of the people of the town that Mayor B. C. Adams, Jr., could answer an offer of help from citizens of Winona by expressing the gratitude of the people of Grenada for the offer, but stating to these good neighbors "Grenada needs no outside help." Damage to business buildings was estimated at $300,000 which, of course was a lot of money at that time. Much of the merchandise housed in the damaged buildings was destroyed, but the Grenada Sentinel reported that, within a few days time, some of the merchants were back in business using temporary housing to display the stock which they had been able to save from the flames. Other merchants who had been able to salvage mostly damaged goods were advertising fire sales. It would seem that the city had already had its full share of fire disasters but the people were destined, within a very few years, to suffer again as flames swept the business section of the town. This fire occurred in 1891, and broke out in the store building of A. Summerfield, resulting in the destruction of that building, and sweeping part of the north side of Depot street and all of the east side of the square. Other stores which were destroyed included the buildings of Pryor & Company; Dry Goods Store of E. Parker; Barber Shop of Henry Johnson and Robert Purdy; Store of Mrs. L. Bernhardt, and some unidentified stores on the east side of the square. The fire destroyed fifteen buildings, eight of which were of brick construction.

Faced with this dismal record of destructive fires, it is not surprising that the people of the town began to demand a better type of fire protection. In 1886 a citizen, who was not identified, in a letter which was published in the Sentinel, had a proposal relative to improved fire protection. He advocated the erection of a tank, similar to the water tanks then used to provide water for railroad locomotives, on the city square with a pump in the well in the square, which tank would be operated by a windmill. The tank would be kept full of water and seventy five to a hundred buckets would be kept in readiness for use when a fire broke out. The citizen claimed to have observed similar provision in other towns. Sometime in 1891, probably after the fire of that year, J. W. Buchanan of the Sentinel published his views on the vital subject of fire protection: "Amongst the hundreds of thousands dollars destroyed by fire in Grenada, a few thousand dollars devoted to a good fire department might have saved a greater part of this...With a first class handworked engine, with sufficent hose, ladder etc. (those were once bought and placed in a house built for that purpose, but if there is any part of them left we do not know it) with a small tank filled with water by a windmill placed in a little enclosure in the square convenient to an inexhaustable well (which is already there) the town might have been richer by many thousands of dollars which have gone up in smoke and flames." This editorial would seem to indicate that the well in the town square was still of considerable public use. This appeal did not, at once, bring about the fire protection advocated by the editor, but in 1892 a Hook and Ladder Company to be composed of volunteers who would be provided with a hand-pump engine was organized. This was, perhaps, the best that could be done under the circumstances. Real fire protection would have to be delayed until a city wide water distribution system could be provided.

The need, especially for fire protection, for such a system, then called "water works", was the impetus which was eventually to bring the city, not only a city water system, but a sewerage system and electric generating plant as well. For several years there was much discussion relative to the need of such utilities with the usual dissenting citizens who contended that the city could not afford the luxury of these utilities. Public opinon in favor of the city providing these facilities so solidified, that on January 25, 1897, the governing authorities of the city set up an election to determine if the citizens of the town would approve a $40,000 bond issue to finance "a complete system of water works, electric lights and sewerage." Having been given the opportunity to express themselves on this vital question, the voters of the city approved the proposed bond issue, and the purpose for which the proceeds were to be used.

Although the people approved the proposal to have electricity available for the city, the need for electricity was not, at that time, as vital as the need for water distribution and sewage disposal. A temporary, and for a time, a satisfactory system of street lighting had been provided some years before electricity was to become available. On January 20, 1891, six years before the approval of the bond issue, the Sentinel ran the following quoted news item: "The street lighting of Grenada was definitely settled for a time by a contract with the Sun-Vapor Street Light Company of Canton, Ohio, for forty lamps at sixteen dollars per year for each lamp, the contract to run for five years, with the provision that the contract could be terminated at the end of two years. The lighting fuel is gasoline and the gas used is generated in the burner and makes a light four times brighter than coal oil. When they are all up and at work our little city will not grope in darkness anymore. We congratulate the Maor and Aldermen on their success in giving us brightly lighted streets. This is no experiment as in Ohio alone, there are thirty five cities using this system, beside its use in other cities." Two expressions in the news item may be of some significence: "definitedly settled for a time" and "the contract could be terminated at the end of two years" would seem to indicate that the editor realized that improvements over the proposed system were anticipated in the not too distant future.

There was some dissatisfaction with the bond issue, some people criticizing the extravigence of such an ambitious program, and others, wiser than most, who felt that the bond issue would not provide sufficient funds to complete the whole project. These people were justified in their position by the subsequent necessity to issue another $15,000 in bonds to complete the project after the funds provided by the original bond issue had proved to be insufficient to complete the project. This second proposal for bonds was approved by the pro-ponents of the issue by a four to one vote over those who opposed the proposal. Evidently the three different kinds of utilities involved were let in one general bid. The Sentinel notes that J. H. Hazelhurst & Company of Atlanta, Georgia, was awarded a contract to construct the water distribution system, the sewerage system and the electric generating plant. In order to provide water for the distribution system the City Board awarded a contract to J. W. Wohl to drill two artesian wells. The contract price was slightly over $38,000 for the work awarded to the Hazelhurst Company. We do not have the price of the well contract.

The Hazelhurst Company began work, and was making rapid progress when work was interrupted by labor trouble. The heavy common labor work was done by negro men who were being paid eighty cents for a ten hour day. After a time these laborers demanded one dollar per day for the work. Mr. Hazelhurst protested that he was paying above the usual wage scale - that he could get all the common labor which he needed at seventy five cents per day. In some way, not known to us, the labor trouble was resolved, and the work continued. Before the project had been completed the city officials realized that the utility should cover a larger extent of the area than had first been contemplated, so then they set up the second bond proposal which has been mentioned heretofore. In less than a year the project was completed. The night of September 25, 1897, was a great night of celebration on the part of the citizens of the town. This was the night when the utility system was to be tested. At the appointed time the current was turned on and some people, for the first time in their lives, saw the wonder of lights provided by an electric current; others who had observed the power of electricity as it was used in other places, now rejoiced that their town had the opportunity to be served by this new source of power. In order to test the pressure in the water mains, a hose was attached to a fireplug near the square, the water turned on in the hose, and the people saw a column of water rise many feet in the air. At last they had the adequate water supply; the distribution system, and the water system necessary to control fires. The people were not so enthusiastic about the sanitary sewerage system. They resented the attempts made by the city officials to induce them to connect their houses with the sewers. It took money to get connected, and it took money to purchase the equipment such as bath-tubs, sink, and indoor toilets which would be connected with the sewer lines. There were angry protests at the cost of such installation. Some complained that the city officials had so constricted the list of plumbers approved for such work that one firm had a practical monopoly of the work. To quell this disturbance the city finally agreed to let workmen connected with the utility plants make such connections and installations at a stipulated price. Still some people refused to take advantage of the utilities. They had averted part of the danger from fire, but were willing to take the risk of illness brought on by un-sanitary conditions.

With the provision of a water distribution system and sufficient pressure to do a good job in fire fighting, the men of the town were ready to form volunteer fire-fighting companies. Three of these companies were organized; two of which were composed of white men and one composed of negroes. Company number one was to keep its equipment on the public square, and its primary responsibility was the protection of the business section of town. The foreman of this company was W. D. Salmon. Company number two was assigned to the East Ward and its foreman was B. E. Moore. Company number three was assigned to the West Ward and it was composed of Negroes. P. S. Golden, a negro shoemaker and shoe repair man was made foreman of this company. H. D. Lowd acted as Fire Chief for the city with J. C. Wilson as Assistant Chief. J. B. Perry was Secretary and Treasurer of the organization. Although each company had its primary assignment, they were supposed to be ready, at the direction of the Fire Chief, to go to any part of the city where they were needed.

At the time these utilities were established in Grenada there were very few towns in Mississippi which had similar facilities. As a result the city officials did not have any well established standards by which they could determine the charges which should be made to consumers of the water and electricity. It was understood that the rates to be announced were only temporary, and would be adjusted up or down as the revenue derived from the charges proved either excessive or insufficient to operate and maintain the services. A Superintendent of the combined operation was secured, and the city officials depended very largely on him to guide them in the establishment of rates. This man, who was supposed to be a graduate engineer, was secured from Yazoo City. The Board, upon his advice, announced the following rates for electric current: Business Houses with less than five lights seventy cents per month per light; those with twenty to twenty five lights sixty cents per month. Residences: with less than five lights thirty five cents per month per light, those with five or more lights thirty cents per light. The water rates were: Dwelling houses with four to six rooms fifty cents per room per year with a minimum charge of six dollars; house with a bath three dollars per year extra. Barber Shops: one chair six dollars per year; with a charge of two dollars and fifty cents for each extra chair; first bath-tub eight dollars per year, with a charge of four dollars for each extra tub. People of the younger generation will find it difficult to believe that, at the time of the publication of these water rates, very few of the homes of Grenada had bath tubs. Many of the men went to the barber shops for their baths. The usual charge for a bath was twenty five cents. Restaurants and Hotels were charged ten dollars per year for their water supply with extra charge for bathtubs. Extra charges were made on additional tubs. These utility charges proved to be unrealistic and it became necessary to adjust the charges. Eventually meters were installed for both utilities, and the people paid for the amount of water or current which they used. At the time the electric generating plant began operation electricity was used almost exclusively for lighting purposes. As various electrical appliances came into general use, it would be necessary to increase the generating capacity of the electric plant. The artesian wells providing the water supply for the distributing system were located in the vicinity of the power plant. One of the wells had a constant external flow of water and became the center of attraction for many of the citizens. Many people would walk down to the well and drink of the water which it gave off.

For a period of approximately thirty years Grenada continued to own and operate all its public utilities. Many other towns in the state were without such facilities. When the use of electricity became popular many small towns desired an adequate electric supply, but were either unable or unwilling to finance the construction of a generating plant and distribution system. This desire for current opened the way for the organization of corporations to generate and distribute electricity over high voltage lines to many towns and cities which would grant franchises for such service. Because of the cost of the construction of these facilities it was to the advantage of those companies to be able to obtain franchises from all the towns in the area through which their lines would be constructed. Towns without electric service were glad to grant these franchieses to the power companies operating in their vicinity, but the towns which had already financed and constructed city owned plants were not so anxious to make a change. The power companies had to do a good selling job to these towns. The first step in this selling job was to convince the city officials that it was practical to generate current at one point and then transmit it great distances for use in towns and cities. In order to do this power company officials invited city officials on expense paid jaunts to see power installations at various places. One such trip made by Grenada officials was mentioned in the Grenada Sentinel on March 20, 1925. The paper reported that a party from Grenada headed by Mayor W. J. Jennings was joined by a similar delegation from Winona as guests of the Mississippi Power & Light Company to observe power property in Alabama, including the Gorgas Reserve Steam Plant. In explanation of the purpose of the trip the paper stated: "The Miss. Power Company is one of those figuring on the purchases of Grenada's power plant." Soon thereafter a meeting was called to be held in Grenada in which meeting other towns approacehd by the power company could formulate some sort of concert of opinion relative to the offers made by that company for either franchises where there were no existing city owned power plants, or for franchises and purchase of power plants in those towns which had constructed such plants. Among the towns and cities represented in the Grenada meeting were Grenada, Charleston, Pontotoc, Senatobia, Water Valley, Oxford, Duck Hill and Jackson. Officers representing two of the rival power companies appeared before the representatives attending the meeting, but apparently no decision was reached by the representatives regarding the desirability of the offers made by the power company representatives. The city of Grenada decided to go it alone in their negoations with the companies. They decided to request bids, or proposals, from the companies interested. We know that two companies interested were the Mississippi Power Company, and the Mississippi Power & Light Company, which was the Mississippi affiliate of the Couch power interests which had large interests in Arkansas and Louisana. When the date for the submission of bids arrived the Mississippi Power Company requested additional time in which to submit their proposal. The City Board refused to grant this extension and accepted the proposal of the Mississippi Power & Light Company. The proposal was for the purchase of the existing power plant and franchise rights. In payment for the plant the Power Company agreed to assume payment of interest and principal on outstanding city bonds in the amount of $81,000. Not all of the bonds were outstanding against the city utilities plant. $14,500 dollars worth of these bonds were designated as "Water & Light Bonds". Another $5,000 issue was designated in the same way. Bonds amounting to $25,000 were designated as "Water, Light, Sewer, Street and Sidewalk" bonds, $31,500 was identified as School Bonds, and $4,000 as Street Improvement Bonds. The deed given by the City in May, 1925, stipulated that the city retained all wells, pumps, water distributing system, and was to have continued access to the lot and building which the pumps and wells were located. Under the agreement Grenada was to obtain electric service from a high tension line coming out from the Greenville Properties of the Couch Interests, which property was furnished electric energy generated by that company's hydroelectric developemnt in Arkansas, and its Sterlington Power Generating Plant. The Grenada Power Plant obtained by the company was to serve as a standby plant to be used when there was any interuption in the electricity delivered in Grenada by the power company's high tension line. It was well that this was done because, during the early years of service by the power company, electric storms were responsible for frequent interruptions of service in Grenada. It was only after the power company had built additional lines into Grenada that the service became satisfactory.

Several years before city owned utilities were provided outside capital became interested in a telephone communication system for Grenada. The first public notice of any activity along this line was a news item in the Grenada Sentinel of January 27, 1883. That item read: "We are glad to announce that the Bell Telephone Company has succeeded in establishing an exchange over Captain McCord's store. The convenience of this thing will be more fully realized when our business people begin to use it. Already they have some ten or twelve subscribers, and wires are being stretched to different parts of town for the purpose of bringing in immediate business relationship. We learn that this place will soon be connected with Memphis by phone, an advantage at once apparent to all business men." In March 1883 The Sentinel had news of progress in the matter of long distance communication: "Representatives of Louisana Telephone Company and Memphis Telephone Exchange met in Grenada for the purpose of establishing telephone connection between Grenada and Memphis." Soon an advertisement appeared in which the Louisiana Telephone Company solicited bids on "600 chestnut poles 28 feet long and seven inches in diameter at the smallest end of the poles, said poles to be delivered along the road between Colliversville, Tennessee, and Holly Springs, by way of Mount Pleasnat." A little later another advertisement by the same company appeared soliciting bids on three thousand poles of the same material and dimensions as set out in the first advertisement, these poles to be delivered in Grenada. It would seem that from 1883 to 1895, a period of twelve years, the Bell System rendered satisfactory, or at least acceptable service, but for some reason, in 1895, a charter was issued to The Grenada Telephone Company, a corporation formed by B. L. Roberts, H. W. Latimer, E. Levy and "such other persons as may associate themselves with them." We have been unable to determine if the newly charted company bought out the Bell System, or just went into competition with it. In September the Sentinel notes that the new company has begun installation of phones under the direction of H. W. Latimer, formerly of Canton, but now the efficient manager of Mississippi Cotton Oil Mill. This statement would seem to indicate that the company was installing a new system rather than taking over the property of the Bell Company. The new company furnished service for a period of about three years and then sold out to the Cumberland Telephone Company, which company was engaged in buying up a number of privately owned telephone companies, and consolidating them into one large system. The Cumberland people raised the rates charged for telephone service; business house phones were raised from two dollars to three dollars per month and residential phones from one dollar to one dollar fifty cents per month. Immediately there was an angry reaction on the part of telephone subscribers. The Grenada Sentinel reported: "Many people have had their phones removed, hardly half a dozen phones now in use." The company survived this reaction and continued to serve Grenada until it became consolidated with the Southern Bell Telephone & Telegraph System. In 1896 L. B. James of Sabougla completed arrangements for a telephone line to connect Graysport, Williamsville, Sabougla and Slate Springs with the Grenada Exchange.

The last utility product to be brought to Grenada was natural gas. During the early years of settlement wood was the chief fuel used for heating purposes. With the arrival of the railroads it became practical to transport coal to Grenada, and there was a gradual increase in its use, although for many years wood remained the primary fuel in use. Kerosene had been used from an early date for lighting purposes and had a limited use as a heating fuel, particularly for use in kitchen stoves. After electricity became available there was a growing use of that source of energy for small heating devices used in small rooms. It would be half a century after the introduction of electric energy as a source of light and power before there would be available in the city another source of heating energy. This would come with the construction of a natural gas transmission line from Greenwood to Grenada. For almost a quarter of a century the Mississippi Power & Light Company has controlled the sale and distribution of electric power. The company did this thru franchise contracts which were negotiated with the city from time to time. In 1947 this company began negotiations with the city relative to securing from the city a franchise to build a gas distributing system and to sell gas to local consumers. There was much opposition to the proposal. Many people looked upon electricity and natural gas as competing forms of energy, and felt that it would not be wise for one company to control the distribution of both electricity and gas. On December 29, 1947, the City granted a franchise to the Power Company to control the sale of gas in the City, and to construct the necessary gas lines to make gas available to people in all parts of Grenada. On June 12, 1948, work began on the job of extending the gas transmission line from Greenwood to Grenada. 164 employees were engaged in the construction of the line. The Power company would expend approximately a million dollars on the project. While the transmission line was in the process of construction, there was feverish activity in Grenada. At the time work began on the Greenwood-Grenada line, 18,000 feet of gas mains had been constructed in the town. It was expected that the gas would be brought to Grenada to be available for use in the Fall of 1948. The transmission line was completed to Grenada in mid-September of that year. On the day the gas was to become available for local use, the Chamber of Commerce had a sort of ceremony by which they welcomed the arrival of another form of energy. A special sort of gas burner had been provided for the occasion, and the use of the gas in Grenada was begun by Mayor Knox Pierce igniting a gas flame from that burner.

The Mississippi Power & Light Company operated both the electric and gas distributing systems until March, 1952, when the power company conveyed its gas franchise and distributing system to the Mississippi Valley Gas Company.

Chapter XVI

Hotels Taverns and Inns

Dating back to the early years of settlement of the area, Pittsburg and Tullahoma were the location of houses of public accomodation called taverns, inns or hotels. The location of the Federal Land office at Chocchuma, a few miles west, and its subsequent removal to Grenada; the existence of a ferry, and the fact that the Memphis-Rankin Stage Line crossed the Yalobousha River in the vicinity of Grenada all contributed to the establishment of these facilities. Later, when Grenada became a railroad junction town, this fact contributed to increased activity in Grenada in the matter of housing accomodations for the many people who passed through the town. The early inns or taverns were rather crude, but not more so than those found in other early settlements. One of the earliest, perhaps the earliest such place in Pittsburg, was the Union Hotel operated by John Smith. In the November 19, 1835, edition of the Pittsburg Bulletin he was advertising his place in the following manner: "John Smith (formerly of Elliot) respectfully informs his friends and the public generally, that he had opened a tavern in the town of Pittsburg, Yalobousha county, at the sign of the Union Hotel, on the South side of the Public square, near the ferry, on the road leading to Carrollton, and a half mile from Belfor's Ferry in Tullahoma, on the road leading to Tuscahoma, Chocchuma, Leflore, Chula, Benton, and Manchester, where he will keep the best of grain and fodder, for horses and teams, and will furnish his house with the best provisions which the country affords." The tavern was located at the northeastern corner of the block south of the early Pittsburg Town Square. The building faced what was then called Vine Street, but which is now called College Street. The tavern building came into the possession of the Yalobousha Female Institute and served for a brief time as the location of that school, and this probably gave rise to the change in street name, although the school was soon moved to a new building on Main street. There were at least two hotels in Tullahoma; one was operated by Major Jack Williams and the other by Mrs. Annie Parker. These two Tullahoma hotels were not advertised in the early issues of the Pittsburg Bulletin.

The first newspaper advertisement of a hotel in that part of Grenada that was once Tullahoma, which we have found was one which appeared in the March 12, 1842, issue of the Weekly Register. In this advertisement Levin Lake who operated the house stated "THE YALOBOUSHA HOUSE:" The subscriber begs leave to inform his friends and the public generally, that he has opened a House of Public Entertainment, at that large and commodious house, formerly known as the Mansion House, in the East Ward of Grenada, on the business square. This house has been undergoing a thorough repairing, and will, in a short time, be entirely comfortable, He is determined no pains shall be spared to render all who may favor him with a call thoroughly pleased; and he hopes, from a strict attention to business to share a portion of public patrongage. P. S. The road leading through East Ward of Grenada is in first rate order, and at the river, there is one of the best Ferry Boats, and most attentive ferry-man in the country. On the north side of the river two miles from town, take the left hand road. On the south side near the edge of town, take the right hand road. Since the Yalobousha House was to use the same building which had formerly been known as the Mansion House and which now needed repairing, it would seem that this building must have housed a tavern or hotel several years earlier, possibly about the same time as that when John Smith was operating the Union Hotel in Pittsburg. In his direction of patrons to his hotel Mr. Lake indicated that the Coffeeville-Grenada road divided two miles north of the river. This was probably due to the fact that there were two early ferries operating, one at Pittsburg, and the other at Tullahoma. One branch of the divided road probably led to the Pittsburg Ferry and the other to the Tullahoma Ferry.

Another early Grenada Hotel was located adjacent to the public square.

On January 4, 1845, the paper, Harry of the West, carried the following quoted advertisement which was inserted at the direction of J. A. Williamson who operated the house: "GRENADA HOTEL: The subscriber begs leave to inform the public generally that he has taken charge of the above establishment. It is handsomely situated on the North-east corner of the public square, east side of Main (sic) street, and is now undergoing repairs. He flatters himself by integrity, assiduity, and strict attention, to merit public patronage. Hoping the good people of Grenada and vicinity (as well as the public generally) by their patronage will assist him in his undertaking, as he pledges himself if sustained, to make the house worthy of the name it has; his servants are first rate; his table shall be furnished with the best the country affords, and charges to suit the times. N. B. My old patrons who favored me while in charge of the Eagle Hotel in Tuscahoma Tallahatchie county; also my old acquaintance from Madison and Yazoo counties are respectfully solicited to give me a call." The location of this hotel raises the possibility that it might have been the same building which Levin Lake was, in 1842, operating as the Yalobousha House. In 1852 the A. S. Brown Hotel on the north side of the square was being operated by Col. J. G. M. Buffalo. Mr. Buffalo later became a sort of publicity man for the Georgia Pacific Railraod System, and spent much of his time away from Grenada in the process of his employment. He maintained a home northeast of the public square, and always managed to be in Grenada on election day. There was an early hotel located on the lot north of the Grenada County Courthouse, and now occupied by the Grenada Theater. At different times this hotel was known as the Carter House, the Pass House, and the Haber House. At times it advertised its nearness to both the courthouse and the town square as a great advantage to potential guests. Another up-town hotel was the Commercial Hotel, located on the north side of the square. It was owned by Mrs. A. R. Davidson, and managed by Walter Crump. A two story wooden hotel building, which was on the south side of Depot street, was first known as the Walthall House, and later it became known as The Central Hotel, Hotel South and Planters Hotel. It was known by the last name when it burned to the ground sometime in the 1930's. At one time W. B. Hoffa was the owner of the building, although he probably never operated a hotel there.

It is very probable that the best known of the early Grenada Hotels was the one located on railroad property and known as the Chamberlain Hotel. In 1871 The Southern Railroad Association, a Mississippi Corporation acting as a kind of holding company for a number of railroads including the Mississippi Central, leased to William C. Chamberlain a designated part of lot number 199 in the East Ward of Grenada. The designated area began a few feet west of the East Track of the Mississippi Central Railroad and extended west, toward the west track of the railroad. This is the area just east of the present railroad station. The term of the lease was for thirteen years, beginning September 1, 1871. For a consideration of one dollar per year the Party of the First part leased the property to the Party of the Second Part for the purpose of the erection of a hotel "according to the specifications attached and signed by G. Burgland, contractor and builder". The building was to cost not less than $12,000, and was to be completed by the first of September 1871. Chamberlain was to "furnish and keep open at all times for the accomodation and convenience of travelers on the trains of the Party of the First Part a waiting room for ladies on the first floor of said building and convenient to the track-said room to be of ample size for the purpose and properly attended and cared for by the Second Party, and to place at the deposal of the First Party a telegraph office, a room on the first floor and in the front part of the said building of ample size for the purpose, having in view the convenience of the operators and those dealing with them, and properly arranged for the business of a telegraph office." One room of the Hotel could be used by the operator of the hotel as a bar-room "provided the business is conducted in an orderly manner". The operator was to keep the building "in first class style in every respect, and to the satisfaction of the Party of the First Part." If representatives of the grantor of the lease should ever find that the building was not maintained to the satisfaction to the grantor, the operator was to make the necessary changes to the satisfaction of the grantor within twenty four hours. Failure to do so would result in forfeiture of the lease, with the grantor paying the cash value of the building to the grantee of the lease.

Since the Mississippi Central Railroad connected with the Mississippi and Tennessee Railroad at Grenada, it would be to the advantage of both railroads to have a hotel convenient to the railraods where passangers could stay while waiting for rail connections. This hotel operated at first by Chamberlain, and then by others, became a focal point for much of the social life of Grenada. Many dances and other social functions were held in the hotel, and many events of importance in the history of post-Civil War Grenada centered about this building. Political figures of the time held frequent conferences here with their supporters. It was at this hotel that the people who came in from Memphis to help during the Yellow Fever Epidemic of 1878 had their headquarters. Out of town sales representatives, then called drummers, made their headquarters here; hired rigs from the local liverystables, and called on the town and country storekeepers in this vicinity. Evidently Mr. Chamberlain became overextended financially in building and furnishing the hotel, since on April 16, 1875, he gave a deed of trust to C. T. Wood in favor of Pickney C. Peeples, Peacock and Powell, Lake Brothers, Loys, Yeager & Vandan, and Flash, Lewis & Company, to secure obligations due the several individuals and firms. P. Q. Peebles was the largest creditor of Chamberlain in the amoung of $824.00. Peacock & Powell were the next largest creditors with the amound due them being $5,453.08. The amount due Lake Brothers was $5,000.00, while Chamberlain owed Loyd, Yeager & Vandam $500.00 and Flash, Lewis & Company $450.00. The last named two firms were out of town creditors, while the others were local men or firms. Ond day after giving this deed of trust, Chmaberlain sold J. C. Brannum an undivided one third interest in his lease of the property. The sale price was $4,000. Evidently Peeples and Brannum satisfied the other creditors since in August, 1880, the Chicago, St. Louis and New Orleans Railroad Company, which had consolidated a number of rail lines, including the Mississippi Central, into a rail system extending from Chicago to New Orleans, made Peeples and Brannum a lease on the lot and building similar to the lease originally made to Chamberlain. These two men began to operate the hotel, still called the Chamberlain House, and soon leased the Edwards House of Jackson, Mississippi for a rental of $300.00 per month. These two men operated the two hotels for a period of two years, after which period Brannum sold his interest in the venture to Peeples for a consideration of $4,000.00. Newspapers of that period referred to Peeples as Dr. Peeples. So far as we can determine, he never practiced medicine in Grenada. For a number of years he was one of the most popular hotel operators in the state. In April, 1894, the Chamberlain House was destroyed by fire. The Grenada Sentinel, in its report of the fire, stated that the building had been constructed at a cost of $20,000 and that it contained $5,000 worth of furniture and equipment.

On November 1, 1894, we find the I. C. Railroad making another lease on Railroad Property for the location of a hotel. The property leased this time was in lot number 202 part of which is west of the Railroad line. It was this portion which was leased as the location of a hotel. The proposed building was to front on Depot street. The lease was given to B. F. Thomas, and was for a period of twenty five years. Mr. Thomas was to pay seventy five dollars per year for the lease of the property, and was required to construct a hotel building on the property within a period of ninety days according to the description; "A good, substantial Hotel-frame building with metal roof." The Leasee was required to charge "fair and reasonable rates, and to operate the hotel in a prompt and careful manner so that neither the Company (Railroad) nor the public will be prejudiced by reason of the Leasee dealing unfairly or negligently in their behalf, or in the transaction of the business connected with the Hotel Building.". At about the same time as the date of the above described lease, B. F. Thomas was petitioning the Board of Aldermen for permission to operate a "saloon on Depot Street, near the Depot." It is possible that Mr. Thomas may already have been operating a saloon in the vicinity of the Depot and was merely requesting permission to continue his old business, or he may have been requesting the permit in order to be able to operate a bar-room in connection with the new hotel. The lease to Mr. Thomas contained most of the stipulations which had been a part of the lease granted Mr. Chamberlain in 1871. It would seem that Mr. Thomas was acting not only on his own behalf, but also for others, when he obtained the lease. On October 17, 1894, the Grenada Sentinel announced the formation of The Grenada Hotel Company. Max Ginsburger was President of the stock company which was to operate the hotel, with F. N. Hartshorn as Vice President. Directors were John W. Griffis, Max Ginsburger, F. N. Hartshorn, B. F. Thomas, G. W. Tribble, S. A. Morrison, while J. C. Perry acted as Secretary and Treasurer. The hotel had thirty rooms for guests, as well as a large dining room. Eleven of the guest rooms were on the third floor, sixteen on the second floor and three on the first floor. Some of the passenger trains which passed through Grenada, but did not have dining cars, scheduled stops in Grenada long enough for passengers to get meals in the hotel dining room. In his news report on the new hotel the Editor of the Grenada Sentinel commented: "While it is not a mammoth concern, it is built in conformity with modern taste and convenience, and will soon be in the front ranks of Southern popular hostelries. Under the management of B. F. Thomas it falls into the hands of no tyro as the Major in this line has made a reputation known from New York to Florida, from Charleston, S. C., to San Francisco, California."

The Grenada hotel was the last hotel of any considerable size to be built in Grenada, although after Grenada College discontinued operation one of the large Dormitories of that college was purchased by a stock compnay which operated it for a time under the name Barwin Hotel. The Grenada hotel continued to serve Grenada until some date during the Second World War, but not under the operation of the company which had constructed it. The construction of motels along the improved highways spelled the doom of many of the small town hotels. Mr. Dinsmore, one of the later operators of the Grenada Hotel, recognized this trend; sold out his interest in the Grenada Hotel, and constructed the first motel to operate in or about Grenada. For over a hundred years the various taverns, inns and hotels of Grenada served the traveling public, and also served as social centers for the people of Grenada. Many social functions such as dances, banquets, and even marriages, took place in the public rooms of these houses of public entertainment. Many of these hotels were well known for the quality and variety of foods served in their dining rooms. We give hereafter the advertised menu of the Hotel South for one particular Sunday." Breakfast: Quaker oats, Fried oysters, with tomato catsup, Calf liver, Breakfast Bacon, Macerel, Biscuit, Butter, Rice, Brains and Eggs, Chipped Potatoes, Milk, Oranges, Apples, Waffles, Tea and Black Coffee." For Dinner, as the midday meal was then called, the guest could have soup, Roast Beef, Chicken, Baked Fish, Stewed Evaporated Apples, Stewed English Peas, Vegetables, Baked Pork and Beans, Pickles, Stewed Tomatoes, Creamed Potatoes, Coffee, Fruit, Nuts, Whipped Cream and Cake." If the Sunday guest was still hungry when the supper bell rang he could be served with "Scalloped Oysters, Steak, Ham, Eggs, Fried Sausage, Potatoes, Hominy, Stewed Fruits, Iced Tea, Oranges, Apples and Coffee."

Although many people took their meals in the dining rooms of the various hotels, there were, from time to time, restaurants which became well known. Many of them were started; prospered for a brief time, and then were unable to meet the rugged, stiff competition. The frequent failure of restaurants is indicated by a comment of the Editor of the Grenada Sentinel in reference to a restaurant which had been able to survive the fierce competition: "The restaurant business has had a very precarious run of luck in Grenada. Sometimes ham, eggs, fish and oysters seemed wanting cusomers at every door, while flaunting signs, inviting the men of hunger to come in and eat, were hanging in all directions. One by one they have failed, or fallen, until but one remain to tell the tale of other, and more plentiful days, when a little silver jingled in the poor man's pocket, and bank bills lined the wallets of the well-to-do. Our old friend Mrs. Lowenstein, still holds her own, is at the same place, well prepared with dainty morsels for the delicate, or a square meal for the strong; of long experience, business knowledge, liberal feelings. She deserves success and wins it. May her days be many and her business a success." This Jewish lady seems to have been a great favorite with the people of Grenada. She had many misfortunes but always seemed to be able to rise above apparent disaster and keep operating. On one occasion her business was ruined by one of the frequent fires which occurred in the town. She had an epileptic son who was the source of more trouble for her. This man got into some kind of an argument with a negro and was charged with murder when he killed the negro. He was convicted of the charge. Not long after this the mother, who had been in ill health for several years but still continuing her business, died and the wife of the son tried to continue to operate the business. After a few months she was forced to discontinue the business. The restaurant, which was in existence as early as 1881, and which operated for a number of years, was officially known as the New Orleans Restaurant, but generally referred to as "Mrs. Lowenstein's". Another well known restaurant which flourished at a much later date was the Dixie Cafe which was located near the Railroad Station. During the earlier years of its existence, the absence of adequate hardsurfaced highways made travel over the roads impracticable for people who were making a journey of great distance. As a result, the railroad station was a site of much activity. In those days many people, who had no intention of boarding the trains, went to the station "to meet" the large number of trains which then ran on the I. C. lines. The Dixie Cafe served, along with the dining room of the Grenada Hotel, the food needs of railroad passangers, as well as the many people who came to the station to meet friends and relatives, or merely to see the train come into and depart from Grenada.

Chapter XVII

The People: Origins and Characteristics

What manner of people were the pioneer spirits who came into the wild Indian land to find little towns along the Yalobousha river, and to carve out small farms and large plantations in the lands adjacent to that stream? Generally speaking, they were people seeking something: better economic, political or social status, or perhaps, all three of these things. They came from many sources, and along a number of different trials, to converge on that part of the Choctaw Cession which is now embraced within the boundaries of Grenada County. The system of primogeniture as practiced in Virginia, along with the exhaustion of its soil by long years of tobacco cropping, caused an exodus of Virginians from their home state into the newer states to the west. Some of those leaving Virginia were younger sons who were given slaves and other personal peoperty, and advised to seek new lands and establish new homes in areas other than Virginia. Then there were those Virginians who were tired of trying to work their worn-out acres at a profit, and who sold their land for what they could obtain for it; gathered up their slaves and other personal property, and moved west. Some of these families made two or three moves before reaching the Choctaw Purchase lands. In some cases these moves respresentated three generations of the same family. In their migration west some of the families first stopped in the Carolinas; then in Georgia or Alabama, and finally in the new Indain lands of Mississippi. Others settled in Tennessee and moved westward, generation by generation, until finally they left Henry County, Tennessee, and came into Yalobousha and the other counties carved out of the land acquired by the Treaty of Dancing Rabbit Creek. A few of the early settlers came directly from their old homes to the area which is now Grenada County. Many of these came by water; down the Ohio and Mississippi rivers, and then up the Yazoo and the Yalobousha. Some of those who came by this water route made brief stops at Natchez before moving on up the Yazoo-Yalobousha route. Most of the people came by the dim overland trails leading into the area. They came down the Natchez Trace from the Nashville area of Tennessee; some came down the Tennessee River to the point where the city of Florence, Alabama is now situated, and there joined those people who were going down the trace. Others came up from the area of South Mississippi which had been settled after earlier treaties had removed the Indians from that area. Those coming from this region came over the Rankin-Memphis road which began near the point where the present city of Jackson is located and traversed the land now embraced in the counties of Hinds, Madison, Holmes, Carroll, Tallahatchie and Yalobousha, and then on through the counties which were to be carved out of the Chickasaw Cession brought about by the Treaty of Pontotoc Creek, to the then small town of Memphis, located on the Chickasaw Bluffs bordering the Mississippi River. It is quite probable that Tennessee contributed more settlers to North Mississippi than any one of the other states mentioned. A great many of the settlers came direct, or as second generation people from the Piedmont region east of the Appalachian mountains. This long stretch of foot hills of that mountain system had early drawn its inhabitants from the states along the South Atlantic sea-board as those states became well settled and land more costly. After several generations of cropping, these hilly farms became exhausted and unproductive, and their inhabitants began to look for new lands in the west. The Indian troubles which brought General Jackson and the milita of the western settlers into the territories of Mississippi and Alabama, and eventually to the Battle of New Orleans, gave those soldiers an insight into the agricultural possibilities of a large region still occupied by the Choctaw and Chickasaw Indians. Many of these soldiers remembered the region. About 1830 the agricultural economy of the Piedmont Region, still depending on tobacco for its money crop, began to suffer from the exhaustion of the soil of the tobacco fields. A type of inland cotton which was adapted to separation of the lint from the seed had been developed, and cotton planters in the southwestern part of the state around Natchez were becoming wealthy.

Whem it became known that the Indians were being removed from the north two thirds of the state of Mississippi, and that land made available, many people of Piedomont connection, directly, or by parents who had moved out toward the area a generation before, began to move into the area which was to become the counties organized from the Choctaw and Chickasaw land cessions. A good example of the Jacksonian soldier coming to the area was George W. Martin who, at one time, acted as secretary to General Jackson. In the battle of New Orleans he served as a staff officer to General Coffee. He came into the Grenada area in 1833 to act as the "locating officer" to locate land for Choctaw Indians who chose to remain in Mississippi. He married a niece of General Jackson and became the paternal grandfather of the late W. B. Hoffa. His Auverigne plantation, located near Obury, was a good example of the extensive plantation development which took place in the quarter century prior to the outbreak of the Civil War.

While doing some research on a project other than this history of Grenada and Grenada County, the writer had occasion to run up on some records which are a good indication of the movement of people from the Piedomont region into the area which is now Grenada County. The records concern three families which lived in Montgomery County, North Carolina. The Crump, Willis and Kendall families lived near the little village of Center which is located near the Pee Dee River. Evidently some members of the three families remained in the area since, as we drove over the area, we found many people living there with the same family names as the three mentioned. Many had given names which are found in the names of members of the three families which came to Mississippi. The Kendall family is a good example of the Tidewater people who moved into the Piedomont area; lived there for a generation or so, and then came by stages into Mississippi. In 1788 several members of the Kendall family moved from their tidewater lands along the Tappahannock River to the area about the town of Center. Later, members of the family moved to Henry County Tennessee, and after remaining there for a few years came on into Mississippi-some settling in Tallahatchie county and others in Yalobousha. It seems that the three families had intermarried while living in North Carolina, although they evidently did not move out together. Members of the Crump family settled near the land office town of Chocchuma about 1834. Members of the Willis family were in the area during the early years of settlement as is shown by early land records. George Washington Kendall, who came to this area later than his uncle James Kendall, was the son of George Kendall who had moved from Virginia to North Carolina. Dr. William T. Willis, who came into the area of the old town of Graysport, is an example of a man who was born in Virginia and came with his family first to Alabama, and who later made the move into Mississippi. Two South Carolina families who seem to have come directly to the Grenada area from their old homes were the Perrys and Ingrams.

Many of the people who were early settlers, in and about Grenada, were people of property, culture and education who came into the new region for purposes which have been related above, but some of the people were less fortunate. They,because of misfortune,lack of opportunity, or economic failure were looking for pioneer lands where they could begin a new life. To them, the rich Indian lands which could be purchased at very little cost was the end of the rainbow where they might find the pot of gold. It would be interesting if we knew what brought each early settler into the Grenada area. For instance what brought Jacob Poirtevent who was born in Brunswick County, North Carolina in 1818 and his wife Mary Jane to Grenada? Both were to die in the Yellow Fever Epidemic if 1878. What was Robert Louis Jones, born in Nottaway county, Virginia during the year 1825, seeking as he came into the new area? We wonder the same about Maria Robbins Buffaloe, born in Raleigh, North Carolina May 2, 1818; Maria Ward Parmel, born in New York in the year 1809, and William H. Winter, born near Huntsville, Alabama. Not all of the early settlers were native Americans. Robert Stevenson and his wife Janet Thompson

Stevenson, born in Ayrshire, Scotland, migrated to this country and died in the Yellow Fever Epidemic. Duncan McKinlay, a native of Kintrye, Scotland, migrated to South Carolina in 1820, became a citizen of Mississippi and died here in 1870. Robert Mullin, born in Belfast, Ireland in the year 1818, arrived in Kentucky in 1820 and came to the old town of Troy in 1838. There was Elder Moore, born in the year 1800 at some place unknown to us, who was to become the father of Jennie Moore, wife the the Grenada Dentist and Mayor who was an early victim of the fever epidemic. Elder Moore died of the same disease.

During the very early years of Grenada, Dr. E. Cahn came to the town and set up a business which was continued many years. He was the first Jewish settler in the area so far as we can ascertain from available records. But others of his race were to follow within a few years. Political disturbances in the German states during the decade beginning in 1840 brought many middle class Jewish people to the United States. Grenada was fortunate enought to attract a number of these cultured, intelligent and thrifty people who became an important factor in the economic development of the area. They came, and for many years were a part of the cultural, economic and social life of the town. At one time there were enough Jewish families living in the town to set up a sabbath school. Nathan Haber was born in the German state of Bavaria in the year 1818. His wife Pauline Kahn, a native of France was born in 1845. We do not know what attracted them to Grenada, but we do know that for several years they operated a hotel located where the Grenada Theater now stands. The building, erected by Colonel W. N. Pass was first known as the Pass House. After the Habers took charge of the hotel it was known as the Haber House and was operated by the Habers until shortly before the death of this Jewish couple, both of whom died in.1888. Meyer Wile, born in Ichenhauser, Bavaria in the year 1828, and his wife Isabella Wile who was born in New York State in 1838 came to Grenada and set up a merchantile business. Mr. Wile was another victim of the Yellow Fever Epidemic. A few years before the death of her husband, Mrs. Wile invited her nephew Max Ginsburger to come to Grenada and become a clerk in the Wile store. After the death of her husband, Mrs. Wile entrusted the operation of her business to her son and her nephew. Later Ginsburger became a partner in the business and soon thereafter established a business of his own. In the same little area in the Odd Fellows Cemetery where the Habers and Wiles are buired there is a grave stone with the simple inscription; "Joseph Strenge. Born in Bavaria March 28, 1802. Died August 27, 1878." This is all we know of this Bavarian who came to this country, found his way to Grenada, died in the fever epidemic, and was placed to rest in the little cemetery area along with four of his Jewish kindred or friends. The headstones in the cemetery give much interesting information relative to the diverse areas and states from whom came the people who built Grenada, but the names mentioned above are representative of the people who converged from many different places to share in the development of Grenada.

Characteristics

Most of the people who settled in Grenada were religious. They were fundamentalists in beliefs, and convinced, beyone the shadow of a doubt, that their own particular church denomination had the most correct and authoritative interpretation of the Holy Writ. Their Churches were the center of both spiritual and social affairs. Since the early churches were the only buildings with any considerable seating accomodations it was natural that many meetings of various sorts took place in or around these church buildings. All of the early churches were called Protestant Churches. They consisted of the Methodist Episcopal Church, The Missionary Baptist Church, The Primitive Baptist Church, The Regular Presbyterian Church, The Cumberland Presbyterian Church, and The Episcopal Church. So far as we have been able to determine the Jewish people never had a synagogue in Grenada, nor a separate cemetery. The church people, particularly the Methodist and the Baptist, placed great stress on, and stood by, what were called "protracted meetings." Today we term meeting of that kind revivals. These meetings ran for ten days or two weeks, and were almost always held in the summer season of the year. Each church would have its own meeting, but on occasion, most of the churches in town would get together and organize jointly, or union meetings. For these joint meetings a well known professional revivalist would be invited to do the preaching. On one occasion, Sam Jones, the most popular revivalist of the day was chosen. Since no church in town was large enough to accommodate the crowds expected, a rough tavernacle was created. The several churches would underwrite the expense of the construction; the honorarium for the revivalist, and all other expenses incident to the meeting. Sometimes there would be a deficit which would have to be met by the several churches; at other times there might be money left over after expenses were paid. Of course the meetings were financed by the collections taken up at the services. The liberality of the people in contributions varied with the eloquence of the minister and the amount of spiritual emotion which had been aroused by the services. On the few occasions when there was a surplus left over after payment of expense, there was more dissention relative to the distribution of the surplus than there was when it was necessary to assess churches their share of any deficity which might have occurred. The people were prone to discuss and debate various theological questions and church doctrines. During the early years of the Baptist denominations in and about Grenada there was a split in the church on the question of foreign missions. At a later date there was another split when a Texas evanglist came for a meeting; preached doctrine contrary to the belief of a majority of the church members; convinced the pastor of the church as to the authority of the doctrine which he was preaching and brought about a division by which the pastor and part of the flock left the First Baptist Church and established the Central Baptist Church. A little later there was a division of opinion in the Presbyterian church-partly over the question of the educational qualifications of ministers. This division resulted in the establishment of the Cumberland Presbyterian Church. There was a Cumberland Church in Grenada for a time.

The Episcopal church was a relatively late comer into the religious life of Grenada. Generally speaking, this church drew its members from families of Virginia Tidewater background. Of course the Episcopal church was the state supported church in Virginia during colonial days, and descendants of those early families had reverence and affection for that church, and were use to the dignity of the church ritual. Many of the settlers who had come in from the Piedomont region had no affection for the Episcopal church-in fact they had resented being taxed to help support that church. Most of these people were inclined to be members of the various other so-called protestant churches. Some of the pre-Civil War churches allowed negro slaves to attend certain services and some of them had negro members. Of course these were more or less inactive members who had no part in the policies and doctrines of the church. After the war negro members of the local Baptist church decided they wanted a church of their own and George W. Ragsdale and other Baptists helped them to build a church house. Ragsdale gave the lot on which the building was to be erected.

Perhaps because of the presence of some Revolutionary soldiers in the community; memories of the not too distant Indian wars and the Battle of New Orleans, and the growing anticipation of trouble with Mexico which was sure to result from the flood of American migration into the Mexican province of Texas, there was much military spirit among the people of Grenada. This military ardor was early indicated by an article appearing in the newspaper The Grenadian in December 1838: "PRESENTATION OF THE BANNER: Many of the citizens of Grenada assembled at the Presbyterian Church on Saturday evening, the 17th ult., to witness the rich donation prepared by the chivalrous female spirits of our town to the gallant Volunteer Company recently organized among us. At 3 o'clock the soldiers were paraded, and a most beautiful and elegantly executed a Stand of Colors, with the following appropriate and soul-stirring address: "Gentlemen and soldiers: the Ladies of Grenada, animated by a love of independence, thrilling as that which propeles the vital current through the heart of the most enthusiastic patriot, are ambitious of fostering your martial spirit by the only public reciprocation etiquette allows them. Accept, then, their banner of Liberty as a pledge of their confidence in your loyalty, in sustaining a cause alike precious to every descendent of 'Seventy Six'. Soldiers! Limit not its glorious aspirations; check not its soarings, entwine its emblem with the thread of your mortal existence." This company was a part of the 1st Brigade, 4th Division Mississippi Militia. The Brigade Court Martial Headquarters was in Grenada. The report indicates the use of an early church building for non-religious meetings; the flowery type of oratory in which so many speakers of the period delighted, and the patriotic spirit of the ladies, which spirit carried over into the Civil War Period. It would seem that Grenada was a center of Militia activity. On October 8, 1842, the newspaper Weekly Register ran the following notice: "The Sixteenth Regiment of Mississippi will parade at Ingram's at six or seven miles east of Grenada, on the Fourth Saturday in October, armed and equiped as the law directs, for the purpose of Regimental Review, at 10 o'clock A. M. "From the same paper of September 24, 1842: "The Company 'D', Sixteenth Regiment of Miss. Militia, will parade in Grenada, on the Second Saturday in October next, at 9 o'clock A. M., armed and equiped as the law directs. This notice inserted by the order of the Captain. Septimus Caldwell, Orderly Sergeant." On November 20, 1839, just about a year before W. G, Kendall had made his flowery speech to the Grenada Pioneers, the Southern Reporter had reminded the people of the presence in their midst of many people who traced their ancestry back to soldiers of the Revolutionary army: "The Revolutionary War could have but little effect on Grenada, for Indians still roamed undisturbed through its forests. Later, when the county was opened to settlement by white, a number of ex-soldiers must have come looking for land, for many Grenada county families trace their ancestry back to soldiers from Virginia. John Hollon, a veteran of the Revolutionary War, died at the residence of his son, Assa Hollon, near Troy, on November 20, 1839, in his ninety second year. The deceased was born and reared in Bedford, Virginia, and from there entered the Colonial army."

Many people in Mississippi were interested in the struggle by which Texas secured its independence from Mexico. Some had sons, and others neighbors, who had migrated to Texas and been a part of the war which had gained Texas independence. Most of them felt that eventually there would be war between the United States and Mexico. Rumors were prevalent that the war was almost at hand. Acting on these rumors, an American Naval officer occupied a California town, and was forced into a red-faced apology to Mexican officials when he learned that these rumors were false. This happened in 1842. The people in Grenada were excited at these rumors of impending conflict. On February 1842 the Weekly Register reported: "A party of three gentlemen have arrived from Corpus Christi: They state that some Mexican robbers have again been making attempts to raise enough men to rob Rancho Corpus Christi, but have not succeeded. Colonel Carns is in the vicinity with a good company of their men, and with them residing at the rancho, they feel able to meet any assault which may be made upon them" Again, on April 9, 1842, the same paper had another comment on the Mexican situation: War and rumors of war, are constantly coming. The many questions between this country and Great Britian most imminently threaten, perhaps compel it. When it comes it will involve France, Mexico and Texas immediately. Every energy of the government ought to be directed to preparation for war, and if declared by this country the declaration should be delayed long enough for that purpose. A tariff for revenue ought at once to be imposed to raise means, 2,000 Paixhan guns ought to be prepared, musket, bombs and ammunition; our forts man'd, repaired and reprovisioned, privateers commissioned, the regular army increased, proclamation be made for volunteers, and then war may be declared to some purpose, backed by a million soldiers, a thousand privateer vessels, and a thousand steam-boats with each a Paxhan gun on board." It will be remembered that both Great Britian and France were interested in annexation of the Independent Republic of Texas at a time when the United States, for political reasons, hesitated to acceed to the wishes of the people of Texas for annexation by the United States. This explains the rather bombastic statement of the editor relative to preparation for war with either, or both of these powers if they intervened when the United States did act to annex Texas.

On July 26, 1845, the paper Harry of the West noted; "From all appearances a little spec of war is likely to call us to action. Fifteen hundred U. S. troops, it would seem however, well fed and well armed, can do the work of Mexico; if they cannot the Grenada Guards may hold themselves in readiness." This rash assumption that fifteen hundred U. S. soldiers could handle the Mexican war is reminescent of the pre-Civil War boast that one Southern soldier could whip five Yankee soldiers. When the Mexican war came, it took many more soldiers, including a volunteer regiment from Mississippi, to end that conflict in a satisfactory manner. The Confederate soldiers were to find a few years later that one Confederate Soldier could not always whip five Union soldiers. On June 10, 1846, The Grenada Hornets, under the command of Captain Judson were taken into a Mississippi regiment intended for use in the war. Of course at the time of the Mexican war Grenada county had not yet been organized, so that it is probable that men, living in what is now Grenada County, fought in units formed from Carroll, Tallahatchie, Yalobousha, and possibly from Chcctaw - the four counties which were to contribute of the territory which eventually became Grenada County. The Coffeeville Guards were under the command of Captain Ephrain Fisher, a lawyer who later became a judge on the Mississippi Supreme Court. The Yalobousha Guards were under the command of Captain A. H. Davidson. There were men by this name living in Grenada and it is possible that some men from Grenada may have been in that unit. Carroll County organized four units: Carroll County Volunteers, Volunteer Company, Carroll County Guards, which was an infantry company, and the Carroll County Guards, a cavalry company organized at Middleton, then in Carroll County, but later to become a part of Montgomery County when that county was organized. Middleton was a town of some importance until the Mississippi Central Railroad was constructed, and then most of the inhabitants moved a few miles east to the place where the new town of Winona was being established on the railroad line. The men in these several companies were assigned to the army of General Taylor and placed in a brigade with John A. Quitman as commander. Through the recommendation of Jefferson Davis, these men were armed with rifles instead of the musket which was the standard infantry arm at that time. The Mississippi troops engaged in the Battle of Buena Vista and also in the capture of Monteray. We know that Boyd Doak, Dr. John Gage and Mather Robinson fought in the Mexican War, but do not know the unit in which they were enlisted. Mather Robinson lost his life in one of the battles of the war.

The early settlers were very much interested in social, political and miscellaneous affairs, and the newspaper men of that period attempted to give their readers the kind of information which they desired. There were no society editors on the small newspapers, but the editors did the best they could in reporting weddings. On October 8, 1842, this report was published by the Weekly Register: "HYMNEAL: Married, on Thursday evening, the 29th ult., by Rev. Asbury Davidson, Mr. E. F. Moore to Miss Pauline Melton, daughter of Michael H. Melton, Esq., all of this place. With the above notice we received a big slice of as rich a cake as we ever smacked our lips over, and a bottle of claret (Bingham's best) which we would praise, but for the reflection that we might be suspected of throwing away our temerance stopper. A health to the bride, whether we drank it or not; and to the bridegroom. Oh take thou this young rose and let her life be prolonged by the breath she will borrow from thee; For while o'er her bosom the soft notes shall thrill she'll think the sweet night bird is courting her still." As an example of the way another editor handled the news of a wedding we quote from the July 6, 1884, issue of the paper Harry of the West: "MARRIED: On Thursday evening last, at the residence of Mistress John Williams in this county, by Rev. T. J. Lowery, Mr. James T. Williams to Miss Eliza Lowery both of this county. So much for Leap Year: Truly, the good work has fairly commenced, and we hope that it will go blithely on; we were not forgotten: consequently, as in duty and pleasure bound, we wish the young couple all imaginable good luck. May their voyage down the stream of time be as much exempt from the snags, sandbars and blow-ups incident to humanity as may be consistent with its proper diversification; may their highest anticipation of future happiness be more than realized: and may the evenness and beauty of their conduct present a shinning example of wedded love and conjugal felicity." People today probably would not like this type of reporting, but people of that far distant day much have loved it. We note in each of the reports the editor has received some token of appreciation for his anticipated writeup.

As early as 1842, the people of Grenada were at odds on the question of the sale and use of alocholic liquors. From the Weekly Register of June 25, 1842, we find a notice of a Temperance Celebration to be held on Independence day: "The Temperance folk are making real preparations for good eating and good drinking too, on the 4th. First the mind will be feasted by an address from the Hon. D. C. Shattuck; and 2nd, the physical man will be presented with a groaning board of good things and a bountiful supply of the fluid elixir-cold water. There will be cakes, pudding, pies, tarts, preserves, fruits, jellies, confections, lambs, shoats, fishes, turtle soup, beef, veal, squirrels, part-ridges, hams, chickens, turkeys, and every variety of meats, vegetables, and pastries. Having feasted the soul, we will eat heartily, wash all down with cold water, smack our lips and be as merry and blithe as the birds, with a good relish." We gather from the tone of the report that while the editor was ready and willing to indulge in the great variety of good things to eat, he was not too interested in the drink which was a part of the celebration. The arrangements for the celebration were rather elaborate. Eight men composed the committee which made the plans. They were A. Gillespie, J. J. Choate, G. D. Mitchell, A. C. Baine, J. C. Abbott, W. H. Stephens, J. A. Wilkins and E. F. Gibbs. President of the day was Col. John C. Abbott. Vice Presidents were Daniel Robinson, Esq., John A. Wilkins, and John R. McRae, Esq. Orator of the day was F. A. Tyler. Esq. Reader of the Declaration on Independence was W. G. Robb, Esq. Rev. E. J. Fitzgerald acted as Chaplain, while Col. G. D. Mitchell, R. D. McLean, Esq., and Levin Lake served as Marshals. N. S. Neal, Esq., was Bearer of the National Flag, and D. M. Beck was Bearer of the Temperance Flag. The badge for members of the Temperance Society was a white ribbon worn on the left arm. The officers wore a scarlet ribbon and the Marshals wore a red scarf. The Sabbath School of the Methodist Church with James Sims as Superintendent, were at the head of the procession which formed in Line street in front of the Presbyterian Church. We wonder if the absence of the Baptist Sabbath School was any indication of the attitude of the Baptist Church members in regard to temperance? We observe that the people were very fond of ceremony and that several of the officers had military titles. We wonder if these were actual titles or merely honorary ones. We also wonder why some of the men had the term Esquire after thier names, while others did not have this distinction. Many of the men named as being participants in the procession have been identified in previous chapters of this work.

Other Independence Day celebrations were of a different nature. The June 15, 1844, issue of Harry of the West gave notice of an event which was to be forthcoming: "We have been requested to note coming events by an invited guest: A grand and social candy stew will come off shortly between this and the fork; probably the 4th of July. The Ladies, of course, will be there and we consider it is the only fit place to spend the 4th of July in this state; young gentlemen of sentiment and thoroughly moralized are respectfully invited to attend." The editor seems not to have been in accord with the people who arranged the affair if we can judge by the following editoral comment which appeared in the July 6, 1844, issue of his paper: "The Anniversary of our National Independence passed off in quietness in this place owing to a fair that was held at the Presbyterian Church. This we did think and yet do think was wrong, as it would in no way have interfered with that matter. On this glorious day party differences, both small and great, should be laid aside; and the pure offerings of the patriot should be placed upon the altar of our country." This statement leads us to wonder if the editor was one of those men not "thoroughly moralized".

Editors then, as now, were critical of the conduct of city business. On December 2, 1843, The Morning Herald had this reprimand for some citizens of the town: "We quietly stepped out of our office yesterday and saw not less than 20 poor perishing cows drooping about the streets. It is a shame that owners of cattle should let them starve in a country like ours." On November 30, 1844, the editor of Harry of the West gave faint praise and considerable advice to the City Fathers: "We are glad to see our town authorities are beginning to pay some attention to our streets. We hope they will not forget Line Street, as our churchgoing people and our school children, as well as others, will be benefited by having that street put in good order, and having a good walk made over the drain." In the December 14th issue of the same paper the editor had this comment: "Sad Accident; Last Sabbath as Miss........... was coming from church in attempting to cross the drain across the street, for want of a foot-way, she unfortunately fell with one foot in the middle of the drain and wet her kid slipper, silk stocking, and foot. We are glad to hear that nothing serious is anticipated from the accident; but we do hope that our town authorities will put a foot-way over the drain as bad colds, coughs and consumption are the consequences of wet feet."

A neighboring newspaper man expressed his dislike of things in general in stronger terms than did the editor of Harry of the West. Soon after Coffeeville was made the county seat of Yalobousha county, E. Percy Howe became editor of a paper published in the new town. For some reason he became angry with some of the people in the town and gave vent to his displeasure in this manner:

> "Upon a hill near Durdens mill
> There is a place called Coffeeville;
> The meanest town I ever saw,
> Save Plummer's town Oakchukamau."

As might be expected Howe did not remain long in Coffeeville. He moved to Tuscahoma where he was editor of The Tuscahomian. Later he moved to South Mississippi where he continued active in newspaper work.

As in other communities of the period, men were very touchy about any question regarding courage, honor or integrity. Then, as now, some parents resented efforts by teachers to discipline children. In the year 1889 a local newspaper reported that Professor Phillips, head of the Grenada Free White School whipped Authur Dubard, fourteen year old son of L. C. Budbard who was employed as a clerk in the store of Roane & Son. When Pbillips went to the store to explain the cause of the punishment inflicted on the boy, the father assaulted Phillips. Dubard was fined twenty five dollars when the case came up in the Mayor's Court. Again, about the same time, the paper reported that: "Mr. Dunbar Duncan whipped Joe Cahn with a hickory stick because of a dispute over a seat at a minstral show." During the same period Captain W. P. Towler shot and mortally wounded Rev. C. F. Stivers who was holding a series of services in the Episcopal church. Towler was a former Grenada druggist who, at the time of the shooting, was a traveling salesman. At the trial relative to the shooting, Mrs. Towler claimed that the minister had made improper advances to her during her husband's absence, and while the minister was a guest in the Towler home. It was reported that when her husband returned home she met him at the carriage house and began to tell him about the conduct of the minister. Towler testified that when the minister saw this meeting and realized that Mrs. Towler was informing her husband relative to the conduct of the minister, Stiver advanced on him with a gun, and that he, Towler, shot in self defense, and in defense of the honor of his home. After this testimony the authorities who held this preliminary trial agreed that Mr. Towler was justified in his conduct. A strong point in favor of Towler was the deathbed statement made by Mr. Stiver that Towler was justified in his action.

There was much criminal activity in the community in the years following the Civil War as, no doubt, there had been during the earlier years of the history of the area. The first Grand Jury to be impaneled in Grenada after the county was created in 1870, was composed of the following men: R. Coffman, S. H. Garner, John P. Flippin, J. G. Gibbs, R. W. Rosamond, J. R. Williams, John Parker, W. B. Willis, G. F. Ingram, F. G. Long, William Bell, B. C. Harrison, R. L. Jones, W. H. Aldridge, James Loring, Richard Holland, John Crump, R. N. Hall, Thomas Koon and J. M. Duncan. This was indeed a "blue chip" jury, consisting as it did, of many of the outstanding citizens of the county. Most of these men had been strong factors in the development of the town and county. The descendants of many of them still reside in Grenada county. This first Grand Jury was quite in contrast with one impaneled in 1890 when the Grenada Sentinel reported; "Three negroes and two white men on the Grand Jury cannot read and write." It will be remembered that it was in the year 1890 that the state adopted the Constitution which made it possible for local white citizens to regain control of local affairs. The make-up of the 1890 Grand Jury is an indication of the need for respectable white men to be in control of public affairs once again. In 1889, just a year before the Grand Jury mentioned, which had five illiterates, there were seven men, two white and five negroes, awaiting trial for murder. During the same year M. J. Cheatham, a white man, was convicted of the murder of a negro, and was sentenced to hang for the crime. The sentence was carried out, and Cheatham became the first white man in the county to be sentenced to death for murder of a negro. In 1887 two negroes who had been accused of murdering a back peddler were taken from the Grenada jail by a mob; carried across the Bouge and hanged from a tree in the vicinity of Futheyville. During this same year rival cotton weighers in Grenada became involved in a dispute, relative to which man should weigh a certain lot of bales of cotton, and the dispute resulted in B. L. H. Wright and his son B. L. H. Wright, Jr. killing A. Melton. Later the father and son were acquitted of the charge of murder. Convictions were hard to obtain in affairs such as the one mentioned above. Perhaps the make-up of the juries was responsible. In 1886 one jury trying a case in the Circuit Court was made up of six whites and six negroes. Because of a lack of educational opportunities before the Civil War, very few negroes had adequate training for jury service, and white men who could be induced to serve on juries loaded with illiterates were probably no fitter jurymen than the illiterates with whom they served. It would seem that fights, quarrels and occasional shootings were a matter of great public interest, and that in times of calm about such matters, the newspapers were bad off for news. In 1883 The Grenada Sentinel, in the absence of more exciting news reported that a big fight took place on Main street the previous day.

Wills made by individuals are oftentimes indicative of the faith, fear, aspirations and frustrations of the person who makes the will. In December 1865, at the beginning of the bitter period of readjustment by the people of Mississippi to the hard results of the Civil War defeat, John Duncan of Jackson, Mississippi made a will which reflected both the uncertainty of the time, and the deep sorrow which had come to him previous to the time when he made the will. He was a property owner in Grenada, hence the presence of the will in the court records of Grenada county. A part of the will reads: "It having pleased almighty God to disolve my Earthly Household by taking to himself all my worldly treasure; Walter my first born; Lucy, the young, the bright and intellectual, the beloved wife of my bosom; Mary, my peerless daughter, and Jannett, the last and youngest of all, and being myself in good health of both body and mind, yet far distant from my home and constantly exposed to peril, I do hereby make and publish this my last will and testament." It is quite probable that this will was made while Mr. Duncan was in military service and only dated after he had returned from such service.

In a previous article on the Yellow Fever Epidemic of 1878 we indicated that the telegraph office in Grenada was closed, and that all telegrams sent to Grenada people were received at a station a few miles north of town. The will of Wyatt M. Redding, dated August 30, 1878, and probated in November of the same year, certainly indicates the resignation of a victim of the dread disease, as well as a possible explanation of the absence of a telegraph operator in Grenada. The will reads: "I, Wyatt Redding being of sound mind but sick of yellow fever do make the following bequests which are my last will and testament. To mother, Mrs. A. Senton of Waterford, Mississippi, (near Holly Springs) two thousand dollars ($2,000) this being secured by a life insurance policy in Protective Lodge Number 2, A. O. W. W. located at Waterford, Mississippi. To my brother A. S. Redding two hundred and thirty dollars, or thereabouts, this sum secured by a deed of trust on Peter Kirby's lot located in Grenada (This deed is in my trunk). To my sister Mrs. W. P. Ford who lives at Laws Hill near Waterford the sum of money due me by the Cincinnati Enquirer, about ($100 - one hundred dollars) also the sum of money due me from the New York Times, about fifty dollars ($50), also the sum of money due me from the St. Louis and N. O. Railroad and the M & T Railroad, about two hundred dollars ($200) from both companies, also the money due me from the W. U. T. Co., about one hundred dollars ($100). I desire my burial expense to be paid out of the sum of money in my trunk, about one hundred dollars ($100). Out of the balance I give to Mrs. Anne Ives ten dollars ($10) for kind attention during my last illness. To Jack Collings, Colored, ten dollars ($10) for faithful services to me during my illness. This money to be a part of the money in my trunk, the balance of which money and all my personal effects, or any other property which is, or may be mine, to be given to my mother." Reading between the lines of the will we conclude that Redding was a telegraph operator serving the Western Union Company, as well as the Chicago, St. Louis and New Orleans Railroad and the Mississippi Central Road. The first named road later came to be known as the Illinois Central line. From the sums of money due from newspapers in Cincinnati and New York we might surmise that the operator, up until overcome by fatal illness, was sending in to those papers reports of the progress of the epidemic.

Another man, bravely facing death which was to come to him before the end of the Yellow Fever Epidemic, dated his will August 27, 1878. The will was probated on November 27th of the same year. The will was made by Dr. W. W. Hall. It read: "In view of the unprecidented fatality of the present epidemic of yellow fever, I deem it proper to make this my last will and testament. If my wife survives me I bequeath to her my insurance policies of two thousand dollars each, minus so much as may be necessary to pay my honest debts. If my wife should not survive me, I bequeath to my parents, if living, fifteen hundred dollars; to my brother C. M. Hall five hundred dollars, and to Mrs. Elizabeth Korn of Colliverville, Tennessee, the remainder of any monies remaining after my debts are paid. To the children of John C. and Elizabeth Stokes I bequeath my interest in house and lot on Main street. If my parents do not survive me, I bequeath the amount set aside for them, one half to the children of my brother F. K. Hall, and the other half to the children of Mrs. E. Hamilton, to be used by the latter for her and their support. I bequeath to my brother C. M. Hall, my horse, buggy, library and instruments, enjoining him to use them for the good of humanity. It is well to state that I am indebted to the late firm of F. K. Hall in amounts to me unremembered, but aggregating several hundred dollars and that I wish them paid. I bequeath my notes and accounts to the children of my late brother F. K. Hall and to the children of my sister E. L. Hamilton equally. In the event of the death of all my family (immediate family?) I direct that my estate revert to my nearest relatives, except as provided for Mrs. Korn. I bequeath to my professional brethren an example which I enjoin them to follow in epidemics." Just how excellent an example Dr. Hall set for his professional brethren is recorded by a simple inscription on a head stone in the Odd Fellows Cemetery which inscription reads: "Dr. William Wood Hall, born August 17, 1839. Died The Christian's Death at his post of Duty August 27, 1878. Buried near his grave, all victims of the epidemic, are the following named family members mentioned in his will: Mary Koen Hall (his wife), Finley Hall and C. M. Hall (brothers), Eliza Hall Hamilton (sister) and his parents Rev. and Mrs. James G. Hall.

Not all of the people who made wills in anticipation of death by the yellow fever plague were people of large means, or of professional training. For instance the Non Cupative will of O. P. Saunders, dated during the dread days of the fever epidemic of 1878, reads: "The last request of Pa to me when dying, writing them as he spoke them. Willie I am going to die. I want you to keep the land that......(name illegiable) was to deed to us as yours forever. The eighty acres of land next to Mr. Moss. I want the children to have ten dollars each in money. I give you everything that I own or have any right to - oxen, wagons, cows, hogs, horses, plows and all debts owing me and all lumber I own. I want you to take the children, move up here and do the best you can by them until they are able to do for themselves, unless Sis Carrie wants some of them. If she does let her have Lena and Clara as Sallie will soon have another babe on her hands. If Sis Carrie does not want them I want you to keep them all and do what you can for them. I know you are not able to do much till you get that debt off your hands, but I hope that you will have no trouble paying that off. I owe two debts to Snyder and Jimmie Fletcher. I want you to pay Snyder. Get the watch and keep or sell it as you think best for your interest. Jimmie F. you can pay or not as you wish. I do not think he has treated us right. Pay the children the ten dollars as soon as you get the place paid for. Make the children mind you as if they were your own and help you as they can. I believe that is all I have to say. Farewell Willie."

Dr. J. L. Milton, Grenada Dentist, who was Mayor of the town at the outbreak of the epidemic, and who was to die during the early days of this time of trial, wrote a letter to Robert Horton, a lawyer friend: "Mayor's Office. Robert Horton Esquire. I wish you to take charge of my business. You will find one note for $300 on Dr. Wilkins, one on Wilkins & Greenhow, one on L. C. Dubard, and some others I don't remember. Also some accounts. You will find one policy in the Equitable Life, one in the N. Y. Life, one on the Mobile Life now the hands of Mr. Kunkindall at Lake Bros., one in the Knights of Honor, the last one is for the benefit of Miss M$_o$llie Poitevent and she is hereby authorized to sign for it. There is also a watch and chain in my upper drawer that I wish given her. You will please, and you are hereby authorized to look after, as guardian, my children and their interest. I wish them to follow such business as their inclination should point. I owe but few debts all of which you will please pay. The last deposit at Lake Bros., of 460 some odd dollars, Martin & McCall of Nashville are entitled to one sixth, $76 or more. My boys and the Judge own land in Dyre County Tennessee, E. G. Sugg Esq. is the agent, Martin and McCall are entitled to one sixth of the running amount, my boys two and one third and the Judge one third of the balance." Judging from the fact that Dr. Milton wrote his wishes in a letter to Lawyer Horton, and the awkward way in which he expressed some of his wishes, we are inclined to believe that he had already contracted the disease which was to claim him a victim within a few days of the date of the letter. When the will offered for probate, the presiding judge accepted it as a legal will, basing his decision on the sworn testimony of William C. McLean, Ben C. Adams Jr., George Y. Freeman and Samuel Lacock. The first three were lawyers practicing in Grenada, and the last was a Grenada merchant.

L. R. Stewart, former Sheriff and Tax Collector of Yalobousha County died a few months before the fever epidemic, but had a troubled mind when he made out the will which was probated February 2, 1878. After appointing "My son, Eugen Henry Stewart, who has suffered great afflictions in early youth" as the executor of his estate, Mr. Stewart touched on family troubles: "To my married daughter Marcella Stuart, wife of F. M. Freely I have given stock of all kinds horses, cattle, hogs, sheep and goats besides other personal property to the value of three hundred and fifty dollars, also maintained and supported her and her husband F. M. Freley, and children for nine or ten years in my house- also gave him, the said F. M. Freley, the free use of as much land as he and what hands he hired could cultivate and plenty of teams to cultivate the same, fed the teams and hands, all for the benefit of my daughter Marcella G. Stewart, wife of F. M. Freley, as aforesdaid beside paying annually heavy store accounts of his, Freley's, contracting. Having spent all the property I gave my daughter Marcella, another draft on my estate bequeathed to my son Eugene must be made for the benefit of my daughter Marcella and her children, and over which the said Freley is to have no interest or control whatsoever, I therefore request that my son Eugene, Executor as aforesaid, pay annually out of the estate bequeathed by me to him, fifty dollars for six years amounting to $300 if it can be done without selling any property to do so; if not said annuity to be paid when convenient without any interest whatever. The ingratitude and dis- respect shown me by the said F. M. Freley has lessend my respect for the said F. M. Freley and increased my love and regard for my daughter Marcella and her children." Mr. Steward thus tells off his son-in-law in a manner which he would probably liked to have done during the long years when he was supporting this seeming near do-well son in law. But Mr. Stewart was also displeased with his daughter Pauline as evidenced by this excerpt from his will: "My daughter Pauline Josephine Stewart, I am sorry to say it, but it is neverthe- less true, has not been to me an obedient and respectful child, but has brought my grey hairs with sorrow to the grave by using harsh, insulting and dis-re- spectful language to an aged parent over three score years and ten. May God have mercy on her. To her, the said Pauline J. Stewart, I will and bequeath the following property (to-wit) the horse bridle and saddle that I have already given her, the gold watch and chain valued at one hundred and thirty dollars, I also bequeath to her one hundred dollars to be paid by my executor afore- said when it shall suit his convenience and ability to do so. If Pauline desires to spend her single life at the old homestead with her brother Eugene she is welcome to do so." This will, which was probated in the early months of 1878, gives the skeleton outline of an unhappy family situation. Was the father unduly partial to his afflicted son? Was his son-in-law Freley as trifling as he is made out in the will? Was the younger girl, Pauline, as bad as her father believed, or was Mr. Stewart just a grouchy old man seeing things with a ju- andiced eye? Of course we can never know the answer to these questions, but they do arouse interesting speculations.

On September 16, 1878, Nathaniel Howard, the transplanted native of New England and descendant from an ancestor who came over in the Mayflower to Ply- mouth, faced the very present danger of contracting yellow fever. It had been thirty nine years since he first reached the area where the little towns of Pittsburg and Tullahoma were to be established. In business he had advanced from an itinerate trader, dispensing his limited wares under the shade of a canvas tent, to an important business man and Director of the Mississippi & Tennessee Railroad line. At this date anyone reading his will would not sense that he was disturbed, perhaps frightened, of the disease which was to soon claim his life. Of all the wills we have found which reflect the urgency of their composition, and the need for immediate recording of the wishes of the testator in the race against the effects of the epidemic, none, other than this one, shows the calm and disciplined emotional nature of a person who does not panic. Mr. Howard was careful to have his will attested by three persons; Panola E. Davis, J. F. Rosoborough and Lea Williamson. He then writes: "I, Nathaniel Howard a citizen of Grenada, State of Mississippi, being sound in mind do make and declare this my last will and testament: I hereby give, devise and bequeath to my daughter Helen Howard Williamson and her heirs all my property, real, personal and mixed of ever nature and character whatsoever, whether situated in Mississippi or elsewhere, and I hereby constitute and appoint her, the said Helen my daughter, my sole exectrix and I hereby direct that she do qualify as such without giving any bond as executrix, or otherwise, and I expressly relieve her from any accounting with the Chancery or any other court in this or any other state, of and concerning any or all of my property herein devised, it being my will that the said Helen, my daughter, shall immediately upon my death enter upon the enjoyment and possession of all my property. I request my executrix to pay immediately after my death all just and legal debts that I may then owe. In testimony thereof I have herewith set my hand and seal the 16th day of September of 1878." With his keen New England developed sense of values, Mr. Howard didn't want his estate diminished by court and legal fees; he wanted his daughter at once to enter into "the enjoyment" of the property devised to her, and wanted his debts payed "immediately" after his death. Mrs. Howard had died some years before the date of the above quoted deed so it would seem that his daughter mentioned in the will was the only close relative who survived him. Like so many other New Englanders who came into the new frontier area of North Central Mississippi seeking to improve their economic status, perhaps expecting to return to their native soil, Mr. Howard made his contribution to the economic, civic and political affairs of the town and remained to die of the dreadful scourge which all but wiped out the town which he had helped establish.

A letter written during the height of the fever epidemic by Henry C. Stokes and quoted in the book, A CHRISIAN HERITAGE, gives about the best description of the people of Grenada as they reacted to the challange of illness and death: "Grenada, Miss. Sept. '78. My Dear Uncle: When you wrote me the other day I was still in bed, having a relapse of yellow fever. But I am now up and improving, as is all the rest of our family. It pains me to talk of our great misfortunes - but as it was God's will, we must console ourselves in the happy thought that we can meet them again. Mother and Jimmie (a brother) died of neglect. We had some nurses that got drunk and went to sleep and neglected us all. They (the nurses) not being satisfied with that, stole every rag I had, 2 good suits, didn't leave me a shirt, pair of drawers or anything else and I can't get in a store to get any. Will you let me have some of Charles? They will do me as much good and I'll pay you for them when you come down. I am getting strong and if I can do anything for you, I'll gladly do so. Dr. Ray is up walking around and Bettie's fever has left her. Aunt Mary's sister (Nannie) who came down to nurse her, is at our house with fever and dangerously ill - little hope for her. We are ever so much obliged for the nice things you sent us and enjoyed them hugely. We managed to get along now pretty well in way of eatables, if we can just keep up. There were only two whites died last night, Dr. Ringgold and a stranger, and about six negroes. It (the fever) is gradually dying out here now. I think, since it has no other to pray upon, and those who are sick, seem to be getting well. About half the people who died, died from neglect. Most of the nurses seem to have come here merely to benefit themselves by stealing everything they can lay their hands on, and I have not seen one, who did not get drunk. Down at the Chamberlain House yesterday there was a great crowd of nurses drawing champaing (sic) for the sick-sitting in the parlor drunk - eating cake and drinking up what they had drawn for the sick, while in every room, you could hear the sick crying for water etc. and nobody to go near them. Among our business men, there's only a few that still live. It (the fever) seemed to be more fatal among them than others. Everything looks fearful gloomy down here - not a store open, and nobody on the streets. Nearly half the people who left here died. Some went to the country and died without any nursing etc. Many got sick and were bro't back in wagons to die. Uncle Jim, I feel as if I could never be happy again - so many of our dear relatives gone, and my dear mother oh! that I could have taken her place. Our home will never be happy again - no never. But she lived and suffered long here on earth and one consolation is that she wears as bright a crown as there is in Heaven. But I must close. Hoping this will find you, Aunt Bell and little baby well, I am, Yr. Aff. Nephew Henry C. Stokes." This young man of twenty three years of age was the grandson of Rev. James G. Hall who served as an early pastor of The Grenada Baptist Church, now called The First Baptist Church. Both Rev. and Mrs. Hall had died during the epidemic as well as several of their children. It is natural that young Mr. Stokes, in his grief at the loss of loved ones, should have resented any neglect of which those nursing his deceased relatives might have been guilty, but his feeling that all the nurses, men and women, white and colored, were guilty of such neglect is not born out by the letters and expressions of others who had great admiration for, and appreciation of, the fine services rendered by many of these nurses. It is conceivable that a number of them did prove unworthy of the trust imposed in them, but it will be recalled that in the chapter of this work on Grenada Newspapers and Newspaper Men, the editor of the Grenada Sentinel, defended the character of the nurses, particularly the female ones, and contrasted their conduct with that of some of the preachers and doctors who, in the opinion of the editor, had not proved worthy of the ethics of their professions.

World wide attention was fastened on the epidemic of 1878 as it struck not only Grenada, Memphis, New Orleans, Mobile, but many other smaller places throughout the South. Evidently there was good newspaper coverage of the suffering of the people. The Book, A Christian Heritage, mentioned above, printed a tribute which the London (England) Standard paid to the spirit of the people who lived in the stricken cities and towns: "It is these people, the flower and pride of the English race, on whom a more terrible, more merciless enemy has now fallen. There can be now no division of sympathy, as there is no passion to excite and keep up courage for the occasion. Yet the men and women of the South are true to the old tradition. Her youth volunteer to serve and die in the streets of plague-stricken cities as rapidly they went forth, boys and grey haired men, to meet the threatened surprise of Petersburg as they volunteered to charge again and again the cannon - crowned hills of Gettysburg, and to enrich with their blood, and honor the name of a new victory, every field around Richmond. Their sisters, mother, wives and daughters are doing and suffering now, as they suffered from famine, disease, incessant anxiety and alarm through the four years of civil war. There may be among the various nations of the Aryan family one or two who would claim they could have furnished troops like those which followed Lee and Johnston, Stuart and Stonewall Jackson, but we doubt whether there be one race beside our own that could send forth its children by hundreds to face, in towns desolated by Yellow Fever, the horrors of a nurse's life, and the imminent terms of a Martyr's death." The end of the Civil War was just thirteen years in the past when the London Standard printed the tribute quoted qbove. Evidently the writer had a very high regard for the soldiers of the Confederacy and their general officers.

Of all those who came to Grenada to help during the dread days of the fever plague it is probable that none deserved more credit than a young thirty three year old minister. Rev. Hiram T. Haddick, who had attended Mississippi College and the Southern Baptist Theological Seminary, came to Grenada in 1875 as pastor of the Grenada Baptist Church. The minister was away from Grenada on vacation when the epidemic broke out. Some members of the church wrote him and advised him to stay away from Grenada until the epidemic had run its course. Disregarding this advice the preacher returned to Grenada and ministered to his people. He contracted the disease and a few days later, on August 28, 1878, died a death which could have been avoided had he listened to the advice of his friends to remain away from his post of duty. What supported Mr. Haddick in this seeming rash action? We will let the minister tell us in his own words. In a letter found on his desk after his death the minister had answered our question. He left for his members the following statement of his reason for coming back to his people: "I came because I felt it my duty to be in the midst of my afflicted, suffering and dying flock. God knows the anxiety I have felt and do now feel for my own preservation, Nothing but the stern dictates of my duty, with the hope of God's special providence in my behalf, ever brought me to the post of suffering and danger. I feel that I have done my duty; I leave the result with God. I am in God's hands; by his help I will trust him, though he slay me. If it should please him to spare me, I shall bless him, and by his grace I will serve him more faithfully hereafter. Should it be his will to take me, I shall cling to his blessed cross as my only hope of salvation. In my hands no price I bring, simply to his cross I cling. For almost eighty eight years this minister has slept in a grave far from his kindred, but marked by a tall shaft erected by the ladies of the church who pledged themselves and others "to keep his grave green forever!"

Chapter XVIII

Six Tragic Years

Grenada had been in existence as a town for just eight years short of a half century when there began the most tragic six years in the history of the Yalobousha river town. The first forty two years of its existence had brought about the usual hardships and triumphs common to the pioneer towns of the region and the times. There had been years of too much rain, or years of too little moisture when crops failed to measure up to optimistic early spring expectations; there had been seasons when the expected rise in the water of the river had not materialized early enough to enable the merchants and planters to bring in all materials needed for local consumption, nor to ship out all the produce upon which the economy of the region depended, and there had been sickness in people and livestock which had slowed up the agricultural production of the region. A period of inflated land values and hectic land speculation, followed by an acute financial panic, caused many men to default in payment of land purchases and lose property in which they had invested considerable money and energy. Lots in Grenada, in large numbers had been sold for taxes. The town and region had just begun to emerge from that period of financial hardship into a few years of prosperity when the dark clouds of the impending Civil War began to forecast another period of disaster. The trials and sufferings of that period have been related in other chapters of this work. But there was never a six year period in its history more tragic for Grenada than the period beginning in the early days of August, 1878, and terminating in December of 1884. In this short period a yellow fever epidemic decimated the town; the failure of its only banks jepordized the financial welfare of most of its people, and a raging fire destroyed the major part of the business houses of the town, and overshadowed by the importance of and publicity given to the above related disasters, the Buffaloe gnats attacked the livestock of the region and brought much loss to the farmers who depended on their livestock to help produce their agricultural products.

In the summer of 1878 the people of Grenada were still very proud of having achieved their longtime dream of becoming the county seat of a new county. A legislature, dominated by republicans black and white, had granted a request which Democratic legislatures every since 1845 had been refusing to grant. Just two years before the summer of 1878, Mississippi had elected a democratic governor, and things were beginning to look up in a political way, although negro voters still were able to place in some offices candidates of their choice. Abandoned plantations had been brought back into cultivation; old businesses re-established and new ones set up, and a fairly satisfactory labor relationship set up between white farm owners and negro tenants. Then came sickness; realization of the prevalence of the dreaded yellow fever, and soon a raging epidemic, the progress and suffering of which have been related in a previous chapter of this work. Although the epidemic was over by late November it took months, even years, for many of the citizens to recover from the shock of those dreadful summer and early fall days of 1878. If a town ever needed a period of peace and security from anxiety during which it could readjust its emotional and economic problems the stricken town needed that period. But this peace did not prevail for the years immediately following the end of the epidemic. There were charges and counter-charges relative to the conduct of different people during the pestilence stricken days and weeks of the course of the plague. Many people had left town during the early days of the epidemic and some of these were accused of cowardice, while the accused and their friends claimed that they had merely been prudent, and that those who had remained in town with their families had been reckless in exposing the lives of their loved ones to the dread disease. In justification of this charge they pointed to cemetery lots in which entire families rested, victims of the fever.

As has been pointed out in a previous chapter, misunderstanding was not confined to disputes between those who remained, and those who fled town. Some of those who remained in town during the entire course of the epidemic were at odds over the way those in charge of political, relief and personal problems had responded to their responsibility. Some of the participants in the general relief work felt that they had received too much criticism and too little credit. One minister, who had rendered great service to the suffering people, intentionally or unintentionally, conveyed the impression that he was the only minister who had remained in town during the epidemic. He was angrily reminded that three other ministers of the town had died while remaining with their stricken people. There were charges that money sent in to relieve the needy poor had been used to help out those people who were able to help themselves. It would take time to heal these scars of a town still in a state of shock over a tragic experience. In their struggle with the republicans, the local democrats had secured a precarious hold on some of the county, and most of the city political offices. Some people, dissatisfied with both of the regular political parties, organized independent voters for the purpose of bargaining with the two regular parties when the independents did not have a large following, or for the purposes of nominating independent candidates when they felt that there was enough dissatisfaction among the members of either, or both of the regular parties to justify the hope that an independent ticket might prevail at the next election. An incident, which has been noted briefly in another chapter, had both political and epidemic overtones. J. J. Williams, employee of the Grenada Sentinel, had been elected to the state legislature by the democrats. He was not renominated by the Democratic Party in the Convention in which they choose their candidates, The Editor of the Sentinel, a staunch democratic, relieved Mr. Williams of his duties in connection with the paper, and a disagreement between the two led to a newspaper argument which was discussed in the chapter of this work relative to newspapers and newspaper men. In their argument over this political question they uncovered an old thread of the charges relative to those who became refugees from the town. In the course of their newspaper letter battle Col. Williams used the New South, a local competiting paper, while Mr. Buchanan, editor of the Sentinel, used his own paper, as the media for the publication of their differences. Mr. Williams referred to Mr. Buchanan as "A refugee who stood at my gate and plead youth, orphanage and friendship for admittance from the ravages of the pestilence then sweeping the best people of Grenada to the graves by scores." He then continues: "Touched with sympathy and rising to the fearless responsibility of Christian courage, he was admitted to the best room and the best bed in my cabin; and that too, when I felt assured that I might be digging my own grave, and that of my helpless family. A ton of gold could not have purchased that which the claim of friendship procured without debate. In order to make him and another young friend more comfortable my good, and then living, wife exiled herself with a darling little granddaughter to a kind neighbor's house for fifteen days that all the room might be given to us to battle with the scourge which I momentarily expected for several days, as both the visitor had been exposed to the dead and dying in Grenada." Mr. Buchanan answered the Colonel in this manner: "When the Colonel referred to us as a refugee during the epidemic of '78, and spoke so feelingly of his lofty display of christian courage in extending the common hospitality of life, he should have gone a little further and told who paid for the meat and bread that was consumed by his entire household. Since the Colonel has thrust this matter upon the public with so little delicacy, it is but just to the editor of the Sentinel and our friend, to say that we paid for what was consumed at the Colonel's hospitable board, as the books of Col. W. N. Pass, Peacock & Powell and others will show. We found the Colonel's larder empty, and had it not been for us he must have suffered for the necessaries of life or have been a pensioner upon public charity. We stopped with Col. Williams about ten days, and we paid well for the enterainment. Having said this much, we now beg pardon of the readers of the Sentinel for devoting so much space to matters that common delicacy and good breeding ought to have prompted the sympathetic old gentleman to have left unsaid. We now dismiss the subject for good, proposing to take no further note of a man who has brought upon himself ridicule and contempt of intellegent people of the county, preferring ourself to be a 'living ass' to a 'dead lion'." But the editor was not done with the subject. Colonel Williams again used the pages of the New South to voice his final leave of any connection with the Sentinel and its editor: "Here I take my final leave of the Sentinel and its hopeful editor, knowing full well that there are papers in and out of the state which may be glad to secure the service of a pen that never grew nervous in an encounter of wits with best talents of a state whose editorial corps, in all the great elements intellectual and moral forces, is equal to the same number in other states in the union; while I shall ever admire a roaring lion rather than a braying ass, I induldge the hope that my quondam friend of the Sentinel will yet arise from the stupidity of the latter, if he never reaches the dignity of the former. If intellect, by any undiscovered mental philosophy comes by absorption, there is hope yet that a few more years of association with men of brains will enable him to venture forth on the fearful experiment of construction of a sentence that Smith has arrived and James has departed."

On October 2, 1881, J. M Patterson, Editor of the New South, joined editor Buchanan in condemning Col. Williams for his changed political loyalty. He quotes part of a statement made by the Colonel soon after his defeat as a candidate for nomination as the democrat candidate for the State Legislature: "So I take my stand in favor of the Democratic ticket with courage undaunted, devotion un-slacked and hope undiminished, asking that many who have spent hours, if not days, misrepresenting my opinions and perverting my purposes shall exercise the same energy and will and honor in behalf of our common political family - and would say to them and especially to the Gallant young Knight (McSwine) who has been placed in the front, lead on, no matter how impregnable the fortress, your old lieutenant will be the first man to salute your standard when waving it in triumph, and applaude the courage that planted it there." The editor then comments: "In borrowing a short extract from Col. Williams' voluminous and redundant literature on which to sermonize, we beg a kind public to make a clear distinction between the genial and innocent old gentleman, socially, and the impractiable, non descript, fossilized, core-hardened, God-forsaken old politican." Although this argument, arising from political differences, became very personal under the stress of the conditions of the time, Mr. Buchanan and Col. Williams became friendly again after the political campaign was over and done with. Dr. McSwine, the man selected as democratic nominee instead of Col. Williams, defeated the other condidates in the general election.

The year 1884 was to rock the economy of the town, and area, in much the same way the fever epidemic had shocked the physical welfare of the people during that past, but not forgotten dreadful period. In August of 1878 the health of the community seemed robust, and no apprehension existed relative to epidemics. In the same optimistic state of mind the people of the area envisioned no serious economic change. The political disputes, such as the one we have related, seemed to be the most serious problems of the moment. Although most of the people had not yet recovered from their business losses of the Civil War and post-Civil War years, most had gone to work with a will and many had begun to build up bank balances in the two private banks serving the town. These banks were owned and operated by local men-citizens of long standing who had the confidence of the town and county. Many of the area farmers depended upon these banks to finance their farming operation in return for deeds of trust given on livestock, agricultural implements and the growing crops. Many of the merchants of the town accepted similar paper as they arranged credit at their stores for the farmers who needed credit, and they the merchants discounted the paper at the banks. A considerable amount of similar credit was furnished by firms of cotton commission merchants of New Orleans and Memphis.

Early in the year 1884 came the first blow at the economy of the region. On that date the Grenada Sentinel reported that the R. P. Lake Bank had failed, and that Mr. Lake had assigned all of his property to G. W. Jones for the benefit of creditors. It was reported that the liabilities of the bank amounted to about $60,000, and it was hoped that, when liquidated, the assets would pay off most of the creditors. At the time of its failure the bank, formerly Lake Brothers Bank, had become the individual business of R. P. Lake. As is usual in such cases, the creditors suffered considerable loss in the failure, although Mr. Jones seems to have done an excellent job in collectin the liquid assets of the bank. Although the bank failure hampered many people in a financial way there was no panic in the business circles of the town. The N. C. Snider & Son Bank was still doing business, and the merchants continued to furnish credit to their regular customers. The Summer months, usually dull times for the merchants of the town, were running out, and the merchants and cotton buyers, anticipating approaching fall business, were getting ready for the expanded business activity which began when the cotton harvest got underway. The season of good business had just begun when tragedy struck a stunning blow. The great fire of 1884 occurred.

The Grenada Sentinel reported the fire in these words: "On last Saturday night a fire swept over a large portion of this town, carrying ruin and dismay in its track. About six o'clock P. M. a white smoke was seen struggling through the roof of S. H. Garner's furniture house; which in a few seconds changed into black, dense volumes, followed by a globe of fire which shot up and disappeared in the darkened sky. The light materials for making mattresses, with a quantity of varnish, turpentine and other combustible and inflammable matterials furnished the fire with both wings and tongues, and the whole building, in less time than we have been writing, was a sheet of roaring flames. As the heat increased buildings both north and south took fire as it leaped from roof to roof of dry cypress shingles, which from the heat of the day were in a ready condition to ignite. To arrest the flames was impossible, and the only resource was in rescuing goods from the contiguous buildings and bearing them to a place of safety, which for a time was in the open street. The heat, however, soon became so intense that these took fire and burned slowly until the row of houses on the opposite side of the street were wrapped in the general conflagration beneath which some of the property of quite a number disappeared, with the all of a few. In less than forty minutes every house on both sides of main street from Phoenix Hall to the corner of Griffis & Duncan, and from Ferguson's stable to the corner of Thomas Brothers caught, and as roofs fell in and walls tumbled, in some instances dense showers of sparks intermingled with flames, they presented a sight of grandure seldom witnessed. Perhaps the grandest exhibition of the fire was when it took in two large livery stables which had just stored in the upper stories large quantities of dry fodder, hay and straw for winter. The roofs were literally raised upon the mad, rushing, roaring sheets of flame that shot up in whirling globes accompanied by masses of smoke as black as the clouds that hang over the bottomless pit.

When the fire had reached every house on main street from one corner of the block to the other, it went east and west on Depot street involving the best and most substantial buildings in the town. Several of them were double-storied and covered with tin or sheetiron and resisted the intensity of the heat for some length of time, but had to yield at last to the devouring element. Now could be seen four lines of fire, with decreasing force in some places, but accumulating energy at others. Rapidly the glow marched until every house from Peacock & Powell's corner to Lake Cottonshed were swept in the angry fires. The larger wooden structures on this line of buildings soon yielded to the ravages of the fiery fiend, while the low wooden buildings on both side of Green Street seemed to whet his appetite for more furious destruction. Thus, in less than two hours, more than two whole blocks had melted away before one of the most powerful forces of nature. During this brief period of cronology, but almost years of agony to our people, everybody was at work, and everything in confusion. Of course the leading idea was to save all the property that could be handled, and this was heaped upon the square in piles, in circles, speriods, oblongs, and every other regular and irregular shape. Fortunately the night was calm; not a leaf trembled on its stem, only as moved by the contending currents of cold and rarefied air, and it was sorryful, to some, at least, as the night that brooded over Pardise when the exiled couple of the world's population looked back upon the expiring lights of their primative, happy Eden. No one was killed or even badly hurt, notwithstanding the many risks that men boldly made and fearlessly accomplished.

Gloomy Saturday night wore along its weary hours and the sun arose on the next morning upon a large part of our town in ashes, with broken walls on every side, and a dozen or two gaunt chimney standing here and there like solemn but speechless sentinels overlooking the ruins. The square was one large bazar of goods and merchandise scattered and heaped in apparently inextricable confusion. The work, however, to moving them to places of safety soon began, and with the aid of practiced eyes and private marks, the recognition of property was made apparent. By noon they were all in places of security, which are now undergoing repairs for future business, leaving the square literally covered with loose papers, boxes, and other debris which ever follow a fire of any magnitude.

In conclusion, we rejoice to say that our merchants and men of business are taking their losses with that calm philosophy which teaches them that the battle of life does not consist of a single engagement, and so far from yielding to despondency, they were busily adjusting their losses and making preparations for a more active campaign in the struggle of life's duty than ever. They have been met on all sides with most encouraging hopes and tenders from friends, and wholesale dealers at a distance not to strike their colors so long as there is a dollar in the locker, one spring of energy left, or one clear idea in the head." Mr. Buchanan relates that he met Charlie Sterle, shoemaker as he passed the Sentinel office one day, leading a fat little mustang, and the shoemaker stated that the animal was all the property he had left after the fire, but that he intended setting up in business again. The Mississippi and Tennessee Railroad generously offered special rates on freight charges for consturction materials brought over its line to Grenada. The freight charge of a carload of 6,000 brick was set at eight dollars, and rates on other types of building materials was proportionately lowered. The Sentinel office, being at that time on the north side of the square, escaped any serious injury although Mr. Buchanan reported about $500.00 dollars damage. Most of the merchants were underinsured, and some of them carried no insurance at all.

On October 4, 1884, less than two months after the fire, The Sunny South, a periodical published by the Illinois Central Railroad System, perhaps in an attempt to boost the prospects of the devastated town, had this to say about the town: "Grenada, which is the junction of the Illinois Central and the Mississippi & Tennessee, has a population of 2500, ninety per cent of which are Americans. It is the county seat of Grenada County, has one Collegate Institute, several fine private schools, and a thorough and efficient public school system. Methodist, Baptist, Presbyterian and Episcopal churches are represented. Has several mills, factories etc." One writer speaking of Grenada says: "This country offers great inducements to emigrants and homeseekers. Fine farming land adapted to every purpose of agriculture ready for immediate cultivation, or only partially improved and developed, can be secured at incredible low prices. The climate is salubrious, and the county for the most part is healthy and free from malarial influences. The soil is fertile, and produces abundantly and profitably all the grains, grasses, fruits, flowers and vegetables peculiar to a temperate and semi-tropical climate. The citizens of the County are generally prosperous, and will compare favorably with any community in intelligence and education, and are quiet, orderly and law abiding. Homeseekers are received with cordiality, and a generous and hearty welcome awaits the coming settlers. In Grenada County are now about 4,000 acres of United States land that can be had for $1.20 per acre, or can be entered as a homestead. Improved farms in the vicinity of Grenada are worth $8 to $20 per acre; unimproved $2 to $4. Grenada offers special inducements to land buyers, and everyone looking for cheap lands in a desirable locality should by all means visit this City and surrounding Count.: The railroad company had on a publicity campaign in an endeavor to bring emigrants into the areas through which its lines ran, so this publicity on Grenada and Grenada County was not altogether unselfish, but was much appreciated by the people of the town and county. Five years later, in the year 1889, Catherine Cole, a representative of the New Orleans Picayune, visited Grenada and wrote an article about the town. Among other comments who wrote: "The chief fault of Grenada is a spirit of indifference to the outside world. Newcomers are welcomed with genuine and lasting hospitality, but they are not invited." This statement confirms the comments of the Sunny South relative to the hospitality of the people, and also indicates an attitude of mind which probably resulted in its slow development while other Mississippi towns were growing at a faster rate. In the year 1900 Grenada and Greenwood had the same number of inhabitants, the number being 2,568; Water Valley (then a railroad shop town) had 3,813; Jackson 7,816 and Vicksburg, the largest city in the state, had a population of 14,834. Grenada increased very slowly relative to population until real industrial development began about thirty years ago.

On October 17, 1884, before the rubbish of the August fire had been completely cleared, and all demolished buildings rebuilt, misfortune again struck the seemingly ill-fated town. The one remaining bank failed. The Sentinel reports the failure: "Our community was very much shocked and excited yesterday (Friday) morning at the announcement that the banking house of N. C. Snider & Son had made an assignment. This was an old, well established concern, and had enjoyed the entire confidence of our people for years, and of course, very naturally caught nearly everybody in this section who had money on deposit. The assets is reported to be between $70,000 and $80,000 and liabilities below the assets. These assets mostly of mortgages on crops, stock and lands, as they have done a heavy advancing business. What the final results we are not at this writing able to state, as everything is in confusion. Surely the county has fallen upon calamitous times, and what the general results will be for the year's business, the deponent sayeth not. Next week we will investigate and give truthful particulars." In the next issue of his paper the editor gives some of the promised particulars: "It is evident from facts, as well as almost universal report, that the smash of N. C. Snider & Son's Bank here has caused more general destruction in its crash than any similar financial institution that has fallen by the wayside for many years in this part of the state. Its liabilities are fully up to the sum of $90,000 or $100,000, while the normal assets are about $65,000, chiefly in notes, one half of which will never be collected. It is well known that after R. P. Lake's failure, Col. Snider repeatedly stated that he was solvent beyond any ordinary contingency, and left the impression with many that he was worth $50,000 to $75,000, and yet several months afterwards we learn, while on his deathbed, he stated to his cashier, partner and confidential adviser, that he was insolvent and desired his son to carry the business through if possible. Here was a secret that should have been used by Mr. J. B. Snider as the turning point of his own life, and perhaps the safety of many others. If he believed his father's statement, he should have examined into the condition of the bank, and finding it toppling, he should not have lost one hour in temporizing by expediencils and hopes, but closed it up at once. He would have saved his own credit to a great extent, and would have saved in some degree the wide spread ruin through the entire community, as fatal to some as the throes of death." The editor seems very severe in his criticism of the unfortunate J. B. Snider who had been made partner in his father's bank just a few months before the father, probably in anticipation of early death, made the reputed confession relative to the condition of the bank. It is inconceivable that the son would have tried to carry on the bank unless he felt that there was a chance of saving it. It is also unlikely that the bank could become to a greater degree insolvent by dissipating the chief assets of the bank, consisting mostly of notes, when these notes were a drug on the financial market. Rather, it would seem that the young man was to be commended for trying to carry out his fathers dying request to endeavor to save the bank.

It is possible that the editor, and the many other people critical of the Sniders, had experienced so many recent reverses that they had to find a scapegoat on which to burden their load of bitterness and frustration. The Editor continued his bitter invective: "The idea of old ladies and old men who have toiled through the light of day and to late hours of the night, in order to lay up a few hundred dollars for the last years of declining life, seeing that pittance disappear as the puff of smoke, can never be known to human intelligence nor to human sympathy. It baffles the pen to portray, the tongue to speak it. But the question will come up, what has become of all this missing money? What has become of the original capital and the many thousands which trusting people have placed in the hands of these bankers? In a well organized bank every dollar received and every dollar paid out should be accounted for. If it has been lost in stock or lands the books should explain it. If it is gone in futures the bank should show it. If it has been lost in high living and extravagence, it should be made apparent to the public. If it has been absorbed in cards, it should be shown. If it has been stolen, some evidence should be left behind. How the money has been lost here, has all gone, we do not pretend to know, nor do we say. We are not sharp enough as mindreaders to intuitively find out these mysterious things. We know that tens of thousands of dollars have gone, and leaving nothing but a blank stare in each face, and perhaps a secret curse in each heart, as the only expression of ruined hundreds." The editor then gives a list of seventy four of the depositors and the amount of their deposits, and states that he has no information on the amount of deposits of many other people who had money in the bank. Significently, he mentions the fact that he had $790.00 dollars on deposit. Perhaps this contributed to the bitterness of his condemnation of the bankers.

The editor of the Water Valley Progress commented on the misfortunes of Grenada: "Snider's Bank of Grenada failed last week. It does seem that our sister city, Grenada, has had a rough time of it, within the last few years. In '78 the terrible scourge, yellow fever, almost depopulated the place. A few months since Lake's Bank made an assignment, which swept away thousands of dollars of hard earnings of its citizens. But a few weeks since the fire fiend raged in all its madness and fury consuming thousands and thousands of property of that devoted people, and now, to cap the climax, Snider's Bank suspends, and the good people of Grenada are forced to take another draught from the bitter cup of adversity."

In view of the bitter criticism and insinuation of the editor of the Sentinel after ther failure of Snider's Bank, it seems only fair to quote from an editorial from the pen of the same editor just a few months before the failure of the bank: "Col. N. C. Snider has long been ranked among the leading private bankers of the state, and his well known habits of promptness, integrity and financial ability has given him a hold upon the confidence of our people that has been unshaken up to this time. Mr. J. B. Snider, after years of tutilage under the direction of his father, is well qualified to fill the junior station in the new firm. (The new firm referres to the change by which the name of the bank was changed from N. C. Snider to N. C. Snider & Son.) This house needs no introduction from us. Their works and their faithful services in our community are their best indorsements."

In a happier state of mind the editor of the Sentinel, on December 20, 1884, reports on the very fine way in which the people of the town has survived fire and bank failure, and had made rapid progress in rebuilding the devastated business section of the town: "Four months ago, when a destructive fire swept through Grenada, it was thought that we were ruined,so great was the distressing consternation of the people. It is adversity and difficulties, that bring out the courage of a community, no less than the grit of a man, and on looking over our town, resurrected from ashes and reconstructed on a heavier basis and with improved proportions, it does seem that blessings sometime slumber in disguise. Now, in the burnt district, twenty two stories, and six one story buildings, with two large livery stables, present to the eye, a transformation almost marvelous. All the new houses that have gone up are creditable to the town, and some of them would adorn cities of greater wealth and population. Besides those that are now up, others are to follow in the spring. The building spirit has infused new energy into the purposes and ambition of our commercial men, and spread amongst all classes a spirit of pride in the beauty of our town, which makes for Grenada a brighter future than ever.

Beginning on the west side of the town, the stranger will see the large cotton shed and wagon yard belonging to Capt. J. B. Lake, of Memphis, in charge of Buck Wright, with impacted yeard, brick walls and iron roof. On the north side of the same street the tidy and substantial business house of Mr. Sidney Kettle and Mr. W. H. Wood will meet the observer's gaze. On Green street are the house of Dr. Barksdale and the neat, two story building of Col. W. M. Pass, all occupied by business men. On the corner of Green and Depot street, stands the large iron and hardware building of Doak & Laurence, severe in its simplicity, with its iron front, smooth walls and large upper story windows. On the south side of the square, extending from Green street some distance, will be seen the large block built by Mrs. Donkin, Mrs. Gerard and the Whitakers with stores, except one, filled with supplies, and that one will be occupied in a few weeks. The upper stories of this splendid block are intended for offices and private apartments, which will soon be occupied, and they present rare attractions with their ample space and splendid lights. The fronts of all the ground floors of this fine block are made with iron, and from their large lighted doors present a business like appearance. Immediate is the handsome and solid structure of Col. W. N. Pass, now occupied as a saloon. The walls of the old Stokes Building on the southeast corner of the square stood the fire from top to bottom better than any other one of the burnt buildings, and has been substantially repaired. Below on Main street, will be seen the tasteful and solid building, now the property of Col. W. N. Pass. Crossing over to the east side of Main street, we see the new, brick stables standing upon the same sites as those burned down, furnished in fine style. Going north from the stables, we approach the Mullin block as it is popularly called, but it belongs to several others, the first of which belongs to John Hughes and is a splendid tribute to his ambition and pride, having its upper and lower stories arranged to his own wants and wishes. The next if the handsome house built for Capt. J. B. McCord on somewhat the same general principles, his own store rooms being peculiarly adapted to his business. In the line of progress northward, we meet with the beautiful and stylish buildings of Mr. Geo. W. Jones and W. C. Mclean. These gentlemen, not merely wished to place on their old sites, houses adapted to business, but something that would add to their fame as public spirited citizens, and something that would reflect upon their architectural ideas of fitness and progress, and they have succeeded. The interior finish of these buildings in the most 'tout ensemble' has an air of beauty and attractiveness that will immediately attract the beholder's eye. In the four beautiful houses of which we have spoken, there is nothing wanted to make them pleasant to look at, and but much more so, to make their design suited to desired ends.

We now approach the grand result of the new order of architecture that has arisen on the banks of our little Yalobousha, to give the final touch of style in the expenditures of the whole of our city. As one good thing exceeds another in proportions and grandure, the buildings erected by Mr. Robert Mullin will long stand as a material monument of his good taste and ambition; and were it not that he will leave behind him (which period we pray may be long deferred) something more enduring than piles of brick and mortar, no matter how artistically furnished, we should have inferred that he intended to erect something, in the splendid proportion of beauty and finish, ti keep alive his memory in after years, but when we examine into the records of our own and other lands and find that the best and noblest of specimens of manhood have lived generations without the aid of iron, bronze or marble, we imagine this splendid building is simply the desire of his old age, to do something for the benefit of the people amongst whom he lived, worked, toiled with no stain to mar his escutcheon. We may say that in the new and splendid house, we have a whole, with its admirable details, that will reflect favorably upon the town, its builder and its architect, and we fearlessly assert, that its equal is not to be found in this state. Its size will challenge comparison, its details are exactly suited to the whole and its ornamentations are works of art. To see in a merchant's apartment English plate glass worth nearly $700 in a town no larger than Grenada, in front of this palatial quarters, is an edivence of the style and cost of the whole. Above is the large and splendid hall devoted to public recreation, public tastes and public education by whatever will amuse, please, instruct and refine the public ear."

Chapter XIV

The Mel Cheatham Affair

In June of 1966 it had been seventy seven years since the Mel Cheatham affair had occurred and accounts of the affair were buried in the dim memory of very old people, and in the faded pages of contemporary newspapers. Then James Merdith started his well publicizes "walk through Mississippi" and was soon peppered with bird shot from the gun of a citizen of Tennessee. This was a period when the Civil Rights issue loomed large on the national horizon, and all the news media played up the stories of racial strive, and professionsal do-gooders were fishing in troubled waters. There was much speculation as to whether the Mississippi Courts would be an impartial forum for the prosecution of the man who had shot Merdith. It was during this period of speculation that a reputable, and usually accurage, T. V. reporter made the statement that there was no record of a white man ever being convicted and executed in the state of Mississippi for the murder of a negro. This statement recalled to the mind of the writer the story which he had once learned from the issues of the Grenada Sentinel printed during the years of 1889 and 1900. That story was about the white man, Mel Cheatham, accused of the murder of Jim Tilgham, who was a negro.

The quarter of a century elapsing between the end of the Civil War and the year 1889, had been troubled years for the town of Grenada and the county of the same name as, indeed, it had been for most people and areas in the Southern states. As a result of the harsh construction policies of the Radical Republicans who controlled Congress in the early post-war years, unlettered negroes, former slaves; had been enfranchised to vote, while many white leaders and followers, because of service either to the Confederacy or to their state government during the war period, were disfranchised. For a period of several years white leaders, with their block negro vote, had dominated political affairs in the town and county, but by the year 1889, white people were pretty well in charge of city and county affairs again. Although there had, from time to time, been flare-ups of racial strife, as a general thing both whites and negroes had adjusted to post-war changes and the two races were getting along very well.

Then occurred an incident which threatened to ruin this relationship. A negro was murdered in a most brutal way, and a white man was suspected of being implicated in the crime. On July 20, 1889, The Grenada Sentinel, a newspaper printed in the town of Grenada, came out with the story: "An infamous and cowardly assassination - one of the most cowardly, cold-blooded and senseless assassinations that ever disgraced the history of Mississippi occured on Thursday night of last week in this county. The particulars we learn are as follows: On last Saturday news was brought to Mr. R. W. McAfee, of this town, that a young negro man, Jim Tilgman, employed on his plantation, nine miles east of Grenada and four miles west of Graysport, had been missing since Thursday night, and his whereabouts was unknown. Mr. McAfee on Sunday morning together with Sheriff G. B. Jones proceeded to the plantation to make an investigation, and on arrival there soon found blood, and they at once became satisfied that Tilgman had been foully dealt with, and at once summoned all the neighbors to prosecute the search. After considerable difficulty they found the body of Tilgman sunk in the Yalobousha river about four miles from the scene of the murder, with eight buck-shot wounds in the back, with two large rocks tied to him as sinkers. The river had fallen and the body was discovered in this way, after some careful sifting of testimony M. J. Cheatham (white), Lee Irvin, Jake Irvin and Cornelius Robertson (colored), were arrested as probably guilty of murder. One other person, James Lemons, (white), who was supposed to be implicated in the assassination fled as soon as he learned that the body had been found, and was not captured until Wednesday morning. As soon as Lemons was brought to Graysport and turned over to the sheriff, we learn one of the supposed guilty parties-Lee Irvin-said it would be death for him to tell what he knew, but he was willing and would tell the truth since Lemons was caught and put under arrest, so he, (Irvin), proceded to make a full confession which was in substance as follows: That he (Irvin) and the four other above named parties were concerned in the assassination, and that he was satisfied that Cheatham or Lemons did the shooting, and that Cheatham had the gun the last time he saw him. There were other statements which give the case a still darker hue, but too lengthy for publication now. A Coroner's jury composed of Messers: W. J. Parker, Silvester Johnson, John Butler, Silas Rayburn, Buck Martin and Jim Williamson, prominent citizens, was impanelled, and after examining about seventy five witnesses and hearing the confession of Irvin, returned a verdict to the effect that Jim Tilgman had been foully murdered by the parties above named. The committing trial at this writing (Thursday) is being vigorously pushed with District Attorney J. J. Slack present.

When it is considered, as well as known to be the fact, that Tilgman was assassinated merely because he was a witness at the last term of Circuit Court against certain of these parties in cases which were only misdemeanors, and that he was to be a witness again at the next Circuit Court term, the absolute sewselessness and the damning brutality of the assassination are both made manifest. If there be a God of Justice and a people here who mean to see justice administered without fear or favor, let this case be pushed to a summary and speedy conclusion. We know that we have that kind of people. We know it from the horror with which the people of the whole county have been struck, and especially in the vicinity where it occurred. There is but one sentiment expressed on this subject, and that is expressed with emphasis on all hands to-wit: That Grenada County will not, and shall not, harbor within its borders men so lost to every sense of duty to society, and that punishment swift and condign according to the forms of law shall be meted out to them. Let it be understood that the people of the county will see to it that the assassination shall result in the hanging of the perpetrators whether the victim be white or black." Later: "Thursday evening about 5o'clock news was received in Grenada that the above named prisoners has waved examination, and that they had been committed to jail without bond. A large number of our citizens congregated on the public square, and about 7o'clock Sheriff Jones, together with twelve or fifteen guards armed with shot-guns, made their appearance with the prisoners, who were taken to the jail and locked up, where they will remain until our Circuit Court meets."

On August 24, 1889, the Circuit Court was in session and the accused were arraigned and all pleaded not guilty. M. J. Cheatham was the first of the four brought to trial, in a case which had the interest not only of citizens of Grenada County, but all over the state of Mississippi. Leading members of the local bar were involved in the case either for the prosecution or the defense. On August 31, 1889, the Grenada Sentinel has this report on the trial: "The public mind has been intensely interested and agitated during the week by the trial of M. J. Cheatham for the murder of Jim Tilgman, a negro, in July, not only was there a large personal interest in the trial, but the public at large became involved in the suspense on account of the momentous question being suggested to every man's mind are we to have the criminal law executed? Are our lives to be under the protection of the law and safe from assassination? The evidence was extremely tragic, and the details bloody and horrible beyond imagination to conceive. Lee Irvin, a negro who was present at the shooting, confessed and gave these details: Jim Tilgman was at church on Thursday night; Cheatham concealed himself by the side of the road Tilgman was to take in his walk home after church; when he came up about 11o'clock at night Cheatham shot him in the back as he started to run. Cheatham, Jim Lemons, Jake Irvin, Lee Irvin and Cornelius Robertson then ran up and threw him on a blanket before life was extinct - put a sack over his head - put him up across a mule in front of Lemons, and after Cheatham had reloaded his gun, the funeral procession through the woods for four miles to the Yalobousha was as follows: Cheatham in front on a mule with a gun; Lemons next on a mule with the dead negro in front of him; Cornelius Robertson behind Lemons on a horse, and Jake and Lee Irvin in the rear on foot. When they reached the river the victim was weighted by rocks and thrown in the river. But providentially, the river was up ten or fifteen feet from heavy rains and the body caught on a log as it sank, and when the river fell it was found the following Sunday evening lodged on the log etc. Cornelius Robertson, (colored) also confessed and corroborated the above details given by Irvin. Besides the confession of these two eye-witnesses, there were many circumstances, all bearing with unerring aim upon the guilt of Cheatham, that were brought out by a great many witnesses white and black. Over one hundred witnesses were summoned and a majority of them were rigidly examined."

On Wednesday evening the testimony was closed, and the speaking began that night. The Court Room was crowded when Judge A. T. Roane arose on behalf of the prosecution, and made an exhaustive, very able and very earnest and effective argument of two and a half hours. He was followed by Hon. J. C. Longstreet for the defendant in a speech of one hour and fifteen minutes. He managed his side of the case with great ability and acumen, and was both forceful and eloquent. He was very highly complimented on his splendid effort. On Thursday morning W. C. Mclean, Esq., spoke for the defense in a speech of three hours. He showed throughout that inflexible determination, perseverance, ability and fertility of resource for which he is noted. His speech was able and eloquent, and brought every possible point in behalf of his client, but the climax was capped by the three hour speech of the original, the uniques, the only J. J. Slack, our District Attorney. He displayed nothing less than genius in his humorous, his pathetic, his argumental strokes. In short, he made a powerful, logical, witty and inimitable speech. Mr. Slack may well feel proud of his speech and the manner in which he conducted the case throughout.

"The argument was concluded by 3 o'clock Thursday evening, and the jury retired. The court then adjourned for an hour, and as soon as it convened again the jury brought in a verdict of 'guilty as charged', which means a death sentence. We learn that the jury was unanimous in their verdict as soon as they retired, a ballot being taken without any discussion of the subject. When the verdict was announced the prisoner's head dropped and tears flowed down his cheeks. The verdict was such as was expected by the people generally, and meets with public approval, not on account of prejudice against the prisoner, but on account of the horrible crime, and a general desire for the just administration of law. The jury was composed of ten white and two colored men, and was considered exceptionally intelligent and able. The unfortunate negro, Jim Tilgham, was assassinated because he testified against Cheatham, Lemons and others in some gaming cases, and was to be a witness against them at the present term of Court. The trial of Lemons was continued until the next term of court because he was too sick to be brought to the Court House; the cases against the three negroes were continued for the want of time to try them, as they called for a special venire, and it was too late to summon some before the term of court expired."

"Yesterday (Friday) evening the prisoner, M. J. Cheatham, was brought before the bar of the court, when a motion for a new trail was argued by council. The motion was overruled by the Court, and Cheatham was then sentenced to be hung October 9th. An appeal to the state supreme court was taken."

At the next term of the Circuit Court which convened on February 1, 1890, Lemons, Jake Irvin and Cornelius Robertson were arraigned and plead not guilty. After a conference between attorneys for the prosecution and defense, the plea was changed to guilty of manslaughter, which saved the accused of the death sentence, but subjected them to long imprisonment in the state penitentiary.

Jim Lemons and Jake Irvin received sentences of thirty years, while Cornelius Robertson received a sentence of twenty five years. The paper does not mention an arraignment for Lee Irvin, so the presumption is that, since he confessed first, and turned state's evidence, there was a deal by which he went free for his evidence which helped convice the other four men. On February 8, 1890, the Sentinel had the following news article: "On last Monday the Supreme Court of Mississippi affirmed the sentence of the Grenada Circuit Court in the case of M. J. Cheatham for shooting and killing Jim Tilgham (colored) on the night of July 13, 1889. Date of execution set for March 19, 1890."

"As the date set for execution neared, the prisoner was removed from the jail at Oxford, where he had been kept during the course of the appeal, to the jail at Grenada." In commenting on this change the Editor of the Sentinel reported: "When, we, last week spoke of Mel Cheatham's removal from the Oxford jail, we had a purpose which in part at least, was accomplished. The facts are that on Sunday morning Sheriff G. B. Jones accompanied by nine resolute, determined young men of the town, armed with double barrelled shotguns and Winchester rifles, proceeded to Oxford and quietly transferred Cheatham to the south-bound train which reached here about 1:30 o'clock. As usual on Sunday, there was a considerable crowd present, which was doubtless increased by the fact that Cheatham would be on the train. Without ado the Sheriff at once proceeded with his charge, followed by his guard and crowd to the fail, where Mr. Cheatham was placed to await his execution."

"Rumors of rescue having got abroad, the Sheriff very properly placed a strong and well armed guard inside and around the jail, with pickets on the outskirts, both day and night, so as to be prepared for any emergency. This may seem supersensitative, but there were reasons, and good ones for the precautions. Up to Monday many people thought that Governor Stone would commute his sentence or give a respite, but when the Governor's letter was received, that last hope on the subject vanished, and the prisoner received the news with little emotion."

"On Monday night Cheatham was so restless that he did not sleep beyond a few flying moments, taking up much of his time writing what he termed a "statement". On Monday he was visited by Revs. E. B. Miller, the Baptist pastor, J. E. Thomas, of the Methodist church and J. C. Carothers, of the Presbyterian pulpit, and manifested a deep interest in the preparation of his soul for its approaching doom. On Tuesday evening Mr. Carothers came accompanied by the deacons of his church, and after the most solemn service, Cheatham was formerly inducted into the Presbyterian Church, having acknowledged conversion in the pardon of his sins. The scene - the surroundings and the facts, made it an hour of serious import, which all present felt, as though standing on the confines of the eternal world."

"Late Tuesday evening the writer proceeded to the jail and requested Sheriff Jones to admit us, when he informed us that at Cheatham's request no newspaper men would be allowed in the jail, much less an interview. This somewhat surprised us, as we were anxious to get all the news for the public possible. Not to be outdone, we got one of the guards and a trusted friend, to avail himself of all information he could get out of Cheatham, and he succeeded beyond our expectations. The following is the conversation of the reporter with Cheatham which we publish from the reporter's own writing, which will no doubt be read with interest to some and surprise to others: The reporter of the Sentinel went into Cheatham's cell at 12 o'clock Tuesday night and entered into a conversation with Cheatham who answered as follows: I am just as miserable as I can be. He then hesitated and appeared to be a little nervous, but continued. Better for me had I never seen Grenada County. He then turned his mind on religion, by asking questions such as what is meant by sinning against the Holy Ghost? This has troubled me ever since last week. I never have been so impressed as of late as to the immortality of the soul. This has caused me so much thought that I have not been able to sleep since the Sheriff brought me back to Grenada from Oxford."

"I never intended to let my people know of my condition, but to my sorrow, my step-mother read an account of my sentence and wrote to me while I was in jail at Oxford. I answered her letters as best I could. I acted very foolish in not making my escape the night I came to Grenada from Graysport to see about getting an attorney. I could have done so, bit I did not want to sacrifice my friend who had me in charge. I wish now that I had done so, and not acted against my judgement. After the Grenad Jury found an indictment against me, in the Court before the trial, I had made arrangement to leave Grenada County and move to a small place west of Harrison. I saw that the people of Beat two were against me, and desired my destruction. I know the people are fully satisfied of my guilt, and, therefore, I have no hope of having my sentence commuted. I thought I had some friends who would come to my rescue, but I find they were false. I never did a wrong to a living white man in my life. I have been a true Democrat and upheld the interest of my country. I don't think that I ever threatened Messrs: J. T. Garner and B. F. Thomas for their action taken against me on the Grand Jury, but I know I said some things against them at the time, bit I regretted it afterwards. I am sure it was not a threat."

After this Cheatham became very quiet for some time, and then proceeded: 'I think a man is doing a very dangerous thing when he preaches that there is no accountability for the moral actions of a man. I do wish that I had never come to Grenada County - for I would have been better off in every way.' At one o'clock he requested the Sentinel's reporter to feel his pulse, and he did so and found it very quick and weak. Cheatham then continued as follows: "I can't sleep, but I find my eye-lids will close in spite of me.' About half past one o'clock he went to sleep and rested very quietly for 25 or 30 minutes. When he awoke he called for a chew of tobacco and sat up and appeared to enjoy it, but did not talk during this time, but often knelt in prayer and requested that the reporter join him. After he prayed the second time he went to sleep. During his sleep he made fearful groans, calling out My Father! My Father! He then became alarmed - sat up and gazed around with a most fearful expression on his face and inquired, What is that? At 2 o'clock the Sheriff came in and Cheatham awoke and called out: I don't want to talk anymore and he did not until after he ate his breakfast, which consisted of a cup of coffee, a sausage, a slice of sweet potato and a mouth-full of bread. After eating he took a smoke, and after finishing the cigar, he knelt in prayer, and as his cry of appeal to God for mercy on my poor sinful soul went up, it was enough to melt a heart of stone, besides the one that had been with him for hours. Never did a soul writhe in prayer for anyone as mine did for the doomed man. After he had prayed he said it was so hard to die 'when I never did the deed.' He said death was more bitter to him when it appeared that the people had made an example of him for his immoral conduct when there were married men, living not far from him, who had good wives and dear children, and acting just as he did. Said many of these men were the first to run him down: 'I think it is so hard that married men who have negro sweethearts and negro children should have acted as they did against me. I might have been a better man, but I never had any relation, or friend to tell me of my wrong.'"

"I left him for a few minutes and on my return to relieve the Sheriff I found him in a sitting position, smoking a cigar, and he appeared to be in better spirits than any time previous. At 3 o'clock he wanted to know if I was going to see him hung. I said I thought not. He said he wished that none of his acquaintances would come to his hanging. He often spoke of those he thought would regret his condition. I asked him if he had made any statement. He said: 'I wrote my statement and gave it to my attorney, and it is the truth. I shall not make another, and it will have to stand. One old negro woman on one occasion stopped me on the road and asked me to quit my bad ways, for people were talking about it. She spoke so kindly to me, I made a resolution to quit my immoral life. The next Sunday after this I attended preaching at Graysport. Rev. Wm. Beane was holding a protracted meeting (note at end of chapter). The sermon on that day sunk deep into my heart, but I soon forgot it all. After my trial at Graysport I would have taken poison but I had some hope of coming clear in Circuit Court. I would have killed myself at Oxford had I known any way to do so. Since I have been confined at Grenada the last five days I have wished for poison - for I don't think it would be wrong to take my life under such circumstances. I had an uncle who committed sucide. He was a prominent lawyer. Tomorrow they will murder me. There is a time coming when they will have to meet death too, and in the hereafter they will see that I never done the killing. On Tuesday I advised a young man, that as soon as he was able to settle in life, to do so and marry.' The conversation here closed and I retired from the cell."

The Editor of the Sentinel then takes up the story: "The above interview, or rather conversation, by the Sentinel reporter speaks for itself. The reporter is an intelligent, trustful gentleman, and put down the conversation exactly as it occurred. On Tuesday night several reporters from the Memphis newspapers came down and made efforts to get inside of the jail to interview the prisoner, but met with no better success than we did. On Wednesday morning Cheatham changed his mind, and stated that he would have no objection to newspaper reporters coming in and, therefore, they were admitted, but Cheatham refused to be interviewed. The writer, having heard that Mr. Cheatham entertained uncharitable feeling against us on account of the stories in the Sentinel in reference to him and his trial, proceeded Wednesday morning to the jail to see him and when our wishes were made known to him through a friend, he stated he had no objection to seeing us. We then went at once to his cell, where he shook hands cordially, and entered into agreeable conversation. Mr. Cheatham acknowledged having had unfriendly feelings toward us, but on mature reflection he stated he was satisfied that we did no more against him than any other man in similar circumstances; that as a public journalist, he believed that we did nothing more than our duty and exonerated us from any blame. During the conversation he said that he was born in Monroe County, this state, and when about two years old moved (with his family) to Chickasaw County. In 1869 he went to Calhoun County and remained there until 1877, when he came to Grenada county and always lived in Beat No. Two, and kept a small store since 1879. We parted with him on the most amicable terms, he saying when we left he hoped to meet us in heaven."

"About 10 o'clock Sheriff G. B. Jones, Mayor B. C. Adams and Capt. R. N. Hall made the last appeal to the Governor for commutation by sending a telegram to him. An answer came back shortly after 12 o'clock, stating in effect that he would not interfere, and the law must take its course. Upon receiving the telegram the Sheriff proceeded to the cell of Mr. Cheatham and told him of Governor Stone's decision; followed it with reading the death warrant in the presence of several men. After this Rev. J. C. Carothers knelt with the crowd and offered up a deeply earnest prayer in behalf of the unfortunate man, and then stood up against the cell, when the prisoner placed his arms tenderly over his shoulder, while the man of God administered the consolations of the christian religion even in this hour of extremity, until the time came for Cheatham's preparation for the gallows. Just before Cheatham was taken from the cage he was asked by the Sheriff if he wished to make any sort of statement on the gallows, when he replied he would not, as he had written out his statement the night before and given it to Mr. McLean, and which was true and correct. When the door of his iron cage was opened he stepped out into the jail room rather firmly, and after having his colar and cravat adjusted by Mr. Frank Smith, he shook hands with the several that were present, and said that he would meet them all in heaven. His hands were then pinioned behind him and the door of the room being opened, he, with Sheriff Jones, Mr. Carothers and others took the short but solemn march to the scaffold. His legs were then tied together and the rope slipped around his neck, and he was asked again if he had anything to say, he replied he did, and looking seriously he said: 'Boys, Good Bye'. Then with solemn and impressive look he raised his eyes to heaven, and clearly uttered the following short prayer: 'O, God, receive my soul, I put in they trust, for they Son's sake, Jesus Christ'. Mr. Cheatham then said: 'I am ready', when the black cap was then drawn over his head, and then in an instant the Sheriff picked up the hatched and with quick movement and steady nerve severed the rope which like a flash dropped Cheatham eight feet below, which sent his soul into eternity. The rope was cut at exactly 1:30 o'clock, and in nine minutes Drs. T. J. Brown and J. B. Gage Jr., pronounced him dead, and in 17 minutes his body was cut down and turned over to Meaders & Garner, who took his remains for interment in the old grave yard east of the railroad. The drop did not break his neck and he died by strangulation, but the doctors think that he did not suffer but little, if any, after the fall."

"Contrary to expectations the crowd from the county was very small and everything passed off quietly. The execution was witnessed by about twenty five or thirty people, in the most solemn silence, while there was not over one hundred outside. The scaffold was built up in front on the east side of the jail, and was encased by a wooden structure eighteen feet high, and about ten feet square, with a light canvass openhead, so that observation from the outside was wholly excluded. Under all the circumstances he met his fate with courage and resolution. As stated above Cheatham was about 40 years old. He was about five feet six inches in height, with light build and wiery form - piercing black eyes and a dark moustache, with a straight nose and wide mouth. Take him all in all, he was rather goodlooking, and ought to have filled a much higher place in society, as he had the ability. He is the first white man ever hung legally in this state since the war for killing a negro, and the second we know of in the South."

"Thus closed on the 19th day of March, 1890, the dark mid-night tragedy of murder enacted in the dense swamp of the Yalobousha on July 11th, 1889, by five men of whom Cheatham is believed to be the leading spirit. The others, save one, who turned State's Evidence, are immured behind prison walls for a period so long that the grave or decrepit age will probably find them before they enjoy as free men the sunlight of freedom, while justice is satisfied and innocence vindicated."

Recently a nephew of one of the men serving on the Grand Jury stated to this writer that his uncle always felt badly about the death of the negro, Jim Tilgman. This young Mulatto was summoned before the Grand Jury because one of the members of the jury felt that he knew something of gambling going on in the neighborhood. Tilgman at first refused to testify because he said if he did testify he would be killed. He was finally forced to tell by being ordered to jail, and in his testimony he acknowledged that he with others had gambled with M. J. Cheatham in Cheatham's house. On his testimony Cheatham was indicted, and Tilgman again testified in the January term of the Circuit Court of 1889, and was to testify in the August term of the same court. Perhaps the concern of the Grand Jury with conditions in the eastern part of the county arose from a mass meeting held by the citizens of Gore Springs, which community was close to the scene of the murder, in which those citizens appointed a committee to appear before the Grand Jury and request an investigation of people guilty of adultery and keepers of houses of ill-fame. This committee was appointed early in 1889, and it is probable that the investigation included gambling houses as well as the alleged houses of ill-fame.

People were very naturally interested in the statement which Cheatham claimed to have given to his attorney, Wm. McLean. Some expected, even hoped, that after having denied his guilt as long as such denial might gain a reprieve or commutation of sentence, Cheatham would leave a confession in the statement left with his attorney. In this they were disappointed when the statement was made public. The statement was in the form of a letter addressed to W. C. McLean, Esq. It read: "My Dear Sir: In reply to your request in the latter days of my life, with grim death almost ready to hurl me into and unseen world, and I do trust and hope and believe to the embrace of my God and Heavenly Father, I shall in as brief manner as is possible state the solid truth and nothing else but the truth, not would I write in this late hour anything else but the truth for a million worlds like this, so help me God. My soul is too precious to me to loose that great hope and Divine invitation to eternal glory, to falsify in the face of my God. As I have said already I shall be brief, as I do not feel able to write you a lengthy letter, for surely you have some idea of the wretchedness of my present life. It is well known that I was in August last, at that term of Circuit Court, tried, convicted and sentenced to death for the killing of Jim Tilgham, colored, and for that crime I am to die Wednesday. My dear estemed council permit me to open my heart yo you in the presence of God, my Savior my only hope, that I did not commit the crime for which I am doomed to die, God knows that I did not do it, and it would be the utter destruction of my soul were I to write a falsehood on this paper. Now I do trust you will believe this statement, and its truthfulness will be duly written in the records of Heaven, and I do sincerely trust that both of us will be able in the life to come to stand side by side at the throne of God, and hear this read by our Savior and Lord Jesus Christ and pronounced by him to be the truth. The truth of this statement is already accepted by Him as the pure truth, and nothing but the truth."

"If I say I killed Jim Tilgman or furnished any money for that purpose, or offered to pay any, I would be telling a lie in the face of my God; this I could not do, nor would I do, for a million worlds like this. Mr. Moore told me today that his idea was or had been that I paid money to have it done, but God is my witness that such is false. Now my dear counsel if you believe this, you will believe the truth so help me God. Thanking you for your kindness and devoted interest in my behalf, I bid you farewell. M. J. Cheatham."

There was a serious difference of opinion among the citizens of the town and county relative to the guilt of Cheatham. Some pointed out the fact that, without the confessions of Irvin and Robertson, one of whom was freed by turning State's Evidence, the evidence was all circumstantial. Others took the attitude of the sage who remarked in another determination of fact "Me thinketh the gentleman doth protest too much". Seventy seven years ago the case was tried, the accused was convicted, and he was done to death by the hangman's noose, but a faint doubt still lurks in the minds of some if the executed man was in reality guilty of the crime with which he was charged.

Note: The "protracted meeting" about which Cheatham spoke was about the same thing as our modern revivals. The Rev. W. Beane doing the preaching was the Principal of a well known High School then located at Jefferson in Carroll County.

Chapter XX

Miscellaneous Items of Interest

In the chapters of this work which have preceded the present one we have attempted to relate the history of the region by the collection of fact and incidents which are hinged about some central thought or event. This, or course, is the most logical way in which to attempt to record the history of a region, vicinity, or town, but in so doing it becomes necessary to eliminate much interesting information which has no place in the logical story of the central thought or important event upon which the chapters preceding this one are based. This is unfortunate because we miss much of the flavor of the day by day life of the people who built the foundations of city and county in which we live today. In order to give some of the social, political and economic atmosphere of those long gone days we give, in no logical arrangement, some interesting events, episodes and attitudes of mind which made up the warp and woof of the fabric into which is woven the history of by gone days.

We know that James Sims, an early merchant in Pittsburg, and husband of one of the daughters of John Smith, was in the little town soon after its establishment, but we would have no idea from whence he came to Grenada were it not for the existence of a deed by which Robert J. Walker conveyed certain land in Yalobousha County to "James Sims of Holmes County". The deed was given in 1833. Twenty seven years later this same James Sims gave a deed to a different piece of land which deed indicates the presence in the community of a former negro slave who, for some reason, had been freed from the bonds of slavery: "Know all men by these presents that we, James Sims, for and in consideration of the sum of one dollar in hand paid by York Smith (a freeman) the receipt of which is hereby acknowledged, and for the further consideration of the friendship and regard we have for the said York (the freeman) we have bargained and conveyed and by these presents do bargain and convey to York Smith (freeman) as aforesaid a lot of land in Survey No. 71, lying and being in the town of Grenada." John Smith, the father-in-law of Sims had died a short time before this conveyance. James Sims died shortly after. This series of connected incidents leads to the interesting speculation that John Smith, before his death, freed the negro, York Smith, and directed James Sims, administrator of his estate, to convey the property to the former slave. The lot conveyed was just south of and adjoined the lot on which stood the house of John Smith. Since the deed given by Sims was a quit claim deed it is probable that the freed slave had been living in some sort of building on lot 71 during the life time of Smith, and that Sims confirmed his right to continue in possession of the property by granting the quit claim deed. Later York Smith, for a consideration of $100.00, conveyed the lot to Mrs. M. M. Ransom. Mrs. Ransom was a daughter of James Sims and granddaughter of John Smith.

Grenada County had been in existence for about one year when the first legal hanging in the new county occured. On October 4, 1871, the following notation was made a part of the Minutes of the Board of Supervisors: "Whereas Frank May has been sentenced by the Honorable Circuit Court to be hanged on the 10th day of November 1871, it is ordered by the Board that said execution shall take place near the South Bank of the Yalobousha River on the land known as McLean's Bend." We have no indication whether May was a white man or a negro. The Board of Supervisors which selected the place of execution had two negro members. In 1872 the same Supervisors who had selected the place of execution of May were instrumental in writing the closing chapter in the history of the early town of Chocchuma - the voting precinct was moved from that place to Tuscahoma.

By the year 1873 R. C. Harrison had become owner of the former Sherman, or "upper ferry" which was located at the approximate location of the north end of Levee Street. Connected with the ferry, and belonging to the ferry owner, was a turnpike built across the swampy area north of the river. Ferry and turnpike fees were regulated by the Board of Supervisors. In April 1873 the Supervisors passed the following quoted order: "R. C. Harrison (a corporation) the owner of the Upper Ferry & Turnpike Road leading there from the city of Grenada are authorized to charge the following stipulated fees, but authorized to change these fees in the fall when the river is too low to use Ferry Boats."

In 1878 the total assessed valuation of the property in Grenada County was $1,303,543,50. About one half of the assessed valuation was on real property and the other half on the personal property of the people of the county. An order of the Supervisors in August 1879 is a grim reminder of the time, just about a year before the date of the order, when Yellow Fever was raging in Grenada. That order reads: "L. McCracken allowed the sum of $24.00 for guarding the Mississippi & Tennessee Road for 12 days during county quarantine." During the June meeting of the Board of Supervisors an order was passed by the Board which indicates a method, now long discarded, by which the county authorities handled prisoners sentenced to jail. The order read: "Ordered by the Board that the prisoners of this county be, and the same are hereby hired to J. M. Liddell Jr., for the term of four years, the said Liddell having this day filed bond with good security with the Board, of one thousand dollars for the faithful performance of his duty as contractor, according to and in compliance with the Act of the Legislature of this state passed March 5, 1878. This contract subject to be annulled at any time by the Board for violation of said Act. Said Contractor is to pay unto the County Treasury 25¢ per day for all persons that have been tried and committed either by the Circuit or Magistrate courts until their fines and costs have been paid, and for all persons that have not been fined and committed, 25¢ per day, until the committment or acuital by the Court, and if there should be any of them acquited then the Board agrees to allow them the amount received from said Contractor and be placed to their credit in the County Treasury. Said Contracotr is required to feed, clothe and treat with humanity all persons intrusted to his care according to the provisions of the Act of 1878. J. H. Willis voted against the motion."

During the years when the western part of what is now Grenada County was a part of Tallhatchie County, the people of the area had to go to Charleston to transact any business having to do with county affairs. Many of these people had to cross the Yalobousha River in order to reach that town. Ferries had been established at both Chocchuma and Tuscahoma. An order of the Board of Supervisors in 1871 would seem to indicate that the inclusion of the area into Grenada County had lessened passage by ferry at these two points to the extent that the operators of the ferries had to have some relief. In order to extend this relief the Board passed the following quoted order: "Whereas it is apparent to the Board from the allegations of J. M. Duncan, R. N. Hall and others that the rates of toll established at the August term of this Board are not sufficient to justify the keepers of the Chochuma and Tuscahoma ferries to keep the same in good repair, it is therefore ordered that the following rates of toll be established for the above mentioned ferries in lieu of those heretofore established towit: Footmen 10¢, Man & Horse 20¢, One Mule, Horse or Ox and vehicle 30¢, two horses, mule or ox & vehicle 50¢, 4 horses, mule, or ox, vehicle 75¢ and 6 horses, mule or ox, vehicle $1.00."

Quick tempers and keen resentment of any word or action which seemed to impunge their integrity or honor brought about immediate action by those who felt that these traits had been questioned. In 1884 we have an example of this action, and the successful attempt by the friends of both parties to avert serious trouble. The Grenada Sentinel printed the following quoted letters: "Mr. John J. Gage Jr. Your language and manner to me in our store yesterday evening, was of such a character that, after reflection, I feel it due to myself to demand of you an immediate apology. This will be handed to you by my friend Mr. Willie Crowder. Respectfully C. E. Goodwin." The answer to this demand came on the same day: "C. E. Goodwin, Esq., Sir! Your communication of this date wherein you require of me an apology for certain language and conduct of mine against you in your store on Wednesday has just been handed me by your friend Mr. Crowder. It might have been well if the demand had been more specific and the offensive language complained of, definitely stated. As I know, however, to what you refer, it is my pleasure to answer fully without any unnecessary preliminaries. You will remember that at the time immediately preceding the conduct and language complained of, you had stated in a most angry and vehement manner that if you voted for the ticket nominated at the Court House on Friday night, that you would consider yourself "no better than a damn negro", and further "that the whole affair was cut and dried and fixed up by a ring and cliue." Therefore, when I knew that you were fully aware of the fact, for you were present and participated in the convention that nominated the said ticket, that my father Dr. J. J. Gage, occupied the most prominent office, that of Chairman, and presided over said meeting, and that I was present also at the same, I gave your language its natural and reasonable construction: Namely that my father and myself had combined with others to fraudulently foist upon the people 'a cut and dried ticket', with candidates selected by a ring and clique, and not by those present; and knowing such to be false, I felt no hesitancy in pronouncing such charges, by whoscever made, so far as they reflect on my father and myself, to be utterly false and untrue. On reflection of my language and conduct, I find nothing for which, in my opinion, it is my duty to apologize. I must therefore refuse to comply with your demand to make apology where I feel none to be due from me. This will be handed to you by my friend Mr. J. C. Longstreet."

Evidently both principals in the quarrel were not tempered men. Their friends were afraid that serious consequences might ensue from the affair, so some of them began to try to work out an understanding which would "save the face" of both of the men. B. C. Adams Jr. and J. C. Branum wrote Mr. Goodwin as follows: "C. E. Goodwin, Esq. Dear Sir: Understanding that there are certain matters of difference between J. J. Gage, Jr., and yourself, we, as the friends of both parties, desire to have the same amicably and honorably adjusted. We, therefore, as such friends, request you to leave the settlement of such difficulties to mutual and dis-interested friends, and respectfully suggest Gen. G. Y. Freeman and W. P. Towler, Esq., as competent gentlemen conversant to the arrangement proposed." A similar letter was sent to Mr. Gage. Mr. Goodwin replied to the request in this manner; "Gentlemen: Your joint communication of this date requesting me to leave the settlement of the difference existing between J. J. Gage Jr., Esq., and myself to Gen. G. Y. Freeman and W. P. Towler Esq., for honorable and amicable adjustment has been received. Appreciating the friendly spirit that prompts you to such request, I can not do otherwise that accede to your request, and will say that I will consent to such arrangement, and agree that Gen. G. Y. Freeman and W. P. Towler Esq., may act in the premise as you suggest, if Mr. Gage also agrees to such arrangement.: Mr. Gage wrote Mr. Adams and Mr. Branum in a similar manner, agreeing to the proposed arrangement. In a formal document the two signed an agreeement to abide by such terms as the proposed mediators should determine: "Agreement: At the solicitation of mutual friends, we, the undersigned hereby submit the matters of difference between us to Gen. G. Y. Freeman and Mr. W. P. Towler, Esq., for amicable and honorable adjustment, and agree to abide by the conform to their action and decision in the premises." After receiving the agreement of the two principal parties to mediation by Gen. Freeman and Mr. Towler, Mr. Adams and Mr. Branum sent the following quoted letter to the two who were to adjust the dispute: "Gentlemen: At the solicitation of mutual friends, Dr. C. E. Goodwin and John J. Gage Jr., Esq., have consented to leave the matter of difference between them to you for honorable and amicable adjustment and settlement, and agree to abide your decision and action in the matter. We enclose the agreement referred to. Will you oblige us by using your efforts in the premises?" Mr. Freeman and Mr. Towler accepted the responsibility and worked out the terms of agreement between the hot-tempered principals: "Terms of Agreement. We, the undersigned, to whom has been referred by requests of mutual friends, the matter of a personal difference between C. E. Goodwin and J. J. Gage Jr., after examining the correspondence, consisting of a demand for a retraction of and apology for certain language and manner used to said Goodwin by said Gage in an interview on the 3rd of May last, in the following words towit:'(Here is set out letter No. 1 above.) To which demand said Gage replied as follows: (Here is set out letter No. 2 above.) We find, upon full investigation, that if Mr. Goodwin will disclaim any intention whatever to reflect upon the character, official or private, of said Gage, or his father Dr. J. J. Gage, or their action in said convention, then the said Gage shall retract any language upon the occasion referred to which was offensive to and reflecting upon the character of the said Goodwin, and we recommend this course to be pursued by both parties." The quarrel occured on May 3rd, and was settled in the manner indicated on May 5th.

Identification of the several men engaged in this "affair of honor" will be interesting to the reader. Dr. Gage, father of the hot-tempered son, was a physician who had long been a leading professional and civic leader in the town and county. He was interested in politics, and served for a time as County Superintendent of Education at a time when the office was appointive and not very well paid. The son was a teacher, who at various times, serves as principal of the Grenada Public School and of a Teacher Normal which he established in Grenada. C. E. Goodwin was a druggist in partnership with J. C. Branum, one of the two men who started the effort to reconcile the two parties to the quarrel. As was the practice of the time, the druggist, Goodwin was frequently referred to as "Dr. Goodwin". B. C. Adams, Jr. was a Grenada lawyer, son of Col. B. C. Adams, and father of the late B. C. Adams who was for a long time an important official in the Grenada Bank System. Gen. Freeman was a Grenada lawyer who later moved to Jackson, Mississippi. W. P. Towler was a former Grenada Druggist who had become a traveling salesman for some out-of-town firm. J. C. Longstreet was a prominent Grenada Lawyer and Mr. Crowder was a young man who, at a later date held several political offices in the county.

Indicative of the troubled financial state of the country at the time is an advertisement by C. W. Jones making known his desire to buy 5,000 bales of cotton to be paid for "In Greenbacks, Gold or Silver". Many people at this time did not consider the greenbacks as safe money, and refused to accept it in trades. Financial hardship may have existed for many, but the cost of living was low. Mrs. Lowenstein advertized thusly: "Lodging 25¢, Table Board $4.00 per week, Board and Lodging $5.00 per week. Transients Board and Lodging $1.00 per day." As a sign of hardtimes, the people were having their phones removed because the Cumberland Telephone & Telg. Company had increased rates. W. H. Wood advertised: "From this date I will sell meats at the following prices for cash: First class steak along 10¢ per pound; steak and roast together at 8¢; shoulder steak cut through 8¢; Rib roast 6¢."

In 1885 the Republican Party, with the support of the enfranchised negroes, still had enough political power to dominate city and county politics from time to time. During that year there were three republicans serving on the City School Board of Trustees. In 1886 the Grenada Sentinel condemned the action of "The good Republicans in re-employing Ann Howard a white Northern woman to teach in the negro school, and who invests her money in the North." At the time the salary of the highest paid teachers in the negro schools was $35.00 per month for a school session of seven months. Miss Howard would not have been able to make any very large investments in the North from the proceeds of her teaching in the Grenada Negro School. When she first came to Grenada another white teacher came with her, but both were so snubbed by the white people that the other teacher left after one session. No white person would rent rooms to the white women teaching in the negro schools, so Captain John Powell built a small house which he rented to them. He was a man of such stature in the community that he could afford to disregard the criticism which would have been bestowed upon some person of lesser stature, who was bold enough to furnish housing for the two northern teachers. It was about this same period in the history of the town when a negro Lawyer, George W. Jones had served a term as alderman from the West Ward and managed to create an atmosphere which resulted in the resignation of Max Ginsburger, a Jewish merchant and civic leader, from the Board of Aldermen. It was shortly after this incident that Jones announced that he had received an anamymous letter in which he was told to leave town in five days never to return. Jones did not leave within five days, but about two years later moved to Kansas. In the same year in which the negro attorney left Grenada a "back peddler" was murdered in the eastern part of the county, and two negroes were arrested and charged with the crime. Soon after their arrest a mob of masked men broke into the jail, made off with the two prisoners, and hanged them on a tree just across the Bogue. Just a year before this incident a case was tried in the Circuit Court and decided by a jury composed of six white men and the other six negroes. In 1888, in an advertisement in the Grenada Sentinel, A. H. Stefens announces the establishment of a negro high school in Belle Flower Church. On Jan. 9, 1886, the Sentinel printed the following account of a difficulty between a white man and a negro: "On last Tuesday night in the back room of Telford's saloon John Phillips (white) of Montgomery County shot at J. P. Sims (colored) the ball passing through his clothing grazing the skin over his heart. Phillips was bound over to the Circuit Court in the sum of $100.00. A woman was at the bottom of it." This is the way in which the Sentinel reported the murder of a white citizen: "August 26, 1882, "We regret to state that a difficulty occured on last Friday night at 11:00 o'clock which may result in the death of Mr. Jno. Greiner, an energetic and useful man by Mr. McKraynes, a painter and a man of not much use to the community."

In 1887 Greenwood LeFlore who had been instrumental in ratification of the Treaty of Dancing Rabbit Creek which treaty opened this region for white settlement, was in Grenada visiting his son J. L. LeFlore who was desperately sick. It had been fifty seven years since the old Choctaw Chief had played his part in a series of events which led to the migration of most of his people to a western reservation. At the time of his visit to his son Greenwood was still living in his Carroll County residence known as Malmason. His son had his residence on the bluff near the present community called LeFlore.

It is hard for us today, in an age of rapid transportation by good highways, to realize what an extensive trade area Grenada served in the years before people of the back country could go to Memphis, Jackson or other points to do their trading. The Railroad which furnished adequate transportation was responsible for much trade which came to Grenada. The Editor of the Sentinel referred to some incidents connected with this trade: "Choctaw generally announces the arrival of her fleet of floats on wheels, loaded to the guards with cotton, by a fusilade of long whips which sounds like a charge of muskets. But Choctaw is a great state within a greater, and we always give her the streets when she comes in with her wealth, Welcome Choctaw, Chickasaw, Calhoun and all surrounding counties to the benefit of our trade." In Novenber 1882, at the height of the cotton season, the editor had another reference to the boisterous conduct of visitors to town: "It is seldom that we have a concert of whip crackers, but when Choctaw and Calhoun agree upon a symphony of the most infernal that ever fell upon an ear this side of the discords of tuneless Erebus, we had it upon the streets of our town on Wednesday. Which took the cake we do not know, but fates deliver us from just such another concussion of air-waves. Yet we welcome Choctaw and Calhoun with their long whips and bovine teams. Boys make yourselves at home, take a drink and open up with this music when we are out of town."

On October 20, 1883, the Sentinel printed an item which indicated a Federal Judical Philosophy far different from that which prevails today: "The Supreme Court of the United States on last Tuesday decided the Civil Rights Law unconstitutional. The law had reference to hotels, railroads and resturants being compelled to serve negroes. There was only one dissenting vote." Although the Supreme Court had knocked down this early Civil Rights Law, there was still a considerable amount of political influence exerted by the Republican Party which claimed the majority of the negro vote. As an instance of this political influence we find that in 1880 Captain M. K. Mister, a planter living near the extinct village of Torrance, was appointed Post Master at Grenada through the influence of the notorious mulatto L. S. Schurlock. This man, for many years, controlled the negro vote in the area of Yalobousha and Grenada counties.

In 1886 B. L. H. Wright and his son were indicted and charged with the murder of a rival cotton weigher by the name of Melton. When the trial jury had finally been completed there were six white and six negro men sitting judgement of the Wrights. The six negroes were G. G. Leonard, Shep Edwards, Esquire Eskridge, Sandy Daily, Jim Conley and Robert Fisher. There was a general feeling on the part of the people that the Wrights would be found guilty, but the jury returned a verdict of "not guilty".

The same issue of the Grenada Sentinel which announced the outcome of the Wright trial also printed the pledge which all students requesting admittance to Mississippi Agricultural and Mechanical College (now Mississippi State University) had to sign before being accepted in that school. The pledge read: "I hereby pledge my honor that is my purpose and intention to pursue as my exclusive, or principal vocation in life, the business of agriculture, horticulture, mechanics or dairyman."

For many years a considerable source of revenue for Grenada was the license fee charged for the privilege of operating saloons. In October 1886 the Board of Aldermen raised this fee from $500 to $750. Evidently there was some dissatisfaction because of this increase since, at a subsequent meeting of the Board, the fees were not only lowered to erase the increase, but were dropped to $300. For many years the money derived from this source was used to help support the public schools. We do not know just what influence the sale of liquor may have had in the matter, but we find that at the time these license fees were being adjusted there were seven men in jail charged with murder, two of the prisoners being white and five colored. From time to time efforts were made, under the local option law, to prohibit the sale of liquor in the town of Grenada. In 1888 one such attempt having failed, and effort was made to get around the will of the voters by an attempt, by the North Mississippi Methodist Conference, to have a bill passed by the Legislature by which the sale of liquor within four miles of a Girl's School would be prohibited if the school officials requested that this be done. Of course the Conference had such a school in Grenada. The bill was introduced and failed to pass.

In these days of inccreased Federal involvement in support and partial control of public schools it is interesting to note that the first Federal grant to public education in Mississippi was in the form of a land grant to Jefferson College which was located at the town of Washington near Natchez. The school later came to be known as Jefferson Military Academy, and operated until comparatively recent times. During the early years of the Choctaw land slaes the United States Congress passed an act granting approximately 1900 acres of land to the school. James A. Girault, an official of the Land Office at Chocchuma, located the land for the school. He selected this land in the area near the present town of Holcomb. Soon after the land had been located Girault bought the land from the school but defaulted in payment, and when the land was sold at public auction, under terms of the Deed of Trust given by Girault, the School bought the land in order to protect its interest. In 1857 B. L. Wailes, President of the college, conveyed 493 acres of this land to C. H. Guy for a consideration of $2,472.99. Before the town of Holcomb was founded the area where the present white school is located was known as Guy's Corner.

The newspaper SOUTHERN REPORTER which was published in Grenada at an early date gives some interesting information relative to property assessment in the little frontier town of Grenada. In the May 25th, 1839, issue of the paper we find the following statement of assessed values on personal property: "Negroes $61,250; Saddle Horses $5,450; Merchandise $74,200; Groceries $61,250; Pleasure Carriages $2,000." We also find that the population of Grenada in 1839 was 1,217. Making up this number were 440 white males and 328 white females. There were 222 black males and 227 black females. We presume that all the negroes were slaves. A study of these figures will show that 37% of the population of the town was made up of slaves. Since most of the planters kept their field hands on their plantations it is probable that most of the slaves living in the town of Grenada in 1839 were house servants.

In 1885 interest in baseball began to develop, and a team was organized. E. Gerard was the pitcher, W. Wilkins catcher, J. C. Longstreet first base and Captain, E. Ransom second base, S. E. Shackleford short stop, S. Garner third base, B. C. Duncan right field, A. C. Thomas center field and M. Summerfield left field. J. T. Thomas was Secretary-Treasurer, and W. H. Whitaker umpire. The name of the team was the Athletics. For a number of years there was much interest in baseball and the local team began to import good players from other towns and some from the colleges. Tosh Sears was a fine pitcher who had played at Oxford. Bob Mitchell, son of a minister who lived for a time in Grenada, was an outstanding pitcher who had played at the University of Mississippi. About this same time Willie Mitchell was pitching for Mississippi Agricultural & Mechanical College (now Mississippi State University). These two faced each in many games both on the college campuses, and in Grenada and other towns which had summer teams.

In 1893 the economy of the region about Grenada was still geared to the production of cotton as the chief money crop, but some far-sighted men were beginning to see the potential which the region had as a cattle producing area. Judge J. C. Longstreet seems to have been the first citizen of Grenada who realized the advantages of the region as a cattle producing region. He first brought in some pure bred milch stock, but later began raising beef animals. He seems to have interested some Texas cattlemen in this area as a good place to winter cattle. On November 11, 1893, the Grenada Sentinel reported that 4,000 head of Texas steers were being fed on the farm of Judge Longstreet. Some years earlier there had been enough interest in stock raising to justify the establishment of the Central Fair & Livestock Association. For a number of years this association drew exhibits from Grenada and neighboring counties, but it fell into financial difficulties and was sold under the provisions of a deed of trust which the officers of the Association had executed. A number of public spirited citizens of the area bought the property which was valued at $9,000 for about one third of the property value. These men formed an association which eventually grew into the North Mississippi Fair. During the more prosperous years of its existence this was one of the better fairs held in the state. The Fair property was eventually donated to the public school system. The Jones Road School and the Football Stadium occupy part of the property.

In 1896 the Memphis Commercial Appeal had this glowing report on conditions at Grenada: "The last empty storehouse in Grenada has been rented, and is soon to be occupied. With its forty seven stores, two flourishing banks, a splendid telephone system, one oil mill, and many other industries, and with Memphis as its wholesale market, Grenada is one of the busiest towns on the Illinois Central Railroad." The publication of this boost for Grenada may have been responsible for the tongue-in-cheek report, published in the Sentinel, of a small village in Grenada County: "Nason is a little town situated at the junction of Grenada, Greenwood and Leflore roads. It contains 40 inhabitants, a telephone exchange, two gins and grist mills, one sawmill, two blacksmith shops, two general supply stores, two livery and feed stables, two public school buildings, one for the whites and the other for the blacks, two Methodist Churches (probably white and colored), a post office, and last, but not least, three old bachelors and two old maids."

Although Grenada was fortunate enough to have Grenada College located in the town, many of the local citizens became very much interested when it became known that the Methodist people were contemplating establishing another college to be known as Millsaps College, the name honoring Major Millsaps who had made a generous contribution to the proposed school. It became known that those in charge of the selection of a site for the college would be pleased to receive proposals from the several towns and cities which would like to have the school established in their towns. In the year 1891 Grenada made its bid for the school. It offered 20 acres of land and $27,000 in cash. Holly Springs offered $40,000, and Winona made an offer of 20 acres of land and $26,000. The trustees of the proposed school chose Jackson as the site. It offered two advantages over the other towns: a larger cash consideration and a more central location. At the time the people of Grenada were trying to induce the Methodist people to locate their new College in Grenada, the Sentinel reported that three illiterate whites and two illiterat negroes were serving on the Grand Jury. Just a few years later, in 1898, a negro rapist was hanged from a cottonwood tree located in the southwest corner of the public square. On June 6, 1891, the Sentinel had reported the death of another negro under different circumstances: "We learn than Ben Tunkett, an old colored citizen living in the western part of the county died on Tuesday last. He was, at one time, a member of the Board of Supervisors and prominent in the politics of the county, but of late years had lived in retirement, attending strictly to his farming interest." As late as the year 1900 Judge A. T. Roane received a visit from a negro who then lived in Marshall County. Their association began after the bloody battle in which General Forrest captured Fort Pillow, then garrisoned by negro soldiers. So many of the negro soldiers were killed that some Federal authorities claimed that Forrest's men had killed captured prisoners. One of those negro soldiers was captured, some say rescued by Judge Roane, and acted as servant to the Judge until his unit surrendered at Gainsville, Alabama as the war drew to a close. This negro was the one who usually visited the judge about once each year. Two years before the visit of the negro, in 1900, a company of Grenada soldiers departed for the Spanish American war. They left in a blaze of glory, but their homecoming after the war was beclouded by having to be quaranteened for a number of days because of having been exposed to some kind of contageous disease. The quaranteen camp was somewhere in the vicinity of Elliott.

    The pace of life was slow in Grenada during the closing years of the nineteenth century and the early years of the twentieth century. People had once been amused by pig fights occuring about the public square, but in 1887 the City Fathers passed an ordinance prohibiting hogs running about the streets of the town. In the Fall of the year the Central Fair and Livestock Association, by an advertisement in the Sentinel, indicated something of the slow pace of the times: "Wanted one hundred and fifty wagons with good spring seats for three days beginning Wednesday October 28, to carry people to the Central Fair and Livestock Association." Since many local people had their own transportation people from the special trains which used to come from a number of different towns during Fair Week. For those Grenada people who did not have their own transportation, and who did not want to ride in wagons to the fair, teams and rigs could be rented from the livery stables. One of these establishments advertised as follows: "Livery Stable charges: Single team and buggy $2.00; Double $3.00; team and surrey $4.50. Day hitching 25¢; night hitching 10¢. Camp house for campers. J. J. Horton located at Weeks Shed." In 1903 one livery stable operator became very much incensed because of strict enforcement of Sunday Blue Laws. He indicated his displeasure by the following quoted advertisement: "Notice. Owing to the strict enforcement of the Sunday Law our livery stable will be closed Saturday night at 12 o'clock and remain until Monday morning. We will not meet trains or attend funerals on Sunday. Doctors as well as others, cannot get horses on the Sabbath. We feel that to try to do a necessary or partial business would cause a great deal of trouble and dissatisfaction, so that is why we have concluded to do no business of any kind on Sunday. Respt. C. C. Penn & Son." Yeager & Son were operating another livery stable at this time, perhaps they did the 'necessary or partial' business which the Penns refused. The pace of life was still slow in 1910 when the City Board of Alderman decided that a new ordinance was necessary to keep things slow. They passed an ordinance which set automobile speed limits at ten miles per hour on the streets of the town, while the speed limit about the public square was set at six miles per hour.

In 1900 the population of Grenada was 2,568, just a little over twice the size of the Grenada of 1839. Greenwood had exactly the same population as Grenada, while Water Valley had a population 3,813. The location of the I. C. Railroad Shops at the last named town had much to do with the rapid increase in the population that town. It may be surprising to many to know that the largest town in Mississippi in 1900 was Vicksburg with a population of 14,834. Jackson had a population of only 7,118. Gradually the old, slow, deliberate pace and tempo of life increased. In 1902 the Grenada baseball team challanged the crack Memphis Chickasaw baseball team to a series of games. In September of 1902 Grenada Merchants and cotton buyers organized the Grenada Cotton Exchange. There was a private wire for market reports. J. R. Scoll was employed to take charge of the exchange. In 1909 a King's Daughters Hospital for Grenada was incorporated, but the incorporators were never able to build a hospital. On May 21, 1910, according to an article in the Grenada Sentinel, D. G. Ross steamed down the Yalobousha in his launch Mary. The boat drew 32 inches of water; was 30 feet long, and headed for Horn Island on the Mississippi Gulf Coast. W. J. Jennings, Jake Kettle, G. W. Fields and G. W. Terrell were passengers.

J. J. Williams was a man of great talent as a newspaper man, but quite eccentric and unpredictable. When young John W. Buchanan assumed ownership of the Grenada Sentinel Williams served as Senior Editor of the paper but soon quarreled with Buchanan and was dismissed from his position with the paper. He served in the Legislature as a democrat, but later ran for the same office as an independent. For a time he was the editor of a paper which was a competitor of the Sentinel. During the elections relative to prohibition of the sale of liquor in the city Mr. Williams was generally assumed to be the one who wrote up most of newspaper propoganda of the liquor crowd. The foregoing being true, it was with a great deal of surprise that the people of Grenada found in the March 23rd 1889, issue of the Sentinel the following quoted notice by Mr. Williams: "If any young man in this town has ever followed me as an exemplar into any house to take a drink, let me take him kindly by the hand and lead him out, and I have quit drinking, so help me God. I have stopped drinking for my own and others good. Signed: J. J. Williams." We have no definite information as to the cause of the sudden change by Mr. Williams. We do know that iw was not unusual for some of the men, to swear off from their bad habits after, or during, some of the high power evangelistic meetings held by such renowned preachers as Sam Jones. Perhaps Mr. Williams may have made his decision under such circumstances.

In the April 6, 1887, issue of the Sentinel the editor introduces his account of a difficulty arising from a matter of school discipline in this way: "It costs more to jump on a school teacher in Grenada than almost any other man. So be careful how you 'monkey' with them." The editor related the incident to which he alluded: "On last Wednesday evening just after the public white school let out, Professor Phillips the Principal gave Arthur Dubard, age about fourteen, a whipping for fighting. Arthur resisted Mr. Phillips, and forced him to use all his strength to control and punish him as he deserved. Mr. L. C. Dubard, the father of the boy heard about the affair and got very angry. About 4 o'clock of the same evening Mr. Phillips walked into the store of Roane & Son where Mr. Dubard clerks, to explain the matter but Mr. Dubard would not listen to him, and according to Mr. Phillips' statement, made toward him, when they had a rough and tumble scuffle which resulted in both of them having their faces somewhat disfigured. Although Mr. Dubard is much the stouter man of the two, judging from appearance, we don't think he got any of the best of Mr. Phillips."

"The news soon spread over ther town, creating much comment and excitement, and as soon as the facts were learned, Mr. Dubard as far as we have learned, was unanimously censured and condemned by all classes, while Prof. Phillips was equally upheld and endorsed for his action in the premises. Thursday moring Arthur Dubard went to school as usual, but was sent back by Prof. Phillips, with the understanding that he could not again be received in the school. A few hours afterward the School Board met at the school house and, after a thorough investigation, unamimously approved Prof. Phillips' course and passed a resolution suspending Arthur Dubard from school. Thursday evening the case came before Mayor Adams, and after statements by both sides, Mr. Adams discharged Prof. Phillips and find Mr. Dubard $25.00 and cost for assault and battery."

"The Sentinel, as well as an overwhelming majority of the good citizens of the town heartily endorsed the action of Prof. Phillips, The Board of Trustees and Mayor Adams in the action. If such things are allowed or continued, we had as well abolish the free school and do away with any further building of new school houses. We believe in the strictest discipline, and if parents don't want their children punished, they had better keep them away. Go on and maintain order and discipline in your school Prof. Phillips, and we assure you that the people of Grenada will sustain and stand by you."

On Sept 9, 1892, the J. J. Williams, who took the temperance pledge, ran a short advertisement in the Sentinel which was indicative of the variety of things which interested this versatile man. The advertisement read: "If there is anyone in this or surrounding counties, who knows anything about making sugar and molasses, or sugar from Louisiana or West India sugar cane and whose time is not too valuable to be rewarded for a fair compensation, such a one would confer a favor on me and perhaps serve indirectly the public, by communicating at once with the subscriber. I have an acre of very fine cane, which I wish to utilize for my own interest and test to some extent, whether such a crop can be made profitable in Grenada County on a small or large scale. Signed: J. J. Williams."

Editor Buchanan who usually gave his opinion on all matters of public concern did not hesitate to criticize public officials and public policies. In 1893 he wrote an editorial in which he protested the remuneration of the Mayor of Grenada. At the time the Mayor was receiving a salary of $500.00 per year, and was allowed the fines collected in the Mayor's Court. The editor argued that the position as Mayor was only a part time job, and that the remuneration derived therefrom was far too much for the service rendered.

For a long time after Grenada enjoyed the advantage of railroad service the people of Calhoun, Webster and Chickasaw counties had no railroad facilities, and Grenada was the town to which they brought their cotton and from which they bought much of the supplies which they needed. Because of the ill maintained roads of that time most of the transportation of cotton and supplies was by ox teams. A trip to Grenada from these points would usually take several days. May of the people who made these trips would camp on the site of the present community Futheyville. The Bogue, during times of heavy rainfall, was a rather turbulent stream and much trouble was experienced in assuring safe passage across that stream. During the early years a ferry was operated by a man by the name of Guthey. At a later date the county erected a wooden bridge across the stream, but from time to time this bridge was severely dammaged by flood waters. On at least two occasions the bridge was totally destroyed, and ferry service would have to be resorted to while a new bridge was being financed and constructed. The members of the Board of Supervisors eventually came to the conclusion that these make-shift bridges would never be satisfactory and in 1898 they awarded a contract to the King Bridge Company of Cleveland, Ohio to construct a steel bridge to be floored with first grade lumber. The contract price was $20,000.00 for a bridge span of 326 feet. At the time it was announced that the bridge would have the longest steel span of any bridge in the South, with the exception of one at Chattanooga. So far as we have been able to determine, this bridge served until the construction of Highway 8 when a concrete bridge across the Bogue relieved the old bridge of its load of traffice. The steel from the old bridge was salvaged, this terminating the service of this historic and vital link in the transportation route which brought much trade to Grenada.

In May 1884 Editor Buchanan had some more advice for the Board of Aldermen: "We call the attention of our City Authorities to the necessity of putting baluster (sic) on the sidewalk all the way from town to the depot, where there are high grades. We say this in the interest of all our citizens who have to travel at all times of night occasionally; and by way of showing the effects of this carelessness we will state that Mr. Tom Phelan, the telegraph operator whose business relations place him in the closest connection with many people, was seriously hurt on last Wednesday night by walking off the embankment in front of the Walthall House. Mr. P. is known to be a sober, faithful and attentive officer who makes many personal sacrifices in his official relations for the accomodation of our citizens, and if he will be liable to such an accident, how will fare the feeble, the infirm and the aged under similar circumstances?"

Some of the leading citizens of Grenada, realizing how much it would mean to Grenada to have a state supported college located in the town, became very much interested in an advertisement appearing in newspapers throughout the state. That advertisement read: "Proposals for the location of Mississippi Industrial Institute and College will be received until August 18, 1884. W. A. Hurt, Secretary of the Board." A movement was initiated to have Grenada offer sufficient inducements in the matter of land and money to bring the new school to Grenada. Other towns had similar ideas. Carrollton, Winona, Kosciusko and Jackson were also bidding for the location of the school. It was expected that the school would be located somewhere near, or on, the I. C. Railroad line preferably at a point somewhere near the center of state population. To the dismay of those towns such as Grenada, Winona and Jackson which had based their hopes on adequate railroad facilities and proximity to the population center of the state, the location selected was Columbus. That city had offered as their inducement buildings worth $50,000 and $40,000 in cash. As the years passed the school at Columbus, often called I I & C, grew in size and importance and today is known as Mississippi State College for Women.

There is little available information relative to the location of the mayor's office of the city of Grenada during the early years of its existence. It is probable that the City Hall, if it went by that name, was located in some rented building. The first documentary evidence which we have been able to find relative to the location of a City Hall is contained in a deed, given on December 18, 1856, by "the Grenada Odd Fellows Lodge to the Town of Grenada" by which deed the Odd Fellows for a cash consideration of $600.00 and a $400.00 note granted the City "an undivided half interest in a fractional part of lot 248 in the West Ward of Grenada towit: 35 feet of said lot fronting on Line street and running back west seventy feet thence south, thence last to Line, together with the lower story of the Odd Fellows Hall situated thereon together with all improvements thereunto belonging or appertaining." For seventeen years this lower story of the Odd Fellows Hall served as the City Hall. In 1873, for some cause, possibly because the building was set apart from the business section of the town, the city conveyed its interest in the Hall to the Odd Fellows for $250.00 in cash and a note for $250.00. For the next quarter of a century the location of the City Hall is clouded with uncertainty. It was not until April 10, 1898, that we have other documentary evidence of the location of the seat of City Government. On that date Mrs. L. M. Winn, in consideration of six hundred dollars paid by the city of Grenada, conveyed to the city a fractional part of Lot 67 which part is described in the deed as "the lot and house formerly occupied by the Grenada Sentinel, and now occupied as a Mayor's office." Just how long the Mayor's office had been located at this place before the purchase by the city we have no idea. It is probable that during the twenty five years elapsing between the time of the sale of the interest in the Odd Fellows Hall and the purchase of lot 67 served at the seat of City Government for a period of forty seven years. On December 10, 1945, the City of Grenada purchased from the Federal Government the building on the east side of Main street which had been used as a white U. S. O. building, and the building on the south side of Bell street which had been the negro U. S. O. center. For the two buildings the city paid $20,000. After necessary renovation, the offices of the City Government were moved to the newly purchased building. The Negro U. S. O. building was sold to the City Schools. On May 21, 1947, the old City Hall was sold to Grenada Auto Company for a consideration of $7,676.00.

During the early years of Grenada County Government paupers were cared for in private homes, with the home owners receiving a small remuneration for each pauper cared for. This course of action necessitated the issuance of a large number of small warrants each month, and also made it difficult, if not impossible, for the members of the Board of Supervisors to determine if the paupers were receiving proper care and consideration. The usual allowance for caring for a pauper was eight dollars per month, and sometimes the person keeping the pauper tried to make too much profit on the deal, with the result that the pauper did not receive proper care. Paupers had to make application to the Board of Supervisors to be certified as entitled to pauper relief. At times such applications would be rejected. In October, 1874, G. W. Hill and wife applied for pauper relief and the application was not approved on the grounds that "Applicants had five sons physically and financially able to care for their parents." The Supervisors soon came to the conclusion that it would be more satisfactory to provide a home in which all paupers would be cared for under the supervision of some person hired to do that job. On October 7, 1883, we find the following notation in the Minutes of the Board of Supervisors: "Whereas the Board having determined to purchase a poor house, and after having considered various propositions have purchased from John Moore a house and lot with the understanding that two additional rooms sixteen feet by sixteen feet be constructed on said land with a stick and dirt chimney." Evidently this statement was a little premature since, in the December 1884 meeting of the Board of Supervisors, that body authorized the Chancery Clerk to issue warrants to the amount of three thousand dollars "in payment of his farm for county poor house and farm." The payment was to be made to J. W. Gibbs who was the former owner of the farm involved. This farm must have been resold by the county since in February of 1886 the Board of Supervisors paid $1,200.00 for the "Boyoworth

Place" located four miles southwest of Grenada at the forks of the Carrolton and Tuscahoma roads. The poorhouse was definitely located at this place, and the road leading thereto was sometimes called the "poorhouse road". In the same month the Board employed William Gibbs to be Superintendent of the poor house. For this service he was to be paid $100.00 in county warrants and two bales of cotton. The cotton was to be delivered to him by the people who had rented the farming land connected with the poor house property. This seems to be a very small consideration for the services of a Superintendent of the poorhouse, so it is probable that some other provision was made for food, clothing and medical attention for the inmates of the poorhouse. We do know from allowances of the Board that different doctors were paid by the county for attention to paupers. It is probable that the new poorhouse had been purchased by the county in anticipation of the city of Grenada sharing the facility and the expenses for the benefit of its indigent citizens. This presumption arises from an order of the Board of Supervisors in April 1877: "Ordered by the Board that J. Portevent take charge of the City poor and place them in the Poor House, the Corporation paying their pro rata share of all the paupers." Mr. Portivent was President of the Board which passed this order. Soon after the establishment of the Poor House the Board began to take bids from interested persons who desired to operate the facility. The prospective bidder would agree to furnish food, clothing and medicine for the inmates at so many dollars per month per inmate. At one time the bid which was low was so inadequate that the Board decided that the inmates would suffer. The low bid was $2.50 per person. At the next meeting of the Board there was another bidding and the person awarded the bid was to receive $8.00 per month per inmate.

The name Samuel B. Marsh, an early lawyer, would probably have been forgotten by this time were it not for a Deed of Trust recorded in Deeds Records Book, Vol. 1, page 45. That instrument reads: "Know all men by these presents that I, Joseph Logan of the county of Yalobousha and the state of Mississippi for and inconsideration of the sum of $1.00 to me in hand paid, the receipt whereof is hereby acknowledged, have bargained, sold and conveyed, and by these presents do bargain, sell alien and convey to Samuel B. Marsh, his heirs and assigns forever 120 acres of land on which I now reside situated in the said county of Yalobousha being, if I am not mistaken, in Section 21, township and range not known to have and hold to the said Samuel B. Marsh his heirs and assigns forever, and also my negro girl slave Betsy age 11 or 13 years old, the condition of the above obligation is an follows: the said Samuel B. Marsh has agreed for one thousand dollars to defend as one of my counsel my two sons Arron and Robert Tyson now imprisoned on a charge of murder in said county of Yalobousha, for which I am indebted to him in the said sum of one thousand dollars. Now if I shall give said Marsh note payable the first of January next for said sum with good security, or shall otherwise pay the sum then the above obligation to be void; otherwise to remain in full force and the said Marsh and his heirs, executor or administrator shall have the power to sell land and slave to pay himself said sum of one thousand dollars provided I fail to pay the sum before the first day of January next the impulsory (sic) to be rendered to me and the sale at public auction. Signed Joseph Logan X his mark." The instrument illustrates the excessive verbage of many of the early legal instruments, as well as the fact that the seat of justice for a large area was then at Coffeeville. The instrument was dated September 12, 1835. Since the deed of trust is recorded in the Deeds Records of Grenada County Mr. Logan must have lived somewhere in the area now within the boundaries of Grenada County. We do not know the outcome of the trial, but trust that the poor, illiterate father of the two wayward sons got the value of his money and was able to redeem his 120 acres of land and his single slave.

The old practice of apprenticing orphan children to those who would accept the responsibility which is generally thought of as a relic of early colonial times, was practiced in Mississippi even after the beginning of the twentieth century. In the year 1903 Douglass and Marietta Lister were apprenticed to Mrs. Rosa Willis and Lewis Willis until the apprenticed children reached the ages of eighteen and twenty one years.

The public square must have been an unsightly and unsanitary place in 1882. On June 10 of that year Editor Buchanan of the Grenada Sentinel published the following quoted comment on the condition of the square: "Have any of the good people of this ancient little borough ever reflected seriously upon the misuse to which the public square has been applied, and the beautiful, higenic purpose to which it might have been consecrated? In its present condition it is neither useful nor ornamental, but a source of suffocating heat in summer, mud and slush in winter. Like a great inverted reflector, its soft, dandy surface receives, all through the summer day, the rays of a blistering sun, to be absorbed for evaporation at night, reflected and refracted by day on the walls that enclose its three sides until past meridian, when the evening air around it becomes thick and stifling. If this be so, and we think that no one who has loitered much upon our streets in front of the square, on summer evenings, will question, why should this inconvenience, to call it mildly, be longer born. In winter it is cut up by the hoofs of mules, oxen, and wagon wheels, until one had as soon plunge into the depths of an Irish bog as to try to cross it. This continued friction cuts up the surface into a soft mass of disintergrated soil ready at the first heavy rain to discharge its thick and slimy contents into the Yalobousha, thus gradually scooping out a basin for the retention of water, from which in the summer, sickening vapors will arise and creep into the parlors and bedrooms of our unsuspecting citizens. This, without the intervention of deeper drains, must be the final issue of leaving the little square an open wagon yard."

"We know but one class of citizen who might advocate the present uses of the square, and oppose converting it into a beautiful, shaded little park, wherein ornamental and forest trees would spread their cooling shadows, whereon green sward would present its carpetlike surface, and rich flowers would bloom to delight the gaze and throw out their fragrant breath in sweet perfumes to enrich and purify the air we breathe, wherein winding walks, hid from the glare and heat of the summer solstice, would be enlivened by the sports of happy children, and people of all classes could sit and enjoy thr refreshing, tranquil evening air, while discussing questions of social life, and interchanging the courtesies of a refined community. The only parties who could oppose any change in the matter would be the merchants, and we hope that we have none so little identified with our material progress, so little acquainted with the laws of health, and the science of pneumatics, as to say all this is silly bosh. Because this has been a wagon yard for fifty years, is no more reason that it should continue so, than that a man should yoke up his oxen to haul a load of goods from Memphis, with a railroad at hand ready to deliver the same in a few hours. Citizens this little square is yours, and you can continue it as a nuisance, or convert it into a little paradise of social joy and health."

This appeal by the editor had no immediate result, and it is doubtful that it had any effect when an attempt was made in the 1890's to improve conditions on the square. It had been the practice, for many years, for the merchants and cotton buyers to weight cotton on scales located on the streets around the square and then dump the cotton on the square until it could be transferred to the railroad station. With the completion of the cotton compress it became much more convenient for the cotton to be weighed and stored at the compress building. Several years after the publication of the article by Editor Buchanan, his paper had an announcement that hereafter all cotton would be weighed and stored at the compress. The farmers who brought cotton to town did not like this. They liked to visit together on the square. Some complained that their teams were afraid of the noise and confusion brought about by the trains which ran by the compress. They claimed that it was dangerous to have their teams near the railroad. At first the cotton buyers did not pay much attention to the complaints. They took the attitude that it was natural for farmers to gripe; that they were never satisfied with the price of cotton and the arrangement for purchase and storing. But they took notice in the cotton season of 1896 when the number of bales of cotton brought to the Grenada market was only two thirds of the number of the previous year. Cotton buyers at Parsons, the eastern terminus of the Y. & M. V. Railroad, were reputed to be paying better prices for cotton than the Grenada buyers. The drop from 15,000 bales of cotton usually sold in Grenada to 8,000 bales indicated that the farmer resentment was serious. Eventually Grenada leaders began to contact the farmers to find out what was wrong. The farmers let them know. In the July 18th issue of the Sentinel 95 citizens of Graysport, Sabougla and Williamsville endorsed a printed statement of grievance, chief of which was that the farmers were being forced to take their cotton to the compress against their will. A little later a similar statement was printed in which 92 citizens of Carroll County voiced the same complaint. The merchant John W. Griffis, who also bought cotton, was the first to give in to the demands of the cotton producers. In a statement printed by the Sentinel he stated that he still thought that the existing system was good, but that henceforth he would have scales placed in front of his store along with a man on duty to weigh the cotton. In the meantime J. G. Weeks has bought the old Alliance Cotton Shed, which was located within a block of the public square, and was ready to store cotton for any farmer who wanted to have his cotton weighed up town. A week later the firms of Kimbrough & Perry, Gerard & Nason, James Pryor & Co., Wright and Williams, Berryhill Bros., G. W. Jones and W. N. Pass, announced that they would buy cotton to be weighed on the streets and stored at eighter the Alliance Cotton Shed or the compress as the seller desired. We do not know if any improvement had been made in the condition of the square during the time the cotton wagons no longer came to the square, but after the change of mind on the part of the merchants and cotton buyers the square reverted to its earlier condition as described by Mr. Buchanan.

It would be a long time after the efforts of Mr. Buchanan before any considerable improvement would be made in the appearance of the square and the streets on the four sides. In fact it would be some years after the death of the Editor of the Sentinel before any kind of street paving was done about the square or in any part of town. In the early 1900's some improvement was made relative to the dust from the dirt streets by beginning to oil some of the streets. This served to settle the dust and to help bind the soil of the streets together, but did not prevent the development of many ruts and pot holes on the streets. During the winter months these were filled with water while in the summer they frequently accumulated dust which would be blown about the adjacent buildings. It was not until the year 1913 that any serious effort would be made to improve the appearance of the streets about the square. In May of that year the Board of Aldermen set up an election to determine if the city of Grenada should issue $25,000 in bonds for the purpose of paving Depot and the other streets about the square. Mr. W. B. Hoffa, always a booster for any civic improvement, wrote a letter which was published in the May 23rd issue of the Grenada Sentinel. The following excerpt taken from that letter will indicate that the condition of the streets about the square was still far from desirable: "Depot street and the south side of the square last winter and the winter preceeding, has been a municipal disgrace and an object of shame to every patriotic citizen." Most Grenada voters were of like mind as indicated by the vote on the bond issue which occured on May 30, 1913. One hundred and twenty five voters were in favor of the proposed bond issue while only sixty four voted against it. With the favorable vote on the bond issue, there was every reason to anticipate a speedy improvement on the appearance of the square and Depot street. But complications arose which would delay this accomplishment. The Board of Aldermen had decided to use creosoted wood blocks as the surface material for paving. These blocks would be set up on a concrete base.

The apparent reason for this choice was that the use of wood blocks would lessen the sound of hoofbeats upon the pavement. At the time the use of motorized vehicles was very limited, and no one realized that within a very short span of years the slund of hoof beats on the streets would be a rarety rather than an ordinary occurance. The paving contract was awarded to the New Orleans Wood Block Creosoting & Paving Company. That company, in a somewhat unusual action, bid in the bonds issued to pay for the paving. For some reason the bond attorneys delayed for several months their approval of the bonds. At least that was the excuse offered by the paving company for delay in beginning work on the project. On January 9, 1914, B. C. Duncan entered a suit to prevent issuance of the bonds. This was a friendly suit filed for the purpose of obtaining a determination as to the validity of the bond issue. In due process the suit reached the State Supreme Court, and on April 17th of the same year that tribunal approved the constitutionality of the bond issue. The paving company still delayed action and the Board of Aldermen, impatient with the long delay, voided the contract for the paving project. For about a year nothing was done to invite new bids on the project. On May 15, 1915, the New Orleans concern entered a suit against the City of Grenada claiming that it had been damaged in the sum of $10,000 because of the action of the City in voiding the original contract. On May 5, 1916, the city Board opened sealed bids for the paving jobs and found that Sullivan, Long & Haggerty of Bessemer, Alabama was the lowest of seven bidders. This firm was awarded the contract for the paving project. The bid was $30,973.00. Although earlier bid specifications had specified wood block material, it would seem that in 1916 the Board needed reassurance as to the durability of this material. Dr. J. H. Dorroh, Dean of the University of Mississippi School of Engineering, was retained to go to Greenwood, Jackson and other places where the wood block payment was in use, and to determine how well this material had served in the several places. Dr. Dorroh reported favorably upon the desirability of the blocks and the small amount of maintenance needed to keep the blocks in good condition. This report confirmed the earlier opinion of the Board, so this was the material used in the specifications when the bidders began to figure on the job. The successful bidder promised to complete the paving in four months, beginning on June 1, 1916. As the work progressed it was decided by the Town Board that Main Street from First to Second street should be paved, this being an area of business houses. In an election relative to issuing additional bonds for this purpose the measure was approved by a five to one margin. A little later the City Fathers decided that Green Street, which had several substantial business houses, should also be paved. Again their proposal was approved by the people. With the completion of the paving project the square was completed encircled by paved streets. Depot Street was paved all the way from its intersection with Doak Street to the Depot, while Main and Green Streets had block long pavement from the square to Second Street. Of course property owners on both sides of the paved streets paid their share of the paving costs. Since the City had assumed ownership of the square, it was necessary for it to assume a greater share of the paving costs than on those streets where there were private property owners on both sides of the street. A white way had been planned to be put in operation as soon as the paving was finished. In late September of 1916 the following excerpt appeared in an editorial in the Grenada Sentinel: "The 'White Way' will adorn Depot Street, the square, and Main street to Second, and the pretty stores, the park, and other attractive places will show to still better advantage." In late December, 1916, the writer on a train trip from Jackson to Oxford, first saw Grenada at night, and he remembers very vividly what an attractive appearance the white way presented. Disinterest, lessening railroad traffic and the passage of time have combined to ruin this beautiful night view from passing rains. 1916 was a good year for the civic pride. Not only did Grenada get its paved streets, but also was sleected first in its class of cities as the cleanest city in that category. This was also the year when the people of the city under the leadership of Mrs. Ed Payne raised money to rescue the East Cemetery, sometimes called "the yellow fever cemetery", from its deplorable unkempt appearance. Money was solicited from individuals, business firms, religious and fraternal organizations and any other available sources. About two hundred and fifty dollars was contributed, and with this money the area was cleared of weeds, briars and small trees which had been allowed to grow up. The entire area was enclosed by a fence composed of heavy wire fastened to white oak posts embedded three feet in the ground and extending five feet above surface. The ground end of the post was heavily tarred, and the upper part painted. Although a few half-hearted attempts have been made to clear the cemetery, it is today a disgrace to a people who claim to be proud of the history and accomplishemnt of those who built the foundations of town in which we reside. We need today some of the spirit of those civic minded people of fifty years ago who were determined that their sacred dead should not lie in an bandoned and forgotten cemetery.

Outside influences and practices were rather slow in coming to Grenada during the first fifty years of its existence. People continued to do things pretty much as they had done in the past. The town and county was a rather closeknit community in which most of the people knew each other. Of course there were the usual differences between the people of the town and those of the county, but these differences were minor in nature. Usually the positions of leadership in the county and town were held by either first, or second generations, of those early pioneers who came into the area during the early development of the region. But changes were due to come about. Business was to become more specialized. General stores began to disappear, and the number of small stores decreased as larger establishments obtained the capital necessary to enlarge their operations. Transportation over the country roads was still primitive, and one shrewd yankee came into the area built his sawmill on the banks of the Yalobousha river; had his timber cut along the areas near the river and floated the logs down river to the mill. He constructed a large artifical lake which was connected with the river. This lake served two purposes; one was to keep the logs from being floated down the river beyond the mill, and the other purpose was to keep the logs in water where they would not be damaged by a kind of larva stage insect known as 'sawyers', so called because of the way they attacked any log which was left unused for any length of time. This method of preserving a large number of logs made it possible for the owner of the mill to keep his mill well supplied with logs. The logs were usually cut early enough to take advantage of the high river stage caused by early spring rains. Farmers and other land owners near the river would cut their own trees into logs and float them down to the Van Osdel Mill. Mrs. Edith Guidry, a daughter of Mr. Van Osdel, remembers living in the vicinity of the mill when she was a dmall girl. She has this to say relative to the operation of that mill: "My family lived at that place for eleven years. My father had not dreamed the supply of timber would hold out that long. The farmers from quite a distance floated their logs down the river to him and they were coralled in the basin formed by the cut-off. My earliest remembrance of my father was seeing him in hip-boots being called out before dawn to see about the in-coming logs. Men with long cant-hooks had to keep the logs separated in order to avoid pile-ups and log-jambs. I think that with each differenct invoice of logs a man, probably hired by owner of the timber, rode a log raft along with the logs to guide them along the river which was said to have a 'mean current'."

The operation of the mill was under the direction of Mr. M. S. Van Osdel. The first documentary evidence of the prospect for this mill is found in a deed to the mill-site. On February 13, 1896, W. N. Pass conveyed to M. S. Van Osdel "a certain parcle of land for a steam mill site situated on Yalobousha River in Grenada County". The deed then went on to establish the location more specifically as being in Section five, Township twenty two, Range Five East. The mill was on the north side of the river almost due north of the present community of Futheyville. The mill operated for a number of years, and many of the substantial Grenada homes constructed during this period, were constructed from lumber cut by the Van Osdel Mill. The mill must have ceased operation sometime prior to 1909, since on March 20th of that year Mr. Van Osdel sold the mill site to J. H. Dunaway.

Not only were outside interests coming in to tap the raw resources of the area, but women were beginning to feel emancipated from old ideas of the restrictions which had been place upon the professional fields in which women were priviliged to work. On October 22, 1915, the following quoted news item appeared in the Grenada Sentinel: "The legal fraternity of Grenada never witnessed before what was seen in Chancery Court this week. Reference is had to Miss Bessie Young, a young lady of Grenada duly and properly equipped for the practice of law. Miss Young graduated from the Law Department of the State University last June and enuoys the distinction of being the first lady ever to receive a law degree from the University. Outside of Miss Young's legal training, she is a most cultured, refined and charming woman, and can be relied upon to apply the rule of reason and good old-fashioned common sense to any proposition she undertakes. She is in no sense an up-to-dal woman. She believes in old time Southern standards and Southern modesty. Miss Young's office will be opened in November over Heath Bros. Store. There is frequently litigation that seemingly only a lady should handle and in due time it is assumed that the people of the county will make her acquantance and consult her expecially about such matters." We do not know just what Editor Lawrence meant by the term 'up-to-dal' nor the nature of the litigation which seemingly only a lady should handle, but in a way he seems damning with faint praise the entrance of ladies into what had been deemed a masculine profession. We do not know just how successful Miss Young was in the Practice of her Profession in Grenada, but we do know that, at a later date, she went to Washington, D. C., and was employed, in a legal capacity, by some agency of the Federal Government.

Index:
History of Grenada County, Mississippi

ABBOT,	53	BAILEY,	110
ABBOTT,J.	23	BAINE,A.C.	23,40,53,125
. J.C.	186	.	186
. JOHN C.	146	. W.B.	167
ABERNATHY,	125	BAINES,T.P.	111
JOHN COOK	124	BAKER,	29,127
ABGEVINE,M.	111	. FRANCIS	126,143
S.S.	111	. J.R.	48
ADAMS,	26,221	. JOHN C.	137
. B.C.	46,84,116-117,134	. JOHN H.	137
.	164,169,209,214-215	. RHODES	128
. BEN	84	. W.R.	119
. BEN C.	191	BAKEWED,IRENE	110
ALCORN,	62,73,78,80,91	BALFORE,JOHN	19
.	95	BALFOUR,ELIZABETH	123
. JAMES L.	94	. JAMES	123
ALDRIDGE,	33	. JOHN	21-23,74
. LEWIS	54,141	BALLARD,MATTIE	57
. W.H.	74,188	BARKSDALE,	202
ALEXANDER,C.P.	25	. J.H.	117-118
ALLEN,	89	. WILLIAM	92
. HENRY	137	BARNARD,THOMAS	28
. WILLIAM	19	BARNES,LOFLIN	11
ALLISON,ALEX	50	BARWIN,	178
AMES,	94-95,129	BASCOMB,	54
ANDERSON,	101-103,106	BATES,H.	160
. B.P.	100	BATTLE,ALFRED	11
. ELIZABETH	11	BAYLISS,J.Y.	53
. R.W.	11	BEA,WILLIE	111
. WILLIAM	11	BEAL,WILLIAM	11
ANGEVIHE,SAXTON S.	107	WILLIAM M.	31
ARMISTEAD,E.R.	78	BEALE,WILLIAM B.	10
ARMOUR,	24,123	BEALL,THOMAS W.	30
ARMSTRONG,COLEMAN	111	. WILLIAM B.	21
J.K.	111	. WILLIAM M.	22
AUSTINE,F.R.	134	BEANE,W.	211
AYER,	163-164	WILLIAM	209
AYRES,A.W.	111	BEARD,WESLEY	74
. I.H.	78	WILLIAM M.	141
. J.C.	104	BEASLEY,	111
. JENNIE	111	JAMES	11
. LIZZIE	111	BEATTY,J.H.	101
. M.C.	57-58	BEAUCHAMP,J.W.	110
. W.I.	111	W.F.	110
BACON,	19	BEAURGARD,	82

230

Index:
History of Grenada County, Mississippi

BECK,D.M.	19,186	BOWMAN,E.L.		61
. DAVID	138	BOYCOFT,CHARLES		83
. W.E.	56	BRADFORD,BENJAMIN		11
. WILLIAM H.	137	BRADY,JOYN G.		44
BEEBE,A.	116	BRAGG,		83-84
BELEW,W.A.	111,134	BRANDON,GERARD C.		149
BELFOR,	157	BRANHAM,		48
BELL,A.S.	108,118,164	BRANNUM,J.C.		177
WILLIAM	62,74,188	BRANUM,J.C.	100,214-215	
BENKE,JAMES	111	BRECKENRIDGE,		82
BERNARD,	29	BREWER,J.H.		118
BERNHARDT,L.	169	BRIARLY,R.T.		137
BERRY,	53	BRIDGES,		24,123
BEW,A.	140	PETER		11
ABSOLAN	19	BRIGGS,CHARLES		207
BEWEN,	82	BRISTOL,C.		110
BIDDLE,	113,120	EMMA		110
NICHOLAS	112-113	BROADSTREET,J.P.		43,118
BIGHAM,CLINTON	61	BROOKS,		60
BINGHAM,HENRY N.	138	WILLIAM		84
BINSWANGER,	166	BROTHER,		34
BISHOP,ADDIE	110	BROTHERS,THOMAS		116,198
. BELLE	110	BROWN,		21,100
. J.M.	110,134	. A.S.	21-23,53,75	
. J.W.	141	.	124-125,140,158,176	
BLACK,	120	. ALBERT SPOONER		124
BLACKBURN,JAMES	11	. J.H.		119
BLAIR,E.	32	. JULIA		89
BLEDSOE,O.F.	164	. R.F.		99
OSCAR	48,101,122	. ROBERT		57
BLOCKER,J.Y.	26	. S.D.		158
JAMES Y.	137	. T.F.		89
BLOODWORTH,TIMOTHY	11	. T.J.		210
BODENHEIMER,	34	. W.H.		79
BODLEY,WILLIAM B.	11	. WILLIAM		125
BOONE,DANIEL	84	BRUNNER,ISAAC		30
BOSTIC,	12	BRYAN,WILLIAM O.		40
BOSWORTH,WILLIAM	74	BRYARLY,R.T.		18
BOTELER,E.L.	119	BRYLEY,R.S.		46
BOUSHE,W.E.	57	BRYNE,JAMES N.		207
BOWLES,MARY	140	BRYON,WILLIAM P.		21
. R.S.	110	BUCHANAN,	98,147,151-153	
. THOMAS G.	30-31	.	196-197,199,222,225	
. THOMAS P.	140	.		226
BOWLING,	11	. ELLEN MALCONSIN		149

Index:
History of Grenada County, Mississippi

. FRANCES M.	149	. AUGUST	124
. J.W.	49,58-59,108,117	. G.W.	110
	153,155,159,167,169	. J.H.	107
. JENNIE	154	. WILLIAM R.	11
. JOHN W.	146,149-150	CARGILE,WILLIAM	11
	154,220	CARL,ELLA	111
. JOHN WALTON	153	. J.A.	164
. ROBERT	153	. JONATHAN	157
. W.H.	154	. PRICE	111
. WILLIAM	153	CARNS,	184
BUCKANAN,JOHN W.	97	CAROTHERS,	207,210
BUCKHAHAN,JOHN W.	97	. A.M.	119
BUDBARD,L.C.	187	. J.C.	209
BUELL,	82-83	CARPENTER,GERMAN	111
BUFFALO,J.G.M.	176	CARROLL,J.D.	25-26
BUFFALOE,		CARSON,SAMUEL	11
MARIA ROBBINS	181	CARTER,	176
BUFFINGTON,THOMAS C.	141	CARTLEDGE,MARY	128
BULLOCK,	53	CARY,	111
BURGLAND,G.	176	CASEY,L.L.	118
BURK,M.P.	141	CHAFFEE,	131,134
BURNES,	134	J.	33-34
BURNETT,C.	11	CHALMERS,	81
BURNS,W.T.	167	CHAMBERLAIN,	100,177-178
BURT,HENRY	111	.	192
BUSH,WILLIAM	138	. WILLIAM C.	176
BUTLER,	103	CHAMBERS,W.C.	19
JOHN	205	CHAMBLISS,PETER	11
BYNUM,	77	CHAMLEY,ROBERT E.	32
CAHN,E.	123,134,182	CHAN,J.	134
. H.E.	167	CHANDLER,WILLIAM	111
. JOE	187	CHAOTE,JOHN M.	53
CALDWELL,ISAAC	15	CHAPMAN,A.	32
. J.W.	159-160	CHARLES,M.B.	119
. L.C.	137	CHEATHAM,	82,84,86,206
. MARY	19	.	208-210
. SAMUEL C.	11,14	. M.J.	203,205-207
. SEPTIMUS	19,184	.	210-211
CAMPBELL,	26,33,85	. MEL	203,207
	101-102,104-105	CHILD,CAWEIN S.	110
. A.B.	61	CHISHOLM,	31-32,128
. A.C.	46	. A.C.	31
. A.L.	26	. ANGUS	30
. A.S.	10,25	CHOATE,	53
. ANGUS	8	J.J.	145,186

232

Index:
History of Grenada County, Mississippi

CHRISTIAN,	57,59
G.W.	58
CLAIBORNE,	120
C.C.	149
CLANTON, MATTHEW C.	11
CLARK,	78
. ADOLPHUS FILLMORE	132
. DAVID	132
. JANE	131
. JESSE	131
. KATE	110
. THOMAS	132
. WILLIAM	11,31,132
CLAW, JOHN J.	21
CLAY, HENRY	112,145
CLEVELAND,	133
. L.	20-22,24
. LARKIN	23,123
COAN,	101,106
G.T.	111
COBB, STANCIL	11
COFFEE, HIRAM	3,11,18,137
COFFMAN,	53,104
. CHARLES	111
. ELIZA S.	108
. J.	122
. J.R.	74
. JOSEPH	19,108,122
. KATE	111
. R.	18,188
. RALPH	19,62,74,108,111
.	122,130,157
COLE, W.T.	106
W.V.	106
COLEMAN, RICHARD	11
COLLEGE, KATE	56
COLLINS, JACK	189
. JOSEPH	11,31,53,140
. MOSES	11,140
. R.A.	111
. ROLAND	92
COLSON, DSMURL	11
CONLEY,	131
. JIM	217
. M.	110
CONLY, WILLIAM	35
CONNELY, D.W.	36
DAVID W.	11
CONNOONTONTAH,	13
COOLY, JOHN	92
COOPWOOD, THOMAS	11
CORDOSA, T.W.	95
CORDS, M.	134
CORRELL, S.M.	129
COVERT, GEORGE S.	76
COVINGTON, WILLIAM G.	21
CRAWFORD, J.D.	74
CRENSHAW,	19
CRITTENDON, J.P.	19
CRITZ, GEORGE E.	57
CROFFORD, JAMES	11
CROMWELL, GEORGE	110-111
JOHN	111
CROWDER,	159,215
. GEORGE	74
. GREEN	11,23,126
. GREEN W.	126,133
. JAMES	3,92,96
. R.B.	11
. R.D.	46,54,126
. RANSOM	126
. WILLIE	214
CRUMP,	181
. JAMES	14,129
. JOHN	188
. WALTER	42,129,161,176
.	207
CRUTECH,	31
CUFF, J.	118
JAMES	164
CURRY, JOHN M.	11
DAILY, SANDY	217
DANIEL, SMITH	64
DANTHIT, W.H.	19
DAUGAN, CLARK	24
DAUGHLIN, DAVID	23
DAVIDSON,	110
. A.H.	185
. A.R.	176
. ASBURY	185

Index:
History of Grenada County, Mississippi

. E.P.	19	DORROH,J.H.	227
. T.P.	53	DOTY,W.S.P.	118,164
. THOMAS	19	DOUTHET,	19
. WILLIAM	74	DRAKE,M.M.	19
DAVIS,	85,95	DRIVER,E.M.	11
. ALEX	57	R.W.	11
. ANDREW	73	DUBARD,	91
. BILL	91	. ARTHUR	187,221
. COLLY	111	. BUD	96
. GEORGE	74	. GREEN	96
. HUGH R.	111	. L.C.	190,221
. J.L.	46	. L.G.	134
. J.T.	146	. M.G.	142,167
. JEFFERSON	78,81,84,125	. PHILIP	131
.	149,185	. SALLY	142
. MARY J.	14	. WILLIAM	74,131,137
. PANOLA E.	192	. WILLIAM M.	131
. RUBEN	78	DUCAN,B.C.	162
. S.L.	111	DUDLEY,	58
. WILEY	11,14,21	. AUSTIN	91
DEJARNETT,	110	. B.S.	86,119,165
SALLIE	110	. BANJO	91
DERRICK,H.S.	110	. BOB	91
DILLARD,GEORGE	128	. BRYON	117
DINSMORE,	178	. P.J.	56
DOAK,	116,130,160-161	. P.S.	56
.	202	DUDLY,	87
. B.M.	111	. B.S.	91
. BOYD	128-129,185	. P.S.	89-91
. BOYD M.	107	DUKLEY,D.M.	19
. LULA	110	DUNAWAY,A.P.	158
. R.	75	J.H.	229
. ROBBIE	99	DUNBAR,WILLIAM	15,128
. ROBERT	43,107,118,129	DUNCAN,	118,198
.	134,163	. B.C.	117,218,227
DOBSON,	77	. BEN	83
DOCKERY,HENRY	44	. DUNBAR	187
DOLITTLE,	134	. J.M.	188,213
DOMAN,PETER	19	. JAMES M.	15,128
DONALDSON,ELIZABETH	120	. JANNETT	189
DONKIN,	202	. JOHN	138,188
GEORGE	138	. L.A.	157
DONLEY,JOHN	2-3,21	. LUCY	189
DONLY,JOHN	11,20,66,125	. MARY	189
	128	. WALTER	189

Index:
History of Grenada County, Mississippi

. WILLIAM	52	FINNER, FRED	110
DUPREE, W.D.	161	FISHER,	82,90
DUVANEY, J.	15	. E.S.	74
EASON, JOHN P.	110	. E.T.	47,134
EATMAN, G.W.	118	. EPHRAIM	185
W.G.	119	. HAL	96
EDGAR, WILLIAM	12	. NICHOLAS	12
EDGERTON, A.J.	56	. ROBERT	217
EDINGTON,	68-69	FISK, ALVON	12
. L.P.	67	FITZGERALD,	134
. L.W.	17	E.J.	186
. ROBERT	132	FITZMORE, N.	19
EDMONDS, CHANCE	74	FLACK, R.D.	19
HOWELL	137	FLACKLY, CHARLES P.	25
EDMUNSON, J.F.	19	FLASH,	177
EDOM, SAMUEL	74	FLEECE,	134
EDWARDS,	24,123,177	FLETCHER, JIMMIE	190
SHEP	217	FLIPPEN, THOMAS	74
ELDER,	148	FLIPPIN, JOHN P.	188
ELDRIDGE,	83	. SAM	111
ELI, ABLES	137	. SAMUEL	111
E.J.	111	FLOYD, ALBERT	90
ELLIOTT,	60	FOLSOM,	8
ELLIS, THOMAS G.	10	DAVID	6
ESKRIDGE,	217	FOOT, SHUBAL	23
. FOX	111	FORD, SAMUEL H.	12
. W.E.	111	W.P.	189
. WALTER	111	FORGAY, JOSEPH	12
EVANS,	34,127	FORREST,	85,219
. FRANK	131,138	N.B.	81,84,86
. J.E.	33	FOSTER,	8,13
. L.E.	34	FRANKLIN, BENJAMIN	28
EVANT, JOHN M.	12	FREELY, F.M.	191
EWING, D.	103	MARCELLA STEWART	191
FAIRFIELD,	80,90,92,132	FREEMAN,	48,215
S.S.	57	. G.Y.	214
FERGUSON,	93,198	. GEORGE Y.	191
. A.P.	14	. JOHN G.	12
. DANIEL	14	FRENCH,	75
. W.P.	108	L.	75,77,91,110
FIELD, GEORGE W.	43	FRIEDMAN, M.	111
FIELDS, G.W.	220	GAGE,	57
. HARRY	110	. ELIZABETH	33
. THOMAS	110	. J.B.	210
FINLEY,	122	. J.J.	46,214-215

Index:
History of Grenada County, Mississippi

. JOHN	185	. THOMAS R.	25
. JOHN J.	33,56,79,213	GIRULT,JAMES A.	14
GARNER,	134,210	GLASS,L.E.	165
. ABB	111	GLEEN,DAVID	12
. J.T.	208	JOSEPH B.	12
. S.	218	GOHAM,HUGH	111
. S.H.	169,188,198	GOLDEN,P.S.	171
. SAMUEL	44	GOLDING,JOHN	92
. TOM	89,95	GOLLADAY,R.H.	134
GARRETT,J.I.	143	GOLLODAY,	48,124
GATE,BEN	111	R.H.	92
GATTIS,ALLEN	12,30	GONDOUGH,LUTHER A.	12
GEORGE,CLARA	56	GOODMAN,J.A.	165
. JAMES Z.	93	L.L.	165
. JOHN	134	GOODSPEED,	19
GERARD,	202,226	GOODWIN,C.E.	214-215
. A.	111,118,167	GORDON,	23
. E.	218	JAMES S.	35
. E.L.	43	GOVAN,A.	114
GHOLSTON,	120	. ANDREW	12
GIBBS,	134,159	. ANDREW R.	21-22
. E.F.	140,186	GOZA,G.R.	119
. EDWARD G.	141	GRANBERRY,J.A.	61
. J.G.	74,188	. LUTHER	141
. J.W.	223	. MOLLIE	86
. JOHN	133,138	GRANT,	81-83,86
. M.M.	133	GRAVES,A.H.	62,74
. THOMAS P.	134	GRAY,	33
GILCHRIST,MALCOLM	10	. ED	111
GILL,	53	. J.C.	111
GILLEM,ALVAN C.	94	. NICHOLAS	12
GILLESPIE,	19,53,111	GRAYSON,E.P.	14
. A.	186	GREEN,	96
. ALLEN	33,122,157	. BERRY	12
. L.C.	30	. DANIEL	12
GILLIAM,LITTLEBERRY	12	GREENHOW,	190
GILLISPIE,	101,103,107	GREER,DANIEL	12
ALLEN	32	GREINER,JOHN	216
GILLON,F.E.	119	GRIFFINS,J.W.	109
GINSBURG,MAX	93	GRIFFIS,	141,198
GINSBURGER,MAX	50,131	. J.W.	117,134,161-162
161-162,178,182,216		.	167
GIRAULT,	207,218	. JESSE	132,140
. JAMES A.	5,8,10,25-26	. JOHN W.	132
.	28,114,128,217	GRIFFITH,	81,150

Index:
History of Grenada County, Mississippi

GRIM, W.L.	78	W.H.	30
GUAGE, MARY	56	HAMMOND, JOHN	12
GUIDRY, EDITH OSDEL	228	HANKINS,	111
EDITH VANOSDEL	228	. S.M.	146
GUY, CURTIS HAYWOOD	122	. W.M.	75
GWIN,	17,67	HARDEE,	86
. S.M.	21	HARDEMAN,	12
. SAMUEL	8,15-16,28-29	C.L.	74
.	120	HARDEN,	80
. W.H.	28-29	J.	80
. W.M.	15,20-21	HARDY,	60
. WILLIAM M.	16,66	HARMAN, LOUIS T.	207
HABER,	176	HARRIS,	33
. NATHAN	182	. DANIEL	12
. PAULINE KAHN	182	. E.G.	33
HADDICK,	110,194	. THOMAS	12
HIRAM T.	108,143,193	HARRISON, B.C.	188
HADEN,	53	. R.C.	212-213
HAGEN, HENRY	14	. STERLING	12,114
HIRAM	14	HART, CLARA	108
HAGGERTY,	227	HARRY	111
HALKENS, DANIEL	12	HARTSHORN, F.N.	163,178
HALL,	98	HASTING, AUGUSTUS	12
. C.M.	189-190	HATHORN, J.C.	61
. CHARLES	111	HAYDEN, JAMES	10,15
. ELIZABETH	127,190	HAYNIE, G.W.	146
. F.K.	111,189-190	HAZELHURST, J.H.	170
. FINLEY	190	HEATH, HENRY	137
. J.G.	111	J.B.	74
. JAMES G.	108,126-127	HENDERSON, GUS	61
.	137,143,190,193	HENDRICK, JEREMIAH	12
. MARY KOEN	108	HESTER, AUGUSTUS	12
. R.N.	42,97,188,209,213	R.H.	61
. S. CLAUDE	61	HICKS, DEMPSEY H.	132
. S.M.	39	HIGHTOWER, J.	74
. W.W.	107,111,189	ROBERT	76
. WILLIAM WOOD	108,190	HILL, BEN	85
HAMES, HILLIARD	62	. G.R.	116
HILLSFORD	74	. G.W.	223
HAMILTON, E.	189	. HENRY	125
. E.L.	190	. HENRY R.W.	21,66
. ELIZABETH HALL	190	. HENRY W.	3
. JOHN J.	145	. JAMES	95
. W.G.	134	. JOEL	140
HAMMER, R.	30	HINES, JOHN H.	137

Index:
History of Grenada County, Mississippi

HOFF,W.B.	36	. MINNIE	106
HOFFA,	37	. S.	110
W.B.	120,176,181,226	. SALLIE	106
HOLCOMB,D.L.	26,43,118	HUGHES,	89,101
HOLLAND,ASA	12	. E.W.	111
RICHARD	188	. J.E.	111,134,167
HOLLOMAN,J.	30	. LIDA R.	108
HOLLON,ASSA	184	. MARY	108
JOHN	184	. W.E.	108
HOLLY,	54	HUGO,FENNER	108
. FRANK	111	HUMMEL,LUNWIG	110
. W.M.	74	HUMPHREY,LOTT S.	138
HOOD,	86	HUMPHREYS,B.C.	94
HUMPHREY	140	HUNLEY,	53
HOOKS,	111	WILLIAM	25
DAVID	111	HUNTLEY,WILLIAM	157
HORN,LIZZIE	60,141	HUNTLY,MARIAH SMITH	121
HORNSBY,K.W.	43,164	WILLIAM	8,69,121,207
HORTON,COWLES	164	HURT,W.A.	222
. J.J.	220	HUTCHINGS,SARAH W.	56
. R.	117,134	INGRAM,	35
. ROBERT	190	. EUGENE	111
HOUSE,JEREMIAH	12	. F.P.	73,77
HOUSTON,A.R.	48	. FLORENCE	111
HOWARD,	18-19,39,53,133	. G.F.	34,126,188
	192,215	. N.B.	126
. A.	53	. NATHANIEL	32
. E.N.	19	. REBECCA D. PERRY	35
. H.	121	. W.I.	134
. HELEN	192	IRBY,	164
. JOHN	100,122	TOM	111
. N.	53,157	IRISH,H.L.	12
. NATHANIEL	44,46,191	IRVIN,	205
. THOMAS	12	. JAKE	203,205-207
. TITUS	12	. LEE	203,205-207
HOWARS,JAMES	19	IRWIN,J.L.	114
HOWE,E. PERCY	26,187	. JOHN L.	21
HOWELL,	111	. R.	111
HOWERY,C.B.	116	. R.A.	111
HOWLEY,JAMES	12	ISIAH,DAVID	12
HUBBARD,J.M.	61	ISOM,	30,39
HUFFINGTON,	134	IVES,THOMAS	29
. M.	110	. THOMAS B.	12,21,53,68
. MARION	106	.	123
. MARY	106	JACKSON,	36,96,112-113

Index:
History of Grenada County, Mississippi

Name	Pages	Name	Pages
. ANDREW	28-29,120	. GEORGE	181
. BOB	124,131	. GEORGE WASHINGTON	181
. J.D.	40	. JAMES	14,181
. LEMUEL	12	. SAMUEL	110
. R.S.	23	. THOMAS	111
. SAMUEL	12	. W.G.	184
JAMES JOHN C.	35	. WASH	135
JAMES,J.C.	74	KENDRICK,LULLA	111
. JOHN C.	126	R.	74
. L.B.	174	KERWIN,E.	40
JAMESON,ROBERT	10	KETTLE	111
JARRETT,BENTLY	12	KETTLE,	106
JENNINGS,W.J.	172,220	. JAKE	220
JENNINS,J.J.	74	. SIDNEY	134,202
JOHNSON,	85-86	KIMBROUGH,	226
. ANDREW	94	O.L.	119,167
. B.F.	33,35	KING,J.W.	19
. HENRY	169	. JOHN A.	19,21,138
. JOSEPH	85	. JOHN S.	141
. SILVESTER	205	KINGSBURY,	6
JOHNSTON,	80	C.	121
. A.S.	82	KIRBY,PETE	110
. ALBERT SIDNEY	79,84	PETER	189
JONES,	83-84-86,210	KIRKMAN,	60
. A.B.	23	THOMAS	12
. ALLEN K.	12	KNOX,J.W.	111
. C.W.	215	THEOPULOS	19
. FRANK	147	KOEN,MARY	108
. G.B.	118,203,207,209	KOON,THOMAS	74,188
. G.W.	55,115,117,198	KOONCE,RICHARD	32
. GEORGE W.	80-81,93,134	KOOPERS,	164
.	167,202,216	KORN,	190
. H.M.	106,111	ELIZABETH	189
. JAMES B.	12	KRWIN,ALEX	74
. JOHN	12	KUNKINDALL,	190
. JOHN G.	137	LACOCK,	134
. R.L.	30,74,188	. ALICE	110
. ROBERT LOUIS	181	. JAMES B.	74
. ROLAND W.	92	. M.	110
. WILLIAM	82	. MARY	111
KAHN,PAULINE	182	. SAMUEL	191
KEETON,	35	LACONT,CHARLES A.	207
KELLY,	91	LADD,J.S.	75
KENDALL,	123	. JAMES	77
. G.W.	122,135	. SAM	99

Index:
History of Grenada County, Mississippi

. WALTER	146	. SAM	116,159-160
LAKE,	24,95,105-106,109	LAWRENCE,MALCOLM	146
.	160,175,177,190,201	. O.F.	146
. A.W.	134	. RICE	147
. ALBERT	85	LAWTON,C.M.	56
. ANNIE	111	LAY,J.T.	117
. CAROLINE	129	LAYCOCK,	82
. DELIA	111	LEA,	131
. G.W.	46	LEE,A.C.	109
. GABRIEL P.	132	. J.W.	118,167
. GEORGE	23,55,115-117	. L.C.	33
.	123,140	. R.E.	86
. GEORGE W.	40,158	LEFLORE,	8
. GUS	109	. GREENWOOD	6,8,21,128
. H.S.	23-24	.	216
. HENRY	123	. J.D.	73
. J.B.	134,202	. J.L.	216
. L.	24	. JOHN L.	128
. LEVIN	23,84,93,123,129	LEIDY,SALLIE	111
.	142,176,186	LEIGH,	29,134
. R.P.	55,115-116,159	. A.C.	118
.	198,200	. J.W.	118
. W.	24	. JOHN TOWNE	129
. W.M.	23	LEMONS,	205-206
. W.S.	55	. JAMES	203
. WILLIAM	23,53,123,138	. JIM	205,207
.	140	LEONARD,G.G.	57,217
LAMAR,	48	G.W.	57,146
L.Q.C.	133-134	LEVY,E.	173
LAMB,EDWARD	74	LEWIS,	177
LAMON,JOSEPH	35	LIARD,	33
LAND,GRIZZELL	138	LIDDELL,J.M.	146,213
SAM W.	53	LIGON,JOSEPH	35
LANDRUM,	148	LINCOLN,	91
LANE,FRANKLIN	12	LISTER,DOUGLASS	225
. JOHN	3,10,18,137	MARIETTA	225
. JOHN A.	3,10,18,137	LOGAN,HENRY	12
.	140	JOSEPH	12,224
LANIER,	81	LOGWOOD,T.G.	19
LATIMER,H.W.	173	LONG,	227
LATLING,R.T.	57	. F.G.	188
LATTING,R.G.	160-161	. JANE	108
R.T.	57	. W.E.	108
LAURENCE,	116,160-161	LONGSTREET,	134
.	202	. J.C.	163-164,206

Index:
History of Grenada County, Mississippi

.	214-215,218	. THOMAS	12
LORD,	163-164	. W.F.	118
LORING,	81	MASON,J.T.	119
JAMES	188	MASS,A.	162
LOVING,JAMES	74	MATHEWS,JAMES	12
LOWD,H.D.	171	MATLOCK,LEWIS	82
LOWENSTEEN,D.I.	134	MAXIMILIAN,	123
LOWENSTEIN,	179,215	MAY,	101,104
LOWERY,ELIZA	186	. FRANK	212
T.J.	186	. W.B.	84,111
LOYD,	177	MAYHEW,BOB	111
LOYS,	177	. FRANK	92
LUCIOUS,A.	141	. J.	74
LUTER,E.	46	MAYNARD,M.L.	31
LYONS,JOSEPH B.	14	MAYS,	35,48
MABRY,DAVID	32-33	. L.M.	34
MAGNARD,D.B.	30	. M.	19
MAJET,LEWIS C.	126	MEADERS,	210
. NICHOLOUS	126	J.P.	119
. NICHOLUS	35	MELTON,A.	188
. SARAH	35,126	. C.W.	167
MALCONSIN,ELLEN	149	. I.	53
MANDEVILLE,W.R.	101	. J.	53
MANN,D.B.	30	. J.D.	23
J.C.	50	. M.	53
MARBLE,JAMES	28,137	. M.H.	19
MARCH,JAMES B.	12	. MICHAEL	18,53
MARSH,JAMES A.	25	. MICHAEL H.	185
. SAMUEL B.	12,25,133	. PAULINE	185
.	207,224	MENDON,B.J.	52
MARSHALL,	24,148	MERCER,	55
. JOHN R.	23	EMMA	54
. SAMMIE	110	MERDITH,JAMES	203
. SAMUEL	111	METCALF,WILLIAM	132
. TOM R.	111	MIDDILL,W.	69
. WILLIAM J.	19	MILBURN,J.D.	159
MARTEN,J.A.	74	JOHN D.	159
MARTIN,	24,37,123,190	MILES,CHARLES	12
. BUCK	205	MILLANDEN,LAURENT	12
. ELIZABETH	-	MILLANDER,LAURENCE	5
.	DONALDSON 120	MILLER,E.B.	207
. GEORGE	21	. JAMES	5
. GEORGE K.	53	. JAMES H.	65
. GEORGE W.	3,10,12,18	. JOHN	25,28
.	20,22,36,120,125,181	. JONATHAN CARL	19

**Index:
History of Grenada County, Mississippi**

. JOSEPH	14	. C.R.	157
. LEWIS	5,137	. G.R.	31
. ROBERT	14	. GRANVILLE A.	19
MILLSAPS,R.W.	117	MORRISON,FANNIE	165
MILTON,J.	107	. J.A.	111
. J.L.	99,111,190	. JOSEPH A.	111
. JOHN L.	73	. S.A.	61,178
MINTER,	29	MORROW,JOHN	111
. JAMES	30-32	MORTON,	24,53
. MACON	140	. G.K.	23,53
. W.M.	30	. GEORGE K.	137
. WILLIAM	12,30-31,128	. GEORGE P.	40
.	140	MOSS,	190
MISTER,J.K.	160	MUFFETT,EDWARD	64
. M.K.	91,97,140,217	MULLAN,	110
. MATTHEW K.	129	MULLEN,R.W.	117
MITCHELL,	60	MULLIN,	105-106
. BOB	218	. ROBERT	77,101-103,106
. C.	12	.	109,127,130,132,161
. C.D.	19	.	182,203
. FRANK	110	MULLINS,	110
. G.D.	186	MUNFORD,	41
. G.E.	186	W.W.	40
. G.W.	52	MURDOCK,ROY	32
. J.A.	23	MURRAY,JOHN A.	33
. J.P.	140	MYER,GEORGE	12
. JOHN R.	126	MYERS,JOHN	12
. WILLIE	218	MYRICK,MORELAN	30
MOLE,MARIE	111	McAFEE,R.W.	203
MONTGOMERY,RALPH	14	McCAIN,	24
MOODY,E.F.	137,140	McCALL,	85,190
EDWARD	141	PITT	83
MOORE,	55,211	McCAMPBELL,	104,143
. B.E.	171	JOHN	111,134
. C.C.	118-119	McCASLIN,	34
. DAVE	111	. A.J.	34
. E.F.	185	. ALFRED	123
. ELDER	182	McCOMB,H.S.	45-46
. JENNIE	182	McCONNELL,JAMES	158
. JOHN	19,23,48,77,124	McCORD,	173
.	130-131,137,223	J.B.	202
. O.J.	117	McCOY,WILLIAM	12
. PAULINE MELTON	185	McCRACKEN,	99,101
. S.W.	54	.	103-106,110,143,148
MORRIS,	19,31	. E.L.	25

Index:
History of Grenada County, Mississippi

. L.	213
. SAMUEL	12
. W.	102
. W.C.	101,103,106
McCRELAH, S.	12
McCRELES, S.	132
McCULLOGH, ALEXANDER	12
McDANIEL, ANDREW	12
McDONALD,	110
McGEE, W.C.	134
McGEHEE, EDWARD	43
McGUIRE, JOEL	12
McIVAN, DUNCAN	12
McKENNIE, JOHN H.	3
McKIE,	134
V.G.	61
McKINLAY, DUNCAN	182
McKINNEY, JOHN H.	123
McKINNIE, JOHN H.	21,24
McKRAYNES,	216
McLAIN,	123
McLAUGHLIN,	26
L.	25
McLEAN,	209,212
. BERTHA	77
. HARRIET J.	108
. LULA	110
. W.	117
. W.C.	76,116,119,134
.	163,202,206,211
. WILLIAM	211
. WILLIAM C.	50,134,191
McLEMORE, JOHN C.	12,21
McLENDON, A.S.	61
McLEOD, J.W.	116,118,167
McMACKEN, THOMAS C.	132
McMILLAM, LEE	82
McMILLIAN, GEORGE	85
McMULLEN, ELI	25
S.	30
McNUTT,	114
McQUAY,	166
McRAE, JOHN R.	186
McRAVEN, J.A.	18
JOSEPH	3,137
McREA,	26
McREE, J.F.	119
R.A.	118
McSHANE, E.M.	118
McSWINE,	98,197
. HESTER	130
. HUGH	80
. JOHN	12,130
. WILLIAM	42,97,130,159
NASON,	226
NEAL,	33,53
. N.S.	23,186
. NATHANIEL S.	32,137
NEELY, E.C.	119
NEWBELL, JOHN	12
NEWBERGER, E.	33
. L.	34
. LEOPOLD	34-35
NEWBURGER, JOE	43
. JOSEPH	123,130,163
. LEOPOL	130
. OSEPH	162
. SAM	167
NEWELL,	143
. CHARLES	111
. J.T.	55
. JOSEPH	111
NEWSOME, CASWELL	12
RANSOM	12
NICHOLS, F.B.	116,161
NICHOLSON, CALVIN	12
NIXON, THOMAS	12
NOLAN, PIERCE	5
NOLAND, JOHN	12
PIERCE	12
NORMAN, WILLIAM	12
NOWELL, JOHN P.	73
OAKS, JACOB H.	12
OBANNON, J.L.	33
OLDHAM, WILLIAM J.	12
ORD, E.O.C.	94
ORMOND, JOHN F.	12
ORWIN, JOHN L.	20
OSDEL, EDITH	228
VAN	228

243

Index:
History of Grenada County, Mississippi

OWDELL, W.S. VAN	119
OWENS, SILAS	116
OWERY, ROBERT	98
OXBERRY,	37
. DAVID	13
. DELIAH	13
. JAMES	13, 66
. SARAH	13
PAINE, W.C.	19
PALMER,	148
PANE, DAVID C.	12
PARIN,	140
PARKER,	34, 42
. ANNIE	24, 157, 175
. E.	169
. G.W.	23
. I.S.	111
. J.T.	117
. JOHN	188
. JOHN T.	35
. T.S.	134
. W.J.	205
PARKHURST, CYRUS	25
PASS,	176
. A.E.	33
. A.S.	91, 134
. J.B.	33
. JOHN B.	23, 32, 35, 127
. R.J.	48
. W.M.	117, 202
. W.N.	35, 116, 127, 134
.	161-163, 182, 196, 226
.	228
PATTERSON, J.M.	197
PAYNE, ED	227
. J.L.	77
. J.S.	108
PEACOCK,	177, 196
. LEVINE P.	141
. MAMMIE	110
. T.E.	110
PEEBLES, FANNIE	111
PEEPLES, P.Q.	177
. P.W.	100
. PICKNEY C.	177
PEETE, C.C.	74
PEGRAM, JOHN W.	12
PEMBERTON,	81
PENN, C.C.	220
PENNYPACKER,	89
PENON, HENRY	12
JOSEPH	12
PENQUITE, ABRAHAM	12
PERKINGS,	42
JAMES W.	12
PERKINS,	34
. JAMES W.	12
. JONES W.	12
PERRY,	226
. C.A.	165
. HARDY	2, 13, 36
. ISAAC	12-13
. J.B.	81, 118, 132
.	164-165, 171
. J.C.	35, 132, 164, 167
.	178
. JOHN	13
. O.H.	33
. OLIVER H.	35, 132
. REBECCA D.	35, 126
. ZADDOCK	132
. ZADOC	35, 126
PERSONS, JOSEPH	12
PETTIBONE, E.E.	93
PETTUS,	78
PEYTON, JOHN B.	12
PHELAN, TOM	222
PHILLIPS,	187, 221
. G.	23
. H.J.	59, 61
. JOHN	216
. TOM	111
PIERCE,	28
WILLIAM	64
PITCHLYNN,	8
JOHN	6
PLUMMER,	4, 18, 20, 67
. FRANKLIN	14
. FRANKLIN E.	3, 16-18, 24
.	56, 66, 68

Index:
History of Grenada County, Mississippi

. FRANKLIN L.	12-13,15	PROPHET,R.L.	117
.	123	PROVINE,C.C.	22,119,124
. J.R.	19,21	PRYOR,	18,133-134,169
. JOSEPH R.	14	PUCKETT,	3,17
POINDEXTER,	15,28	. G.M.	18
GEORGE	149	. SAMUEL	137
POIRTEVENT,JACOB	181	PURDY,ROBERT	169
MARY JANE	181	RAFALSKY,ALEX	111
POITEVENT,JACOB	137	RAGSDALE,G.S.	55
. MARY	137	. G.W.	159
. MOLLIE	190	. GEORGE	55
POLK,	80,86	. GEORGE W.	142
. JAMES	29	RAIPE,JOHN J.	104
. JAMES K.	28,69	RANSOM,E.	218
PONTIVENT,JOHN	137	. M.H.	57
POOL,SAMUEL	19	. M.M.	56,58,134,212
PORTER,	32-33	RATALSKY,HENRY	111
. THOMAS C.	32	RAY,	118,192
. THOMAS I.	32,35	RAYBORN,D.M.	132
PORTEVENT,J.	224	RAYBURN,	35
PORTIVENT,J.	224	. SILAS	205
POTTEVENT,M.	111	. W.A.	115
POWELL,	29,110,131,134	. W.O.	74
.	177,196	READ,JAMES M.	141
. JOHN	92,95,101-103,105	REDDING,A.S.	189
.	109,116-117,124,131	. WILLIAM M.	107
.	141,159,161,216	. WYATT	107
. M.L.	134	. WYATT M.	111,189
. THOMAS	111	REED,BOB	92
. W.H.	48,62,74	REID,S.P.	106
POWER,J.L.	104	REVELS,H.R.	64
POWERS,J.B.	61	HIRAM R.	64,94
. J.N.	61	RHEA,JOHN S.	12
. LEWIS B.	12	RICHARDSON,	74,153
. N.E.	12	. J.D.C.	74
. THOMAS	12	. JOHN	74
PRENTISS,S.S.	28	. R.	46
SARGENT S.	15	RILEY,S.	64
PRESSLEY,	30	RINGGOLD,	192
PRICE,	68	RINGOLD,	101,106-107
. BEN	116-117	.	110-111,192
. E.F.	134	. R.S.	141
. MATILDA	23	RIVER,	111
. STERLING	81	ROAN,	40
. WILLIAM	91-92	A.T.	117

Index:
History of Grenada County, Mississippi

ROANE,	167,187,221	OLIVER PERRY	107
A.T.	50,59,134,206,219	SATTERFIELD,JENNIE	111
ROBB,W.G.	186	SAUNDERS,A.P.	106
ROBBINS,MARIA	181	. O.P.	190
ROBERTS,B.L.	173	. W.B.	59
CHARLES	84	. WILLIE	190
ROBERTSON,CORNELIUS	203	SAVAGE,	39
.	205-206	G.M.	25
. DONALD	141	SCANLIN,	110-111
. JAMES	141	SCHURLOCK,	91-92
ROBINSON,C.N.	44	L.S.	217
. C.W.	116	SCOLL,J.R.	220
. DANIEL	186	SCOTT,ABRAHAM	4
. JOHN	12	ABRAM M.	149
. MATHER	157,185	SCURR,JOHN L.	132
ROGAN,	106	LYDIA	132
THOMAS J.	101	SEAGERS,JOHN	12
ROLLINS,O.B.	111	SEARS,TOSH	218
ROOK,B.J.	74	SEMMES,D.O.	118,164-165
ROOSEVELT,TEDDY	153	SENTON,A.	189
ROSAMOND,A.	141	SHACKLEFORD,S.E.	218
. J.R.	62,74	SHANKLE,E.	110
. R.W.	188	ROBERT	111
ROSE,BARRY	111	SHARKEY,ALLEN	21
ROSECRANS,	89	WILLIAM L.	94
ROSOBOROUGH,J.F.	192	SHARP,J.W.	164
ROSS,A.S.	46	SHATTUCK,D.C.	186
. D.G.	220	SHAW,	110
. JOHN B.	46	J.N.	19
. WILLIAM	30	SHEPHARD,KATTIE	110
ROSSER,IDA	111	SHERMAN,	79,85-86,111
ROWLES,JOHN	12	. E.T.	103
RUNDLE,JOHN	60-61	. ED	103
RUNNELS,	4,16,20,125-126	SHIELDS,	3,17
. H.G.	21	JOHN	18,137
. HARDEN D.	12	SHUMATE,M.G.	26
. HIRAM	3,11,18,66	SHURLOCK,	92
. HIRAM G.	21-22	SIDNEY,	54
. HIRAM J.	15	SIGNAIGO,ALICE	111,150
RUSSELL,DANIEL R.	53	J.A.	146
SADLER,ROBERT	111	SIMPSON,A.J.	74
. ROSA	111	SIMS,	18-20,53,69
. WALTER	111	. HARRIET SMITH	134,157
SALMON,W.D.	171	. HARRIETT	19,54,68
SANDERS,A.P.	111	. HARRIETT SMITH	7,18

Index:
History of Grenada County, Mississippi

.	121,140	SOMERVILLE,T.H.	117
. J.P.	216	SOUTHERY,LEWIS	32
. JAMES	3,7,17-19,54,69	WILLIAM	32
.	121,134,138,140-141	SPEARS,ELI C.	33
.	157,212	SPENCE,	111
. WILLIAM	12	J.H.	119
SKINNER,JOHN S.	12	SPICER,R.M.	138
SLACK,	134	STACEY,A.F.	25
. HESTER McSWINE	130	STAEEN,HENRY	12
. J.J.	130,205-206	STAHAM,BEN	92
SLEDGE,D.D.	146	. CRAWFORD	96
SLIDER,JAMES	137	. D.H.S.	90
SLOAN,W.G.	51	STANDLEY,JOHN	19
SMITH,	19,35,53,101-102	STANFORD,	81-84-85
.	111	. DANIEL	14
. ANDERSON C.	12,141	. T.J.	80
. ANN	141	STANLEY,JAMES	19
. FRANK	209	STATHAM,	79-80,86,134
. HANNAH	6,19,121,134	W.S.	78
. HARRIET	134,157	STATTON,E.P.	137
. HARRIETT	7,18,121,140	STEFENS,A.H.	216
. J.P.	106	STEPHENS,M.D.L.	95
. JAMES	46	. M.P.L.	89
. JOHN	3,5-8,18-19,53-54	. W.H.	186
.	69-70,121,134,136-137	STERLE,CHARLIE	199
.	157,175,207,212	STERLING,	13
. MARIA	69	ROBERT	14
. MARIAH	121	STEVENS,	53
. SAM	23	STEVENSON,	
. SAMUEL	137-138	. JANET THOMPSON	181
. W.B.	74	. ROBERT	108,111,181
. W.E.	89,117,119,134	STEWARD,L.R.	31
. W.G.	100	STEWART,EUGENE HENRY	191
. WILLIAM W.	35	. L.R.	191
. YORK	212	. MARCELLA	191
SNIDER,	53,55,201	. PAULINE JOSEPHINE	191
. A.C.	64	. VIRGIE H.	12
. CLARA	108	STIGHER,LOUIS	12
. J.B.	167,200-201	STIPE,J.W.	43
. JACOB	108,146	STIRLE,CHARLIE	134
. N.C.	106,115-116,127	STIVER,	188
.	134,198,200-201	STIVERS,C.F.	187
. N.V.	95	STOKES,CHARLES	192
SNYDER,	190	. HENRY C.	192-193
JACOB	53	. J.C.	111

Index:
History of Grenada County, Mississippi

. J.G.	108	THOMAS,A.V.B.		142,161
. JAMES	111	. A.W.		74
. JIMMIE	192	. ADRIAN V.B.		132
. JOHN	111	. B.F.	117,163,177-178	
. JOHN C.	48	.		208
. R.H.	118	. J.E.		207
STONE,	209	. J.T.	117-119,163,167	
STOWE,C.H.	101	.		218
WARREN	101	. JOHN		111
STRANG,	111	. MARY		132
STRATTON,E.P.	53	THOMASON,J.D.		23
STRENGE,JOSEPH	182	THOMPSON,JANET		181
SUDLEY,OLIVIA P.	56	. PARHAM		12
SUGG,E.G.	190	. W.A.		19
SULLIVAN,	227	THRELKELL,STEPHEN		12
SUMMERFIELD,A.	169	TILGHAM,		206
SYKES,GEORGE H.	12	JIM		203,207
TABB,JOHN	12	TILGMAN,JIM		210-211
TALBERT,	29,141	TILLER,W.T.		75
. HILLARY	140	TILLHON,BERRY B.		32
. HILLIARD	33	TILLMAN,P.		46
. HILLIARY	32	RICHARD		32
. J.T.	46,53,157	TILMAN,		35
. JAMES B.	128	TIMBERLAKE,H.C.		55
. JEREMIAH T.	137	TINDALL,G.W.		159
. MARY CARTLEDGE	128	JAMES		132
. MICHAEL	128,140	TOPP,GEORGE W.		30
. MICHAEL D.	127	TOWLER,		188,215
. ROBERT D.	119	W.P:	187,214-215	
TARPLEY,J.P.	140	TOWLES,W.P.		134
TATE,J.M.	19	TOWNES,		29
TATUM,S.T.	119,163-164	. FREELAND		73
TAYLOR,	53	. HENRY C.		74
. CHARLES R.	137	. J.L.		23,124
. E.F. PRICE	134	. WILLIAM		74
. H.G.	74	TOWNSEND,		102
. ISAAC	137	J.B.		75,91,161
. JAMES M.	95	TRIBBLE,G.W.		178
. JERRY	19	TRIMBLE,G.W.		132
TELFORD,	216	GREEN W.		137
TERGARTERN,WILLIAM	14	TROTTER,JAMES		137
TERRELL,G.W.	220	. T.R.		80
TERRY,WILLIAM	21	. WALTER		117
THAMES,S.M.	59	TRUIT,WILLIAM		12
THERREL,	153	TRUSSELL,HENRY		33

Index:
History of Grenada County, Mississippi

. JAMES	35
. JAMES S.	33
. W.M.	164
TRYHAN, JAMES A.	69
. JERRY	17,20,67-68,70
. PEGGY	2-3,13,16-18, 20-21,66-69,125
. SARAH	68
TUBBY, TUCKLOON	13
TUBY, TOOKLOON	2
TUCKER, EDWARD	12
W.F.	47
TULLIS, WILLIAM	140
TULSON,	26
TURATT, J.A.	46
TURNBULL,	36
. JESSIE	13
. JUDY	8,13
. WILLIAM	13
TURNER, R.H.	42
. ROBERT H.	133
. WILLIAM	74
TWIN,	3
TYLER,	26
F.A.	145,186
TYSON,	20
. S.	23
. U.	137
. URIAH	21
VANCE, C.F.	44
J.D.	74
VANDAM,	177
VANDAN,	177
VANDORN,	78,81
VANOSDEL,	228-229
. EDITH	228
. M.S.	228
VANOWDELL, W.S.	119
VEASY, H.A.	101
VEAZIE,	101
VERHINE, JESSE	141
JESSE L.	32
VINSON, E.E.	111
WAILES, B.L.	218
WALFON,	83
WALFORK,	110
WALKER,	28-29,120
. ALLEN	12
. ROBERT J.	5,10,15,28, 30-31,120
WALLACE,	101
WALTERS,	35
. ALICE	108
. J.	34,42
WALTHAL, E.C.	46
WALTHALL,	80,109
E.C.	92-93,109,133
WALTON,	102,105,110
. THOMAS	101
. TOM	111
WARD, ENOS	12
WARDLOW, S.W.	119
WATHALL,	101,222
WATSON,	101,105
. ELIJAH S.	12
. THOMAS	109
WATT,	125-126
JOHN	3,11,18,21,66
WEATHERLY, JOSEPH	141
WEAVER, PHILIP A.	12
WEBSTER,	112
WEEKS, J.G.	226
WEIGART, A.J.	104
A.S.	102
WEIGERT, CHARLES	111
WEIR, JAMES	32-33,35
R.C.	74
WELLS, MOSES	30
WELSH, SIDNEY	111
WEST,	78
EDGAR	117
WHITAKER,	53,202
. W.H.	218
. W.W.	146
WHITE,	165
. A.	40
. DONALD	44
. F.L.	44
. F.M.	44,46
. T.W.	44

Index:
History of Grenada County, Mississippi

WHITESIDE, W.H.	53
WHITFIELD,	134
WHITTAKER,	164
WIDDON, PERRY	12
WILBORN, F.G.	61
WILBOURN, JOHN	140
WILCOX,	26
WILDER, C.A.	162
. C.L.	161
WILE, EMANUEL	111
. I.	116,131,134,161
. ISABELLA	182
. M.	111
. MEYER	182
. SAM	131
. SAMUEL	167
WILEY, D.B.	117
WILKINS,	57,190
. J.A.	186
. J.R.	111
. W.	218
WILKINSON, JAMES	149
WILLARD, J.E.	164
WILLIAMS,	26,38,121,197
. B.P.	74
. CAROLINE LAKE	129
. ELIZA LOWERY	186
. GEORGE W.	141
. J.	33,157
. J.A.	111
. J.H.	42,161
. J.J.	64,97,151,167,196
.	220-221
. J.M.	59
. J.R.	188
. JACK	24,35,129,175
. JOHN	12,23,32-33,74
.	123,133,186
. JORDAN	12
. L.S.	6
. P.C.	163
. R.D.	118
. ROBERT	12,19,23,32
. THOMAS	19
WILLIAMSON,	
. HELEN HOWARD	192
. J.A.	176
. JIM	205
. LEA	192
. T.B.	141
WILLIS,	35,181
. J.H.	213
. LEWIS	225
. ROSA	225
. W.B.	188
. WILLIAM T.	35,126,181
WILSON,	110
. E.S.	109
. J.A.	23
. J.C.	171
. ROBERT	85
WINN, L.M.	223
WINTER, THACKER	10,132
. W.H.	89,95
. WILLIAM	12,74,132
. WILLIAM H.	181
WITTY, P.D.	117
WOLFE,	60,107
. EUGENE	134
. W.B.	161
WOOD, A.W.	77
. C.T.	177
. I.K.	111
. W.H.	202,215
WOODWARD, J.H.	61
WOOTEN, ISHAM	12
WRIGART, A.	101
WRIGHT,	53
. B.L.H.	188,217
. BUCK	202
. GEORGE	74
. R.H.	119
WYATT, JOHN D.	12
YALMON, JOHN	129
YEAGER,	177,220
YOUNG,	229
. HENRY	103
. J.W.	167
. ROBERT A.	111
. WILLIAM S.	12

Index:
History of Grenada County, Mississippi

ZOLLICOFFER, 79

www.ingramcontent.com/pod-product-compliance
Lightning Source LLC
Chambersburg PA
CBHW050629300426
44112CB00012B/1720